Reconsidering the Postmodern

Reconsidering the Postmodern

European Literature Beyond Relativism

Edited by Thomas Vaessens and Yra van Dijk

AMSTERDAM UNIVERSITY PRESS

Cover design: Liesbeth van Warmerdam, Amsterdam
Lay-out: Mulder van Meurs, Amsterdam

ISBN: 978 90 8964 369 8
e-ISBN: 978 90 4851 515 8
NUR: 617

© T. Vaessens & Y. van Dijk / Amsterdam University Press, 2011

All rights reserved. Without limiting the rights under copyright reserved above, no part of this book may be reproduced, stored in or introduced into a retrieval system, or transmitted, in any form or by any means (electronic, mechanical, photocopying, recording or otherwise) without the written permission of both the copyright owner and the author of the book.

Contents

Introduction: 7
European Writers Reconsidering the Postmodern Heritage
Yra van Dijk & Thomas Vaessens

I – European Literatures 25

1. **Russian Literature: Reviving Sincerity in the Post-Soviet World** 27
   Ellen Rutten
2. **British Literature: Residual Traces of Postmodernism** 41
   Sebastian Groes
3. **Dutch Literature: Stripping the Novel of its Harmlessness** 59
   Thomas Vaessens
4. **Italian Literature: The Epics of Reality** 77
   Monica Jansen
5. **French Literature: Post-Realism and Anti-Realism** 93
   Sabine van Wesemael
6. **Post-Yugoslav Literature: The Return of History and the Actuality of Fiction** 115
   Guido Snel
7. **Norwegian Literature: The Return of the Narrative** 133
   Suze van der Poll
8. **Flemish Literature: Questions of Commitment and Authenticity** 149
   Sven Vitse
9. **Polish Literature: Saving Men and Nations** 167
   Arent van Nieukerken
10. **German Literature: The Dialectics of Readability** 185
    Ewout van der Knaap

II – The Transatlantic Connection 205

11. **Spanish and Spanish American Literature: Memory, Evil and the Rhetorics of Authenticity** 207
    Brigitte Adriaensen & Maarten Steenmeijer

12 American Literature: A New Aesthetic of Sincerity, Reality and   225
   Community
   Allard den Dulk

Notes   243
Bibliography   275
About the Authors   307
Index of Subjects   312
Index of Names   317

Introduction

European Writers Reconsidering the Postmodern Heritage

Yra van Dijk &
Thomas Vaessens

Now that we have reached the point in which postmodernism, rightly or wrongly, has been declared defunct, it is time to critically evaluate its literary legacy. What has been the effect of postmodernism? Have we gone beyond it in literature, and why would we want to go beyond it? What criticisms have been leveled against it in the last decennia by writers and critics? What have they put in its place? To what extent do they rely for this on (conceptions of) literature that postmodernism had consigned to history?

This book is about the postmodern legacy in European literature of the last few decades. From the moment postmodernism was considered to belong to the past, writers and critics have searched for new paths. Young authors increasingly situate themselves by means of a critical discussion of their postmodern predecessors. Older authors, who themselves were seen as exemplary postmodernists in the 1980s and 1990s, are wondering what answers postmodernism can give to today's questions. Postmodernism, in demolishing the essentialist cultural ideal of liberal humanism, has had an important historical function. Postmodern discourse, already a half-century old, has become a reference point for anyone active in the field of literature. Even when they are not out to proclaim the end of the postmodern era, critics and writers are seeking new ways to relate to this discourse, which legitimates the question of whether we are justified in speaking of a late-postmodern or post-postmodern condition.

We focus on the era in which the literature of various European countries questioned the value of postmodernism. These are the moments when writers and critics became aware of a turning point and tried to think themselves beyond postmodernism, but not because they wanted to throw doubt on the beneficial effects of postmodernism. In fact, postmodernism proved an excellent medicine against the essentialist underpinnings of the liberal humanist conception of literature. Under discussion, however, are the unpleasant side effects the medicine appeared to have had, especially in literature: relativism, cynicism, and noncommittal irony.

Postmodernisms

In a book as broad and international in outlook as this one, very divergent writers are profiled, from divergent literary fields. There is, after all, not one single European postmodernism, but rather many different local variations of it. In countries with greater political tension, for example, it shows a stronger ideological coloring, as the contributions to this volume from Russia, Poland and even Spain demonstrate.

The very term postmodernism can refer to different ideas and literary forms. Hans Bertens and Douwe Fokkema have extensively documented the variations in the conception of postmodernism according to a country or linguistic area in their monumental: *International Postmodernism. Theory and Literary Practice* (1997).[1] If European postmodernism has many faces, so does the criticism of postmodernism. Moreover, some language regions have had a more elaborate critical debate than others: Italy more than Germany, and Belgium more than Norway. These differences concern specific cultural situations in respective European countries, and obviously the differences in philosophical, cultural and ethnic background of the writers play a role as well. One writer formulates his criticism after a thorough study of post-structuralism; for another, the desire to loosen ties with postmodern discourse is more intuitive; and there are many nuances between these two extremes. We are dealing with fundamentally varying interpretations of postmodern thinking (whether first-hand or not) which resonate in the literary debate and to which writers attribute literary consequences. As several critics have suggested, definitions of postmodernism form a discursive field, rather than a coherent concept.[2] That is why this book does not start from one definition of postmodernism. Instead, it aims to show the variety of nuances of the criticism of postmodernisms formulated in Europe. We are not in the first instance interested in a 'kernel' of postmodernisms (if one could find such a thing), but rather in the borders of a large and varied territory that we could call postmodern.

This does not diminish the fact that participants in the critical debate about postmodernism agree on a few main points. Therefore, the question addressed in this book – the question of the postmodern legacy in European literature – is based on a global but guiding concept of postmodernism. Now that we have evoked the notorious polysemy of the term postmodernism, we can sketch the contours of this leading concept, contours which can be recognized in each of the following chapters.

Postmodern thought evolved parallel to and under the influence of French post-structuralist theory with protagonists such as Barthes, Derrida and Lyotard. It rose against the great Theories of Everything which we had begun to take for granted in our modern Western world as the bedrock of our thinking and behavior.[3] These theories seemed universal in scope, but postmodernism revealed them to be ideological constructs that needed interpretation and deconstruction. Values are not universal, but context-bound. Not discovered in some Platonic sky, but fashioned by historically and socially situated human beings. For these reasons, values object to change.[4] A word often used in this context is relativism: postmodernism relativizes Western cultural values.

In literature, postmodernism chiefly took aim at the values of 'Liberal Humanism,' an ideology which had no doubts about the beneficent workings of 'true' literature. It worked on the assumption that the canon had a universal status and that the literary text was honest and the result of an authentic voice. Literature was believed to have a timeless quality in which form and content were one and indivisible.

Literary postmodernism questioned such values as sincerity, originality, authenticity and truth. It demonstrated that the liberal humanist belief in these values as eternal and universal, suppresses the historical, political, material, and social context of art.[5] The postmodern criticism of this essentialism found divergent expression in literature, from intellectualist, aesthetically challenging fiction (whether explicitly leaning on French Theory or not) to 'popular' forms of postmodernism such as literary pop-art and minimalism. In the following chapters the way postmodernism found expression in various European languages will become clear, as will above all how it was critically evaluated and even came to be seen as 'passé' by all sorts and conditions of writers all over Europe.

The Death of Postmodernism?

From the early 1990s and onwards, critics started to doubt the viability of postmodernism. Minsoo Kang dates 'the death knell of postmodernism in the U.S.' to 19 June 1993, when the standard postmodern devices of self-reference, ironic satire, and playing with multiple levels of reality suddenly also seemed to appear in an Arnold Schwarzenegger film, *The Last Action Hero*. This appearance, Kang argued, made the 'intellectual idea's final demise' a fact.[6] In this view, put forward by many, postmodernism simply became a victim of its own success. In the words of Maggie Humm: postmodernism came to an end in the 1990s, when its commodification was a business success story.[7]

Ever since, everywhere in the world where the idea of the postmodern has played an important role in discussions about literature, authors and critics have brought the idea itself and its consequences into question. According to Jeremy Green (*Late Postmodernism. American Fiction at the Millennium*, 2005) 'the demise of postmodernism' in literary criticism has even become commonplace since the start of the new millennium.[8] It is highlighted by publications such as Frederick Crews's satire on postmodern literary and cultural studies and their fashionable professors (*Postmodern Pooh*, 2001) and Andrew C. Bulhak's *Postmodernism Generator* (written in 1996), a computer program that automatically generates academic-style texts filled with postmodern jargon, meaningless, but superficially plausible (claiming that this is just like a 'real' postmodernist essay).[9]

Not only postmodernist jargon has been criticized, but in particular postmodernism's deconstructive mode and, in cultural matters, its skepticism towards the cultural tradition of the West – equating the canon with Eurocentrism, exclusion, and cultural imperialism. Early postmodern criticism of the universalism that underlies Matthew Arnold's infamous definition of culture ('the best which has been thought and said in the world')[10] seems in this day and age to have resulted in an inert relativistic stance in relation to both the canon and the Western values that it embodies. It is striking that this criticism has been formulated precisely by those authors and critics whose work was initially a product of postmodernism. They criticize postmodernism because of the relativistic assumptions in which it is rooted. Those assumptions turned out to have unforeseen and unsettling consequences for everyday life and for literature.

And many critics have pointed to social events to further explain the waning influence of literary postmodernism. An obvious, and hence often-cited, end-date for postmodernism is 11 September 2001. The attacks on New York and Washington and the resulting political climate in the Western world seemed a logical endpoint for the kind of relativistic thinking associated with postmodernism. In the days following 9/11, various international commentators established a link between the terrorist attacks and 'the end of postmodernism'. Whatever the rhetorical force with which postmodernism had fought universal values, the commentators agreed on one thing: there would be a very strong temptation to fall back on such values after the attacks. 'Postmodern Outlook Objectively Smashed' (*The Washington Post*)[11]; 'Attacks on U.S. Challenge Postmodern True Believers' (*The New York Times*)[12]; 'The Age of Postmodern Irony Comes to an End' (*Time Magazine*)[13]...

Novelists, too, saw the connection between the critique of postmodernism and social actuality. According to Martin Amis, on 9/11 we witnessed 'the apotheosis of the post-modern era', through which 'all the writers on earth were considering the course that Lenin menacingly urged on Maxim Gorky: a change of occupation'. Amis notes that an unusual number of novelists chose to write some journalism about September 11 instead of continuing their work on a new novel: 'I can tell you what those novelists were doing: they were playing for time. The so-called work in progress had been reduced, overnight, to a blue streak of autistic babble'.[14] Amis's colleague and friend Ian McEwan also said that the events of New York and Washington initially withheld him from writing fiction ('journalism seemed more adequate than fiction at that moment'),[15] and that he had to almost reinvent for himself the genre of the novel afterwards.

McEwan's post-9/11 novel *Saturday* (2005) is situated in the midst of the debate about the 'the clash of civilizations', 'the axis of evil', and – in intellectual or literary circles – 'the apotheosis of the postmodern era',[16] or 'the end of postmodern relativism',[17] that followed the attacks. In the novel, in which the literary tradition plays an important role, two elements of postmodernist criticism can be detected that are central to many of the following chapters. First, we can speak of an overt criticism of the way postmodernism is articulated. For example, the way in which the main character portrays the vaguely postmodernist, 'relativist' professors of his daughter. This reminds us of the uproarious professors in Frederick Crews's satire on postmodernist criticism, with their tendency to deconstruction and skepticism about the values of Western modernity.[18] Second, the novel probes into the meaning of the literary (canonical, liberal humanist) tradition for the world today. The latter is treated most overtly in the scene where a murderous burglary is prevented from taking place by the timely quotation of a poem by, of all people, the man who epitomizes the liberal humanist tradition: Matthew Arnold.

Whatever one makes of this episode – some critics regarded it as otherworldly, ludicrous and kitschy[19] – it certainly puts Arnold's liberal humanism back on the agenda. Not as a model worthy of imitation, but as a challenge: when postmodernism has succeeded in hedging its pre-eminently literary values with suspicion, can those humanist values now be reclaimed for literature without returning to their old essentialist underpinnings? What we see in McEwan's representative novel is a definite gravitation towards the values made taboo by postmodernism. In recent literature, authors and critics are engaged in a search for confirmation about the function of literature and the usefulness of exactly those literary values dismissed by postmodernism: sincerity, authenticity, truth... The attempt is not to reinstate these values as if postmodernism had never been, but rather to examine if and how they can be redeployed in a less absolutist way, in the current literary discourse. These authors and critics combine a critical reconsideration of postmodernism with a reorientation towards the deconstructed values of liberal humanism.

It is important to stress that all this is not a post-9/11 phenomenon. However logical the association of critical reflection on the legacy of postmodernism and the attacks of 2001 might be, questions about the consequences of postmodern discourse were already being asked quite some time before. It is true that the contours of this became more visible after 9/11 because we were suddenly more sensitive to them. In this book, we examine how criticism of postmodernism developed in European literature, before 9/11 and even before the 1990s. The coming chapters follow the trail of criticism back that leads us to the 1980s. Even then the literary legacy of postmodernism was approached critically with the question of whether the literary discourse was not ready for new directions. What does this body of criticism look like?

Critique of Postmodernism

The first thing we are forced to note is how self-critical postmodernism has actually been from the beginning. This is obviously true for the self-reflexive critical thought of its Founding Fathers such as Baudrillard, Derrida, Lyotard, Foucault or Deleuze, but also holds true for the literature that is based on it (sometimes loosely).

Already in the early 1980s, a number of postmodern critics realized that the politics of literary postmodernism were threatening to become ineffective because it dawned on them that deconstructionist artistic strategies could be as readily commodified and marketed as anything else (the Schwarzenegger example was certainly not the first token of the perversion of postmodernism). Moreover, the avant-gardist left gradually acknowledged that a cultural politics based on anti-representation was ineffective. The critique implied by a deconstructionist artistic practice remained immanent to the discourse of art, and it seemed to be high time to come up with a strategy to save a postmodern cultural politics from futility.[20] Critics who took this view did not abandon postmodernism but did seek strategies that could give postmodern cultural politics a less theoretical and more pragmatic turn. This self-critical tenor of postmodernism became more manifest as it became more mainstream, and as the authors linked to it became more canonized. The forms of criticism of postmodernism explored in this book slot into this development.

Secondly, there was the criticism from without. Postmodernism has been under pressure in the last few decades from critics who would have preferred that postmodernism (or the literature associated with it) to never have existed at all. Alan Sokal and Jean Bricmont, for example, described the 'fashionable nonsense' and the 'intellectual impostures' of postmodern intellectuals,[21] and critics like Frank Furedi attacked postmodernism with their cultural pessimism.[22] Within international debates, engaged voices lamented that because of postmodernism, many of the ideals associated with the exercise of intellectual authority had become targets of skepticism. In their view, the search for knowledge, the application of reason, and the acknowledgement of literary quality remain unquestionable.

It is not our aim a priori to promote this anti-postmodern, neo-conservative criticism (which often also targets 'the spirit of '68' or 'the ethos of Cultural Studies'). This criticism exists and it is influential, but it is not the focus of this book. The authors featured in this collection do not ask 'how do we keep postmodernism out' but 'how do we continue from within postmodernism?' This is true regardless of whether this continuation takes them outside of or beyond postmodern discourse. We therefore do not aim at forms of anti-(post)modernism, but criticisms of postmodernism which are well-disposed, criticisms that are not restorative (of some sort of pre-postmodern condition or essentialist worldview).

How do we distinguish these two forms of criticism? The difference lies in the fact that well-disposed criticism does not necessarily take issue with the ideas that are at the root of postmodernism, whereas restorative criticism does. The critique this book is concerned with is primarily aimed at the literary consequences of postmodern thinking and not always at that thinking itself, although we admit, of course, that it is not possible to focus on the literary consequences of postmodernism without addressing that thinking itself.[23]

Two different attitudes are possible in this criticism that stem from postmodernism itself. It may be self-criticism from within on the one hand, or a criticism so fundamental as to take us outside of postmodern discourse on the other. In the first case, we are dealing with late-postmodern concerns about some offshoots of postmodernism such as rampant irony turning into cynicism; in the second, we could speak of a post-postmodernism. It is striking that the first criticism occurs considerably more often in this collection than the second. Some of the following chapters show us a changed postmodernism that is not turning its back on postmodern theory (late postmodernism), but certainly not a completely new discourse in which the wheel is turned more radically: a criticism for which the term post-postmodernism would be more fitting.

In both forms of critique, authors have to deal with a problem. Their late- or post-postmodern 'rhetorics of sincerity', and 'reality' and 'truth' don't have a universal and absolute base. This problem didn't occur for prototypical postmodern authors because they categorically declined the possibility of 'sincerity', 'reality' or 'truth'. Even the most convinced advocate of the idea that postmodernism is over and done with could not deny, after reading the following chapters, that it is precisely notions of the postmodern which have shaped both literature and commentary after the 'death' or end of postmodernism. In that sense we are conducting an autopsy on a breathing body.

Challenging the Borders of Postmodernism

Most of the writers discussed in this volume see postmodernism as a necessary reaction to authoritarian certainties from the past, but one that has been carried too far and is not practically tenable in its consequences. In the slipstream of postmodernism, they share the postmodern critique of the unspoken assumptions of the modern canon, but they think that too little thought has been given to alternatives after the deconstruction of these assumptions. A certain justified skepticism has hardened into cynical relativism, it is argued, also with respect to the possibilities of literature. Upon reflection, the postmodern deconstruction of everything we have ever held sacred cannot be the answer to all questions.[24]

We shall see in the following chapters that four points recur in the criticism of postmodernism, four supposed attributes of it to which, even in literature, there is resistance: (1) its irony, (2) its asocial quality (indifference to or separation from society), (3) its academic jargon, and (4) its relativism.

1. Postmodern Irony

Irony, wrote David Foster Wallace, 'has permeated the culture. It's become our language; we're so in it we don't even see that it's one perspective, one among many possible ways of seeing [...] irony's become our environment'.[25] Irony can mutate into cynicism. 'Cynicism,' says Timothy Bewes in *Cynicism and Postmodernity* (1997), 'is a concept mobilized by politicians, critics, and commentators as a synonym for postmodernism.'[26] In the last decennia authors from several literary traditions have resisted this equivalence. The New Sincerity-movement, begun in Russia, explicitly turned its back on irony and cynicism qualified as 'postmodern'. This does not mean that the reflections on irony by postmodern theorists such as Richard Rorty in the 1980s and Linda Hutcheon in the 1990s are being revoked, on the contrary.[27] The authors in question are fully aware of the fact that irony can have a liberating and highly critical side – they only refuse the permanent and all-penetrating irony which has become an end in itself. The arrows are aimed at a disengaged literary practice that, though referring for legitimization to a postmodernism, has at the same time detached itself from that postmodernism. More than literature, in greater society too, there is criticism for an irony which devalues all values. The Dutch author Arnon Grunberg explicitly rejects irony, comparing it to a cancer overgrowing all: 'it makes our food inedible and many books unreadable'.[28] As Allard den Dulk describes it in the last chapter of this collection, the main objection is that irony does not replace anything that it breaks down: it renders any form of commitment impossible. This ambivalence about irony goes back to the early days of postmodernism: the Russian writer Dmitrii Prigov already tried to find a 'sincerity' that went together with irony in the 1970s.

Postmodern critics tend to resist the idea of 'postmodern irony', for instance by referring to postmodern theorist Linda Hutcheon's *Irony's Edge* (1994) and pointing out (rightly) that Hutcheon's theory of irony certainly has nothing to do with the ironic pose of the (mainstream) postmodernist. Hutcheon continued to defend the critical impetus post-structuralism and postmodernism gave to the field of literature and literary studies (while theorists such as Fredric Jameson and Christopher Norris dismissed postmodernism as a reflection of the ideological confusion in late capitalist society). Still, the intellectual fashion of the easy ironic pose of postmodernism exists, irrespective of Hutcheon and other postmodern theorists of critical (as opposed to easy, destructive) irony. In line with the argument of this volume, one could qualify Hutcheon's remarks on irony as late postmodern (without suggesting that *Irony's Edge* is merely a response to the popularizing or commodification of postmodernism).

When Hutcheon had just submitted the final version of the manuscript of her book on the theory and politics of irony to her publisher, she walked into a bookstore. While browsing there, she came across the cover of an English magazine entitled *The Modern Review*. On it was pictured the equivalent of a 'no smoking' sign, but this time the barred red circle of forbiddenness surrounds a pair of inverted commas, reinforcing the headline: 'The End of Irony? The Tragedy of the Post-Ironic Condition'. A few years later in an essay Hutcheon asks her reader to imagine what it was like to read this headline in her particular situation:

> *You might be somewhat nonplussed: you know you delivered the manuscript a bit later than you had promised – but you had not really counted on the book being utterly out of date before it was even published.*[29]

In reality, it was the other way around. The volume of *The Modern Review* proved the timeliness of Hutcheon's book.

2. Postmodernism's Alleged Indifference to Society

Ian McEwan is not the only one who turned to journalism in recent years – the impulse to enter the world is present in many contemporary novelists. This 'return of the real', as Hal Foster called it,[30] is not a reaction against any original postmodern idea. The point is not that a postmodern thinker such as Derrida neglected reality (he did not) but that his statement 'il n'y a pas de hors-texte' was often misunderstood. The complex postmodern ideas about the relation between language and reality were, in the practice of some postmodern novels, reduced to a minimalistic inwardness. Today, history and memory are omnipresent in literature, whilst authors are fully aware of the Deriddean certainty that their words mediate that past.

The antisocial tendency criticized in postmodernism was confined to the West; in Eastern Europe postmodernism was precisely subversive politically. Even in post-war Italy, Germany and Spain, postmodernism was the opposite of disengaged. A Yugoslav author like Danilo Kiš was perhaps fêted in Paris as a postmodernist, but he himself was critical of the lack of political reality in the work of Borges or the French literature of his age. The minimalism of the 'nouveau roman' was also called asocial by other critics, as the world portrayed in it is limited to the consciousness of the protagonists. The main criticism uttered in the West was aimed at another genre, however; the 'narcissistic' literature that was influenced by pop-art and that flirted with mass-culture. The potential subservience to the culture industry was seen as a threat. It was seen as prose without hope in which irony had unmasked all value, a prose whose model also in Europe was the work of American author Bret Easton Ellis.

Theorists also dispute postmodernism's alleged indifference. In the 1990s critics such as Teresa Ebert were opposed to the common view of the political as outside of and opposed to the postmodern by trying 'to write the political back into the postmodern'.[31]

3. Postmodern Jargon

A third line of criticism aimed at the opposite of this pop-literature: the intellectual and leftist (and according to some, radical) postmodernism. It arose in the 1960s and, after its introduction into the Anglo-Saxon academies, produced a certain ideological and discursive orthodoxy with all the attendant jargon.[32] On this side we find, for example, the 'tenured radicals' of which Michael Ignatieff spoke: members of the 'protest-generation' who had received academic posts and, consequently, cultivated a hypercorrect discourse from within the campus walls (and therefore turned away from the world).[33] Andrew Bulhak's already mentioned '*Postmodernism Generator*' from 1996 showed how easy it was to ridicule this discourse. It is one of the weakest points of postmodernism that its critical discourse has become so specialized as to be no longer understood or even heard outside of the campus enclosure. This led to a lack of efficiency in postmodern theorizing about literature and culture. Again this criticism is not aimed at postmodernism (its 'content'), but at its proponents in academia and their rigid and unworldly attitudes, attitudes that were mercilessly exposed in Philip Roth's *The Human Stain*.

4. Postmodern Relativism

Something similar applies to our last example, the postmodern relativism so often criticized in literary debates. It is hard to call the first postmodern thinkers 'relativistic', but the argument against a unified subject and universal values has produced an extremely skeptical attitude towards values in general (and Western values in particular) in many critics tinged by postmodernism. It is this relativism that is now under critique. A German manifesto by four authors in *Die Zeit* rejected it in these terms: 'But those, who have now turned towards a post-modern game of 'anything goes', should realize that this game remains – as it has always been – deadly serious.'[34]

Critics point to two actual developments that make cultural relativism undesirable: the growing impact of mass-culture and the radicalization of society. In 2009 the manifesto of the Tate Gallery-triennal *Altermodern* declared that postmodern relativism 'gives us no weapons against the twofold threat of uniformity and mass culture and traditionalist, far-right, withdrawal.'[35] The argument is that relativism makes postmodernist theory practically incapable of furnishing either an ethics or a politics. The late postmodern question then becomes how literary politics and ethics are still possible when concepts such as 'truth' and 'foundation' have disappeared. At the same time, critics are aware that the postmodern settling of scores with modernism (or, in Rorty's terms, with modern metaphysics) was necessary. This ambivalence has led to a complex position in which authors have put their own relativistic literature under the microscope. Dutch author Arnon Grunberg conducts this type of self-criticism, as does French writer Michel Houellebecq. In his *La Possibilité d'une île* (2005, English translation 2005: *The Possibility of an Island*), a character becomes so tired of his own ironic and relativizing art that he literally throws up.

Grunberg and Houellebecq are not the only authors whose battle with the postmodern legacy has become the very subject of their novel. This internal ambivalence is one of the most striking characteristics of the new novel.

Towards a New Novel: Six Features of Late Postmodern Literature

After the application of irony and relativism had reached a dead end, the question arose as to the foundations that literature rested on. In the contemporary novel, a search for confirmation about the function of literature is plain to see. It is a search which can explain why so many authors, in their critical reaction to postmodernism, end up with exactly those literary values dismissed by postmodernism: sincerity, authenticity, truth...

This gravitation towards the values made taboo by postmodernism occurs not only in the novel but can also be seen in literary criticism. Thus, Andrew Gibson begins his *Postmodernity, Ethics and the Novel* (1999) with a direct provocation of postmodern discourse by referring to a precursor of the reviled tradition. 'It is time to go back to Leavis,' he writes: an opening which, with its reference to one of the most influential twentieth-century representatives of liberal humanism, courted yawns of boredom or disbelief, wry smiles, and ironical jeers. Unnecessarily, according to Gibson, because even the most convinced postmodern theorist has already converted himself anew to a neo-humanistic focus on ethics.[36]

This reorientation towards humanism is one of the characteristics which many contemporary novels share. Without pretending to be able to sketch a complete picture of the variety of European late postmodernism, something the other chapters do in rich detail, we can note a number of strongly connected tendencies in contemporary novels. We list six of them below: the problematizing of irony, the blurring of boundaries between fiction and non-fiction, increasing social commitment (*engagement*), neo-realism, reflection on the use of literature and a new relation to the audience. The first two were already touched upon earlier when we set out our four examples of criticism of postmodernism.

1. Problematizing Irony

In many recent novels, the kind of postmodern irony that has become a way of life is problematized. The striving towards a negative independence from all things is seen as an incomplete strategy. Characters that cling to this position are forced to re-evaluate their place in the world, often because the world makes an ethical demand on them. A complex mixture of irony and seriousness is a characteristic of recent late postmodern novels. Irony is not rejected radically but problematized, and its alternatives (sincerity, authenticity) are not celebrated unrestrainedly but reconsidered cautiously. The work of the Polish writer Gombrowicz shows the complexity of the attitude towards sincerity and authenticity; in this respect Arent van Nieukerken (chapter 9) uses an expressive phrase: 'authentic inauthenticity'. Still, authors are in search of what one could call a new sensibility: 'new sensibility novels' such as A.S. Byatt's *Possession* (2005) display an apparently unremitting belief in the possibility of genuine love.

2. A Turning Towards Reality

There is talk of increasing activity in the border area between fiction and non-fiction. Some novelists base their stories on reality and events from real life: Jonathan Safran Foer (*Eating Animals*, 2009), Aifric Campbell (*The Semantics of Murder*, 2007), Thomas Brussig (*Wie es leuchtet*, 2004), Ted Conover (*Newjack*, 2000), François Bon (*Daewoo*, 2004)... In this (non-)fiction, literary means and techniques are employed: the texts are emphatically subjective and rhetorical. When Dave Eggers wrote about hurricane Katrina in *Zeitoun* (2009), his work was even compared by critics to that of Charles Dickens.[37]

Conversely, there are non-fiction writers who choose fiction to convey their message. Thus, Pulitzer prize-winning journalist Lorraine Adams recently moved from investigative reporting for English newspapers to writing fiction because 'fiction is much more equipped to capture the complexity of our lives than the missives and reports that come out of newspaper organizations'.[38] Fiction and non-fiction make alliances, and writers from both ranks use each other's techniques. As is the case with other features of the recent, late-postmodern, literature mentioned above, we need to stress that this blurring of boundaries concerns a new move on the part of the postmodern legacy and not a radical new departure. Mixing genres is not new: a postmodern author such as Kiš wrote fictionalized history too.

The material of the novelist increasingly consists of history: there is a wealth of autobiographical family histories in Dutch, French and Scandinavian literature, for example. In the context of 'nostalgia', stories are written about childhood. Suze van der Poll points out in her chapter on Norway that the 'small narratives' are an attempt to keep narration alive despite Lyotard's declaration of the end of grand narratives.

The 'documentary imperative', according to which history could only be written in a non-fictional manner, has been broken. Instead, one could say that 'documentary fiction rules', as the chapter on German literature has it, and in which it is also clear that this hype is immediately parodied, for example in Klaus Modick's *Bestseller* on the Holocaust (2006). In documentary fiction, the emphasis is on the potential of literature to remember and re-tell the past in a subjective manner. The hybrid between literature, autobiography and documentary is summed up in novels with lists and summaries, following the example of postmodern authors such as George Perec. Even the photos appearing in so many European novels are a characteristic of documentary fiction – from Orhan Pamuk's *Istanbul* to Sebald's *Austerlitz* and Aleksander Hemon's *The Lazarus Project*. Rather than pointing towards a historical 'truth', they reflect the fragmentary nature and subjectivity of our knowledge of the past, and of personal memories in general.

3. Commitment

Many contemporary novels get their bearings from current themes and social problems, and critics observe a 'reality hunger' (among writers).[39] Of course, for some regions this is nothing new: Yugoslav postmodern literature has never been apolitical, for example, and received an even stronger impulse to turn towards political reality after the siege of Sarajevo in 1992. As Guido Snel argues in the chapter on the Balkans: a 'blessed post-political Zeitgeist' never arrived there, because communism immediately crossed over into nationalism. However, former Yugoslavia does show a late-postmodern way of telling stories about the war in which the 'documentary imperative' again plays a role. Authors just describe the reality but without reflecting on the ethnic and representative difficulties it entails.

For Northern and Western-European authors, political reality has increasingly been an obvious choice of subject since the 1990s: novels about terrorism, war, nationalism, refugees and ecological questions are no longer the exception. It is rarely about accusations – the position of the witness or author is not univocal. Every position can be defended, and it is more often about teasing out all the opinions than about passing judgment. The postmodern legacy is present in the impossibility to draw conclusions about reality. One could say that these novels pose ethical questions but rarely become moralistic. When they are, it is a moot point whether we are speaking of post-postmodern literature or a complete harking back to the humanistic values of yore. Often (e.g. in Italian literature, as Monica Jansen shows in chapter 4) the accent is put on cultural activism, on building participatory communities through transmedial storytelling: the collective dimension of literature is back again, relying on a kind of interconnected subjectivism.

4. A Return to Conventional Forms

'New readability' it is called in Germany, but the phenomenon can be found in all European literature. Novelists choose accessible and conventional forms more and more often: postmodern experimentation is on its way out. They mention a 'return of the narrative', which means a reassessment of the conventions of the realistic novel: clear character drawing, determinism and causality, linear course of action, daily parlance, social criticism, detail.

Again, this is not a simple throwback to the past (the nineteenth century novel for example): the impossibility of representing reality is always invoked. In the chapter on French literature, Sabine van Wesemael proposes the term 'post-realism' for the work of Michel Houellebecq, to emphasize that his realism is not devoid of the realization that we live in language-like structures. In Scandinavia, a similar development is designated as 'postmodern realism': the work of the playwright Jon Fosse would be a case in point. Another characteristic of this neo-realism is that it sometimes describes extremely aggressive and transgressive situations – and the work of Houllebecq can serve as an example here, too. In less violent novels as well, the body plays an important part. As Hal Foster argues, the body is a way of getting closer to 'the real'. In this way reality is not described but represented in a more direct and visual manner.[40]

5. Self-Reflexivity

Many recent novels reflect on the task and function of literature and its impact on today's world. Divergent authors such as Saabye Christensen, Aifric Campbell, Jonathan Coe or Marjolijn Februari all wrote novels in which literature itself is the subject, and others (like Martin Amis and the Dutch author Joost Zwagerman) wrote novels about writer's block, a theme that reflects the uncertainty contemporary authors feel about the radiance and status of literature in today's world. In many of the novels described here, the protagonists are writers and just as often, in college halls, book clubs or friendly conversations the question is what the function of literature might be. After the tendency of (post)modern authors to retreat into autonomous and self-reflexive fiction, these writing characters are in search of a new place for their work. Often the conclusion is that literature helps to interpret reality, sometimes even that the novel is directly engaged in attempts to save the world.[41]

As is shown in chapter 3, a number of recent Dutch novels ask whether literature can matter in the world, and what the writer can do to reach the people with power and responsibility again. In this respect, they fit in a broad trend in international literature. As in Zadie Smith's *On Beauty* (2005), for example, two stereotypes are often presented: the uncommitted, ironic, postmodern writer on the one hand, the worrying, humanist, 'sincere' author on the other hand. Instead of authors, the protagonists may be academics, journalists or teachers: professions that demand an intellectual and ethical stance.

Contemporary literary critics also point to the saving power of literature, a function which for a long time was taboo in considerations of it. Again, literature offers 'equipment for living' (Kenneth Burke) and company ('the company we keep', Wayne Booth).[42] It offers thoughts that come back in discussion, like the ones uttered, for example in Declan Kiberd's *Ulysses and Us: The Art of Everyday Living* (2009)[43] and also in *Un coeur intelligent* (2009) from philosopher Alain Finkielkraut – a book that received the subtitle in the Dutch translation: 'How novels can help you in life'.[44]

6. Rapprochement with the Audience

This new and more important role for literature also means that the attitude of writers towards their readers changes. One way to open up to the audience is to take on the role of the public intellectual, as many European authors seem to be doing. Now that the cultural impact of literature is diminishing, writers express their opinions in media that bring them into immediate contact with the audience: television, radio and newspapers. The ethics already present thematically play a role here, too: the author has descended from his ivory tower and engages with the reader. This is because of a new commitment with the external world shared by both author and reader, because of a new 'readability' (avoiding unnecessarily puzzling and hermetic forms), and because of literally coming outside, in the form of readings, blogs or forums. The autobiographical trend, giving the author himself the key role in his fiction, is another factor in this rapprochement between author and reader.

This growing autobiographical character of literature means that the subject re-enters fiction, and even non-fiction, which has become more subjective and personal.

The Following Chapters: Along Established Lines

As stated before, a quick summary such as the present one cannot do justice to all the subtleties and national variations that characterize European literature. That is why the following chapters are dedicated to recent novels, poetry, and debates in ten countries; Russian, English, French, German, Italian, Polish, Norwegian, Dutch, and Flemish literature are discussed, as well as literature from the Balkans. The last two chapters, despite the book's focus on the European situation, concentrate on what we have called 'The Transatlantic Connection': Hispanic literature (Spain and Spanish America: chapter 11) and American literature (chapter 12). American debates about the postmodern legacy form an important reference point in many European traditions. Conversely, European, especially Russian, postmodernism has influenced the American discourse.[45]

The chapters all follow the same pattern. A first part explains how postmodernism has manifested itself in the literature in question: which postmodernism is given body in the local discussion? A second part explores the question of how this construction has functioned in the discussion as a terminus: how was that postmodernism criticized? The third and final part, analytically examines three exemplary authors to discover what has been put in its place in literature: what attempts are made to go beyond postmodernism?

As editors and authors of this volume we don't take sides: we tried not to identify with a position in the present literary debate, neither a postmodern nor a pre-, anti- or late-postmodern position. To some (postmodern) readers the argument of this volume might seem supportive of conservative tendencies in politics or culture, but the surpassing of postmodernism is by no means the purpose of our analysis. Neither did we consider it to be our task to defend the 'seminal', 'original' or 'genuine' postmodernism of founding fathers such as Derrida and Foucault against writers who reconsidered the postmodern heritage (possibly without being versed in postmodern theory). It was not our goal to criticize (implicitly) the superficiality of some 'late-postmodern' interventions in today's literary debate or to impute the champions of 'new sincerity' of philosophical ignorance or naivety.

Although we didn't want to take a stand for or against postmodernism, we focused on one specific position in the debate on postmodernism's heritage. We tried to explain literary texts and authorial strategies by analyzing them as parts of the search for a Third Way in literary and cultural politics: a new position that tries to reconcile postmodern and pre-postmodern, humanistic elements.

Part I
European Literatures

Chapter 1
Russian Literature
Reviving Sincerity in the Post-Soviet World
Ellen Rutten

I just want sincerity so badly!... Sometimes I cry and how, how do I save myself?! In the old traditional way: I write and pour my feelings into euphonic and heartfelt lines! But that is precisely what I am doing.! — DMITRII PRIGOV[1]

Introduction

At the 2009 exam show of Amsterdam's Rietveld Academy for Fine Arts, visitors could purchase a box with postcards made by the graduates. The cards included a somewhat hazy photo of a Dutch soccer player in action. With ballpoint, the maker had drawn a text cloud from the player's mouth, which read: 'I am not saying postmodernism is dead'.[2]

The soccer card captures feelings which are central to this edited collection: first, the sense that postmodernism is increasingly becoming obsolete; and second, the thought that the very articulation of that idea – saying that postmodernism *is* obsolete – is itself becoming passé. By the late 2000s, talk of postmodernism's demise and a dawning 'post-postmodern' age was so ubiquitous that it became grateful material for parodic imagery of the Rietveld-card type.

Less ubiquitous is the notion that 'post-postmodern' talk is not unique to the US and Western Europe. As recently as the autumn of 2009, I heard a colleague claim that writers raised in post-WWII Arabic countries simply had 'better things to do than undergo the postmodern experience'.[3] In truth, the postmodern project has been anything but limited to 'Western' countries. Neither is the 'what-comes-after-postmodernism' (or 'into-which-new-forms-does-it-morph') question exclusive to those countries. Since the early 1990s, artists and critics have pondered it in a much wider range of cultural and geopolitical settings than many scholarly analyses suggest.[4]

In this chapter, I probe 'post-postmodern' talk in one of those less well examined world regions: post-Soviet Russia. Russia has not only gone through the postmodern experience, but ever since the 1990s, debates on a shift to 'late' or 'post-postmodern' thinking have thrived there no less than in Western Europe or the US.

A buzzword in the Russian debates is 'sincerity', and visions of a 'new sincere' world view – one that renounces postmodernism's alleged cynicism – are omnipresent in post-Soviet literary culture. The following pages zoom in on these literary discussions of a Russian 'new sincerity'. More pointedly, they scrutinize the nexus between post-Soviet 'new sincerity talk', on the one hand, and a trend in which literary-intrinsic and political-historical spheres blur on the other: the current Russian preoccupation with cultural memory and the nation's recent history.

Postmodernism Versus *Postmodernizm*

In the 1970s, poet-cum-performer Dmitrii Prigov – a name with cult status within non-official Soviet art – devoted lyrical odes to a mythical Soviet official, the consistently misspelled 'Poliseman':

> *Now when he, the Poliseman,*
> *Wakes up early on his day off,*
> *He goes out to the fields and gently*
> *Skims over a flower with his wing.*[5]

Using icons of Soviet culture as readymades, Prigov and other artists of the late-Soviet underground stood at the cradle of a new cultural mentality – one which, in retrospect, is clearly recognizable as postmodern. The exact outlines of this 'Soviet-born' branch of international postmodernism are debated to this day,[6] but scholars more or less agree on its distinctive features. They include the conviction that all ideologies and hierarchies are relative; the pursuit of semantic pluralism, transgression, play, and all-pervading intertextuality; theoretical self-reflection on one's work; a distrust of meta or master narratives; and a tendency toward the demythologization or critical deconstruction of cultural myths and stereotypes.[7]

So far, the list of stock features will sound familiar to the non-Slavist: the above is a blueprint of postmodernism as we have gotten to know it elsewhere. Russian postmodernism does not converge completely with its West-European-cum-American pendants, though.[8] Most importantly, Russian-style *postmodernizm* arises within a totalitarian context. If American postmodernists responded to late capitalism and commercial mass culture, their Russian colleagues lived in a society that generated ideological content rather than consumer satisfaction. In that sense, it is akin to the Central European brand of postmodernism that Guido Snel describes elsewhere in this volume rather than, say, its Dutch, French, or North American variations.

As a result, more than its American pendant, Russian postmodernism is politicized: one of the key languages that it deconstructs is that of socialist realism.[9] Not coincidentally, a recurring motif in (post-)Soviet postmodernism is that – in the words of the linguist Irina Skoropanova – of 'evaluating Soviet history, refracted through the prism of cultural history'.[10] Following a venerated national tradition, Russian postmodernists keenly travesty myths of national identity,[11] and many a critic has read their work in terms of a commemorative tool, a vehicle for digesting Russia's fraught recent past.[12]

'It's Him or Me': Proclaming *Postmodernizm* Dead

Political history has been no less relevant to Russian postmodernism than to discussions of its purported successors. Those discussions followed swiftly after international postmodern theory caught on in Russia, as late as the 1990s. Reaching a broader audience only when postmodern devices had long since marked Russian artistic culture, the theoretical vocabulary of such postmodern thinkers as Derrida and Lyotard had hardly gained ground in Russia before a weariness of postmodern effects set in.[13] Revealingly, the first Russian conference on postmodernism was held in the same year – 1991 – that artist Anatolii Osmolovskii labeled one of his installations '*After* Postmodernism (All One Can Do Is Scream)'.[14]

In subsequent years, the thought that Russian postmodernism – or its prime Soviet exponent, Moscow Conceptualism – was either 'dead' or mutating into new forms thrived in theoretical thinking.[15] It was discussed in publications by leading writers, critics, and academicians[16]; and in 1994, artist Aleksandr Brener took the idea of postmodernism's 'death' to its literal extreme with a hunger strike, which called for the end – 'it's him or me' – of postmodernism.[17]

Brener soon relinquished his strike, but the idea of a new, 'post-postmodern' (to coin a much-hated term)[18] cultural era started crowding the pages of scholarly publications more and more towards the end of the 1990s. Between then and today, it has been discussed in lengthy sections of book-length studies of Russian postmodernism. At first, this happened mostly in Russian-speaking editions which reached a relatively modest international audience.[19] From the mid-1990s onwards, that audience grew somewhat as scholars outside Russia picked up and expanded the debate on a Russian 'post-postmodern turn', in literature as well as cinema and contemporary art.[20] International attention for Russian 'post-*postmodernizm*' grew yet again in the 2000s, when American writer-bloggers eagerly turned to the writings on 'post-postmodernity' of the Russian philosopher-cum-cultural-theorist Mikhail Epstein.[21] From the mid-2000s onwards, textbooks and university courses on post-Soviet literature have also started warranting regular attention to 'post-postmodern' trends, or to the idea that in Russia today, postmodernism's peak has passed.[22] They do so again, however, mostly within Russia, having been written primarily in Russian.

In other words, the idea of a Russian 'post-postmodern' age is commonly discussed today in Russian-speaking intellectual circles. In order to define to what extent non-Russian examples fuelled the discussions at stake, additional analysis is needed; but Epstein's influence in the US does indicate that Russian 'post-postmodern' thought, in turn, also impacted on contemporary American cultural criticism.

'Post-*Postmodernizm*': Renewing Sincerity

On an international level, a poignant philosophical category within the 'post-postmodern' debate has been that of sincerity. In countries as varying as the US, France, the UK, Germany, the Netherlands, China, and Indonesia, the concept of sincerity – and especially the phrase 'new sincerity' – has been employed in flagging an alleged turn away from postmodernism towards a spanking new cultural mentality.[23] According to one theorist of the term, anthropologist Aleksei Yurchak, 'new sincerity' is a persistent 'contemporary cultural trend in global popular culture', which 'takes the form of a close and interested attention to the subject matter; cynicism and sarcasm are avoided'.[24] Within the current volume, Allard den Dulk touches upon the outlines of a similar striving for sincerity and 'irony-criticism' in recent American writing.

In post-Soviet Russia, the phrase captures a similarly anti-cynical *Zeitgeist*. '*Novaia iskrennost'*, as the Russian equivalent of 'new sincerity' sounds, is today embraced as a novel philosophy of life by Russians from a variety of social and professional backgrounds, from bloggers to curators, from scholars to poets, from philosophers to PR assistants, and from literary or film reviewers to visual artists. 'New sincerity to the bone', 'that's really new sincerity': as we speak, these and similar definitions jostle both the Russian-speaking Internet and Russian print writing. In the past years, when I subjected the phrase to a blog search, its most recent usage never dated back to more than a few days or even hours ago.[25] In the 2000s, the phrase appeared regularly on the pages of renowned Russian academic journals.[26] Yurchak – the same scholar who discerns 'new sincerity' as a global trend – brands 'sincerity' the prime aesthetic mode of 'post-post-Communist' art;[27] and in the literary sphere – which holds centre stage here – 'new sincerity' was singled out as a salient cultural trend by such leading commentators of perestroika-era and post-Soviet culture as Mikhail Epstein, Svetlana Boym, and Mark Lipovetsky.[28]

What, then, is the 'new sincerity' which occupies so many Russian minds today? This chapter does not solicit a watertight answer to that question: I am not interested in establishing what the Russian 'new sincerity' 'really' stands for, or in demonstrating that author X or Y 'actually is' a 'new sincere' writer. I do not think 'new sincerity' is *the* leading cultural trend following Russian postmodernism, or that it necessarily follows postmodernism at all. Instead, I adopt the analytical perspective of a cultural historian – one who does not partake in Russian 'new sincerity' debates herself, but does observe their vital role in the processes of contemporary cultural production and consumption. One, moreover, who feels that the 'new-sincerity' discourse forms a major point of departure for current Russian thinking on such diverging but primary mental categories as subjectivity, reality, identity, language, politics, and cultural memory.

This cultural-historical perspective does not comply with developing an ironclad interpretive framework – but a working definition of Russian usages of the phrase 'new sincerity' is not inappropriate here. Despite its widely diverging appropriation (how does one unite highbrow literary definitions with the 'that's sooo new sincerity!' of excited Russian bloggers?) the term does occur in discursive situations that share a set of common features. Most importantly, those include the – explicit or implicit – reference to postmodernism. Both inside and outside Russia, as a rule references to a 'new sincerity' signal disaccord with a fixed set of supposedly postmodern features. They inevitably include: excessive relativism, cynicism, mockery, an anything-goes mentality, and ethical indifference. In the place of these – as a rule, rather caricaturized – 'postmodern' traits, apologists of the 'new sincerity' propose an alternative cultural condition. In the words of Russia's best-known advocate of the trend – the same Mikhail Epstein whose ideas are cherished so ardently by American writer-bloggers – they defend an aesthetics

> *defined not by the sincerity of the author or the quotedness of his style, but by the mutual interaction of the two, [...] [whereby] the elusive border of their difference ... allows even the most sincere utterance to be perceived as a subtly quoted imitation, while a commonplace quotation may sound like a piercingly lyrical confession.*[29]

In the 'new sincere' aesthetics, according to Epstein, 'words such as "soul", "tear", "beauty", "truth", and "the Kingdom of Heaven"' – favorite targets of postmodern deconstruction – have been

> *purified by being kept out of circulation. After going through a period of radical deadening and carnivalesque derision, they are now returning to a transcendental transparency and lightness, as if they were not of this world.*[30]

That Epstein's – markedly mystical – writing is no immediate source of inspiration for each Russian 'new sincerity' adept is beyond doubt. Russian bloggers, for one, often employ 'new sincerity' as a slogan in pop-cultural contexts – contexts that have little in common with Epstein's fleshed-out theoretical concept. His is not the final critical investigation of the topic either. In recent years, theoreticians of Russian 'new sincere' trends define them as an offspring of new- or mass-media culture no less often than of postmodernism.[31]

But Epstein's observations do capture precisely the ideas from which the concept springs. They also point to the preoccupation with history that has my interest here. According to Epstein, the words which 'new sincere' thinking revitalizes have been tarnished by 'centuries of traditional, official usage'.[32] In other words, they are tainted by *history*. If Epstein presents that history in general terms, then the examples with which he illustrates his case point in a narrower direction: that of the recent Soviet past. As one of the 'new sincerity's' leaders, Epstein singles out Dmitrii Prigov, saying that the latter proposed the new aesthetics in response to the Soviet-era underground artistic trend labelled Moscow Conceptualism, 'which parodied models of Soviet ideology'.[33] Epstein sees another prime exponent of the trend in the poet Timur Kibirov, whom he brands the 'bard of Soviet daily life' *par excellence*.[34]

Epstein's references to the Soviet experience are not coincidental. In post-WWII Russia, literary 'sincerity talk' has consistently dovetailed with the ongoing debate on the recent past. The two already interlaced in the 1950s, when a discussion on 'Sincerity in Literature' – as a heatedly debated 1953 literary essay was called – paved the way for critical reflection on the Stalinist era.[35] And they do so again during and after the collapse of the Soviet Union. The (post-)perestroika era – and the events that led to it – is not only a background against which debates on a 'new sincerity' take place: it also forms one of their key preoccupations. In those debates, writers, critics, and scholars avidly revert to socio-political and historiographic categories. A closer look at representative participants shows that a political-historical bias – and the idea that the Soviet trauma is formative to 'the new sincerity' – resonates throughout post-Soviet sincerity discourse as a *continuo basso*.

Dmitrii Prigov: Sincerity after 'What We Have Been Through'

In post-Soviet 'sincerity talk', authors locate sincerity in political spheres rather than in the private domain. Take Dmitrii Prigov's thinking on the concept, for instance. Having gained fame in oppositional circles in the 1970s, Prigov is today internationally known for his artistic appropriation of Soviet clichés – apart from the 'Policeman' cycle cited above, his most celebrated creations include a series of quasi-hagiographical 'Stories about Stalin', and theatrical performances in which the author mimics the language (verbal and body) of the Soviet authorities. By the time of his death in 2007, Prigov's status as a leading figure in contemporary Russian literature was undisputed. So was his reputation in a spectacularly wide range of other artistic disciplines, including painting, sculpture, performance, rock music, dance, opera, and cinema.[36]

Prigov's best-known metaliterary achievement is the 'behavioral project DAP', or Dmitrii Aleksandrovich Prigov, which is perhaps best explained as a long-term, consistent attempt to present the authorial *persona* – including his work, his physical presence, and his biographical self – as a discursive or cultural product. In the artist's own words, formative to 'DAP' was the idea of a 'shimmering relationship between the author and the text ..., in which it is very hard to define (not only for the reader but for the author, too) the degree of sincerity in the immersion into the text and the purity and distance of the withdrawal from it'.³⁷ In its most tangible and easily accessible form, this 'shimmering' behavioral strategy can be seen in a set of short (undated) videofilms, available on Youtube: in the videos, Prigov adopts the identity of a stereotypical representative of Soviet ideology – something between the figure of the wise but stern leader and the prophetic writer-thinker³⁸ (I purposefully write 'adopts' rather than 'imitates': instead of mimicking or parodying stereotypical Soviet identities, Prigov insisted that he immersed himself in them.)

Not surprisingly, among contemporaries the 'DAP project' has stirred heated metaliterary debates regarding performativity, theatricality, and authenticity – debates in which the question 'Can we trust this poet or is he mocking readers?' was perennial. Critics and scholars often characterize the man behind 'DAP' as a hardcore postmodernist, for whom irony and playful relativism are an artistic *sine qua non*.³⁹

Yet, although it is indeed principally impossible to discern earnestness from play in Prigov's authorial stance, the traditional view of his work risks reading it in reductionist terms. Prigov himself – although in ambiguous language and without explicitly opposing postmodernism⁴⁰ – consistently warned against one-sidedly ironic, 'non-serious' readings of his writings from the start. Just like Western European postmodern writers self-critically strove for a move 'beyond' irony and relativism from scratch, so Prigov emphasized from the early 1970s onwards that such concepts as sincerity and love were pivotal to his creations.⁴¹ Admittedly, in his hands those concepts never turned into unreflected sentimental categories. 'Sincerity has two modes,' he argued on one occasion, 'that of a truly sociocultural construct and that of some non-articulated principle ...The mode which I take up and which I experience and criticize is the cultural mode'.⁴² At the same time, Prigov defines his own 'shimmering' strategy as an attempt to shift from the cultural mode to a more 'generally human, pre-articulated' sincerity: in the somewhat jargonistic terms without which Prigov wouldn't Prigov, the poet explains that

> *if one correctly traces [sincerity's cultural mode – ER], it evokes a classical reaction of sincerity. ... In fact, at some point I sincerely enter into a discourse. The problem is not that of deceiving the reader ... The problem is that you yourself have to be beside yourself in that respect.*⁴³

That sincerity (this highly analytical form of it) was pivotal to Prigov's artistic project suggests the persistence with which the concept keeps emerging throughout his *preduvedomleniia* – the theoretical introductions with which he opened most of his verse collections. 'I just want sincerity so badly!' he exclaimed, quasi-involuntarily, in the one which I picked as a motto for this chapter.⁴⁴

In pondering that avidly desired sincerity, Prigov systematically framed the concept as a counter-official longing that clashed with the 'hypocrisy' of the Soviet experiment. The first to use the phrase 'new sincerity' as an artistic motto inside *and* outside Russia,[45] he formally introduced it in a 1985 lecture addressed to postmodernist-to-the-bone Vladimir Sorokin. Hadn't Sorokin's literary devices exhausted themselves by now? Prigov asked his colleague. Instead of the Conceptualist disavowal of exalted ideas and feelings, wasn't 'a New Sincerity conceivable?'[46] Prigov went on to answer his own question positively, coining his new poetic device as a primarily sociopolitically motivated strategy. 'New Sincerity', he explained, was unique in allowing the writer to speak 'clearly, sincerely and directly', but 'without forgetting the entire scorching experience of what we have been through'.[47] After all, he concluded, 'we need ideology!'[48]

That Prigov's sincerity was a complex, non-one-dimensional entity – one intricately interwoven with rather than strictly opposed to irony – is beyond doubt. But the references to 'scorching' past experiences and to the need for 'ideology' do unequivocally show something else: the fact that for *this* artist, reflections on sincerity were inextricably interlaced with thinking about the Soviet past. In that respect, the Sorokin lecture is not unique within Prigov's oeuvre: when the poet conceptualized sincerity, history was never far away. This is true not only for his early writings; in the late 2000s, Prigov still answered the question 'how can one be sincere?' entirely in terms of a political discussion. Is the genuinely experienced trauma of victims of Soviet repression, he ruminated in the 2006 essay 'Sincerity: That is What We Cherish Most of All', more heartfelt than the equally earnest enthusiasm of pro-Stalinist veterans? And if not, don't the two complement rather than contradict one another?[49]

Prigov, in short, configured contemporary sincerity primarily in response to Stalinist repressions and in reaction to the Soviet experiment. His writing suggested it is sincerity that paves the road to coping with that experience as an artist: whether the notion is blemished by historical trauma or not, the poet can express himself only by embracing, rather than defying, sincerity.

Kirill Medvedev: 'New Sincerity' and the Conflicted Post-Soviet Mind

The memory topos is far from restricted to Prigov's writings on sincerity: in fact, it forms a continuous thread in the post-Soviet debate on the topic. This does not mean that its status within the 'new sincerity' discourse has been static between the mid-1980s and today. With the advent of new media, the orientation on public memory decreased at the cost of more intimate conceptualizations of sincerity. By the mid-2000s, a younger generation of Russian writers and bloggers presents *their*, substantially more privately oriented, definition of 'new sincere' art and literature.

This younger generation sometimes adheres to the vision of a 'new sincerity' as a reaction to the past, but it also roots that concept in more personal-intimate and globally informed discourses. 'New sincerity' now becomes the Russian blogger's slogan for such diverse phenomena as pop bands, popular films, fashion shops, or favourite cafes. 'This is the new sincerity,' runs blogger flippi754's comment on two attractive girls at Starbucks: 'little drops of spring rain on your cheeks, and hot coffee in your mouth'.[50] That the phrase similarly serves as a social identity marker ('I am a new sincerity afficionado and therefore I love phenomenon X'; 'I proclaim phenomenon X "the new sincerity"') for American bloggers, implies a mildly parodic list of 'official additions to the New Sincerity Movement' by the Californian writer Alex Blagg. In November 2005, Blagg invited readers of his blog to submit weekly nominations for 'things you think might be considered New Sincerity'. He opened the floor with a long list of 'New Sincerity things' that included 'Best Friends, High Fives, Lemonade Stands, Ron Popeil, Arena Football, Forts, Catapults, Retarded People, Hammer, Dodgeball, Camping Trips, Big League Chew, Backpacks, Andrew WK, Astronauts, Tenacious D'.[51]

Needless to add, it is a long way from Prigov's literary-historical writings to Blagg's and flippi754's pop-culturesque vision of a 'new sincerity'. In Russia, however, the debate at large still shares a number of features with those early conceptualizations of the phrase. The Russian 'new sincerity' discourse, for one, is still dominated today by readings of the concept as a soundboard for sociopolitical discussions – discussions in which recent history and the Soviet trauma take pride of place.

Emblematic for new developments in the debate is a 2007 critical essay on the role of 'The Writer in Russia' by the poet Kirill Medvedev (b. 1975). A critically acclaimed poet and translator of Charles Bukowski, Medvedev (not to be confused with his presidential namesake) announced a self-imposed ban on his literary activities in the mid-2000s: he needed to rethink his position in Russia's cultural landscape. Refusing to this day to publish new poems, Medvedev began concentrating on radically leftist political activism instead. He is now known as the founder of a Marxist publishing house and as an organizer and participant of neo-leftist political actions – think literary 'solidarity evenings' for striking workers, or a street protest against the staging of Brecht in a purportedly 'bourgeois' theatre.[52]

Medvedev explains his interest in Marxism in terms of a protest against the postmodern condition, as 'a response to the illustrious "postmodern sensitivity", to the rupture of all sorts of bonds between words, objects, people, acts, to that entire shimmering of fragments in people's heads, to the inability to construct even a minimally coherent world view'.⁵³ In his essay on the Russian writer, he incorporates this anti-postmodern rhetoric in a critique of contemporary Russia – one within which 'sincerity' is the pertinent emotive category. According to Medvedev, under Putin, Russia's artistic climate has become determined 'not so much by "money" and "celebrity"…, but by the "new sincerity"'.⁵⁴ The poet sketches this 'post-postmodern' mentality, with its foregrounding of 'direct expression' and 'biographical experience', in critical strokes:

> *It [the 'new sincerity' – ER] is President Putin and contemporary poetry and the broadcasters on television. It is Alexander Lukashenko admitting that his party falsified the elections – lowered Lukashenko's numbers from 93 percent to 80 percent – because, Lukashenko very sincerely confessed, 'the European Union wouldn't have accepted the results otherwise'. This is simultaneously unbelievable and symptomatic. The new sincerity is the blogosphere, with its absolutely sincere poets in one corner and its equally sincere Nazis in the other.*⁵⁵

Putin, Lukashenko, neo-Nazis: Medvedev's is a highly politicized view of 'new sincerity', in which poetry goes hand in glove with politics. Not surprisingly, Soviet history looms large over the 'new emotionalism' – as Medvedev alternately calls the new mind-set. According to him, if arising partly in reaction to postmodernism, it responds no less to another cultural condition: the 'confused and conflicted (post-)Soviet consciousness' that marks today's Russia.⁵⁶

In Medvedev's rendering, then, 'the new sincerity' of the post-Soviet mind has a markedly instrumental, near-therapeutic social function. In his words, it emerged as 'a tool that could force open' existing cultural discourses – discourses among which 'the rough, ideologized Soviet one' plays first fiddle.⁵⁷ Ultimately, Medvedev believes that 'the new sincerity' does not succeed in fulfilling that curative promise. The current-day sincerity and emotionalism, he argues, have proven non-productive attempts to deal with either the postmodern or the Soviet legacy – and he concludes by pleading for a new socialist project.

Mark Lipovetsky, Alexei Yurchak: Conquering Trauma, Reassessing the Past

By the time Medvedev published his essay, the view of sincerity as a tool – fruitful or not – for coping with the recent past had become rampant in Russian critical theory. This is not the place for an extensive survey of the discussion, nor of the many contributions made to it by additional individual authors.⁵⁸ For a more inclusive view it does make sense, however, to halt briefly at a different type of voice in the discussion: that of the scholarly commentator. A closer look at two scholarly perspectives reveals that Soviet history colours metatheoretical takes on the 'new-sincerity' discussion no less than those of literary practitioners.

Emblematic is the view of post-Soviet sincerity of the renowned literary scholar Mark Lipovetsky. In his *Paralogies* – a recent publication that attracted much attention among scholars of contemporary Russian culture – Lipovetsky discerns a 'late postmodern' trend in recent Russian writing that attempts to restore the grand narratives of the past. In his view, in non-fictional genres this 'late postmodern' tendency inclines 'towards what D.A. Prigov ... labeled a "new sincerity"'.[59] Although sceptical of the phrase 'new sincerity' himself, Lipovetsky does use it to cluster the essayistic writings of a number of contemporary Russian authors. Crucial to his analysis of these 'new sincere' writers are, once again, history and memory. For example, Lipovetsky ascribes a downright therapeutic historical function to the essays-in-prose of poet-cum-publicist Lev Rubinstein. Rubinstein's authorial position, according to Lipovetsky,

> *is for him the single accessible form of* historical consciousness, *which allows him to reconcile himself with trauma and to conquer it through laughter, while at the same time refraining from* identifying ... *with the ideologicized discourse of 'grand history'*. (italics original – ER)[60]

The passage from which this citation stems is crystal clear about the type of shock that Rubinstein seeks to overcome: rather than historical trauma per se, his battles target the *Soviet* trauma.

Similarly historicized views are articulated by another icon of post-Soviet cultural studies: Alexei Yurchak, whose analysis of 'post-post-Communist sincerity' I mentioned earlier. Yurchak explains the Russian pendant of global 'new-sincere' trends as marked by a preference for Soviet myths – among young artists in particular. He defies the common reading of that turn to Soviet aesthetics as reactionary nostalgia. Reverting to curative metaphors, Yurchak prefers portraying it as a purposive attempt to 'engag[e] with the Soviet past' in order to 'enable an aesthetic construction of the future'.[61] Exploring 'new-sincere' trends in concrete works of musical and visual art, he summarizes them in glaringly politico-historical terms. In his argument, they offer an 'aesthetics [with] its own political potential ... based on the redeemed categories of sincerity and idealism'.[62] Both the artists' own turn to a 'new sincerity' and the popular demand for that trend are, so Yurchak concludes, *instances of the same contemporary phenomenon of reassessing the history of Soviet modernity, exploring its meaningful aspects, and separating the original ethical aspirations of that modernity from the political regime which relied on them for its ends.*[63]

Conclusion: 'New Sincerity' and Memory

A creative reassessment of Soviet history to one, a coping tool for the 'scorching' Soviet experience to another, a vehicle for 'reconciling' with historical 'trauma' to a third, and a response to 'the post-Soviet consciousness' to a fourth: in Russian literary *and* metatheoretical discussions on a 'post-postmodern', 'new sincerity', thinking about sincerity inextricably intertwines with attempts to deal with the recent past.

That orientation on collective memory is, of course, not unique to Russia – or to contemporary culture, for that matter. Even a cursory peek at history tells us that at times of cultural paradigm shifts, the wish to 'solve' or 'cure' recent traumatic socio-political experiences is never far away. To mention but one example, wasn't the Romantic answer to the Enlightenment partly informed by a shock reaction among intellectuals to late eighteenth-century revolutionary events? The same is true for international pendants of the 'new sincerity' debate: more than once, the shift to a 'reanimated', 'post-postmodern' sincerity has been presented as an artistic response to the attacks on the World Trade Center on September 11, 2001.[64] This is true for the US, as could be expected; but a similar causal relation has been discussed with reference to Western European countries – think of Thomas Vaessens's analysis, elsewhere in this volume, of a 'late postmodern' reaction to the 9/11 attacks in Dutch literature. Vaessens links that response directly to American 'new sincere' trends. Similarly, the 'search ... for lost innocence' that Guido Snel – in another contribution to this collection – discerns in 'post-postmodern' writing and visual arts from Central Europe and the Balkans emerges primarily in response to concrete political-historical traumas.

But political history looms large over 'new-sincere' talk, particularly in post-Soviet artistic and literary debates. This should not surprise us, perhaps: in studies of contemporary Russian literature, the Soviet trauma has repeatedly been singled out as a major concern. '[W]hat it emulates and struggles with, is history,' says Alexander Etkind about post-Soviet literature; and Rosalind Marsh argues that 'Russian society's confrontation with its past' is a leitmotif of post-Soviet literature.[65] The preoccupation with the Soviet past in the Russian literary culture is inevitable, according to Etkind: since post-Soviet society lacks 'hard memory' (monuments, state laws, or court decisions that critically assess the recent past), reminiscences of Soviet terror tend to adopt 'soft' forms (literary, historical, and other narratives).⁶⁶ Etkind has explored 'soft memory' primarily in literary texts; but the discussions on a 'new sincerity' that I mapped here suggest that critical debates *about* literature (by the writers themselves or by academic commentators) form another 'soft' space permeated by strivings to digest the past.

That those debates single out sincerity as an artistic coping tool for the Soviet trauma is not surprising either. In their recent collected volume *Rhetoric of Sincerity*, Ernst Van Alphen and Mieke Bal argue that sincerity is always foregrounded 'in times of intercultural tensions and conflicts'.⁶⁷ The post-9/11 pleas for a 'post-ironic sincerity' confirm their claim. So do other historical examples, and I agree with Van Alphen and Bal – but I think that the post-Soviet literary debates still have something more to teach us about the rhetoric of sincerity. They demonstrate that interrogations of the concept thrive not only at times of *intercultural* conflict, but also in periods of *inner cultural* tumult. In modern Russia, sincerity debates flourished after Stalin's death; and they revived during and after the downfall of the Soviet Union. Russian discussions on a 'post-postmodern', 'new sincerity' developed emphatically in the aftermath of this internal political crisis. In order to analyze these discussions, taking into account their commemorative dimension is inevitable. That dimension may be more or less pivotal to other local manifestations of 'post-postmodern' discourse, but in the post-Soviet cultural space, as the above analyses showed, it is unusually prominent.

Chapter 2
British Literature

Residual Traces of Postmodernism
Sebastian Groes

Introduction

This chapter traces the various ways in which British writers have responded to and shaped the legacy of postmodernism. The main argument is that the deeply moral English tradition and its rootedness in humanist thinking have always been distrustful of relativistic narratives of the more radical thinkers of high postmodernism, resulting in an intellectual disappointment with, and rejection of, the possibilities offered by postmodern culture.

I would like to focus on five specific moves made by writers after high postmodernism, which runs from the early 1980s to the mid-1990s. First, we see a 'reality hunger' manifesting itself in the writing of the 2000s that rejects any interest in the textualization of the world beyond the subjective self in favour of reconnection with material culture, which it finds unable to attain due to epistemological complexity and uncertainty. Second, after relativistic accounts of history and culture that claim our knowledge of the world is limited and partial, and therefore profoundly uncertain, we see the reassertion of the boundary between fact and fiction in what has been termed the 'new historical novel'. Indeed, a form of 'New Humanism' is manifesting itself in reaction to postmodernity's ideological challenges by rescuing some of the important underpinnings of the artistic and philosophical concepts that come to us from the European tradition beyond the confines of the Enlightenment. Third, the optimistic, cheerful accounts of the possibilities offered by the so-called 'international novel' that emerged in the early 1980s make way for narratives by immigrants who are more cautious and distrustful of the possibilities of the multicultural society. Fourth, there is a marked return to the legacy of modernism (late) and its obsession with the workings of the mind and consciousness, sparking what could be termed a new inward turn. Fifth, and in conjunction with this return to modernist preoccupation, there is a renewed interest in formalist analysis. This layering of responses can be traced in writers who contributed to shaping British postmodernism, such as Ian McEwan and Julian Barnes, as well as those who started writing in the shadow of these high postmodernists, such as Zadie Smith and Tom McCarthy.

In the conclusion I will argue that the postmodern era has a lasting legacy because it has continued to complicate and destabilize our perception and understanding of the modern world. Despite a move away from the concerns of hardcore postmodernism, this does not mean a permanent and wholesale rejection of the issues that its critics and writers raised but a renegotiation and realignment of narrative accounts of our cultures and world that will continue to make a major contribution to shaping our understanding of our post-postmodernist, or late modernist cultures.

Postmodernism in Britain

Postmodernism has now become a taboo subject within English Studies in the UK in various ways, an obsolete concept, in Philip Larkin's words, 'pushed to one side/Like an outdated combine harvester'.[1] Traditional English reserve and a distrust of things continental created some initial suspicion of the 'highfalutin' postmodernist theory and intellectual ideas. Especially the Leaviste tradition of English fiction, with its rootedness in liberal humanist values and its staunch convictions about reality and morality, pre-empted the unalloyed success of postmodernist fiction in Britain. In his influential and provocative book on English fiction, *The Great Tradition* (1948), F.R. Leavis identified 'great' writers (Jane Austen, George Eliot, Henry James, Joseph Conrad and D.H. Lawrence) whose work promoted the values and virtues of liberal humanism and displayed 'a marked moral intensity'.[2] This traditional moralist outlook established a scepticism which prevented a blanket adoption or embracing of the cultural relativism of the more hardcore postmodernist thinkers and writers.

British intellectuals are equally distrustful of cleverly clever philosophers, and in contrast to the major thinkers that the continent has spawned over the centuries, the nation lacks a 'great' tradition of philosophy. The post-war boom in French theory, and post-structuralism in particular, had come to Britain mainly via Frank Kermode, who introduced continental philosophy and *avant garde* literary criticism in the hugely successful course at University College London in the late 1960s. Although embraced by a small club of academics, the 'theory-led' practices of the 1980s were generally frowned upon. Derrida was booed at a lecture he gave in Cambridge, and Baudrillard was dismissed as an amoral relativist. English culture has continuously been averse to over-intellectualizing debates, and favours stories over theory and philosophy as a way of thinking about the world.

Yet British fiction certainly contributed greatly to shaping our understanding of postmodernism. Authors such as Peter Ackroyd, Martin Amis, John Banville, Julian Barnes, A.S. Byatt, Angela Carter, to an extent Ian McEwan, John Fowles and certainly Salman Rushdie are all authors belonging to the hypercanon of literary postmodernism. Although John Berger and John Fowles, both influenced by French post-structuralist thinkers of the late 1950s and 1960s, had already introduced various concepts and representative models into British fiction in the 1960s, it is the aforementioned group of authors that popularized postmodern intellectual concerns in the UK in the 1980s and early 1990s. Ackroyd and Julian Barnes practised what was to become known as historiographic metafiction by writing novels which emphasized the constructedness of any narrative so that the boundary between fact and fiction became porous if not non-existent, whilst our knowledge of the past gained through textual documents is fundamentally unreliable. In short, all our relationships to the world and other people are 'narrated' and, to a large degree, textual, and therefore uncertain.

Martin Amis became a specialist in self-referentiality and exploitation of simulacra. In novels such as *Money* (1983) and *London Fields* (1989), we find an exploration and criticism of the constructedness of 'the real', of the weakened traditional status of the author as an omniscient moral authority, and the ways in which texts determine the nature of our experience. Amis's own interest in the postmodern came to a dead end with *The Information* (1995), the third instalment of his London triptych, another sprawling novel that has problems of finding anything useful to say about anything.

Salman Rushdie became perhaps the most obvious, and controversial, embodiment of British postmodernism when he was fatwa-ed by Ayatollah Khomeini for his supposedly offensive novel *The Satanic Verses* (1988). His early work, and *Midnight's Children* (1983) in particular, was adept at deconstructing grand narratives and rewriting established historical narratives. Beyond the controversy, *The Satanic Verses* was important because the novel posited the world, and the city of London in particular, as a textual construct that can be rewritten. Rushdie spectacularly renames London, in its Indo-Pakistani iteration, as "Ellowen Deeowen".[3] Indeed, one of the protagonists, Saladin Chamcha, imagines hearing 'the noise of some approaching doom, drawing closer, letter by letter, ellowen deeowen, London' (*SV* 136) whilst his antagonist, Gibreel Farishta, imagines conquering London by means of his maps: '*London shareef, here I come*. He had the city in his pocket: Geographers' London, the whole dog-eared metropolis, A to Z'.[4]

Rushdie also promoted a concept called the 'International Novel', a concept born in the early 1980s, which was long overdue for many writers living in Britain. Since the 1980s Rushdie's postmodern ideas about the migrant, nomad, cultural cross-fertilization and hybridity have created internationalization of the British novel. The migrant and the nomad have provided powerful images for the postmodern sense of the incomprehensible global networks of capital and also of the new international novelist: a figure no longer tied to any one national tradition but rejoicing in the fluid, the disseminated and the rootless. The novel, like Britain, had to acknowledge and invite the *dissemination* and loss of national identity. Embracing an ever-expanding flood of immigrant stories, Rushdie refers to his contemporaries: 'we are inescapably international writers at a time when the novel has never been a more international form'.[5]

Martin Amis's classic postmodern novels also presented shifty, globetrotting individuals – one may think of *Money*'s porn and fast food addict John

Self – yet undercutting these protagonists is a moral force that ultimately draws the novelist world back into the realm of the Leavisite tradition and the certainties of the humanist tradition. Despite the apparently ever more open and fluid identities that globalization enacted upon the penitentiary island consciousness of England, a deliberate retrenching into bounded, closed forms of identity and nationhood also implied a rejection of postmodern issues and concerns.

Understanding Postmodern Heritage: The New Postmodernists

It is clear that the late capitalist modes of production that underpinned the intellectual foundations of postmodernism have not retreated; instead, the early twenty-first-century world has continued to be shaped by ever increasingly post-industrial forms of production whereby science and technology have radically and irrevocable altered the nature of the way we live.

The absence of postmodernism as a major category for the definition of literary work in the books by two important critics of contemporary British fiction, Dominic Head and Richard Bradford, suggests that the British intellectual landscape is actively repressing what it now has come to see as an embarrassing intellectual blip or a philosophical dead end. In both critics we see a return to more conservative, conventional forms of organization of artistic production via, on the one hand, the reassertion of distinct social categories, such as class, gender and sexuality, place, and ethnicity, and on the other hand, literary form and aesthetics. Indeed, Bradford's *The Novel Now* (2007) opens his critical work by pinpointing a wider struggle between realism and modernism's experimental impetus, whose reverberations can be felt throughout the twentieth and early twenty-first centuries. Dominic Head also warns against appropriating writers in the name of postmodernism as a reactionary rejection of an antimodernist backlash and return to realism in the 1950s because the postmodernist project is much less coherent than some of the critics pretend: 'The problem with enlisting these writers – perhaps any writer – in the name of postmodernism with a beneficent political underpinning is that to do so implies a uniform ideological conviction about the novel that is unconvincing.'[6] Similarly, the appealing thesis of Brian McHale's *Postmodernist Fiction* (1987), which presumed a clear-cut shift from the modernist concern with epistemology to postmodern issues regarding ontology, seemed a convenient yet overly sweeping, generalizing thesis.[7] Indeed, these grand conceptions themselves are at odds with most theses about postmodernism's interest in shifting away from grand narratives.

However, despite this wholesale rejection of postmodernism within English criticism, there is an intellectual pocket that has continued the postmodern project in a modified form. Bradford does single out a small group of writers whom he calls 'The New Postmodernists', a category that includes the fiction of Will Self, John Lancaster, Nicola Barker, Candia McWilliam, Ali Smith, Toby Litt and David Mitchell. These writers eschew a critical tendency that treats the work of authors indiscriminately as undiscerning functionaries of an all-encompassing postmodern condition which it exemplifies. The above-named authors, and to an extent the ones discussed in detail below,

> *execute a calculated and premeditated shift away from an implied mindset, outside the novel, that involves the plausible, the rational and the predictable [...] The writers themselves are as astutely aware of the taxonomy of postmodernism as its theorists. [...] Their novels incorporate many of the mantras that their readers [...] would recognize as guarantees to intellectual hauteur, but while the theorists write in a manner that variously bores and alienates the ordinary reader, the novelists invite them in. It may or may not be the case that we are, as participants in the Postmodern Condition, experiencing an unprecedented intellectual and cultural apocalypse, an unbidden and all-pervasive state of nihilism, but what is evident is that fiction writers have seized upon this as a saleable commodity. Their style is alluring, by varying degrees elegant, friendly and transparent, and once the reader becomes attuned to this they are offered commodified thrills: multinarratives with no cohering pattern, horrible descents into the grotesque, arbitrary switches between the plausible and unimaginable. The New Postmodernists are in truth engaged in a programme that undermines the jargon-ridden pomposity of their academic counterparts.*[8]

Beyond these new postmodernists, intellectual life in Britain has seen various 'turns'. One of the most important ones was the turn towards New Historicism, which revalued detailed historical research and favored literary narratives that did not wear their relativity on their metafictional sleeve and the limits of factual knowledge. A good example of this is Julian Barnes's *Arthur & George* (2005). After exploring historical relativity in his *über*-postmodern text *Flaubert's Parrot* (1983), in which an amateur biographer attempts to reconstruct a mystery in the life of Gustave Flaubert and discovers that he is unable to do so and left unable to resolve his quest, this more recent novel investigates the life of another writer, Arthur Conan Doyle. In contrast to *Flaubert's Parrot*, *Arthur & George* makes much greater use of factual research, and the novel reasserts the boundary between fact and fiction. Another, even more recent turn within English studies sees a revaluation of formal analysis and the close reading of text instead of the exploration of theoretical paradigms in relationship to literary texts. There is in general a more grounded research activity.

Indeed, one important marker of this return to realist modes of representation comes in the form of the New Puritans, whose manifesto-anthology *All Hail the New Puritans* (2000), edited by Nicholas Blinchoe and Matt Thorne, is a clear shift away from the postmodern baroque of writers such as Rushdie and Amis. This new generation of writers, including Alex Garland, Geoff Dyer, Toby Litt, Rebecca Ray and Scarlett Thomas, shunned poetic license, rhetoric, and moved away from the imaginary, rooting their prose narratives in very real places and times. Indeed, in one of the conveniently numbered ten points, they also declared themselves moralists whose texts feature a recognisable ethical reality, which is a clear rejection of the amoral cultural and social relativism with which postmodern thinking in its more radical (i.e. Baudrillardian) form had come to be associated.

A more recent book is David Shields's *Reality Hunger: A Manifesto* (2010), in which the author sets out to 'write the *ars poetica* for a burgeoning group of interrelated (but unconnected) artists in a multitude of forms and media (lyric essay, prose poem, collage novel, visual art, film, television, radio, performance art, rap, stand-up comedy, graffiti) who are breaking larger and larger chunks of "reality" into their work.'[9] One may think of American writers such as Dave Eggers whose first novel *A Heartbreaking Work of Staggering Genius* (2000) reasserted a need for 'the real' while necessarily acknowledging its attainability, and in a British context, Zadie Smith and Monica Ali, whose work attempted to reassert a historical and material reality. This movement is characterized, according to Shields, by a

> *deliberate unartiness: "raw" material, seemingly unprocessed, unfiltered, uncensored, and unprofessional. [...] Randomness, openness to accident and serendipity, spontaneity; artistic risk, emotional urgency and intensity, reader/viewer participation; an overtly literal tone, as if a reporter were viewing a strange culture; plasticity of form, pointillism; criticism as autobiography; self-reflexivity, self-ethnography, anthropological autobiography; a blurring (to the point of invisibility) of any distinction between fiction and nonfiction: the lure and blur of the real.*[10]

Although Shields appears to deliberately distance himself from postmodern, both the rhetoric and content show residual traces of postmodern thought. The proliferation of form seems to be a product of the voracious postmodern appetite for absorbing a multiplicity of literary and cultural forms of expression. In particular, the effacing of the distinction between fiction and nonfiction seems informed by the postmodern thought that all narrative acts are mediated and discursive and therefore constructed and artificial. Although there is a clear hunger for 'the real', this real has itself, especially in the light of continuously new developments within mass media and technology, become postponed and contentious.

Late (Post)Modernism in British Literature

This section traces the ways in which three writers in various and different ways representative of British fiction have engaged with, challenged and moved beyond the confines of postmodern intellectual thought. Although all three were deeply influenced by postmodern culture and thinking, the recent work of Ian McEwan, Zadie Smith and Tom McCarthy shows a clear shift away from high postmodernism whilst acknowledging its continued value and heritage. All three writers are also public intellectuals who have spoken openly about their problematic relationship with postmodernism whilst acknowledging their desire not only to go beyond postmodernism, but also to return to the concerns at the heart of late modernism, such as time, consciousness and memory. This re-diction should be considered within a more general revisioning of modernity that runs from the later Dickens of the 1860s to the present moment, and in which postmodernity forms a distinct, late twentieth-century branch that is part of a late, or later, modernism.

Ian McEwan

Ian McEwan was not much of a postmodernist to begin with, yet the trajectory of his work forms an important indicator of the various shifts that British culture, and literary responses to these changes, has been going through. Not only is McEwan obsessed and unconditionally committed to understanding what is going on in private and public life today, but the work itself has been an important shaping force upon British literature. Still, compared to some of the other authors that make up the astoundingly talented generation of writers to which he belongs, Amis, Barnes and Rushdie, he is the one most suspicious of the more radical branches of postmodern thought, and the later work of McEwan sees a intellectual retrenching and return to Leavisite values.

McEwan's early work was dominated by a crisis of representation, and he sought refuge in writing for film and television. In an interview he states that he rejected the high and late modernist of Kafka and Alain Robbe-Grillet: 'I had lost faith in writing. I had been tied to a restricted aesthetic of the novel that I now find quite puzzling. It was the existential trap, the novel cleansed of all reference to place or recognizable public spaces, with no connection to time or historical context. This mode of writing didn't permit itself the luxury of describing inner states; it was all down to what someone said or did.'¹¹ Equally, McEwan shunned the postmodern narratives of Ackroyd, Rushdie, Amis and Barnes because he has always been interested in understanding the state of the present at a more direct level, at a sometimes even journalistic level, as his screenplay about the implications of Thatcherism, *The Ploughman's Lunch* (1983), shows for instance.

Yet there is a 'postmodern' moment in his first proper novel, *The Child in Time* (1989), where the protagonist is spying on his parents who are discussing potentially aborting him at the time when he is still a fetus in his mother's womb. The discussion leads to an epistemological, or even ontological, conundrum that is worthy of profound Borgesian mind games or, at least, the epoch-defining film *Back to the Future* (1985).

McEwan denounces this mode of writing as a self-indulgent flight of fancy in *Saturday* (2005) where the protagonist, the *über*-rational neurosurgeon, Henry Perowne, makes a case for the realist tradition of fiction. Indeed, whereas his idealistic, artistic children, Daisy and Theo, and the poet Grammaticus represent the humanist tradition and its belief in the redeeming values of art and culture, Perowne is a calculating rationalist who has no truck with experimental literature or the imagination in general. His curative vision and Enlightenment beliefs cause him to have a staunch faith in his predominantly rational and materialist vision of civilization as a machine that can be controlled through cold-blooded calculation and interpretation. Whilst stuck in a traffic jam in London, the narrator notes the limits of his imagination: 'He can't feel his way past the iron weight of the actual to see beyond the boredom of a traffic tailback, or the delay to which he is contributing, or the drab commercial hopes of a parade of shops he's been stuck beside for fifteen minutes. He doesn't have the lyric gift to see beyond it – he's a realist, and can never escape.'¹² Perowne is unable to see beyond the materiality of the world around him.

Yet interpreting McEwan's fiction is never easy. One narratological detail of the novel that throws a spanner in the works of McEwan's own presupposed embracing of realist modes of writing – the conflating the narrator with the author's point of view, a trap that many lazy critics fell into easily – is the gap between the protagonist's consciousness and the narrator, who constantly mocks and ironizes Perowne by showing his imaginative limitations. The novel makes it constantly clear to the reader that Perowne's experience is at the mercy of the narrator, and what is actually at stake in the novel are the very limits of our ability to interpret the contemporary world dominated by mass media and technology that have become extensions of our consciousness.

An important factor is McEwan's representation of Perowne's experience as a fictional construct. The British writer J.G. Ballard contributed hugely in defining the postmodern experience by writing that we live in a world in which 'reality' is 'ruled by fictions of every kind – mass-merchandizing, advertizing, politics conducted as a branch of advertising, the pre-empting of any original response to experience by the television screen'.[13] In McEwan's *Saturday* there is an overwhelming sense that our contemporary experience at the beginning of the early twenty-first-century world has become completely intertwined with and mediated by technology and mass media. The result is not only a loss of a potentially authentic experience, but also an increasing gap between the private experience and a sense of 'the real' beyond the subjective self, the public life we share collectively. For instance, Perowne's obsession with round-the-clock news broadcasting is an indication of his thwarted desire to connect with the general public in a communal narrative. Mark Currie suggests that in the representation of Perowne's experience, there is a 'sense of corroboration between the public narratives of news and private experience. This sense of the gap between public and private [...] extends more generally to Perowne's relation to his historical moment, and to his position in the modern city'.[14] McEwan's novel suggests that our understanding of the contemporary self is a fantasy about the collective mediated by the narratives and discourses provided by the state, but in particular by commerce and mass media. This is also a clear indicator that the postmodern has had a lasting impact upon our understanding of the world.

Yet the way in which McEwan frames this differs from the knowingly self-reflective account of twenty years ago; his narratives show that in fact we have lost a particular ability to *know* the world around us. This sober conclusion also expresses itself in the form of McEwan's writing. A bird's eye view of McEwan's work is also important because it shows a trajectory that has slowly circled back towards an important literary period in British literary history, namely, modernism. Beneath the apparent foregrounding of realist modes of writing, we are trapped in Henry Perowne's stream of consciousness, but it is McEwan's masterpiece *Atonement* (2001) that forms an even clearer case in point. The ending of this novel contains a major manipulative plot twist, which many of the critics have regarded as postmodern trickery.

In a furious attack on McEwan's *Atonement*, Alistair Cormack suggests that McEwan's increasing conservatism and return to Leavisite tradition and its belief in mimesis, as well as his belief in science, undermine our very trust in the novel form as an idiosyncratic but very valuable mode of knowledge itself:

> *By referring to Austen, the novel implicitly attacks postmodern novelists and their celebration of the fictive. These latter-day Jacobins – one thinks*

> *perhaps of Angela Carter and Salman Rushdie, and, ironically, McEwan's earlier self, who wrote* The Child in Time *– are guilty of making overelaborate claims for the novel, and the literary imagination in general. Against the dangers of relativism and self-delusion implicit in postmodern poetics,* Atonement *pits a tradition of English empiricism.*[15]

Although Cormack's dismissal of McEwan as a Leavisite traditionalist is perhaps slightly reductive given that the author's work is so complex and contradictory, there certainly is an intellectual and aesthetic retrenching in McEwan's work that aligns itself with more realist modes of representation as well as anti-postmodernist accounts of understanding the contemporary experience. However, we do find a clear indication of the legacy of postmodernism in McEwan's foregrounding of uncertainty at the heart of early twenty-first-century life, and more generally in the intensification of his focus upon memory, time, and the subjective consciousness and experience.

Zadie Smith

The work of Zadie Smith (born 1975) forms an important 'hinge' between postmodern culture and its aftermath, beyond profoundly shaped by its various forces yet also rejecting its gravitational powers. The overwhelming critical and popular reception of her first novel, *White Teeth* (2000), at the beginning of the new millennium, and her next two novels, the less well-received *The Autograph Man* (2002) and her homage to E.M. Forster, *On Beauty* (2005), suggests that Smith had a major impact upon the contemporary British literary imagination. Smith's critically acclaimed, popular, prize-winning *White Teeth* turned her, almost overnight, into a global literary superstar. The novel shows us, perhaps naively optimistically, how the multicultural society could triumph – at least in the imagination. Its subject matter and aesthetic move us away from Rushdie's earlier euphoric, totalizing narratives as well as his tropes that involve the celebration of the rootless postmodern nomad. Instead, Smith presents us with a cautiously upbeat account of a globalized culture with at its heart an ever more uncertain and troubled society drowning in the currents of contingency.

Smith's work consciously shifts away from postmodern literature's obsession with the textuality of experience and the world beyond the subjective self in favour of a more grounded vision that reasserts materiality and roots the human subject within a historical context. Whereas Rushdie's characters in *The Satanic Verses* still imagined the possibility of literally rewriting the world around them, the protagonist of *White Teeth*, Irie Jones, is more sceptical of the utopian powers of the imagination. She observes 'lives that were stranger than fiction, funnier than fiction, crueller than fiction, and with consequences that fiction can never have'.[16]

Smith's dynamic and energetic *White Teeth* is the result of her time at Cambridge University, 'the regurgitation of the kind of beautiful, antiquated, left-side-of-the-brain liberal arts education', yet it also emerged from, and represented the euphoria of, New Labour's election triumph in 1997, which ended 18 years of Conservative rule, in the year Smith graduated.[17] Whether this was a coincidence or not, Smith and her novel became the New Labourite blueprint for the ways in which the multicultural society might triumph, even though Smith herself cautioned against this reading of her novel.

It might be said that *White Teeth* offers itself as the new literary middle ground – a term that critic Lorna Sage uses to describe the realism of women writers such as Iris Murdoch and Margaret Drabble – that would allow the heterogeneous, diverse social and cultural communities to be able to live and flourish together in harmony.[18] The novel begins in 1974, when after a failed suicide attempt, the father of the protagonist, Archie, meets Irie's mother Clara at a party. The narration of this encounter is illuminating because it reveals how Smith moves away from Rushdie's magical realism towards a carefully controlled reassertion of the boundary between 'the real' and the fictional:

> *But first a description: Clara Bowden was beautiful in all senses except maybe, by virtue of being black, the classical. Clara Bowden was magnificently tall, black as ebony and crashed sable, with hair plaited in a horseshoe which pointed up when she felt lucky, down when she didn't. At this moment it was up. It is hard to know whether that was significant.*[19]

The reader is confronted with a set of rules of semi-realistic representation. We are back in the sphere of naturalism, where a description of external appearances allows the reader to understand the character's mental make-up. The plaited hair, for instance, acts as symbol of Clara's mental constitution; we can conveniently 'read' her inner world via her outward presentation. Simultaneously, this traditional realistic mode is undermined by the knowing foregrounding of the description *as* a description, and by the irony in the narrator's voice. The modified realism, which has a clear postmodern knowingness and self-reflexivity about it, is further complicated again in the final line, which stresses the uncertainty of this late twentieth-century world: there are limits to knowing the world and ourselves.

The scene that follows continues to question any comfortable idea of what the narrative status of this represented world is. Smith appropriates a cliché from the history of narrative – the Cinderella fairytale in which a poor, plain girl changes into a stunning princess – and sprinkles it with 1930s Hollywood iconography. When Archie looks at Clara float down the stairs, the spectators below go silent:

> *In real life he had never seen it. But it happened with Clara Bowden. She walked down the stairs in slow motion, surrounded by afterglow and fuzzy lighting. And not only was she the most beautiful thing he had ever seen, she was also the most comforting woman he had ever met. [...] She gave him a wide grin that revealed possibly her one imperfection. A complete lack of teeth in the top of her mouth. (p. 24)*

The description knowingly sets up an epiphany whereby fiction is infiltrating reality. Yet the 'scene' turns into a deflatory experience, which ruptures and questions the representative power of fictional narration. *White Teeth* attempts to restore realism and to restore materiality after a postmodern literature dominated by an emphasis on the textual nature of experience and world beyond the subjective self. Smith is knowingly distancing herself from Rushdie's ecstatic attempt to represent experience as a purely mediated construct, and she constantly foregrounds the hiatus between the experience of England through his immigrant's eyes and its novelistic representation: '"The gulf between books and experience," intones the bosom friend of Irie's father Archie, Samad Iqbal, solemnly, "is a lonely ocean"' (p. 240).

This also has implications for our understanding of Smith's vision of the multicultural society, optimism about which is often rooted in postmodern fantasies of the culturally hybrid and porous subject. Pilar Cuder-Domínguez's assertion that *White Teeth* strikes 'at the very heart of the middle-class, heterosexual, patriarchal values that have persisted to this day in the English identity. [Smith suggests] that the class struggle is as prominent as the racial one' is certainly not true, yet Dominic Head's claim about Smith's naïve subscription to the multicultural society is a slight misrepresentation as well.[20] Bruce King comes closer to understanding the more ambivalent currents within *White Teeth*:

> White Teeth *was the desired multicultural novel of a new multicultural England, a celebration of London as an international city in which peoples and cultures of the world were cross-pollinating. It did not show, however, a new multicultural homogeneity which was replacing old England. The new generation knew each other from school and lived together, but* White Teeth *was also a story of conflicts, of new resentments, of new stereotypes, novel of an England still in turmoil. It was not going to be easy to get beyond race, class, difference.*[21]

White Teeth is, as King suggests, infinitely more ambiguous in its assessment of multicultural society, as the following passage indicates:

> *Because we often imagine that immigrants are on the move, footloose, able to change course at any moment, able to employ their legendary resourcefulness at every turn [...] and step into their foreign lands as blank people, free of any kind of baggage, happy and willing to leave their difference at the docks and take their chances in this new place, merging with the oneness of this greenandpleasantlibertarianlandofthefree [...] weaving their way through Happy Multicultural Land. [...] Because this is the other thing about immigrants [...] they cannot escape their history anymore than you yourself can lose your shadow.*[22]

This passage subverts the idea that Smith's work is a one-sided, optimistic celebration of metropolitan London as a utopian space of multicultural harmony. In the light of this excerpt, Smith's novel contains a much darker vision where the ethnic and religious tensions manifest themselves.

Yet despite the critics' focus on Smith's discussion of the problems and potential of the multicultural society, there is another possible reading that shows how the novel picks up on and develops the postmodern interest in questions about the limits of 'the human'. One sub-plot involves Marcus Chalfens's creation of FutureMouse©, a genetically modified mouse. This particular strand, although it has been read by many critics as a metaphor for miscegenation, should also be read literally: Smith is engaging with developments in science which are renegotiating traditional notions of the human subject drastically. In fact, the novel ends with the creature escaping from the exhibition at which Chalfens's work is unveiled, presenting us with an ambiguous yet comic image that symbolizes our inability to control the world that has emerged out of centuries of scientific revolutions, and which is now challenging received ideas about what it means to be human. As a mapping of the contemporary, the novel is not just attempting to re-align ethnic plurality of the modern cosmopolis with humanist values, it is making a clear statement about the fundamental instability of knowledge in the present, post-postmodern world.

In her criticism, too, Smith has been strikingly explicit in her thinking about postmodernism and its heritage. In an essay called 'Two Directions for the Novel', published in her collected non-fiction work *Changing My Mind* (2009), she notes that a 'breed of lyrical realism has had the freedom of the highway for some time now, with most other exits blocked'.[23] In a move that reminds one of Iris Murdoch's division of the modern novel into either crystalline or journalistic categories in her canonical essay 'Against Dryness' (1961),

Smith suggests that the most exciting form of contemporary writing is a criticism of this realism, building on a tradition of resistance that has its roots in the high modernism of James Joyce and Virginia Woolf and the late modernism of Alain Robbe-Grillet: 'They all of them note the (often unexamined) credos upon which realism is built: the transcendent importance of form, the incantatory power of language to reveal truth, the essential fullness and continuity of the self. Yet despite these theoretical assaults, the American metafiction that stood in opposition to realism has been relegated to a safe corner of literary history, to be studied in postmodernity modules, and dismissed, by our most prominent public critics, as a fascinating failure, intellectual brinkmanship that lacked heart.'[24] There is the sense that Smith wants to rescue postmodern fiction and thought as a radical mode that also fits into a longer tradition of resistance against forms of realism. This tradition hinges on self-reflexivity and a knowingness (in various degrees) about its undertaking, which postmodern fiction shares not only *with*, but also as a form *of*, modernism.

Tom McCarthy

This 'reality hunger' and epistemological uncertainty are continued in the recent work of the *avant garde* artist and writer Tom McCarthy (born 1969), one of the writers that Zadie Smith singles out as a major innovative writer taking fiction after postmodernism into interesting, significant developments. McCarthy's first novel, *Remainder*, 'clears away a little of the deadwood, offering a glimpse of an alternative road down which the novel might, with difficulty, travel forward. We could call this constructive deconstruction,' notes Smith.[25] McCarthy invented the fictional Necronautical Society in 1999, which led to publications including 'Navigation was always difficult' (2005), installations and exhibitions at, for instance, Tate Britain and ICA in London, and New York's The Drawing Centre.

His first novel, *Remainder* (2006), tells the story of a nameless, amnesiac narrator who, after being traumatized by an accident which involves 'something falling from the sky', receives 8 million pounds.[26] He experiences an epiphany in his bathroom and proceeds to reconstitute this memory of his former self by recreating it. He buys a building and uses 're-enactors', actors who have to play specific parts and generate phenomenological associations (smells and sounds) to evoke the memory. The attempted recovery of his former self fails, sparking an ever deepening quest for control over 'the real' by replicating real events. The novel ends with the attempt to enact a carefully rehearsed bank robbery in reality, a project which again fails, and we leave the protagonist after he has escaped on a private plane doing endless loops, postponing his capture by the authorities.

The novel seems to draw on some of the key postmodern tropes and obsessions, including ahistorical amnesia, the proliferation of simulacra, and the perpetual deferral of a conclusion. Yet McCarthy's novel in fact cleverly and knowingly distances us from postmodernism and returns us to high and late modernist obsessions with time, consciousness and memory. There is no postmodern celebration of the eternal postponement of understanding 'the real', but a return to a profound desire to somehow regain – in vain – a sense of history, reality and a whole self. The reconstruction of the memory is equated with a reconstitution of the self, which at first seems to succeed: 'I'd merged with [the memories] and run through them and let them run through me until there'd been no space between us. They'd been *real*; I'd been real – *been* without first understanding how to try to be: cut out the detour. I remembered all this with the force of an epiphany, a revelation.'[27] The attempted negating of the 'detour' here is exactly the idea that memory, just as our relationship to the real in more general terms, is mediated. The point that McCartney's novel makes is that this attempted circumvention of mediation and narration *fails*: our hunger for 'the real' and authenticity remains thwarted.

McCartney's paired down style and obsession with permutations is derived from Samuel Beckett while the obsession with control over perception he gets via the *nouveau roman* experiments of Alain Robbe-Grillet, both late modernists. Another important source of inspiration is Belgian novelists and the filmmaker Jean-Phillipe Toussaint, whose surreal *The Bathroom* (1986) features as one of the key intertexts. This return to surrealism again confirms the realignment of intellectual and metaphysical values with those of modernist rather than postmodernist writers.

The rejection or, perhaps, renegotiation of postmodernism and return to modernism is even more pronounced in McCarthy's Booker Prize-nominated novel *C* (2010). The novel tells the story of Serge Carrefax, born in the last year of the nineteenth century, who journeys through the birth of the various technologies that lie at the heart of our modern consciousness. The novel foregrounds some of the key obsessions of modernist literature and surrealism, from the machinery of modernity (the motor car and airplane) to the labyrinth, and adds to this an interest in wireless transmission that opens up an increasingly internationalized human consciousness, and drugs.

In many ways the novel speaks to our contemporary concerns: from the technological revolutions of the Internet and mobile phone to war and surveillance, but *C* works against postmodernism's open-endedness and exhausted metaphors of nomads and identity in a state of flux, by metaphorically locking the world and the self back into the image of the labyrinth:

> *When the corridor forks, cutting at right angles in opposite directions, he chooses a branch and follows it until, after performing several more right-angled turns and forking twice more, it comes to a dead end. He doubles back to the last fork, advances down another branch and follows it until it, too, runs out—at which point he doubles two forks back and takes a new branch. There's no need to stick to the paved section—the maze is wall-less, two-dimensional as the figures on the block, and the grass is short and wouldn't slow down his trolley—but he continues working his way along the abruptly turning corridors, held by their pattern, until they deliver him back out, through the same doorway, to the footpath once more.*[28]

This is no ordinary labyrinth but an image that 'deconstructs' the nature of modernity. It posits the modern world as a maze which we need to acknowledge in order to understand the nature of the relationship between our modern private selves and the public world. This image describes a relation to complex and proliferating power structures that are present everywhere but visible nowhere, because modern power structures create a condition of being a subject in relation to knowledge he or she does not possess. There is always an order, system, logic or command to which we are subjected, but which never will or can be disclosed because the logic is held in secret and the former centre of command is no longer in control of itself. McCarthy's work then stresses a fundamental uncertainty and ambivalence at the heart of a modern existence that stretches to long before postmodernism, and is likely to persist into the future.

Conclusion

The moralistic tradition of English fiction, which finds its expression most clearly in F.R. Leavis's *The Great Tradition*, and Britain's often insular attitude to the outside world prevented postmodernism from taking a firm hold in the popular consciousness in the first place. After the waning of high postmodernism (found particularly in the work of Martin Amis, Julian Barnes and Salman Rushdie) in the 1990s, there appears to be an abandonment of postmodern concerns and preoccupations. Whereas writers in other countries have perhaps started to reconnect and rethink their previous engagement with postmodernism, British writers placed a moratorium on the use of postmodern ideas; indeed, in critical theory the very lexeme itself has become a taboo word whilst writers have responded violently to its ideas by retrenching into various modes of realism that reassert the boundary between the real and fiction, revalue historical context and seeks to restart some sort of unified self. Yet, if we open up postmodernism as stressing that our relationships to the outside world are mediated and narrated, we can embed it in a longer, subversive tradition that works against conventional forms of realist writing. Rather than return to key concerns of postmodernism, many authors have returned to the interests that lie at the heart of late modernism, and an engagement with the moment at which our modern, and postmodern, cultures sprang into being at the beginning of the twentieth century. Rather than abandoning the key ideas that lie at the heart of modernity, and postmodernity, such as the limits of our ability to interpret and understand – to *know* – the world, British writers today are continuing to embrace the different productive ways in which the uncertainty and ambivalence at the heart of the modern world can be explored.

Chapter 3
Dutch Literature

Stripping the Novel of Its Harmlessness
Thomas Vaessens

The idea that in the name of literature everything should be allowed in novels or poems pushes literature to the periphery of society. – ARNON GRUNBERG[1]

Introduction

In this chapter I will show how Dutch authors reoriented themselves from the late 1980s onwards in relation to the postmodern tradition they inherited. Postmodernism started as a reaction against the liberal humanist[2] (and structuralist) suppression of the historical, political, material and social aspects in the definition of art as eternal and universal.[3] However, in the course of the 1990s it was criticized for being relativistic. The anti-essentialist assumptions of postmodernism appeared to have unforeseen and unsettling consequences for everyday life as well as for literature. During the last few decades these consequences have increasingly come to the attention of postmodern theorists[4] and writers.

I will discuss the critique of postmodernism formulated by Dutch writers in the light of the following hypothesis. A new, late postmodern position has gradually emerged from the Dutch debate about literature and its function. The authors in question consider literary postmodernism as a necessary but insufficient counter-reaction against liberal humanism and its self-assured conception of literature. The question that therefore arises is what, if anything, can be saved in terms of values such as sincerity, authenticity, originality and truth when postmodernism has succeeded in hedging these modern and pre-eminently literary values with suspicion. Can they be reclaimed for literature without returning to their old, essentialist, rationalistic and humanistic underpinnings? Postmodernism is now seen as a medicine against the liberal humanist conception of culture, a medicine which, in the course of the 1980s and 1990s, revealed unpleasant side effects, such as relativism, cynicism and noncommittal irony. I will try to explain the tendency towards *engagement* (commitment) in Dutch novels, not as a late-in-the-day rejection of postmodernism, but as a reaction to its side effects.

Two of the three authors that I discuss in this chapter were part of the postmodern tradition at the start of their careers: Joost Zwagerman and Marjolijn Februari, both born in 1963 and both making their debut at the end of the 1980s. Both will, however, eventually distance themselves from their initial affinity with postmodernism in the course of their careers, albeit without rejecting it outright. Although starting from different viewpoints in their critique of postmodernism, they nevertheless draw similar conclusions regarding the status and significance of writers in today's world. This is also true of the third author I will examine in this chapter, Arnon Grunberg (1971). His debut in 1994 is rather more recent, however, and he mostly associates the postmodern tradition, of which he is critical without rejecting it, with a previous generation of writers.

Therefore, the main witnesses in this chapter are three Dutch writers reconsidering their postmodern heritage. It should be stressed at the outset that these authors feel especially uncomfortable with the increasingly questionable *reputation* of postmodernism in the Netherlands, and that this reputation is based on postmodern theory (and in particular on its frequently biased representations in the mainstream cultural discourse). In the course of the last few decades, postmodernism has been compared with abstraction, 'anything goes' and radical relativism. The fact that postmodern practice (fiction, poetry, drama) was sometimes absolutely anti-relativistic and explicitly engaged could not prevent this. The authors in question tried to escape postmodernism's reputation of being relativist (based on postmodern theory), thereby changing their own authorship (postmodern practice) entirely.

The next section of this chapter ('Postmodernism in the Netherlands') explains how postmodernism has manifested itself in Dutch literature: which postmodernism is given shape in the local discussion? Subsequently, in the section 'Redefining the Postmodern Heritage', the chapter explores the question of how this construction has functioned in the discussion as a terminus: how was that postmodernism criticized? The final part ('Late Postmodernism in Dutch Literature') analyses three representative authors to discover what has replaced postmodernism in literature: what attempts have been made to challenge (or even go beyond) postmodernism?

I want to make two preliminary remarks. (1) My main concern is not to discuss in detail the specificity of the situation in contemporary Dutch literature, which would take me beyond the scope of this chapter. Rather, by using Dutch authors and Dutch literary texts, I would like to contribute to the international debate about the relevance of postmodernism.[5] (2) This chapter does not claim to be a 'realistic' inventory of what is happening in Dutch literature or to be exhaustive. It seeks to explain a few established patterns in the recent literature proceeding from an explanatory model which is, of course, necessarily simplified and sketchy.

Postmodernism in the Netherlands

Postmodernism was remarkably late in entering the literary debate in the Netherlands. It hardly interested journalistic critics.[6] The agenda of leading reviewers in newspapers and magazines in the 1980s and 1990s never departed from the liberal humanism that postmodernism had just consigned to history. When the term did put in an appearance in Dutch literature reviews in the mid-1980s it was with a considerable reserve.[7] Critics showed that they were aware that postmodernism had been a buzzword for some time in other circles (architecture, history of art, fashion, lifestyle, etc.) and, for this reason, they used it sparingly and with a certain reluctance.

Academic circles hardly showed any interest in postmodernism either until well into the 1990s.[8] Academics studying Dutch literature at Dutch universities were generally suspicious of it because of its fashionable character.

When a Dutch academic summarized the position of literature in the Netherlands in 1993 for an international audience (German in this case), he wrote:

> Seit kurzer Zeit hat der Begriff 'Postmodernismus' auch in die Niederlände Eingang gefunden. Es ist bezeichnend, daß er vor allem die Phantasie der Journalisten anregte und wie jedes andere Modewort innerhalb kürzester Zeit an semantischer Inflation litt.[9]

Because of this journalistic and academic reserve in respect of the 'P-word', the Dutch chapter of the conceptual history of postmodernism has remained rather thin. Nevertheless, it is possible in retrospect to identify two forms of 'postmodernism' in the Netherlands, two broad orientations, which bring some order to the rather chaotic debate around the issue hitherto characterized by terminology confusion and 'semantischer Inflation' (semantic inflation): a playful postmodernism (predominant in literary journalism) and an intellectualized postmodernism (predominant in academia). The word postmodernism as I use it here refers to a construction that can be recognized in critical discourse, not to any literary reality (writers, movements, novels, etc.). It is a postmodernism-in-inverted-commas (although I will leave the inverted commas out, as I will be needing them frequently later).

1. *Playful postmodernism* (not to be confused with what Teresa Ebert has called 'ludic postmodernism').[10] In the world of literary reviews this concerns a 'postmodernism' (allow me to use the inverted commas just this once) centred upon American mass or popular culture. The keywords of this playful version are zeitgeist, eclecticism, pastiche, relativism and the blurring of boundaries between high and low culture: anything goes.[11] Patron saints: Warhol, Madonna, Fukuyama. A seminal publication for this playful postmodernism in the Netherlands was a special 'Pomo' issue of the trend-sensitive weekly *Haagse Post* of 18 April 1987, compiled by a young Joost Zwagerman.[12] In his ambitious introduction Zwagerman sketched the outlines of an anti-modernistic postmodernism concerned above all with rejecting the elitist rigidity of High Modernism.[13] In this way 'postmodernism' came to be understood in the late 1980s and early 1990s in Dutch literary reviews as the collective name for the texts in which the existential emptiness of the 1980s received form and substance by means of the unbridled cutting and pasting of quotations, especially drawn from popular culture. Zwagerman's zeitgeist novel *Gimmick!* (1989) is a good example. With this novel Zwagerman sought to align himself with what Bret Easton Ellis and Douglas Coupland were doing in English.[14] The writings of Zwagerman, known as playful postmodernist, have also been linked with international authors such as Paul Auster and Martin Amis.[15]

2. *Intellectualized postmodernism*. Academic circles reacted with boredom to Zwagerman and others' playful postmodernism. Academics used terms such as 'postmodern pop art' or 'literary pop art' to describe it: a not very complex and essentially conservative and affirmative literature which never forces the reader to change his reading attitude.[16] These negative epithets also reveal what was considered in academic circles to be the 'real' postmodernism. This intellectual postmodernism was rooted in French philosophy which had started challenging the pretentions of modern thought in the wake of 1968. Keywords: anti-humanism, dissemination, deconstruction and the end of the Grand Narrative. Paragons: Derrida, Foucault, Lyotard. The texts associated with this intellectualized postmodernism were found hermetic by its opponents, as was the poststructuralist theorizing with which it linked itself. These fragmentary texts were supposed to resist any presumption of understanding reality from within an ontological or metaphysical system. They unmasked the 'I' and 'reality' as fictions and lacked any 'centre'. According to a respected study of intellectualized postmodernism in the Dutch novel, writer and philosopher Marjolijn Februari is 'one of the most typical postmodern authors', especially since her first novel *De zonen van het uitzicht* (Panorama's sons, 1989) is constructed around 'the absence of a centre'.[17] From an international point of view this experimental and philosophical novel is reminiscent of the work of authors such as Thomas Pynchon, Julian Barnes and Italo Calvino.[18]

Zwagerman and Februari have a different background but, as soon as they started criticizing postmodern tradition(s), they took exception to the same things. It will become clear later that self-criticism in both postmodern orientations shows remarkable similarities. This comes as no surprise, since the two variants of postmodernism I distinguish share a number of important assumptions. A significant starting point, for example, for authors from both orientations is the rejection of all forms of cultural hierarchy or authority (the canon, high and low art) on principle and the questioning of notions of 'originality'. The critique of postmodernism of both orientations is aimed at the underlying relativism of such assumptions and on the paralyzing effects of this relativism on the writer.

Redefining the Postmodern Heritage: Late Postmodernism

Before I turn to Februari, Zwagerman and Grunberg and their respective struggles with postmodernism, I will go through the four definite themes in the wider discussions about the heritage of literary postmodernism in Dutch newspapers, literary and cultural magazines, book reviews and academic criticism from the late 1980s onwards. In doing so, I will try to formulate a hypothesis for discussing the individual writers in the next section. These four related points are:

the alleged relativism of postmodernism, the supposed devaluation of literature (even though it is postmodernism that accepts literary narrative as a truth narrative equal to discursive writing), the relation between literature and its public, and the relation between literature and ethics. I want to make their interconnection more explicit by reformulating them in general terms (and in a somewhat lapidary manner, leaving aside local curiosities or controversies between individual Dutch authors and critics).[19]

1. *Alleged relativism.* Postmodern thought is associated by critics in both its manifestations with relativism (cultural). In playful postmodernism there is an eclectic relativism of 'anything goes', and in intellectualized postmodernism it is a cultural relativism which refuses to accept universal criteria for fair or morally responsible actions and thinking. Postmodern man is supposed no longer to have independent foundations that are beyond discussion, no pure leverage point from which his actions and thinking can be directed. Postmodernism has unmasked the 'universal values', with which a modern and humanistic West liked to skirmish, as context-bound ideological constructions. Critics of postmodernism point out that this relativism of both manifestations makes any claim to authority virtually impossible, and that this has consequences for the literature, too.[20] They do not want a return to the kind of authority that liberal humanism clung to, or to a world in which a homogeneous cultural elite successfully mystifies the ideological content implicit in their taste. The return of the liberal humanist suppression of the historical, political, material and social in the definition of art as eternal and universal is even less desirable. They do, however, question the disavowal of reality which seems to characterize much of postmodern literature. They also pose the rhetorical question of whether the postmodern deconstruction of everything the West held holy (humanistic values such as *Bildung*, emancipation and progress, the canon, etc.) is the final answer.

2. *Devaluation of literature.* The second theme arising in the Dutch reconsideration of the postmodern legacy in literature (discussed in relation to authors such as Februari, Zwagerman and Grunberg) is the changed status of literature and its culture in the world. In reflecting on the legacy of postmodernism, the general feeling that literature has a less prominent role in today's postmodern culture and pluralistic society is a crucial point. The authors are confronted with, in Antoine Compagnon's words, 'the erosion of literary culture' and with William Marx's 'devaluation of literature': the diminishing impact of bestowing literary value on the outside world by experts in the field. As Compagnon puts it:

> *La littérature devient une zone marginale, un appendice périphérique de la culture; elle disparaît du discours social.*[21]

The liberal humanist idea of a restricted category of authors and literary works that have an absolute model value while serving as a general quality standard corresponds to a hierarchically stratified society which is now firmly consigned to the past: a society whose upper echelons defined a stable order of values that was cemented by the institutions and supposedly endorsed by the entire community. Today, however, we are living in a pluralistic society, differentiated by function instead of rank, and which has few common values. The values associated with literature are not part of this limited consensus.[22] As we will see, the authors studied in the next section do not deny this postmodern reality, but they do not take it for granted either. They are seeking a new legitimacy for the writer's authority, one that would allow him to interact with the world.

3. *Literature and the public.* The third recurring point in Dutch literary discussions since the late 1980s is intimately linked to this reflection on the conditions and the possibility of literary authority, namely the relation between literature and public. There has been a moment in the career of many a Dutch author (including the three discussed here) where they started reflecting upon the form and, consequently, the accessibility of their work. Against the backdrop of the shrinking influence of literature on social discourse, these authors broke with the experimental postmodern features which also typified their own work at that time. They experienced the formal and compositional elements of postmodernism (such as fragmentation, indeterminacy, the 'Russian doll'-effect, the severing of all links between language and reality, etc.) either as too playful and non-committal or as unnecessarily puzzling and hermetic. In the more recent works of authors such as Februari, Zwagerman and Grunberg, any postmodern form experiment has been rejected or watered down. These authors revert to relatively conventional forms (storytelling, plot, readability, character, etc.) that critics have interpreted as a conventional overture, whether appreciated by the reviewer or not, to the reading public.

4. *Literature and ethics.* The fourth and final point that reappears in Dutch discussions on the legacy of postmodernism is the fact that critics of postmodernism focus on moral and ethical problems, both within their novels and outside (columns, journalism). Februari, Zwagerman and Grunberg all wrote novels embedding a reflection on the possibility of literary *engagement*. Thus, they echo (or pioneer) a tendency also highlighted in the last few years by Dutch literary criticism. 'It has finally happened,' noted a critic of the authoritative book section of the daily newspaper *NRC Handelsblad* in 2008:

> *Literature has been chased out onto the street. After years of toing and froing about whether writers should concern themselves with social problems, the question has been answered.*[23]

When, in early 2010, the weekly *De Groene Amsterdammer* asked critics and other experts to compile a Top 21 of twenty-first-century novels, the editorial noted:

> *The time of great psychological and philosophical novels is over [...] as is that of the purely aesthetic novel. What seems relevant now is actuality. More and more fiction and non-fiction form an alliance, and increasingly the fear of terrorism and concerns about immigration and the environment seep through in literature. The clash between civilizations as a result of globalization is a fertile topic. Many novels are about 'The Other'.*[24]

The new attitude of Dutch authors in relation to postmodernism, as examined in this chapter, therefore correlates with a revaluation of the moral and ethical dimensions of literature. Authors try to write the political back into the postmodern.

In the last few decades, the image conjured up in Dutch literature by the convergence of these four points is that of a writer trying to think himself beyond the relativism that has been compared with postmodernism. Postmodern theory challenged the essentialist premises of liberal humanism with great rhetorical virulence. The idea that literature stands above politics as an universal form of expression was unmasked as an article of faith, and the absolutism of the 'white' canon as an eternal and universal standard came to an end. This postmodern 'victory' over liberal humanism initially went hand in hand with a certain triumphalism, but the writers discussed here have distanced themselves from this. They realized that the breakdown of the aristocratic cultural ideal of liberal humanism was only a first step. It was undoubtedly necessary, but in itself was not a tenable (over)reaction. The postmodern deconstruction of old presuppositions and certainties has been mired in cynical relativism, including with respect to the possibilities of literature which, according to a considerable number of contemporary writers, fails to respond to the needs of an evolving culture. The historical usefulness of postmodernism is therefore accepted, but its offshoots are being criticized: an unbridled relativism, an ironical stance in life where nothing is real anymore, and the terror of the 'anything goes' slogan.

The three authors discussed in the next section of this chapter have candidly faced the consequences of these offshoots for writers. They may have settled scores with an outmoded cultural ideal but have also sidelined themselves in the process

Late Postmodernism in Dutch Literature

The basic assumption of this section is that three representative voices in Dutch literature expressed a desire to go beyond postmodernism. Februari, Zwagerman and Grunberg have abandoned their postmodern literary posts. They are no longer positioned as more or less prominent players within the closed realm of literature but as public intellectuals whose new playground is the public sphere. Their search for new connections between literature and the world marks a new phase in what is called postmodernism, which is characterized by a reorientation in relation to everything that postmodernism had vigorously dismissed in an earlier phase, maybe too vigorously. This very reorientation makes them late postmodern authors.

Marjolijn Februari: The Writer as a Public Intellectual

Following her first novel *De zonen van het uitzicht*, Marjolijn Februari was described by critics and journalists as a 'notorious postmodernist'.[25] Although she had already distanced herself from the relativism associated with postmodern thinking ('the infinite relativizing of postmodernism is absolutely not the message I am giving,' she said as early as 1990),[26] reviewers concluded that the author of *De zonen van het uitzicht* 'narrowly followed in the postmodern wake' or 'took the postmodern tour'.[27] Even academic criticism placed the young Februari in 'the inner circle of postmodernism'.[28]

When her second novel *De literaire kring* (2007; English translation 2010: *The Book Club*) was published, the chosen form was much less experimental and immediately labelled by critics as less postmodern (and even anti-postmodern). 'Februari has converted to linear prose,' a critic remarked, and another noted that Februari had renounced 'postmodern theory' in favour of 'pragmatism and worldliness'.[29] *The Book Club* is 'an easy read'[30] which, in contrast to her earlier work, 'excels in its accessibility',[31] and in which the author displays evidence of a 'wider view of society', said the reviewers.[32]

The Book Club concerns a literary circle of self-satisfied, rich and powerful dignitaries of a Dutch village. Februari sketches a picture verging on a caricature of this club's liberal humanism. Its members entertain idealized notions about the healing and character-building powers of high culture in general and canonical literature in particular. They obviously hate 'the extravagances of postmodernism'[33] more than anything: their exalted conception of culture has barely suffered from the onslaught of postmodernism which has failed to enter the world of *The Book Club*.

Februari's book club novel reads as an indictment against the hypocrisy of a self-appointed cultural elite of white males and their outdated liberal humanism. In this respect *The Book Club* fits in a broad trend in international literature, from Martin Amis's *The Information* (1995) to Zadie Smith's *On Beauty* (2005). One character in Februari's novel typifies the presumptuous members of the reading group sarcastically as 'right-thinking humanists' and their reading club based on high culture as a 'moral money-laundering organization' ('morele witwasorganisatie').[34]

The Book Club is more than a postmodern settling of scores with liberal humanistic pretensions, however. The novel – which in many ways reminds one of Zygmunt Bauman's analysis of globalization and the newly acquired independence of global elites from territorially confined units of political and cultural power[35] – thematizes the decreasing importance of the public sphere (Habermas's *Öffentlichkeit*) and therefore the decreased social relevance of the writer who, more than anyone else, breathes in the public sphere.[36] The activities of the book club members have ever-increasing financial and moral consequences as they manage branches with annual turnovers in excess of the turnover of the government of the country they live in. Yet no one oversees them. They do business in each other's backyards, invisible to the public and its representatives in the public arena, politicians, journalists and writers. In the world of the book club members, public discussion is seen as a rear-guard action, fought between people without either reach or muscle. The fact that the members, high on high culture, place the writer on a pedestal is therefore mere chutzpah: indeed, they have a stake in ensuring that the writer and other potentially embarrassing snoops are kept as powerless bystanders. In their world, literature is but harmless wallpaper.

A crucial question raised by the *The Book Club* is what the writer can do about it. How can he reach the people with power and responsibility? Certainly not by losing himself in what one character calls 'the extravagances' of a failing postmodernism. Februari's novel sketches an alternative answer. When a young woman from the village makes waves with an international bestseller, the fact that the book club will discuss it is par for the course. The members try to prevent this by all means, and it slowly transpires why. The bestseller describes the true story of how a fellow villager, a former member of the book club, knowingly sold impure glycerine to a medicine manufacturer in Haiti with the result that seventy people died, including many children.

Although the powerful club members succeeded at the time in burying the story, they have no wish to face it again. They try to disqualify the book by dismissing it as pulp fiction ('bedside novel', 'girl's diary').[37] Autobiography does not seem highbrow enough for them, convinced as they are that True Literature should above all raise the reader above the banalities of everyday life. This diametrically opposes two things in the novel: on the one hand, the exalted notions of the book club members about what literature does and allows (which dictate that literature is above all a question of abstractions), and on the other hand, the more modest opinions of a bestselling writer who prefers the concrete. 'Seen from the writer's point of view, there is no such thing as political culture, no world history nor tragedy,' she says in *The Book Club*, but only 'the individual reactions to them'.³⁸ She pleads for concrete *engagement* rather than inflated abstractions.

It would be difficult to call *The Book Club* chick-lit or a bedside novel, but the fact is that Februari comes much closer to it with her second novel than with her first experimental postmodern one. She has repeatedly reflected on this reversal in interviews and essays since the publication of *The Book Club*. Soon after, for example, she looked back on her debut as follows:

> *Politics rippled, the money flowed and writers had collectively taken a sabbatical [...]. Paradoxes, mirror effects, echo chambers, illusions and the derailing of illusions: those were the literary techniques during the glory days of postmodernism. They were techniques of literary criticism and philosophical reflection.*³⁹

But politics no longer gently flows, Februari concluded in 2007, since 'the storm is also raging over the West'. In a short time 'a completely new experimental situation has arisen', and writers have to adapt and set themselves up as public intellectuals. Februari does it herself in her politically and socially oriented columns, but fiction also requires it. 'The windows have been blown open,' she writes, and the writer needs to find 'new goals' and a 'new public':

> *A new necessity has arisen to personally take responsibility, in writing, in the public domain [and] to transpose social, ethical and religious theories into concrete social, moral, religious problems.*⁴⁰

Literature can feed public discussion by leaving the safe level of abstract convictions and descending towards concrete and small stories. As early as 2004 Februari wrote that with these little concrete histories, she wanted to raise the level of 'literary sensitivity', especially among the social elite that normally does not concern itself with individual histories but only with the general rules and laws to correlate these histories.⁴¹

After reaching a small group of cultural insiders with her first novel, Februari aimed at a wider public with her second. She looked for an alliance with readers whose daily work confronts them with moral issues and with 'the real world'. In this respect one could say that *The Book Club* investigates what is tenable in liberal humanism, after its postmodern deconstruction, in the culture and society of today.

Joost Zwagerman: The Writer and the Devaluation of Literature

When poet and novelist Joost Zwagerman came onto the literary scene at the end of the 1980s, everything about him was qualified as postmodern: his work, his interest in popular culture, his obstreperous way of assailing the established order in the world of poetry, his dynamic handling of the media. He was seen as 'the zeitgeist expert',[42] someone well up on the 'Amsterdam pomo-scene'.[43] His novel *Gimmick!* was described by one reviewer as the 'cynical diagnosis of postmodern culture'.[44] The word postmodern itself appears frequently in the novel and refers to an anti-pretentious kind of art and culture, a culture despairing of ever producing something original or real. The self-presentation of the young and career-making Zwagerman reinforced this idea of postmodernism. Pretending all along that postmodernism could not be taken seriously was part and parcel of the playful postmodern prose which was becoming fashionable in the Dutch literature of the time.[45]

Zwagerman's flirtation with the postmodern zeitgeist did not last. Shortly after *Gimmick!*, he appeared quite sceptical about the type of disengaged and remote postmodernism he had initially represented. During the 1990s he began to engage himself more and more as a writer. He came to view postmodernism as a phenomenon stranded in its own cynicism which was responsible for literature turning in on itself. From that point onwards he called on his fellow writers to engage and to show a raised awareness of the needs of society. Thus, he speaks repeatedly of the scandalous fact that there is no trace in the European literature of the 1990s of what he called 'the most burning issue of Western Europe: the question of immigration'. 'In Dutch literature all the protagonists are white,' he said in 1994, 'as if we did not live in a multicultural society'. [46]

In 1994 Zwagerman lent weight to this call for literature to connect with the world and topical issues. His novel *De buitenvrouw* (The Mistress) deals with the multicultural society and the lack of understanding between its supporters and its opponents. The writer allows his protagonist to conclude a monologue over the xenophobia of the Dutch with an outraged judgment on artists and intellectuals:

> *Now that it was really necessary to kick a conscience into the citizen,*
> *the cultural vanguard launched into easy camp and postmodern irony.*[47]

De buitenvrouw has clear overtones of self-correction in its political and ethical dimensions. Zwagerman himself was in any event no longer taken by the seductions of postmodern irony. He no longer wanted to be a camp artist. In other words: in the 1990s, Zwagerman constructed his identity by rejecting his former 'postmodernism' whilst looking for direct *engagement*, which he found in multiculturalism (for many progressive people in those days, this was indeed a welcome new interpretation of their engagement).

Three years later he covered this reinvention of himself as a writer in the novel *Chaos en rumoer* (Chaos and Commotion, 1997). This novel pits two stereotypical types of writers against each other: the protagonist (a worrying liberal humanist who finds *fin de siècle* 20th-century culture superficial and calls literature 'a minority sport'[48] while struggling with writer's block) and his opposite (a slick, successful author versed in literary fashions who wins prize after prize). In the protagonist's eyes, his popular opponent is a 'non-committal postmodern joker'[49] who does everything that can be expected from a postmodern author in line with the stereotype. He keeps using quotations (as authenticity or originality no longer exist in the postmodern worldview) and plays postmodern games with the relation between fiction and reality.[50]

Zwagermans's *Chaos en rumoer* reads like a critical self-examination in which both types of writer are held against the light as reflections of Zwagerman himself.[51] With his caricature of a (self)portrait of the 'non-committal postmodern joker', he again distances himself from his former position as an author. He challenges the playful postmodern conception of literature with the high-minded liberal humanism of the protagonist. However, that liberal humanism is also portrayed as a caricature: the writer with writer's block is the loser who never takes off in the cynical world of *Chaos en rumoer* and whose splendid isolation is not taken seriously by anyone. His seriousness and his somewhat naïve striving for truthful words are not really held up as a worthy alternative for the playful, anti-pretentious and disengaged postmodernism of the successful author (and the former Zwagerman). But this postmodernism is definitely qualified by it.

At the end of the novel, after developments we will not go into here,[52] a kind of synthesis is achieved: thanks in part to his opponent, the protagonist overcomes his writer's block and writes a book that aims to be an improved version of his opponent's. His attempt at synthesis can be interpreted as Zwagerman's view on writing: the author takes a step back from his own postmodern position, not by falling back on the completely isolated and necessarily blocked position of his protagonist (who does not suffer from writer's block) but by renouncing the cynical, fashion-conscious and superficial aspects of postmodernism and reorienting himself towards the values and expectations of what postmodernism had ended: the values and expectations of liberal humanism.

With the conceit of writer's block, Zwagerman proves to be acutely aware of the problematic situation of the writer as a public figure in today's expanding and diversifying culture.[53] The protagonist arrives at an impasse because he has to operate in a world in which there is barely agreement as to who is worth reading and who is not. In *De buitenvrouw*, the reflection on the dwindling public interest in literature also plays a part when the protagonist, a Dutch language teacher at a secondary school, realizes that for his pupils, writers 'had become as abstract as the kings and *stadhouders* (governors) from history lessons'.[54] As a literature teacher, traditionally one of the gatekeepers of High Culture, he experiences the fact that postmodernism's scepticism towards universal standards has made any authoritative attribution of quality impossible. The consequence is that literature highly regarded by experts and insiders is no longer guaranteed a place in a widely shared canon.

Zwagerman's critique of postmodernism (a critique to which he paradoxically gives shape in a novel, *Chaos en rumoer*, that ultimately is thoroughly postmodern: in the final section, 'reality' appears to be fiction and vice versa) is also a reaction to the crisis in which the literary culture has found itself under postmodern rule. In *Chaos en rumoer* he portrays a cynical literary crowd which no longer believes in the power of literature and who consider it as an insider joke for cognoscenti. In the course of the 1990s, Zwagerman reached the conclusion that his own earlier postmodernism was the wrong answer. He exchanged uncaring cynicism for a new *engagement*. Zwagerman divested his own postmodernism of its cynical and superficial sides. He tried to tone down the postmodern scepticism that prevented writers (like himself) from tackling ethical and moral issues. His own novels have increasingly dealt with precisely these issues, and in doing so, the writer deliberately chose an accessible style. (Zwagerman himself considers his *Chaos en rumoer* to be proof of his competence to write a postmodern novel that is still readable.)[55] Beyond his novels, the writer Zwagerman has also expressed himself through columns and other journalistic interventions in the public sphere which are increasingly politically motivated, whether in books, newspapers, magazines or radio and television.

Arnon Grunberg: The Writer's Hunger for Reality

No matter how much Februari and Zwagerman differ as writers, their reactions to postmodernism are similar. Both want to use literature to reflect on moral and ethical issues, they choose accessible literary forms, and they intervene explicitly in public discussions, including outside their novels. As the heyday of postmodernism recedes into the distance, the differences between the two manifestations of postmodernism in the Netherlands also disappear from view, and the critique of postmodernism results in similar author strategies.

As happened with Februari and Zwagerman, the early work of Arnon Grunberg was also qualified as 'postmodern' in the second half of the 1990s. The work of this undeniably *jeune premier* of contemporary Dutch literature clearly shows both playful postmodern traits and more philosophically oriented characteristics of intellectualized postmodernism. Critics decried Grunberg's two faces, sometimes in one and the same review.[56] On the basis of novels such as *Blauwe maandagen* (1994, English translation 1997: *Blue Mondays*), Grunberg's first novel about a young Jewish boy who struggles with his identity, he is labelled as an unfettered ironist who is deadly serious when describing love as illusion and truth as a lie. He actually contributed himself to this image with a number of cynical one-liners.[57] At the beginning of his career, Grunberg seemed to have associated himself with what Douglas Coupland in *Generation X* (1991) has called the 'Cult of aloneness': 'the need for autonomy at all costs, usually at the expense of long-term relationships'.[58]

While some critics saw in Grunberg's early work yet another, almost routine, exercise in postmodernism,[59] others (including the author himself) declared that on the contrary this work marked a departure from it. This peculiarity was also true of the early reception of his contemporary and spiritual kinsman Dave Eggers. The fact that all reviewers, whether for or against Grunberg (or Eggers), had nothing positive to say about postmodernism is telling for the new constellation that has been in place since the turn of the century: for many critics, postmodernism is passé.

'As you know, so-called postmodernism is already behind us' starts an interview with Grunberg in 2007. Not only is the interviewer convinced that postmodernism ('all stories are already told') is dead and buried, the writer himself is critical. 'The idea that all stories are told seems complete nonsense,' he replied. 'As soon as society begins to disintegrate you can no longer hold this position.'[60]

We can see that in the course of his career, Grunberg himself tired of the postmodern pose of detachment that he still supported in the mid-1990s. He turns away from the pernicious indifference of the 'anything goes' doctrine, and he explicitly rejects the very irony he saw before as his salvation. In line with David Foster Wallace and subsequent New Sincerity writers such as Eggers and Jonathan Safran Foer, Grunberg criticizes the ironic stance that seems to be ingrained in postmodernism because it can get mired in relativism. In this vein he spoke in 1999 of 'irony as a cancer stifling everything. The irony that has rendered our food inedible and many books unreadable'.[61] His own reputation as a writer hiding behind the play of irony increasingly irritated him. 'My God, how I long to be taken seriously,' he wrote in 2007 in a text about the task of the writer, a text which, he assured his readers, was 'guaranteed to be irony-free'.[62]

The way Grunberg sees the task of the writer can be distilled in the first place from his novels, in which he shows himself more and more committed and concerned. In 2003, his book *De asielzoeker* (The Asylum Seeker) provides a pointed reflection on the (im)possibility of literary *engagement*. The novel paints a damning portrait of a failed writer who suffers from 'the postmodern drive to unmask'.[63] With *Tirza* (2007) Grunberg proceeded to write one of the most remarkable Dutch 9/11 novels. *Onze oom* (Our Uncle, 2008) is a novel about the moral dilemmas in the context of war and terror in a South American dictatorship.

The end of that novel lifts the veil a little on Grunberg's working methods. A journalist – clearly Grunberg himself – is visiting one of the protagonists, an arms dealer, for an interview. The suggestion is that he is gathering material for the story we have just read. The interview the journalist carries out with the arms dealer is the kind Grunberg has conducted himself in real life. During interviews at the time of publication, he repeatedly stated that he had researched arms dealing and spoken to dealers.[64]

If Grunberg's early work was often a mixture of autobiography and at times aberrant fantasy, his subsequent work is increasingly based on thorough fieldwork: the writer Grunberg is leaning more heavily on the journalist Grunberg who, since 2005, has visited Dutch soldiers in Afghanistan and camped with the American army in Iraq in the course of reporting for leading Dutch newspapers.[65]

In the novel *Onze oom* the arms dealer asks the journalist the reason for his visit. 'I try and get as close as possible,' he answers quietly, 'to danger, destruction, death.'[66] That is exactly what Grunberg is doing in his recent novels. He is interested in making literature out of real experience, out of the proximity of others and realities that cannot be deconstructed away in relativism. Literature has to return to the essence of life and, with this in mind, the writer starts to work in a documentary manner. His novels are increasingly based on journalistic fieldwork. In *Onze oom,* for instance, not only did he incorporate the results of research into the illegal arms trade but also interviews with imprisoned women in Peru. In this respect Grunberg joins the recent trend towards non-fiction, documentary fiction or 'non-fiction novels' typical of authors such as the Americans Eggers (*What Is the What, Zeitoun*) and Foer (*Eating Animals*), but also Europeans like François Bon (*Daewoo*), Aifric Campbell (*The Semantics of Murder*) or Thomas Brussig (*Wie es leuchtet*).

Critics have reacted in different ways to these changes in his work. The new seriousness is valued. One critic noted that 'the mature and serious tone' of his recent journalism contrasted starkly with the 'reckless, boyish and sarcastic tone' of earlier work.[67] Another, however, regrets that with *Onze oom* Grunberg has left the domain of literature in order to bring us 'arid pamphleteering prose' which conveys 'one-sided moral messages'.[68] Grunberg has parried this criticism, aimed at style and form rather than content, as follows:

> *Criticism of style is always the means of choice to pacify reality [...], a means of not having to talk about the book and what happens in it, to keep the*

novel at arm's length from the reader so that his worldview does not have to topple, that everything can stay as it was.[69]

A more frequently recurring element in Grunberg's reflection on literature and authorship is his criticism of writers and critics who hold on to old literary conventions, without re-examining them in the light of a fast-changing culture. Primacy of style is one such convention. According to Grunberg, today we should be asking ourselves whether style has not become an obstacle to the writer who wants to be in touch with reality and his public. Literature is threatened, he said in 2001, 'by the ignorance of those who want to continue practising it against the grain'.[70] They are making a reserve out of literature. This has to be prevented, he wrote in 2009, 'because the idea that the park of literature is a paradise is less obvious than some of its inhabitants like to think'.[71]

According to another literary convention, the author can never be held accountable for what his characters say. While this convention is taken for granted by insiders (breaking it is taboo), Grunberg has re-examined it. When an interviewer spoke critically of the utterances of one of his characters, Grunberg conspicuously did not use this opportunity to distance himself from his character. 'No, I would not call it fiction,' he said, 'I appreciate it if someone takes the words of my character seriously.'[72] Of course it does not mean that Grunberg has to endorse what is said by his character, but neither does he believe that what is said in the novel has a clearly defined function outside of its fictional world. The novel is not a work of art that only refers to itself but an attempt to intervene in real debates. As Grunberg put it in a recent blog-posting: 'The idea that in the name of literature everything should be allowed in novels or poems pushes literature to the periphery of society.'[73]

Since Grunberg's attempt to overcome the cynicism of his early work, which was generally held to be 'postmodern', he no longer tries to hide behind literary conventions or behind postmodern ideas about the crisis in language and the complexity of reality. 'Ah, the exquisite complexity of reality,' he quipped in 1996, 'it can serve as an excuse for almost everything.'[74] Statements such as these should alert the reader to the fact that Grunberg wants him to focus on content and abandon his suspicions of postmodernism.[75] They are characteristic of his genuine pursuit of a literature that breaks free from its isolation and that does not seek to please the reader (aesthetically) but shake him up (ethically).

Conclusion: Late Postmodern Ambivalence

Two things have come to light in this chapter. The first is that the authors discussed started criticizing postmodernism after initially embracing it. Their critical reconsideration of postmodernism implied just as much affinity as repugnance. Still, they searched for a new position and did not shun inspiration from traditions and forms associated with the liberal humanist position that postmodernism was supposed to have left behind. The second is that this quest for a new third position can be interpreted as a reaction against a changing literary climate and the devaluation of literature. The authors seek new ways of exercising their trade in order to revitalize a marginalized literature. They are no longer ashamed of having certain expectations of their work (the public effects), and they strive to strip writing of its harmlessness.

From their late postmodern position, Februari, Zwagerman and Grunberg have taken an ambivalent stance in relation to the postmodern legacy. They endorse postmodern criticism of the universal pretensions of liberal humanism, but they are also forced to conclude that it has failed to put the historical, political and ethical dimensions of literature back on stage. As a response to a changing culture, it is unsatisfactory. This is why these late postmodern writers have turned again to postmodern taboos such as *authenticity* and *originality*.

Late postmodern ambivalence clearly came to the fore after the 9/11 attacks, when commentators all over the world, including in the Netherlands, announced the end of postmodern relativism. Dutch journalist and literary critic Michaël Zeeman wrote on 14 September 2001 in a newspaper that on 9/11 'a few hits' had put an end to the 'feeble cultural relativism of postmodernism'. It seemed that history had not yet come to an end.[76]

It is tempting to interpret the literary forms of the critique of postmodernism, such as the New Sincerity movement, as a literary variant of the general confusion that followed the attacks of 9/11. Yet if, with today's knowledge, we follow the critical trail back in the literature, we can see, long before 9/11, some elements that can be interpreted as 'late postmodern' coming to the surface. This is true for Zwagerman and Grunberg, as we have seen earlier, but also for the work of dissenting Dutch writers like Frans Kellendonk, Leon de Winter, Robert Vernooy, Dirk van Weelden or Charlotte Mutsaers from the late 1980s and early 1990s.[77] Literature is not just a reaction to a social reality. Often it is one step ahead of that reality.

Chapter 4

Italian Literature

The Epics of Reality

Monica Jansen

Introduction

This chapter on late postmodernism in Italian literature investigates, firstly, whether it is possible to speak of Italian postmodern literature, and how this literature has addressed the questions put forward in the intellectual debate on postmodernism of the 1980s and 1990s. After 9/11, the coming to terms with a crisis of experience was put on the literary agenda. From that date on, postmodernism is generally considered an 'anything goes' culture: inadequate to formulate new forms of literary *engagement* beyond its proclamation of the 'End of History'. The ensuing series of debates about an alleged return to realism is the second concern of this chapter. This return of the real is best achieved, according to critics and writers, through a highlighting of the artificial approaches of literature to reality. This implies that we should speak of a definition of *late postmodernism* rather than *post postmodernism*: late postmodern authors do not leave the paradigm of pluralism behind but criticize postmodernism's excessive relativism and ironic detachment.[1]

The difference between postmodernism and late postmodernism is to be found in the interpretation of ontological doubt, which is 'reactive' in postmodern and 'active' in late postmodern criticism.[2] Metafiction still functions as stylistics, but is not so much the expression of fictionalized truth as of 'true fiction', of reality 'authenticated' by fiction, or the process of 'fictionalizing' reality.[3] In this sense, Italo Calvino's assumption that the world is only accessible through writing is still valid. A postmodern aesthetics should try to reformulate the dialectics between the 'written' and the 'unwritten' world, working precisely on the artificial limits between fiction and reality.[4] The three case studies of Italian late postmodernism presented in this chapter aim to show that the postmodern absence of Grand Narratives is the starting point also for those writers who are in search of some kind of relational, if not relativist, truth. All of the selected authors, Antonio Tabucchi (1943), Alessandro Baricco (1958) and Niccolò Ammaniti (1966), represent a line of continuity with Italian postmodern culture, its aesthetics (Tabucchi), its condition (Baricco), and its performativity (Ammaniti). In my analysis of these authors, I intend to speak of 'New Italian Postmodernism' (NIP), in response to 'New Italian Epic' (NIE). NIE is a literary movement publicized on the Internet by the writers' collective Wu Ming in 2008 and transformed into a booklet in 2009,[5] grounded in a politics of rupture with the 'anything goes' postmodern culture. It is my assumption that if postmodern *impegno* (commitment, *engagement*) has a right of existence, a new ethics of writing has to be valued first of all in relation to the condition it criticizes or aims to oppose.

Antonio Tabucchi is perhaps the most paramount example of an author whose work has been regarded, positively and negatively, as typical of an aesthetic postmodernism. In view of the debate on commitment and realism after the events of 9/11, Tabucchi has been 'rehabilitated' as a writer whose commitment goes against the grain of the status quo and is now considered as one of Italy's most critical voices.[6] Central to his aesthetic as well as to his engaged narratives is the paradox of 'true fiction', which will be elaborated in the first case study of NIP authors.

An author who, on the contrary, has been highly criticized in Italy for being too commercialized and 'integrated' in the 'society of spectacle' (Debord), while being hailed abroad as one of Italy's leading voices in the debate on cultural change,[7] is Alessandro Baricco. This second case study investigates not so much his literary work[8] as his columns on what he senses to be a cultural 'mutation'. Just as in other Western countries, in Italy a blurring of boundaries between literary and non-literary genres has produced the ambivalent category of 'non-fiction', which includes Baricco's essay-journalism, where he blends aesthetics with everyday life experience.[9] His openness towards both 'high' and 'low' cultural pluralism implies a mobile and horizontal concept of meaning, irrespective of the vertical dialectics between surface and depth. Analyzing the debate stirred up by his latest essay on cultural barbarism, I will address the question of whether his postmodernist approach to the aesthetic experience could be explained as an 'integrated' version of NIP.

Another exponent of the 1990s, though pertaining to a younger generation, is Niccolò Ammaniti, who can be seen as an example of what has been defined as a 'genetic postmodernism'. Launched in 1996 on the literary scene as one of the 'giovani cannibali' (young cannibals), his exuberant 'pulp fiction' has been compared to that of filmmaker Tarantino. Ammaniti, however, considers himself first of all a realist who, even in his most grotesque vein, never leaves the limits of the 'plausible' behind. His exploration of the 'noble' and 'trash' dimensions of popular culture runs parallel to that of the different roles of storyteller and entertainer requested by the cultural industry. This third case study therefore poses the question of whether the cultural logic of late capitalism also dictates that of late postmodernism: is Ammaniti's invitation to celebrate culture's and society's apocalypse perhaps a 'too late' postmodernism?

Postmodernism Italian Style

The debate on postmodernism in Italian literature and culture has been suspicious from the very beginning, in the early 1980s, towards a cultural concept that was imported from the United States. This postmodernism, bearer of a 'playful' kind of aesthetics, contrasted with the 'serious' dimension of post-war *impegno*.

The post-war Italian literature is characterized by an ambiguous position between the historical materialism of Neorealist *engagement* on the one hand, and cultural industry and mass (pop) consumer culture on the other. This started with the Italian Neo-avant-garde of the 1960s, an artistic movement that can be regarded as 'the first formulation of postmodernist theoretical discourse in Italy'.[10] The divide between a democratic 'close the gap' position like that of Leslie Fiedler and one of distinctive cultural critique – to create an 'Indian reserve'[11] for critical literary resistance against the cultural dominance of late capitalism – was bridged by the literary 'compromises' of Umberto Eco's *Il nome della rosa* (1980, English translation 1983: *The Name of the Rose*), and Italo Calvino's *Se una notte d'inverno un viaggiatore* (1979, English translation 1981: *When on a Winter's Night a Traveler*). What their authors propose, and theorize, is a quality bestseller which can be read at different levels and – contrary to the avant-garde credo of 'non-literature' – as such stimulates, first of all, the pleasure of the complementary acts of storytelling and reading.

Eco's definition of postmodernism's 'double coding' – a conscious, ironic attitude towards intertextuality and the elitism of high culture – in his *Postscript* to *The Name of the Rose* may be an exception in the Italian postmodern landscape,[12] but it has nevertheless become a 'classic'.

In 2008 a counter-definition was proposed by the writers' collective Wu Ming's Memorandum on the *New Italian Epic*. It opposes Eco's idea that the originality of the postmodern author, who can only repeat what has already been said, consists in the ironical distance of inverted commas. Wu Ming claims that the post-postmodern – or NIE – writer should dare to take the already said seriously again, notwithstanding the risk of banality. In reply to Eco's witty pun of postmodern love, as expressed in his *Postscript* 'Come direbbe Liala, ti amo disperatamente' (As Liala – or Barbara Cartland, as the English translation has it – would say, I love you desperately), Wu Ming's reversal reposits the faith in the written word: 'Notwithstanding Liala, I love you desperately'.[13] As I mentioned earlier on, the *New Italian Epic* Memorandum was first published online on the initiative of Wu Ming 1 in 2008, and was transformed – in interaction with its readers (version 2.0) – into a collective paper edition in 2009 (version 3.0). Thus, the readers' agency is not limited to the passive pleasure of postmodern 'word play' but extended to an interactive practice of post-postmodern 'world play'.

The importance of being postmodern was at stake in the critical debate of the early 1990s, following on the simultaneous publication in Italy of philosopher Gianni Vattimo's *La società trasparente* (1989, English translation 1992: *The Transparent Society*) and Fredric Jameson's *Il postmoderno o la logica culturale del tardo capitalismo* (1984 'Postmodernism, or the Cultural Logic of Late Capitalism', Italian translation 1989). Literary critics embraced neo-Marxist Jameson, who envisions possibilities for mapping a critical postmodernism along the lines of dialectics.[14] Most rejected Vattimo, who in Adorno's shadow reforms dialectics into ambiguity, the continuous 'oscillation' between opposites, and who sees a plural dialogism of historically mobile and un-foundational truth. The Italian debate is centered on how to value and counter the feared homologation of postmodern culture and culminates in *Raccontare il postmoderno* (Narrating the Postmodern, 1997) by Remo Ceserani. Ceserani, an expert of comparative literature, exhorts Italy's literary critics and writers, with the help of Rimbaud's famous words, to be finally postmodern: 'Il faut être postmoderne'. His 'story' of a cultural change that at the same time aims to convince the Italian literary field to join the international debate may sound a bit *passé*, as international postmodernism in 1997 has already entered its reflexive phase,[15] but it also reveals Italian postmodernism to be essentially of a meta-critical nature. Furthermore, Ceserani's main focus is on the 'functionality' of postmodern literature, and therefore he is more interested in postmodernism as a meta-historical 'cognitive strategy'[16] rather than as historical stylistics.

Raccontare il postmoderno is also the personal account of an Italian generation that witnessed the cultural change towards the information and consumer society in the late 1950s, a change which has often been regarded as an 'anthropologic mutation' in the prophetic words used by writer, filmmaker and journalist Pier Paolo Pasolini in 1974.[17] What's more, Ceserani's publication coincides with the introduction of a new phase in Italian literature by the next and perhaps last postmodern generation. With their bestseller anthology titled *Gioventù cannibale* (Cannibal Youth, 1996), the 'giovani cannibali' (young cannibals) turned the literary contamination between highbrow and lowbrow fiction of the 'young writers' of the 1980s into the mainstream emancipation of youth literature and B-culture. The literary examples for the *cannibali* generation were not 'fathers' Eco and Calvino but rather 'elder brothers' Enrico Palandri (1956) and Pier Vittorio Tondelli (1955). Rather than the 'cultural' postmodernism, which plays with the literary forms of tradition, they appealed to a 'direct' postmodernism, which expresses the faith in the written word – through the so-called 'romanzo generazionale' (youth novel) that expressed the truth of experience and the 'sound' of a generation.

This is a 'genetically' postmodern generation, an Italian Generation X that grew up with the media of consumer culture (cinema, television and video, comics and computer games). Critic Pierpaolo Antonello saw in them an 'ironic postmodern detachment'. What makes their gesture – if fully inserted in the literary circuit – radical and post-avant-gardistic, Antonello concludes, is 'their absolute awareness and consciousness of such homologation [...] that constitutes the new given of such literary and cultural operation'.[18] As such, this generation represents, according to critic Alberto Casadei, that component of the avant-garde that has fused the aesthetic into the daily life sphere and contributed to the decomposition of the traditional 'absolute value' into modifiable 'semi-values', which follow trends set by public success or by marketing strategies.[19]

This generation of 'cannibalized' consumer postmodernism has recently been 'written out' of Italy's literary history by a concomitant one, that of Wu Ming and its acolytes, who consider themselves not the heirs of the avant-gardes but the problematic children of popular culture.[20] In their Memorandum, which explicitly is not a Manifesto, Wu Ming dates the eruption of popular culture in Italy to 1993. This means fueling it with historic pregnancy, 1993 marking the beginning of Italy's Second Republic, after the corruption scandals and the collapse of the whole party system. Popular culture in the writers' collective's view is distinct from mass culture; it centers on community building rather than marketing. Essential for their view of making literature *popular* is therefore the concept of transmediality, the mobility of narratives traveling between media and between participatory reader communities.[21] The narrative essence to be transmitted is historical experience, the best example being the historic novel *Q*, written by the collective under the former name of Luther Blissett (2000).

In the 'New Italian Epic' which the group writes, the 'epic' has to be understood as the tale of the multitude whose voice has been silenced by official history.[22] This emancipatory outcome of postmodernism's deconstruction of the teleology of history and progress is best achieved, in the view of Wu Ming, through a conscious manipulation of pop icons, which can propel a collective counter-narration. Hence, Wu Ming's literary movement NIE aims to counter the *cannibali*'s commercialized 'fantasy-poesis' with the interstitial guerilla of 'mythpoesis'.[23]

It seems that playful postmodernism in Italy has become the most recognizable as well as the most contested form of what can be called a postmodern art of contamination of styles and genres. According to literary critic Filippo La Porta, the tendency to 'de-realize' the real, proper to new Italian crime fiction and genre fiction in general, best illustrates the celebration of Italy's culture of appearances and spectacle.[24] Instead of bestowing depth on the present, these narrations then perform a stereotype of national identity.[25]

In other words, where contemporary American literature has been able to reach the depth of a truly critical postmodernism, after a phase of 'anything goes',[26] Italian writers – playing around with horror, SF and pulp – are stuck on the surface of the comic, of auto-irony at best, and unable to interpret the tragic dimension of existence. This, at least, is the starting point for those Italian literary critics who try to redirect a general cultural pessimism towards other, more promising, literary trends within and beyond postmodernism. Alberto Casadei, for instance, in his critical survey of contemporary Italian fiction, singles out the international examples of Don De Lillo and Michel Houellebecq to identify a new group of Italian novelists. From the second half of the 1990s and after 9/11, they position themselves on the crossroads between reality and fiction in order to question the impact of the de-realization of the human experience.[27] This new group of writers, now in their forties and often the object of discussion rather than subject, has gained a voice on the pages of the *La Repubblica* newspaper with a programmatic article by Giorgio Vasta (2009). This Sicilian writer living and working in Turin argues that the literary decade of the 1990s is often treated as a 'limbo', hosting a generation of epigones that is valued for what they are not, and for what they have borrowed from their predecessors of the 1980s. However, their condition of 'orphans without certainties', without paternal authorization, is the major selling point of these authors and puts them in the right position to analyze today's complexity as a rule, and not an exception, of our human condition of uncertainty.[28]

Italy, representing an avant-garde of televised culture – television's invasion of the life sphere has been marked as typical of postmodern Italian culture[29] –has also produced an avant-garde culture of resistance, dating back to the violent but also creative revolts of the 1970s. In the above-mentioned NIE Memorandum, this precedent of new imaginative activism is grounded in the country's 'anomalous' condition during the Cold War,[30] and built on Italy's experience of political crisis and social anti-State movements. Philosophers Paolo Virno and Michael Hardt speak of an 'Italian laboratory' of radical thought and propose, in their edited volume *Radical Thought in Italy*, that 'in the 1990s [...] Italian exceptionalism has in fact come to an end, so that now Italian revolutionary thought [...] can be recognized as relevant to an increasingly wide portion of the globe in a new and important way'.[31] The inhuman consequences of the material shift towards post-Fordism exploded on an international level with the tragic events of 9/11, preceded in Italy by the violent clashes between police and No Global protesters during the G8 at Genoa, in July 2001. The autobiographical touch given to these traumatic moments in Wu Ming's Memorandum – NIE is conceptualized in the afternoon of 11 September 2001, with the wounds of Genoa still open – recalls Ceserani's personal experience of modernization, which made him decide to become postmodern; for Wu Ming postmodernism has dramatically come to its end. The question remains of course of *which* postmodernism has reached its expiry date, and if postmodernism's criticism of ideology can still, in new ways, function as a 'cognitive strategy'. In that case, would it not be more appropriate to speak of NIP (New Italian Postmodernism) instead of NIE, the crisis of modernity still being at the heart of today's condition of uncertainty?

'Late' from the Start: Janus or Proteus

We have seen that the debate on postmodernism of the 1980s and 1990s is fed by Italian intellectuals from a dominant neo-Marxist position, on the one hand, and by the (contradictory) legacies of the Italian Neo-avant-garde, on the other. Postmodernism is treated either as philosophically superficial or as aesthetically post-avant-garde, representing normalization and progressive integration into the new technologies of the cultural industry. In 1964 Umberto Eco coined a fortunate distinction between 'apocalyptic' and 'integrated' intellectual parties, the first holding on to dialectics and the second opening up to the bi-directionality between art's autonomy and the cultural industry's economy. This distinction still seems valid for today's debate on late postmodern literature. The epochal moment of rupture represented by the assault on the Twin Towers has, for instance, encouraged neo-Marxist critic Romano Luperini in his 'apocalyptic' belief that the end of postmodernism has finally become an historical and material fact, showing once and for all that the postmodern liberation of ideologies has been nothing but an a-historical alibi for disengagement.[32] Writer Alessandro Baricco, on the contrary, is confirmed by 9/11's 'surrealism' in his belief that it is the writer's task, from an 'integrated' position, to 'imagine' the consequences of the fusion between reality and fiction and to resist its violent extremes with narratives that enable us, with the help of fantasy, to become a creative and at the same time transformative part of the 'dream' of globalization.[33]

Within this binary opposition between integrated and apocalyptic parties, what risks being left out is precisely the hybrid 'in-between' of a 'critical' form of postmodernism. This ambivalence in the end best characterizes the Italian postmodern literature and has marked the start of the aesthetic and philosophical debate in the early 1980s. It can be traced back to the First International Exhibition of Architecture held in Venice in 1980, which aroused the attention of, among others, Linda Hutcheon, Jürgen Habermas and Jean-François Lyotard. Postmodern architect Paolo Portoghesi introduced the metaphor of the Janus head to typify the postmodern cultural helmsman that hovers between the Scylla of historicist dialectics and the Charybdis of the ambiguity of pluralist thought.[34] The 'double-bind' of the Janus head looking forward and back in history at the same time inspired Hutcheon's famous definition of the politics of postmodern metafiction.[35]

This postmodernism 'in between' has been put into practice in Italy by a group of poets founded in 1989, who called themselves Gruppo 93. These poets created their own form of critical postmodernism, in opposition to and continuity with the Neo-avant-garde Gruppo 63 of the 1960s. Founding member Lello Voce even vindicated the right for his own generation to be postmodern: if the economic boom and the bi-polar world belonged to Gruppo 63, the ideological void of post-1989 Italy was claimed by Gruppo 93: 'So, please, at least leave this to us: postmodernism is ours ... Hands off!'[36]

The search for a third way within the binary opposition between Marxist-oriented critics and hermeneutic ones has been theorized by postmodern Italian philosophy in the 1980s and 1990s, though its critical potential has not been recognized in the literary debate. Gianni Vattimo's *Weak Thought* has been categorized by Italian literary criticism as a celebration of the 'heterotopy' of the information society's relativism and as the end of a utopian project. The existentialist humanism introduced by Vattimo in French poststructuralist antihumanism, however, has not found the resonance in Italy that it did elsewhere. In philosopher Giuseppe Stellardi's view, for instance, Vattimo's *Weak Thought* could be described as the 'ethics of weakness': a tolerant experimentation of the possibilities of thought and action, open to the other (or, more precisely, to the others) and to the future, not deaf to the voices of the past, constantly prepared to re-negotiate identities and positions.[37] The special attention paid to existentialist ontology, which in Vattimo's case originates from Heidegger's concept of *Verwindung*, an open-ended and distorted process of 'becoming' without leaving the traces of past diseases behind, has been developed further in other, post-human, directions by Italian philosophers such as Giorgio Agamben and Roberto Esposito, from the late 1990s onwards. They start, instead, from Foucault's concept of 'biopolitics' and its dangers and potentials for the community and the singular.[38] Both thinkers are more concerned with the insidious and intrinsic power structures of 'surveillance' than with the emancipatory pluralism of network society, which was central to Vattimo's *Transparent society*.[39]

If the Janus head had been a popular metaphor in the theorization of postmodernism's 'double-bind' between past and future in the early 1980s, in 2008 crime writer and critic Girolamo De Michele introduced the figure of Proteus, to fight precisely the indecisive and repressive proteiformity of postmodernist ambivalence[40] and to transform it into 'performative knowledge'.[41] Allegory, in De Michele's view, has been granted the noble task of helping meaning escape from the fictional plot and bringing it back into the great 'book of the world'.[42] However, De Michele's rejection of a postmodern aesthetics can still be conceived within, and not so much beyond postmodernism.

This resembles the 'critical postmodernism' defined by Angello Petrella, of which Luther Blissett's *Q* would be another example.[43] According to Petrella, Gruppo 93's critical postmodernism was still conceived within the boundaries of language. The leap beyond the *impasse* of postmodernism can only be accomplished with the literary creation of new, collective myths that impose themselves on and at the same time exploit the myth-making machinery of consumer culture. Thus, an epic of the 'multitude' is created, as well as a new political art that reenacts Jameson's enduring resistance within and against the cultural logic of late capitalism.[44]

Late Postmodernism and the Epics of Reality

In its latest literary forms, critical postmodernism thus becomes a cognitive strategy or, better, a performative knowledge to actively overcome the pitfalls of postmodernism's passive relativism. The fact that ethics and *impegno* (commitment) – in Italy associated with the overarching social agenda of communism in the 1950s – are not necessarily at odds with postmodernism's deconstruction of the modern project is the starting point of *Postmodern Impegno*, a collection of essays published in 2009. As the editors state in their introduction: 'What postmodernism challenges [...] is not *impegno* as such, but its essentialist, rationalistic and humanistic underpinnings. To describe postmodernism as an expression of nihilism means to misunderstand this specific challenge to established totalities'.[45] The fragmentary lens of postmodernism rather frees *impegno* from any restrictive ideological embrace and brings to the fore the relational connotations of commitment, attached more to the private than to the public sphere.[46]

In its reduction to 'postmodernismi da quattro soldi' (tuppenny ha'penny postmodernisms), Wu Ming's NIE does not take into account the possibility of an ethical turn within postmodernism, as is explored by Antonello and Mussgnug in *Postmodern Impegno*. Raffaele Donnarumma (in a 2008 special issue of the literary journal *Allegoria* on Italy's young writers' return to the real) polemically suggests that the authors of NIE, trapped in the postmodern frames they grew up with, are themselves 'radicalizing' postmodernism instead of overcoming its pitfalls.[47] Donnarumma summarizes the alternatives of literature, after the end of the poetics of postmodernism, with the return to realistic modes from the past and the search for new modes of subjective realism: 'Not school realism, but a realistic tension is maybe what is needed today more than anything else to give back to literature its meaning [...]. Realism is a social operation'.[48]

According to the NIE Memorandum, what is crucial in this 'active' sense of post-realism is the shift from the denotative and objective representation of the real to the 'epic mode' in which narrative is first of all a connotative and affective experience.[49] The accent is put on cultural activism, on building participatory communities through transmedial storytelling. The collective dimension of literature relies on a kind of interconnected subjectivism, in line with Nicoline Timmer's analysis of the 'post-postmodern syndrome' in contemporary American fiction.[50]

Two novels, both published in 2006, have been paradigmatic for the debate in Italy on late postmodernism and, more precisely, for the debate on post-realism: Walter Siti's *Troppi paradisi* (Too many paradises), welcomed as Italy's first really postmodern novel American style,[51] and Roberto Saviano's international bestseller *Gomorra* (English translation 2007: *Gomorrah*). In both cases, the borders between reality and fiction are explored in narratives or, better, in 'unidentified narrative objects' that cannot be pinned down to pre-established genres and that generate the hybrids of 'autofiction' (Siti) and of 'non-fiction' (Saviano).[52] Siti, in his multiple roles of author, narrator and protagonist, shows where televised and lived 'reality' meet and intertwine into postmodern 'irreality'.[53] Saviano, on the other hand, denounces the 'system' of globalized organized crime, Naples' camorra, through a personalized and connotative realism in which identification with the other is the cement for a new pact with the reader: sensitized by the narration, he can freely prolong the effects of his reading outside the limits of the private. Again, in these post-realist fictions, the connection between literature and ethics is not to be found on the level of unchangeable truth claims but in the process, on the 'path to the acquisition of a possible truth'.[54] It is therefore also possible to consider them as examples of New Italian Postmodernism (NIP). This personalized kind of commitment may permit us to see where visions of literature and politics can meet, within and beyond postmodernism.

The three selected case studies present the working through of postmodernism and its critique in three authors who have been successful internationally, and who have started writing at crucial moments in the Italian debate on postmodernism. Their works, after the end of postmodernism, seem to reflect the passage towards a new kind of connotative and personalized late postmodern *impegno*.

Tabucchi's Paradoxes of 'True Fiction'

Writer and intellectual Antonio Tabucchi combines writing 'highbrow' postmodern stories and novels with a type of 'angry' intellectualism that does not eschew polemics.[55] A representative of hyper-literary intertextual and metatextual postmodernism,[56] his elliptic and visionary fictions express the disquiet of ontological doubt. In his journalistic essays *L'oca al passo* (2006), he seems to claim that Gramsci's notion of the organic intellectual, despite its 'expiry date', is still valid in postmodern society.[57] The starting point of Tabucchi's analysis of contemporary culture and politics is the crisis of 'lapalissian truth', which suggests that its obvious, unquestionable constituents no longer coincide with moral transparency but are perverted instead into monstrous paradoxes. The essays, which won him the prestigious Spanish Premio Cerecedo for freedom of opinion in 2004, follow the matrix of binary oppositions common to the values of democracy as well as to those of totalitarianism, two opposite values which risk coinciding dangerously, if historical memory fails to recall the difference. The geopolitical space of Italy is set within the context of globalization, that of Western democracy, but is referred to by Tabucchi in terms of *regime* and *regimetto*, with frequent parallels to fascism.

Readers, throwing their dice, can choose between different trajectories to discover the causes and consequences of the crisis of Lapalisse truth, and by doing so they perform an active role in the themes that are presented by the author with biting satire. The presence of the framework and the dimension of literary play make it clear that, for Tabucchi, the critical function of art can be put into practice only on one condition: to create a self-conscious and fluctuating dynamics between dialectics and ambiguity.[58] For this reason he can be considered an exponent of late postmodernism or, in Foster's terms, a testimony of 'the never-complete passage to the postmodern', which the art critic connects with Freud's notion of deferred action.[59]

How do we explain Tabucchi's most recent work of fiction, however, the collection of stories *Il tempo invecchia in fretta* (Time Runs out of Time, 2009), which seems to go back to the writer's early phase of neo-Baroque intertextuality? The reader is first caught by a sense of loss and melancholy, though at a second reading one is seduced by the possibility of change, generated by the incongruity between anagraphic and spiritual time. The book cover shows a man before a mountain landscape, contemplating nature's immensity, a typical figuration of the sublime in the style of Caspar David Friedrich's Romanticism. In this case, however, the man – photographed from behind by artist Philippe Ramette – is elevated on wooden implements which enable him to create a distance from his contemplation, and thus to escape from the risk of being crushed by the vastness of nature and reduced to human finitude.

Perhaps a reference to the English philosopher Simon Critchley's *Infinitely Demanding*, quoted by Mussgnug and Antonello to back their statement on postmodern ethics, may be appropriate here. According to Critchley, the ethical subject is configured as divided between a limited self and the unlimited ethical demand posed by the Other, to which he is unable to respond completely.[60] The 'consciousness' of this 'dividuality' of the self configures ethics as 'the experience of an infinite demand' at the heart of our subjectivity, a demand that composes and decomposes us and that urges us to do more, 'not in the name of some sovereign authority, but in the namelessness of a powerless exposure, a vulnerability, a responsive responsibility, a humorous self-division'.[61] Thanks to this consciousness of the limit, a multiple and anarchic 'meta-politics' can be composed which puts state authority continuously into question.[62]

Similarly, the characters of Tabucchi's stories, consciously manipulating the limits of the real with artificiality, create their liberty to act while at the same time being reverted by memories that fix them to feelings and experiences fundamental for their lives in connection with others. The climax of metafiction is reached when the protagonist of the last story, 'Controtempo' (Time reverse), succeeds in subverting the effect of *dejà vu* into a future life and is open again for new possibilities: 'It was not the already seen which swallowed him in a never lived past, but it was he who was capturing it in a future still to be lived'.[63] In these stories, the characters thus show themselves to be not only virtuosos of metafiction, but also to be skeptical just to the point of not being poisoned by their political disappointments. Modeling the limits of 'true fiction', they also act (and not only react) to the real.

Baricco's Dances with Barbarians

Baricco is definitely one of those authors who plunge themselves into what critic Renato Barilli has called the infinite mediatic ocean of the third wave of *neo-neoavanguardia*.[64] The multi-talented writer is not afraid of being exposed to the debilitating effects of the cultural mutation he describes and experiences. His essays on (post)modern culture are coherent from the start,[65] and in line with philosopher Vattimo's 'weak' concept of postmodernist pluralism. This makes him an easy target for anti-postmodernists[66] as well as an excellent guide on the consequences of cultural barbarism – who even speaks from the future. His lesson, brought to us from the year 2026, twenty years after the publication of *I barbari* (The Barbarians), is that we should not resist superficiality but inhabit it instead, and be conscious of the fact that depth is nothing but an optical illusion: 'The surface is all, and meaning is inscribed there. Or better: there we are able to trace a meaning'.[67] The 'soft' postmodern spirit of the 1990s made us believe there are no final answers, that meaning is a process and never structural. In Baricco's futuristic view this consciousness of imperfection is just a compromise, and today we should dare to commit ourselves to a new kind of horizontal truth.[68]

Although earmarked as the advocate of Disney culture,[69] Baricco's cultural analysis has also been taken into serious consideration by Eugenio Scalfari (1924) and Claudio Magris (1939), venerable intellectuals and themselves the melancholic sons of modernity.[70] Both have discussed Baricco's assumptions on barbarism not as an effacement, but as a dislocation of meaning. Scalfari, founder of Italy's leading newspaper *La Repubblica*, answers to Baricco's 2026 call by expressing his dissent with the simple fact that Baricco himself is not a barbarian at all. Instead, he is equipped with historical memory and, thus, a 'modernist' (like Scalfari himself) who declares the end of modernity but who, at the same time, fights the dangers of barbarism's culture jamming.[71] If the barbarians are still looking for themselves and for a future, it is the task of modernity, with its cultural legacy, to safeguard the present. This is the bottom line of Scalfari's own personal account of modernity in *Per l'alto mare aperto* (On the High Open Sea, 2010).

Claudio Magris's response can be put on the same line of resisting postmodernism's apocalypse, without entirely rendering the modernist dream of utopia. His thoughts on barbarism have an ethical vein: 'We must try to reconcile a maximum of openness, of ethical relativism, of dialogue with other cultures and their differences, with a minimum, with a *quantum* of inalienable values, not more negotiable values, which are the basis of every civilization'.[72]

In other words, there are ethical and aesthetic limits to Baricco's openness towards mass culture that should be further addressed. If not, his plea to follow the vectors of 'convergence culture' might lose credibility. Baricco's optimistic view, for instance, of the potential of virtual reality to enlarge our modes of aesthetic experience contrasts with the caution professed by younger generations, who are aware of the dangers of Internet surveillance and fear a general crisis of 'inexperience'.[73] Youth is not so much fascinated by cyberspace subjectivity, which it takes for granted, but by its 'dispositif': the concern is with how it can be turned into an interactive tool for self-expression and cultural activism. A reference can be made here to the way young writers and activists in Italy employ transmediality to voice one of the major risks of post-capitalist risk society: the economic and existential consequences of flexibility, namely precarity.[74]

Ammaniti's Party-Apocalypse

Niccolò Ammaniti, finally, in his latest novel *Che la festa cominci* (Let the Party Begin, 2009), seems to have gone back to his early *Cannibali* stage and its 'close the gap' contamination of high and lowbrow ethics and aesthetics. It can be read as a parody or carnival of cultural industry, and the protagonist – star writer Fabrizio Ciba – could be Ammaniti himself, or perhaps alludes to other literary celebrities like (why not?) Alessandro Baricco. Is this a literary perversion of postmodernism brought to the extremes of the 'society of spectacle'? Or can this novel also be interpreted as a deforming mirror for those writers and critics who claim they can bring literature back to its commitment with reality, by-passing that other inconvenient truth, literature being a mediated commodity as well? Ammaniti's claim of being a realist could be a statement of postmodern 'sincerity' in the sense that his work 'can help cast light on the point at which creative labor as aesthetics, and creative labor as *work*, may overlap and interpenetrate'.[75]

Ammaniti is a bestselling author in Italy and abroad, and his imaginative style lends itself well to transpositions in other visual media such as film and comics, of which the young writer is also a passionate consumer.[76] This makes him an example of what Stefano Calabrese has termed the 'new global novel', which follows on postmodernism's abuses of metafiction and hypertextuality, and takes care instead of dispersed individual identity, disintegrated by the waves of transnational globalization.[77] Furthermore, Ammaniti's acquaintance with videogames could make him an author of 'allegorithm', a paradigm that combines allegory with pattern recognition, and is used by Kenneth McKenzie Wark[78] to describe how gamers become immersed in and manipulate gamespace. Allegorithm has become one of the pillars of NIE and has been redefined by Wu Ming 1 as not simply allegoric writing but the recognition of allegory in the process of interaction.[79]

L'ultimo capodanno dell'umanità (The Last New Year's Eve of Humanity) was published for the first time in the short stories collection, *Fango* (Mud, 1996), and republished as a separate volume in 1998 after the film *L'ultimo capodanno* by Marco Risi. A comparison with *Che la festa cominci* brings to light the point where the postmodern author Ammaniti[80] begins and possibly ends. In both cases different life stories are combined in a simultaneous celebratory event, New Year's Eve in the first case and an extravagant mega-party organized by a megalomaniac criminal in the second. Both parties end up in an auto-destructive rapture with only a few, privileged survivors who represent the future of (post)humanity. These narratives are a combination of an uninhibited fantasizing drive for storytelling and a sincere commitment towards the farcical reality of personal lives and of the affective transmission of experience.

L'ultimo capodanno has been analyzed by Irina Rajewsky as a masterpiece of what she calls a 'Dramaturgie des Aufpralls', a dramaturgy of impact between violence and comicality, between everyday life and excess. Its climax is reached in the collapse of internal and external communicative situations, which enables the narrator and the reader to free themselves from the moral constraints of normality and to abandon themselves to overt fictionality and the contrasting emotions it generates.[81] The difference with *Che la festa cominci* is what Baricco means when he suggests that, after postmodernism's relativism, we have to commit ourselves to the depth of the surface and take our responsibility in it. The 'allegorithm' that brings writer and reader nearer to a possible escape from barbarism writes itself inevitably in the icons of consumer culture it wishes to oppose or simply leave behind. Ammaniti's evolution is towards a progressive involvement of the writer in the 'bad' fictions that are put in circulation, and the depth in the surface is his space of imaginative freedom, which can be gratuitous, opportunistic as well as ethical and sincere. That is left for the reader to decide.

Conclusion: The Beyond Is Behind: How to Survive the Apocalypse

Waiting and maybe even hoping for the apocalypse to happen ultimately means escaping our responsibilities towards the present. Young writer Mauro Covacich, who thinks of himself as a 'saboteur' of mass culture, has formulated this hypothesis in his 'reality show' novel *Fiona* (2005): 'I, for apocalypse, would be prepared. [...] Only there will be no apocalypse at all and the world will still go on very slowly in its oval orbit, leaving me and a rather big number of posterior generations in the comfortable condition, oh yes, really comfortable, to have to decide for its own future'.[82] Therefore, the conclusion of this chapter is that New Italian Postmodernism means to transform the 'cognitive strategy' of postmodernism into the 'performative knowledge' of late postmodernism.

Chapter 5

French Literature

Post-Realism and Anti-Realism

Sabine van Wesemael

Introduction

There are two types of modern writers: those who respect the conventions of the realistic novel and those who are opposed to them, having to a greater or lesser degree departed from the ambition to represent the non-literary reality. This is what the French postmodernist Alain Robbe-Grillet argues in a metafictional comment in his novel *Le Miroir qui revient* (1984). Modernists such as Proust and Larbaud wanted to express an intermittent, inner reality. Breton set out to understand surreality. Perec followed strict, mathematical rules while writing his experimental texts which his readers could reconstruct only with difficulty. Alain Robbe-Grillet wrote fragmented novels which seemed to deny any link with the non-literary reality: 'Un roman ne renvoie qu'à lui-même,' he said in his theoretical text *Pour un nouveau roman*. And authors such as Jean-Philippe Toussaint and Jean Echenoz, both from Minuit (the publishing house that became the hallmark for a formalist kind of prose), more recently chose to approach reality in a minimalistic way. In their novels, the characters hardly develop, reflections in a psychologizing manner are not to be found, the plots have not been arranged in a causal order, both authors display an aversion to realistic descriptions. Novels such as *Je m'en vais* and *La Salle de bain* express a postmodern view to humankind and society where alienation and ontological doubts are the central points.[1]

In addition to these anti-realistic movements, twentieth-century French literature has always known a more traditional tendency, too. For instance, one could think of authors such as Marguerite Yourcenar and Michel Tournier who, for good reason, are often referred to as 'classiques modernes'.

Postmodernism in France

Postmodernism was a dominant movement in France in the 1960s and 1970s, featuring authors such as Robbe-Grillet, Sarraute, Duras, Simon and Butor who published theoretical writings that put forward their poetic ambitions, such as *Pour un nouveau roman* by Robbe-Grillet and *L'ère du soupçon* by Nathalie Sarraute. The movement found theoretical support in structuralists such as Genette. The often-quoted remark of Robbe-Grillet of "un roman ne renvoie qu'à lui-même" clearly expresses the fact that these *nouveaux romanciers* were not sympathetic to the non-literary reality, and harboured no wish to express any commitment, considering the literary text a closed entity within which any form of traditional realism had to be undermined: no clear character drawing (Robbe-Grillet was even of the opinion that the personage itself had to disappear from the novel), no reflections in a psychologizing manner, special focus on the object that in the action often takes the place of the personage (here, the French will speak of 'chosification'), no chronological, causal narrative style, and an aversion to analogical usage because reality fails to be captured, even in a literary way. For instance, the novel *La Jalousie* by Robbe-Grillet amounts to little more than an incoherent collection of text fragments that the reader-puzzler is supposed to reconstruct. The personages of the novel have no or scant descriptions. The man from whose point of view the narrative is told is likely to be a jealous husband who is peeping at his wife A through the Venetian blinds as he suspects her of having started an adulterous relationship with their neighbour Franck. The shape of the text excellently expresses the narrator's emotions; descriptions of A and Franck enjoying a dram on the verandah or reading an African novel together are endlessly repeated, with the usual variations and inconsistencies, but without the narrator having any certainty about their relationship. This French structuralist and experimental postmodernism intention to express epistemological and ontological doubts broke with the conventions of the realistic novel, going back to authors who had done so previously: Proust and Breton had been shining examples to both Robbe-Grillet and Sarraute.[2]

A Reaction to Postmodernism

French historians of literature such as Dominique Viart and Bruno Blanckeman (*La Littérature Française au présent*) state that from the 1980s postmodernism gradually had to give way to a (neo-) realistic movement that no longer engaged in the above-mentioned experiments of form and style. They mention a 'return of the narrative', a reassessment of the conventions of the realistic novel: clear character drawing, determinism and causality, linear course of action, daily parlance, social criticism, detailism, etc.

In *Le Miroir qui revient* Robbe-Grillet is reacting against these modern authors who are distrustful of the experimental formalism of postmodernism:

> *Nowadays the reaction to any attempt to escape from traditional representation is so vehement that the daring remarks I used to make will be drowned out by an old discours, seemingly restored, against which I have always spoken out so passionately. [...] So should we resume these terrorist actions of the 1955-1960s? Sure, we should.*[3]

Viart and Blanckeman put forward a number of arguments to enforce their proposition about a 'return of the narrative'. First of all, the modern novel puts the impersonal nature of much post-modern literature behind it, as for instance the infinity of ego-documents published from the 1980s goes to show. The former 'nouveaux romanciers' also write autobiographical texts: *Enfance* by Nathalie Sarraute, *L'Amant* by Marguerite Duras, *Le Jardin des plantes* by Claude

Simon and *Le Miroir qui revient* by Alain Robbe-Grillet are a few striking examples. Furthermore, many modern authors are opposed to the hermetic nature of many post-modern texts, and display an ambition to describe a non-literary reality. Annie Ernaux, Virginie Despentes, Marie Darrieussecq, François Bon, Michel Houellebecq and Frédéric Beigbeder each in their own way try to make comments on contemporary society. However, not only the individual views on humankind and society are back at centre stage, history, too, is again the subject matter of literature. Over the last two decades numerous novels have been written about the First and Second World Wars, ranging from Jean Rouaud's *Les Champs d'honneur* to Philippe Claudel's *Les Âmes grises* and from Patrick Modiano's *Dora Bruder* to Lydie Salavaire's *La Compagnie des spectres*. Still, Viart and Blanckeman are right in admitting that at the moment it is not a matter of slavishly imitating nineteenth-century conventions, and that all disruptive, modernist, twentieth-century tendencies did leave the contemporary French novel with deep marks:

> *Contemporary literature is not characterized by restoring tradition. The indications of 'retour du sujet' and 'retour du récit' give a distorted view of what is really going on. The 'I', as the large quantity of autofictitious texts demonstrates, is surely back at the centre, the 'story' is quite in vogue again. This is not to say, however, that authors reapply traditional literary forms. A more correct claim would be to say that 'sujet' and 'récit' (but 'réel', 'Histoire', 'engagement critique', 'lyrisme'... as well) have a compelling presence again, but will, at the same time, be problematized, frequently still raising insoluble problems.*[4]

The contemporary French novel is often rather a hybrid form, converging realism and postmodernism. Not by any means could *Le Miroir qui revient* (1985) and *L'Amant* (1984) be considered traditional autobiographies. They may be specified as 'nouvelles autobiographies', as the 'nouveau roman' strategies that undermine realism still affect them. To be sure, the novel *Les Âmes grises* by Philippe Claudel, dealing with the brutal murder of a little girl at the time of the First World War, is punctuated with realistic descriptions of setting and character, yet the novel is permeated by postmodern characteristics, too. The very title of *Les Âmes grises* alone indicates that reality is not black or white – nor can it immediately be known – but multi-interpretable and doubtful instead: ultimately, the murder will not be solved. Jean Rouaud's description of the First World War in *Les Champs d'honneur*, too, is markedly impressionistic, differing strongly from the realistic descriptions in the patriotic novels written at the time of the *Grande Guerre* of which *Le Feu* by Barbusse and *Le Croix des bois* by Dorgeles are fine examples. The novels by bestselling author Michel Houellebecq, too, are prize examples showing that nowadays authors frequently opt for combining traditional narrative techniques and postmodern principles.

Post-Realism and Anti-Realism: Late Postmodernism in French Literature

French literature since the 1980s may be characterized by this negotiation between the two strands of literature that were prevalent in its literary tradition: realism on the one hand versus experiment (postmodern) on the other. What emerges therefore is a hybrid novel, which will be illustrated by three cases in this section. I will discuss two contemporary authors (Houellebecq and Claudel) whose novels express this hybrid postrealism. They will be compared to an author who claims to hold to postmodern principles, repudiating any form of realism, Alain Robbe-Grillet, but whose work is undoubtedly influenced by the turn to the narrative as well.

Michel Houellebecq

Michel Houellebecq is quite averse to the experiments of form and style of postmodern literature. In *Interventions*, a collection of essays, he writes about this, in his view, objectionable formalism:

> *There is something sad in this spectacle. I myself will always feel anxious whenever I see the riot of techniques that any 'Minuit-formalist' will put to use for so poor a final result. So as to put fresh heart into myself, I would often in my mind repeat Schopenhauer's statement: "The first rule, indeed by itself virtually a sufficient condition for good style, is to have something to say".*[5]

Viart and Blanckeman assign Houellebecq to the 'hyperréalistes' because, like his personage Daniel1 considering himself a modern Balzac, he aims to provide our modern society with comments, sure enough choosing a form and style with a nineteenth-century touch. With iron logic Houellebecq demonstrates that not only our economy but our emotional lives, too, are under complete control of the deterministic market forces of demand and supply. The physically unattractive narrator of *Extension du domaine de la lutte* has little success with women, losing himself in an ultra-nihilistic view on humankind and society as a result. Over forty and starting to wear woollen pyjamas in bed, Isabelle, in *La Possibilité d'une île* (2005, English translation 2005: *The Possibility of an Island*) is traded in by Daniel1 for the much younger and sexually more active Esther.

The opening passage of *Les Particules élémentaires*, describing Bruno's and Michel's childhoods, could very well be read as a contemporary application of determinism, known from Zola's 'roman expérimental'.[6] For lack of his mother's love, Michel is driven to science whereas Bruno is bound all his life to try and compensate for this lack of affection by compulsive sexual conquests. Houellebecq's characters will be realistically drawn, the course of action is often linear, his novels are permeated by reflections on contemporary society, his style being ordinary and accessible; it is rare for him to employ rhetorical figures. The scenario-writer Daniel1 who, as has been mentioned before, considers himself a 'commentateur social' and idolizes Balzac, is noticing at the same time that he is having difficulty with identifying himself with his characters, as nowadays there is no place for conquerors of the world who are completely driven by their ambition to bend reality to their will. Like Daniel1, the writer Michel Houellebecq maintains a love-hate relationship with realistic authors such as Balzac; he does use realistic conventions of the novel, yet he will also ridicule them, the breach with postmodernism being much less radical than might be thought on cursory reading. The Freudian causality the narrator of *Les Particules élémentaires* finds between the early childhood experiences of Bruno and Michel and their future emotional developments is so simplistic that it eventually fails to enhance the realistic value of the text. What are the postmodern characteritics of Houellebecq's novels?

Firstly, there is the loss of identity. Like many postmodern writers, Houellebecq will opt for average anti-heroes, nihilistic incarnations of man, who have been completely alienated from themselves and their surroundings and thus suffer from a lack of identity. For instance, in *Plateforme* can be found numerous passages that are critical of contemporary individualism, and where, on the contrary, the lack of authenticity of modern humankind will emerge. When Michel decides to go and live together with Valérie, it comes to him, while moving house, that he has no personal attachment to any of the items, and he is losing himself in the following shocking reasoning:

> *Nor did I have any photos of myself: I had no memory of what I might have been like when I was fifteen, or twenty or thirty. I didn't really have any personal papers: my identity could be contained in a couple of files which would easily fit into a standard-size cardboard folder. It is wrong to pretend that human beings are unique, that they carry within them an irreplaceable individuality; as far as I was concerned, at any rate, I could not distinguish any trace of such an individuality. As often as not, it is futile to wear yourself out trying to distinguish individual destinies and personalities. When all's said and done, the idea of the uniqueness of the*

individual is nothing more than pompous absurdity. We remember our own lives, Schopenauer wrote somewhere, a little better than a novel we once read. That's about right: a little, no more.[7]

The novels of Houellebecq illustrate the theories of the much-praised French philosopher/sociologist Gilles Lipovetsky as he explained them in *L'ère du vide* and *Les Temps hypermodernes*. Lipovetsky holds that, as a consequence of the disintegration of ideological and moral frames of reference, modern humankind has been left quite to its own devices and is in danger of losing itself in lamentable narcissism. Houellebecq has adopted this criticism on individualism and continues to show that unicity is not the main characteristic of contemporary man. This idea of a soulless humankind is developed in the most consistent way in his latest novel, *La Possibilité d'une île*, where cloned, robot-like figures are leading virtual and detached existences with all their consequences. Daniel24 commits suicide and his successor Daniel25 decides to leave the guarded compound in order to go and seek for the human emotions he has had to do without.

Many a postmodern novel will focus on this erosion of the 'I'.[8] For example, the novels of Robbe-Grillet, where dummy-like figures are roaming about without any depth at all being given to their inner selves or, more recently, the texts of the so-called 'impassibles' such as Toussaint, Oster, Gailly and Delville. Like Toussaint, Houellebecq writes about people who suffer under a feeling of moral and emotional poverty, about marginal figures painfully aware of the meaninglessness of their existences. The narrator of *Extension du domaine de la lutte* says that smoking cigarettes is the only form of freedom left to him, and the main character in *La Salle de bain* of Toussaint shuts himself in the bathroom so as to escape reality.

This dismantling of the 'I' results in personages weighed down by psychiatric symptoms:[9] The depressed narrator of *Extension du domaine de la lutte* and Bruno in the *Particules élémentaires* both find themselves in a psychiatric clinic, and Daniel1, too, has a complete nervous breakdown when the young Esther runs out on him. Houellebecq chooses to give expression to the mental confusion in his characters in the form and style of his novels, though he does not go as far as Robbe-Grillet whose *La Reprise* is a chaotic sequence of psychotic hallucinations. The final argument in *Les Particules élémentaires*, where Michel's view of the future is explained, will be considered an alarming delirium by many a reader; the nihilistic and misogynistic thoughts of the narrator of *Extension du domaine de la lutte* result from his depressed disposition and will be brushed aside by many people as too morbid; and neither will people take seriously Michel's plan (*Plateforme*) to open posh brothels throughout the world where the sexually frustrated Westerner could have his every whim fulfilled.[10] Characters in Houellebecq, but not Robbe-Grillet, are identifiable up to a certain point, but they are also marked by depersonalization and the neurotic symptoms that go with it, making them, after all, less realistic than one initially tends to think.

This loss of identity also results in the tendency for Houellebecq's personages to lose touch with reality. They play a role in their own fiction. Though Houellebecq would certainly not deny the referential function of language completely, he seems in part to subscribe to the postmodern conviction that a breach has occurred between language and reality. Many of his personages are slaves to their own construction. Michel (*Plateforme*) can see the Thai exotic reality only through the eyes of hotel brochures and travel guides, Daniel24 and Daniel25 have to submit themselves meekly to the directions of the *Sœur Suprême*, and *Extension du domaine de la lutte* is a long-winded treatise on the disastrous consequences of the soulless telematica revolution for modern humankind. One of the narrator's colleagues, Jean-Yves Fréhaut, thinks himself to be merely a leading figure in this revolution:

> *His own life, as I would subsequently learn, was functional in the extreme. He was living in a studio flat in the 15th arrondissement. The heating was included in the rent. He barely did more than sleep there, since he was in fact working a lot – and often, outside of working time, he was reading* Micro-Systèmes. *The famous degrees of freedom consisted, as far as he was concerned, in choosing his dinner by Minitel.*[11]

A second postmodern aspect of Houellebecq's novels is the conviction that humankind is caught in linguistic structures. The consequence is that, like many postmodern novels, Houellebecq's work is distinctly eclectic and intertextual. *Plateforme* abounds in quotations from travel guides such as *Le Guide du Routard* and the *Guide Michelin*; *Extension du domaine de la lutte* is permeated with the jargon as used in the IT sector; and both *Les Particules élémentaires* and *La Possibilité d'une île* are heavily relying on physical science theories such as the quantum mechanics of Bohr and Heisenberg as well as on eugenetic laws. Houellebecq opts for this pastiche approach to demonstrate that contemporary humankind has become alienated from itself and its surroundings, being just a slave to its own structure, that is to say to the thought patterns enforced on it from the inside and outside. Besides, it seems almost impossible for him as an author to evade this theme altogether, as another main characteristic in his novels is that they will rely on strategies and techniques derived from popular genres such as travel books, utopias and sci-fi stories. Like many postmodern authors, Houellebecq, too, undermines the dividing line between serious and popular arts with great satisfaction. For instance, Jean Echenoz's ambitions are to undermine the traditional conventions of the serious novel by deriving narrative techniques from popular genres such as detective novels, biographies and adventure novels. His novel *Ravel*, describing the French composer's last ten years of his life, is also distinctly eclectic because Echenoz is amply drawing from existing biographies, not shrinking from occasionally reproducing whole text fragments verbatim. So rather than a novel in the traditional meaning of the word, *Ravel* is a 'biofiction', that is to say a text that is continuously alternating between historical facts and fiction.[12]

For instance, the protagonist of *La Salle de bains* by Toussaint, like the main character in Houellebecq's *Extension du domaine de la lutte*, considers himself a minor actor who created a role for himself because it fits in very well with his strategy of survival: he is trying to put in practice Pascal's thirteenth *pensée*, 'divertissement'. But where Toussaint's personage dozes off into a lethargic sleep in the bath, Houellebecq's and Robbe-Grillet's figures will show an ultra-violent response to their sense of alienation. They will overstep the mark in order to feel alive after all. Transgression is in fact a main characteristic in Houellebecq's novels and may well explain the reason why they caused such a fuss. The narrator in *Extension du domaine de la lutte* wants to chop off the lovely legs of the disco dancers with an axe, and he incites his companion in misfortune Tisserand to murder a young black man who is quite successful with the same girls. Michel in *Les Particules élémentaires* and Savant in *La Possibilité d'une île* proclaim the end of the human race, and Michel in *Plateforme* would like to avenge his father's death by killing a number of Muslims. Violence seems to be the alternative for depersonalization. Still, this aggression is not aimed only at the other. Many of Houellebecq's personages will mutilate themselves because self-mutilation makes them feel that they exist. As I have shown in my book, *Michel Houellebecq. Le plaisir du texte*, almost all dreams in his novels express castration fantasies. Bruno indulges in fantasies about being a little pig that is slaughtered in a slaughterhouse, his half-brother Michel dreams about rubbish bins filled with cut-off genitals, and the narrator in *Extension du domaine de la lutte*, when waking up in the morning and seeing a pair of scissors sitting on his bedside table, can hardly resist the temptation to cut off his sex organ. Sure enough, it is particularly in the field of sexuality that the personages are in danger of taking up bad ways. All of them feel drawn to sexual acts that overstep the mark, some to neutralize their fear of the opposite sex, others to satisfy their uncontrollable sexual impulses. The narrator of *Extension du domaine de la lutte* is a misogynous masturbator who vomits whenever he sees a girl, because in this world of market and combat, only ugly women such as Catherine Lechardoy ('God has not, in truth, been too kind to her'[13]) are responsive to him. Michel (*Les Particules élémentaires*) has been living chaste ever since Annabelle cheated on him. On the other hand, his half-brother Bruno, Michel (*Plateforme*) and Daniel1 maintain pornographic views on the opposite sex, sexuality being to them the only source of comfort in their otherwise pathetic existence. Bruno has wild nights with the accommodating Christiane; and while promoting sex tourism, Michel and Valérie are only too happy to be indulged by the chambermaids whom they engaged on behalf of their customers; and Daniel1 feels most attracted to the young Esther as she devotes herself with conviction to her exclusive sexual services, her inspiration being the performances by porno stars. While playing a role, she, too, likes to imitate the behaviour of others:

> *'Don't worry...' she said; then she knelt down to suck me off. She had a very honed technique, doubtless inspired by porn films – it was immediately obvious for she had that gesture, which you learn quickly in films, of throwing back her hair to allow the boy, for want of a camera, to watch you in action. Since their beginnings, fellatio has always been the jewel in the crown of porn films, the only thing that can serve as a useful model for young girls [...].*[14]

Extension du domaine de la lutte excepted, the novels by Houellebecq are punctuated with lovemaking scenes that leave nothing to the imagination, expressing the pornofication of our society. Though Houellebecq's figures do find again a sense of symbiosis and oneness in the brevity of physical love, still the pornographic sexuality they often take to will not in the end give them any satisfaction. At the end of *Les Particules élémentaires*, the profligate Bruno goes into a psychiatric clinic where he is chemically vasectomized, and Daniel1 regrets the fact that Esther is driven by sexual desire alone and that she fails to attach any significance at all to love; she leaves Daniel1 for a younger lover. Whereas transgression is an 'opération sacrée' to Bataille that is to deliver mankind, Houellebecq in the end judges it negatively. He shows that by now all taboos have been broken and that on this score, too, contemporary humankind is left empty-handed: the act of overstepping the limit will give a brief moment of pleasure, yet in the long run it will only feed precisely those feelings of depression and disappointment which it had sought to compensate.

The criticism of modern consumer society is one of the main differences between Houellebecq and his postmodern predecessors. The author voices Lyotard's conviction that modern man's inner void is easily accounted for due to today's absence of any ideological frame of reference. Robbe-Grillet does not have the ambition to voice his opinion about contemporary society; his is a much more abstract approach, wishing to describe the human condition in a separate way from principles restricted to time and place.

Like any author, Houellebecq also has, to a certain extent, the ambition to say something general about the fate of humankind, but his trademark is unmasking lofty, social ideals. In *Plateforme*, Michel pokes fun at communism when he lets himself be indulged by the chambermaid in a luxury hotel in Cuba; in *Les Particules élémentaires* the high ideals of the May '68 movement are ridiculed in the figure of Janine Ceccaldi, the unconventional, egocentric mother of Bruno and Michel, *La Possibilité d'une île* being a prolonged satire on the salvation doctrine of various religious convictions. Even elohimism, which wants to realize immortality by cloning humans, fails to bring relief as the soulless, dehumanized clones end up deeply unhappy: Daniel24 commits suicide, and Daniel25 decides to break the genetic chain and sets out on a tough hike straight across Spain only to immerse himself in one of those pools surrounding the former Lanzarote. Whereas the personages of Houellebecq continue to put forward ideas critical of society, the *engagement* remains a more implicit element in the postmodern novel. As its title indicates, *Extension du domaine de la lutte* is about the excesses of our modern consumer society, about capitalizing on our emotional lives and the pornofication of contemporary society resulting from it; *Plateforme* ridicules Islam, the Western perception of sexuality being depicted as poor and without any sincere empathy; Michel, one of the two half-brothers in *Les Particules élémentaires*, felt like inventing an alternative for our society that, to his mind, is directionless and close to ruin, etcetera.

Still Houellebecq cannot be said to be bringing the 'roman engagé' as promoted by Sartre back to life; rather, like in many postmodern novels, the possibility of social engangement is brought up for discussion. Houellebecq's criticism on the capitalist consumer society and the May '68 ideals seems leftish, whereas his diatribe against Islam and his disillusioned analyses of the consequences of the sexual revolution caused critics to classify him among the 'nouveaux réactionnaires'.[15] As has been remarked, his personages will not choose unambiguous social commitment, but end up stranding themselves, like many postmodern novels, in a nihilistic ideological vacuum. Houellebecq's novels do make use of the strategies of the Utopian novel (there is a long discussion on Huxley's *Brave New World* in *Les Particules élémentaires* – and not for nothing), at the same time ridiculing any utopian wish; rather, they are dystopias. For instance, *Lanzarote* is a parodic rewriting of the Grail myth where Rudi, a Belgian policeman seeking rescue from his oppressive existence, joins a sect preaching the raping of small children, and in *Les Particules élémentaires*, the chaste academic Michel is sublimating his sexual frustrations by designing a new human characterized by his immense sexual potency: the surface of his skin is covered with Krause-bodies creating unbeatable erotic experiences.

Houellebecq makes his anti-heroes dream about a better life and a happier humankind, but he will never make their wishes a reality; indeed, the clash between high ideals and the disillusioning reality will irrevocably lead to the tendency to destroy themselves and the other. Annabelle, Christiane, Tisserand and Daniel24 take their own lives, Michel and the narrator of *Extension du domaine de la lutte* decide to disappear without a trace, the sensual Valérie is killed in a bomb attack by Muslim extremists who took offence at the luxury brothels she and her compagnon Michel opened all over the world, and the narrator of *Lanzarote* feels more depressed than ever following his stay on the volcanic isle that bears the promise of regeneration by the primeval elements. Houellebecq makes use of all standard satirical devices to bring home to the reader that his ideas of social criticism are not meant to be taken too seriously: he is putting them into the mouths of failures, ridiculous individuals who are treated by the author with a good deal of irony and sarcasm, the stories of their lives all the time taking the edge off the meaning of the message. Bruno and Daniel1 feel happy only when they know themselves loved by the sexually unconventional Christiane and Esther, and, as a result, their fates show that the sexual revolution brought about many good things, too.

Daniel distinguishes three types of artists in *La Possibilité d'une île*: the revolutionary, who thinks his art would get the masses going; the 'decorator' who withdraws into his ivory tower, not caring about the world around him; and the humorist who has no wish to change the world either, but wants to make it an acceptable place by transforming the violence required for any revolutionary act into a laugh. Daniel1's and his friend Vincent's careers unerringly illustrate Houellebecq's position in the debate on the fundamental assignment facing the artist. Vincent starts his career as a committed artist but soon has to acknowledge that his serious art fails to mobilize the public; abandoning his revolutionary ideals, he retires to his basement. On the other hand, the scenarios of Daniel1 express a provocatively moral and ideologically ironic relativism so characteristic of the writings of Houellebecq himself and the much more formalist 'nouveau nouveau roman'. For instance, think of the hilarious way in which Toussaint, in *La Télévision*, makes his main character go through the various stages of detoxification after he decided to stop watching TV. In his book *Crépuscules*, Lipovetsky argues that in our current Western society, all higher values in fact become parodic: 'Postmodern unbelief, the neo-nihilism that is taking shape is atheistic nor moralistic, from now on it will be humoristic.'[16] Daniel1 comments on the success of his latest show bizarrely entitled 'Forward Snowy! Onwards to Aden', as follows:

> *From the outset, I got on to the subject of the conflict in the Middle East – which had already brought me a few significant media successes – in a manner which, wrote the Le Monde journalist, was 'singularly abrasive'. The first sketch, entitled 'The Battle of the Tiny Ones', portrayed Arabs – renamed 'Allah's vermin' – Jews – described as 'circumcised fleas' – and even some Lebanese Christians, afflicted with the pleasing sobriquet 'Crabs from the Cunt of Mary'. In short, as the critic for Le Point noted, the religions of the Book were 'played off against each other' – in this sketch at least; the rest of the show included a screamingly funny playlet entitled 'The Palestinians are Ridiculous', into which I slipped a variety of burlesque and salacious allusions about sticks of dynamite that female militants of Hezbollah put around their waists in order to make mashed Jew. I then widened this to an attack on all forms of rebellion, of nationalist and revolutionary struggle, and in reality against political action itself. Of course, I was developing throughout the show a vein of right-wing anarchy, along the lines of 'one dead combatant means one less cunt able to fight', which from Céline to Audiard, had already contributed to the finest hours of French comedy [...].*[17]

The morbid humour that is so characteristic of Daniel1's texts also typifies the work of Houellebecq, but like his personage, his creator eventually has to acknowledge that this ironic relativism offers no relief, that humour eventually is of no use. Daniel1 is struck with a feeling of utter dejection when he is watching the tapings of his shows, he has to vomit when he sees the audience burst out laughing because in his view laughter is the ultimate expression of cruelty, and the following disillusioning comments of the narrator of *Les Particules élémentaires* expresses Houellebecq's criticism on ironic relativism: 'You can look at life ironically for years, maybe decades; there are people who seem to go through most of their lives seeing the funny side, but in the end, life always breaks your heart.'[18]

To Thomas Vaessens, professor of Dutch literature, this criticism of irony is typical of late postmodernism. In his view, Dutch authors such as Grunberg, Zwagerman and Februari have had enough of the unproductive postmodernist cynicism.[19] The situation in France is somewhat more complicated due to the fact that texts by most prominent French postmodernists such as Robbe-Grillet, Butor, Sarraute, Duras and Simon certainly could not be characterized by frequent use of satiric stylistic devices such as irony and sarcasm; on the contrary, they are generally not particularly humorous. Nor should it be taken for granted that Houellebecq would distance himself from the books that every so often are humorous novels indeed, by minimalist authors such as Echenoz, Toussaint or Delville; in his frame of reference, they play no role at all. So rather than betraying an aversion to postmodern literature, Houellebecq's criticism of the ironic relativism shows a wish to radically break with the postmodern mentality so clearly described by Lipovetsky.

Even acting in an aesthetic manner will fail to offer any rescue. Michel (*Plateforme*) is convinced that his novel about his love for Valérie will not keep him from oblivion, Daniel1 harbours deep doubts about whether his cloned descendants will be interested in his life story, and the narrator of *Extension du domaine de la lutte* does not consider art to have any purifying influence at all:

> *If I don't write about what I've seen, I will suffer just the same – and perhaps a little more so. But only a bit, I insist on this. Writing brings scant relief. It retraces, it delimits. It lends a touch of coherence, the idea of a kind of realism. One stumbles around in a cruel fog, but there is the odd pointer. Chaos is no more than a few feet away. A meagre victory, in truth.*[20]

The narrator would prefer to spend the remainder of his days reading. The only escape open to him seems to be to cease taking part, to step out of his role.

Like the postmodernists, Houellebecq radically breaks with the elitist conception of art of the modernists, but unlike the postmodernists he is drawn by the nineteenth-century realist 'esthétique du laid'. Like them, he opts for an everyday, marred style as this style effectively expresses the shallow emotions of his personages, and he puts earthly characters on the scene whose life stories and neuroses are to a large extent deterministically defined by their social contexts. As has been mentioned, however, he is also making fun of the realistic conventions of the novel as the referential illusion continues to be undermined by the merciless deconstruction of mankind and society, so that in the end there is hardly anything left of them.

Alain Robbe-Grillet

As we have seen, with his intertextual, transgressive novels, conscious of ontological doubt, the rift between language and reality, the alienation of humankind from itself and its surroundings, Houellebecq is closer to a postmodern author such as Robbe-Grillet than might be thought at first. Robbe-Grillet's novel *La Reprise* (2001) also deals with dismantling the 'I'. The story is about a French secret agent on a mission in Berlin who is ignorant of the facts of his assignment. He is constantly changing his identity, his name being now Franck Matthieu and now Henri Robin. Moreover, wherever he goes, he sees lookalikes pursuing him, and eventually he loses himself in psychotic delusions. The personages in Robbe-Grillet's latest novel, *Un roman sentimental*, are also explicitly anti-realistic: they will be referred to as personages, fictitious creations of a narrator whose status, too, remains obscure as he now expresses himself in the first person singular, now merges with one of the figures filling a central role in the string of perverse scenarios the reader is being presented with. Since the 1950s Robbe-Grillet has claimed that he wants to banish the character from literature, and *Un roman sentimental* shows he never sought to repudiate this basic principle. At the start of the novel, we are introduced to a narrator who expresses himself in the first person singular, describing how he finds himself in a white, neutral room ablaze with light. He wonders where he is: in a morgue, a coffin, a ward or a cell? On one of the walls is a picture of a landscape with a few figures painted in it. The text suggests that all personages fulfilling a role in the perverse scenarios told in the novel are coming from the mind of the narrator, who brings the painted characters to life. So the reader will wonder what the status of the text and the personages might be: are we dealing with a description of crazy hallucinations, or is the text expressing the dreams and imaginings of the author, who has time and again indicated his fascination with perverse sexual acts with underage girls in real life, too. Anyway, it is a fact that the personages have been represented unrealistically; Gigi, her father, and all young girls who, in the course of the narrative, are being raped, tortured or prostituted hardly have any identities of their own; they are characterized by their perverse sado-masochistic acts only.

So Robbe-Grillet and Houellebecq both seem to describe the alienation of modern humankind in relation to itself. However, a significant difference between both authors is that like Lipovetsky, Houellebecq explains this phenomenon in a sociological way, always harping on the alienating effects of contemporary disideologized society for humankind, whereas Robbe-Grillet takes the philosophical view, interpreting the problematical perception of one's own individuality as inherent in the human condition.

The novels by Robbe-Grillet, like those of Houellebecq, mainly contain robot-like figures caught in linguistic structures that transform reality. The neutral narrator of *La Jalousie* presents the reader with a completely incoherent story about the alleged adulterous affair between his wife and the neighbour. Having no grasp of reality, he is giving himself fully to his runaway fantasies. Rather than describing reality in an objective way, he is thinking it up, thus getting caught up in his own delusions. Gigi and her father in *Un roman sentimental* are only fictitious figures with no true identity because the perverse scenarios in which they play the leading part overstep a mark to such an extent that they could be attributed only to the disordered fantasies of the author/narrator. Robbe-Grillet calls his latest novel a 'fiction fantasmatique', being quite aware of the fact that if he were to put his perverse fantasies in practice, he would simply get taken to court.

Transgression, in particular in the sexual sphere, is a main characteristic in many postmodern novels. Houellebecq's texts have caused the usual outrage, but still, in recent years the most amazing novel has certainly been *Un roman sentimental* (2007) by Robbe-Grillet. As has already been said, this novel tells the shocking story of a perverse father who abuses his accommodating daughter Gigi in brutal ways. Father and daughter completely give themselves over to sado-masochistic games, organizing cruel torture parties they enjoy immensely. In *Le Miroir qui revient*, Robbe-Grillet had already confessed that only perverse scenarios managed to rouse his desire, and that he felt attracted to very young girls in particular, indulging these fantasies to the full in *Un roman sentimental*. The postmodernist Robbe-Grillet, as a matter of fact, is working more along the lines of Bataille and does not express any negative value judgment like Houellebecq: in the postmodern novel, transgression is another means of escaping the suffocating straitjacket of norms and values, whereas Houellebecq seems, on the contrary, to subscribe to the importance of this straitjacket.

However, it is true of both authors that their breaking of taboos spoils the quality of realism of the text, though in this case, the breach with realism in the postmodern novel is more radical than in the case of Houellebecq. *Un roman sentimental* is, as has been said, a chaotic sequence of perverse scenarios the status of which never becomes quite clear. On the other hand, Houellebecq and Robbe-Grillet do share the opinion that transgression is the natural outcome of a lack of identity. So alienation and its resultant violent transgression are characteristic of both the 'hyper-realistic' writings of Houellebecq and many a postmodern novel.[21]

Philippe Claudel

So, is Robbe-Grillet wrong when claiming that the contemporary French novel is too indebted to nineteenth-century realism? Is his call for resuming the terrorist actions of the 1955-60s falling on deaf ears? I think that Viart and Blanckeman are right in observing that every age will develop its own realism and that the 'return of the narrative' as observed by them in no way implies that postmodernism has had its day once and for all.

This is also true for authors such as Philippe Claudel who seem to be breaking radically with postmodernism. His novel *Les Âmes grises*, which won the Prix Renaudot, is often quoted as an example of a contemporary novel that succeeded in holding on to a large readership precisely because of its classical, realistic set-up. It is a fact that Claudel is less indebted to postmodernism than Houellebecq, which makes a comparison with an author such as Robbe-Grillet less obvious, but for Claudel's novels, too, it is still true that they have been positively permeated by postmodern principles. In *Les Âmes grises*, a novel with a First World War setting, a policeman is trying to reconstruct what happened in a small French village near the front line twenty years after the fatal murder of a little girl, Belle de jour. In order to do so, he refers to his own memory and to the testimonies of others. He tells about the soldiers at the front who, to escape the horrible reality of the trenches, hang around the local pub and brothel, and about young Lilia Verhareine, volunteering for a job as a teacher because she wants to be close to her fiancé who was sent to the front as a soldier. He describes how the villagers are only too keen to deny the reality of the war, but that death is found to be infectious: Lilia commits suicide after her fiancé is killed or else she is murdered by the prosecutor Destinat, the little Belle de jour is strangled, and the policeman's wife dies in childbirth in the absence of her husband, who had been unable to come home due to the roads being obstructed by battalions of soldiers on their way to the front. *Les Âmes grises* is a sort of detective novel, but one in which the crimes go unsolved. We will never know whether Destinat or a deserter killed Belle de jour no more than we will make sure about the rights and wrongs of Lilia's death. The novel does make use of the nineteenth-century realistic conventions of the novel, but undermines them at the same time; it is far less conventional than one might be inclined to think on cursory reading. *Les Âmes grises* is peppered with long-winded realistic descriptions that support both the dramatic course of the action and the psychological profiles of the personages and that are not to be found in novels by Robbe-Grillet. For instance, the policeman gives a detailed description of Destinat's life story, he talks about Destinat's parents, his marriage, the early death of his wife, his unrelenting attitude as a prosecutor, portraying him as an unapproachable and solitary man who might be capable of committing a murder; Lilia nicknamed him 'monsieur Tristesse'. The following description of Destinat's bedroom might just as well be found in a novel by Balzac:

> *Destinat's room was nothing like the others. The bed was narrow, a monk's bed: iron bedposts and a simple mattress, no trimmings, no tester hanging from the ceiling. The walls were simply lined with grey, no paintings or decorations. Beside the bed stood a small table with a crucifix on it. At the foot of the bed there was a washstand with jug and basin. A high-backed chair. A little desk with nothing on it. No book, no paper, no pen.*
> *The room was like the man himself. Cold, silent, it made you uncomfortable, but it inspired respect. It had drawn a sense of distance from the man who slept there, impervious to laughter forever. The very orderliness of the place endorsed the idea of dead hearts.*[22]

This extract, for example, brings strongly to mind the pages-long description of the lodging-house of Madame Vauquer with which Balzac opens his famous novel *Le Père Goriot,* ending it with the remark: 'Toute sa personne explique la pension comme la pension implique sa personne' – 'her whole person, in short, provides a clue to the boarding-house, just as the boarding-house implies the existence of such a person as she is' (quote translated by Marion Ayton Crawford). However, whereas with Balzac the subsequent course of the action follows naturally from this opening extract, the descriptions in *Les Âmes grises* are only an expression of the narrator's persistent longing to find out the truth, but no confirmation of it. Much as he does his best, Destinat will remain an inscrutable man to him, like the husband in *La Jalousie* by Robbe-Grillet:

> *For years, I have been trying to understand, but I do not think I am any cleverer than the next man. I fumble, I get lost, go round in circles. In the beginning, before the* Affaire, *Destinat was just a name to me, an official position, a house, a fortune, a face I encountered two or three times a week and to which I would raise my hat. As for what went on behind the face, I had no chance of knowing! Since that time, having lived with his ghost for so long, he has become quite the old acquaintance, the companion in misfortune, a part of myself you could say, and one that I have tried to persuade to speak, tried to bring back to life so that I can ask it one question. Just one. Sometimes I tell myself that I am wasting my time, that the man was as impenetrable as the thickest fog, and that a thousand evenings with him would not be enough.*[23]

The very title *Les Âmes grises* gives a clue that nobody is solely good or solely evil, that we all are wandering souls whom morality has a scant hold on. This implies that unambiguous character drawing is impossible. Man can only be known in part. This notion in itself is not exclusively characteristic for late postmodernism, but falls back on the principles of the *nouveaux romanciers* from the 1950s and 1960s, who were already of the opinion that we cannot know the truth, everything being dependent on the point of view. The young Lilia has long been described as a pure soul, as a lost fragrant flower in a village steeped in hatred and violence, but in the end even this pure soul will not go unspoiled. She is prepared to kill if by doing so she could save her fiancé's life. For instance, she flies into a rage when, in the hills surrounding the village, she meets the policeman who, exempt from military service due to his position, is bearing a shotgun:

> *He stood there like a clown. At that moment I hated him more than anyone else in the world. He stammered a few words that I could not make out. I turned my back on him.*

> *I would give the lives of thousands of men like him for a few seconds in your arms. I would cut the heads off them myself, just to feel your kisses on my lips again and look into your eyes. It doesn't matter to me if I'm hateful. I couldn't care less about other people's opinions and morals. I would kill to have you alive.*[24]

The policeman started to write after his wife's death so as to fill the void she, and other deceased people with her, left behind. However, he is aware of the fact that his project is doomed to fail because reality cannot be known:

> *If anyone asks how I have filled the years leading to this point, today, I would not be able to answer them. I did not see time pass, even though it seemed to pass so slowly. I kept a flame burning, and I interrogated the darkness without gleaning more than snatches of answers.*[25]

The result is a kaleidoscopic, non-chronological tale that is less coherent than, for instance, *La Jalousie*, but in which various realities continue to be compared to each other. Schoolmaster Le Contre is unable to come to terms with the facts of the acts of war and, hit by madness, he daubs the verses of the *Marseillaise* on the walls of his staff residence with his own excreta: 'The madman had written those verses, written them and rewritten them, like a demented litany, so that we felt trapped inside the pages of some hideous book.'[26] Once an essential defender of Dreyfus, Corporal Matziev turns out to be a merciless and godless sadist during the war: he tortures a deserter to make him confess. The deserter Rifolon, confessing the murder of Belle de jour in order to escape the war crimes tribunal, shows in his statement that in a time of war, different rules and laws apply. When Judge Mierck calls him a murderer, Rifolon replies: 'Of course we've killed. That's what we were meant to do. Kill the other boys, the ones who look like our brothers. We kill them, and they kill us. It was your lot that told us to do it.'[27] The difference between good and evil has grown vague. Moreover, not omniscient, the narrator is permanently forced to resort to the often dubious interpretations of others. In this way, he reconstructs the story, filling in the gaps with his imagination, which lends the narrative its speculative nature: 'I kept a flame burning, and I interrogated the darkness without gleaning more than snatches of answers.'[28] Often the narrator himself was not on the scene when crucial events happened. It is Barbe, Destinat's chambermaid, who over a bottle of brandy tells him about the evening that Lilia and the prosecutor spent together. The narrator wonders whether he was fooled, whether her memory might have been warped by alcohol. The policeman, too, is refusing to state or examine certain facts. For instance, he fails to question the prosecutor about the evening of Lilia's suicide. The manuscript the reader is presented with turns out to be hardly more than an incoherent collection of memories and interpretations: 'This must all seem a terrible muddle, hopping shambolically from one thing to the other, but that's how my life has been, little snippets chopped up and impossible to stitch back together again.'[29] Like in *La Jalousie,* the shape of the text expresses the narrator's emotions; no jealousy this time, but a devastating sense of guilt due to his failure as both a human being and a policeman.

The narrator is in constant doubt, not expressing any unambiguous moral value judgment, and so he seems to subscribe to the ontological doubt so characteristic of postmodernism. Yet, unlike an author such as Robbe-Grillet who would flatly reject any reflection of the non-literary reality, Claudel intends to convey a certain message, because in the end the chaotic interpretations of the narrator do express a judgment about the events of the First World War. The narrator is sympathetic to the mangled soldiers taking out their anger at the factory workers who were not under mobilization orders ('Lucky devils', 'Draft dodgers'[30]) and he shows that France, too, is to blame for the war: 'Thanks to pride and stupidity, one country was ready to throw itself into the jaws of another.'[31] The soldiers sent to the front are portrayed as victims who are, with vacant stares, going to meet their doom:

> *But they weren't laughing now. They were as stiff as statues, the same dark iron colour as well. Their eyes were not eyes but bottomless abysses, open onto nothing.*[32]

In this way Claudel means to convey a balanced picture of the role played by France during the First World War, and to demonstrate that France, too, is to blame for the atrocities that occurred at that time. Worshipping French soldiers as heroes and pretending all of France was united in facing the enemy is then unbecoming: there was great tension between the soldiers and their French compatriots, exempt from military service, who would prefer to deny the reality of the war:

> *In the beginning, after the first fighting, it felt very strange seeing these fellows coming through with their faces rearranged by exploding shells and their bodies carved up by machine-gun fire, while we, the same age as them, kept nice and warm and quietly got on with our little lives.*
> *Of course, we knew the war was going on. We saw the mobilisation notices, and we read about it in the papers. But, deep down, it was all a pretence. We'd found a way out of it. We coped with it as if it was a dream, a bitter memory. It wasn't us, it didn't touch our lives.*[33]

Reality is not black or white, but grey. Via his account of the First World War, Claudel means in general terms to show the effects of violence, madness and sorrow on humankind. Since her fiancé was sent to the front, Lilia has felt an inner void, and the narrator, too, has lost all touch with life after his wife died: 'I have been dead for a long time. I pretend that I am alive, but my sentence has been deferred, that's all.'[34] So as to survive, every personage clings to the role that has fallen to them: the prosecutor 'pursued his profession with clockwork precision',[35] the insensitive, sadistic Judge Mierck is pleased with Belle de jour's death because he has to solve a real murder at last, and about the mayor's attitude during the interrogation of the two deserters, the narrator remarks: '... his small duty complete. What happened now was of no concern to him'.[36]

Conclusion

So *Les Âmes grises* is, then, a fine example of postrealism because the novel shows that contemporary realism radically breaks with the hermetic nature of much postmodern literature, at the same time being permeated by postmodern principles such as ontological doubt, the melting together of various realities, discontinuity and alienation of humankind from itself and its surroundings. And so Viart and Vercier are right whenever they claim that today traditional literary forms are being reconsidered, and that in this way a hybrid form will arise in which, in various degrees, realism and postmodernism come together.

The main principles of postmodern poetics could also be found in the novels by Houellebecq: ontological doubt, the rift between language and reality, the alienation of humankind from itself and its surroundings, the transgression of norms and values, eclecticism, the desecration of Art, the blurring borderline between serious and popular expressions of art, the minimalist style. Houellebecq's œuvre most evidently shows that postmodernism is still rampant in the contemporary novel which, sure enough, at the same time opposes this formalist poetics by its very neorealist characteristics. The concept of 'postrealism' may well cover the hybrid nature of the work by one of France's most successful authors. Daniel1 outlines this renewing postrealism as follows:

> *I don't mean that my sketches were unfunny; they were funny. I was indeed a cutting observer of contemporary reality; it was just that everything now seemed so elementary to me, it seemed that so few things remained that could be observed in contemporary reality: we had simplified and pruned so much, broken so many barriers, taboos, misplaced hopes and false aspirations; truly, there was so little left.*[37]

Chapter 6
Post-Yugoslav Literature

The Return of History and the Actuality of Fiction
Guido Snel

Yes, we have the Third World, but we have lost the Second and the First […] The Barbarians are at our gates, and we know – we, the Former First plus the Former Second World – that we are losing. We are becoming more and more illusory, and they are becoming more and more real. – EMIL TODE[1]

Introduction

Central to this chapter is the question of how Yugoslav postmodernism evolved after the demise of the former Yugoslavia. Crucial to establishing the forms and meanings of postmodernist writing in Yugoslavia is the work of Danilo Kiš (1935-1989). The three writers whose work is discussed here, Semezdin Mehmedinović, Aleksandar Hemon and Daša Drndić, each take a different approach to what seems to have been a central concern in Kiš's work: the blurring of fact and fiction, and how that can be related to the politics of literature.

Same Stories, New Realities

There is an old belief that until 1989, in what we used to refer to as the Eastern Bloc, politics might have been oppressive, but the arts, as well as a culture of reading, thrived precisely because the politics was oppressive. In the West, according to the same belief, democracy came jointly with superficiality and the law and logic of the market. Hence, postmodernism in Western Europe – and for that matter in the United States and Canada too – was considered to be playful, uncommitted and free-floating, whereas in Central and Eastern Europe it could not be dissociated from political life. Even if a poem or novel claimed, in postmodern fashion, to refer only to its own textual reality, readers hardly ever failed to detect a political meaning, whether they were reading secretly in the underground culture of samizdat or officially, as censors.

While democratization, EU enlargement and the precipitated introduction of a neoliberal free market thoroughly changed the face of the literary cultures in East and Central Europe,[2] politics continued to interfere with cultural life after 1989. As Andrei Pleşu, writer, dissident under the Ceauşescu regime and Romanian minister of culture (1989-1991) and foreign affairs (1997-2000), states with some regret:

> *During communism there was no such thing as an innocent reading [...] When Hamlet said: 'Something is rotten in Denmark,' audiences would applaud. After 1989, I hoped that the possibility of an innocent reading would return. To enjoy reading for reading's sake, without political agendas. But then a different discussion emerged. Now we are reminded that people like Eliade have been fascists.*[3]

Of course, direct political interference in the arts and literature has greatly diminished since 1989, becoming, with a few exceptions, more or less restricted to those countries where semi-authoritarian regimes succeeded the communists, for instance in Moldova, Russia, and Belarus. But Pleşu's complaint signals something else. What he deplores is that the end of communism failed to bring the 'end of history', a blessed post-political state in which the arts had entered what Chantal Mouffe has critically called the 'post-political *Zeitgeist*' of the 1990s. What occurred instead was a thorough re-evaluation of history, as the part played by the canonical writers in twentieth-century literature was revaluated, with some who had been left out of the canon being rediscovered.[4]

There is still more to Pleşu's statement than meets the eye, for it also signals that the Western attitude toward the former communist countries has not changed, for the Western expectation is still that literature in East/Central Europe functions first and foremost as an expression of a political condition. That is a second aspect of the ongoing and direct presence of politics in the literary cultures of East/Central Europe, which can hardly be overestimated. While the Cold War division of Europe into an Eastern and a Western part is history, a new, velvet curtain appeared during the 1990s, identifying not just a new East in Europe (Belarus, Ukraine, Russia, Moldova) but more especially another, quasi-Oriental Southeast Europe, in the shape of the Balkans. The Western reception continued to stress the political meaning of literature from the East, now as an antidote to nationalism and intolerance. Goran Stefanovski, prominent post-Yugoslav playwright, bilingual in Macedonian and English and part-time expatriate from his native Skopje, signals a new or rather renewed inequality in an essay entitled 'A Tale from the Wild East':

> *The luxury of artists in the West is that they can stay away from politics and still have ample space for discourse. In the East, because of the centralization of society, there are no avenues for alternative discourse and no parallel spaces. Staying away from politics looks like retreating into autism.*[5]

When critics in the West today tend to signal an end to postmodernism, an end to playfulness and mere self-reference of art and literature – following the assumption underlying this collection of essays – then this ending is usually ascribed to new ideological antagonisms in our societies in the aftermath of 9/11.

The case of the former Yugoslavia, Stefanovski's cultural Heimat with which this chapter is concerned, should warn us precisely that such a position pertains to a very narrow sphere of literatures: those of Western Europe, Canada and the US. It could be even claimed, not just for the former Yugoslavia but for the whole of East and Central Europe, that ideology never ceased to be relevant, that there never was a 'post-political *Zeitgeist*', even though writers and critics believed that history had finally left them in peace.[6] Perhaps, looking back at the 1990s, East/Central Europe, while trying to 'remain relevant', to keep pace with the West, was in fact not lagging behind at all. Perhaps it was in fact the avant-garde of a new era.

Danilo Kiš and Postmodernism in Yugoslav Letters

Yugoslav postmodernism ended in 1992, when the siege of Sarajevo began (see the section on Mehmedinović in this chapter), but where were its beginnings? One possible starting point[7] for a postmodern aesthetic in the former Yugoslavia is the activities of Medijala, a group of painters, architects and poets operating out of Belgrade. By far the most important artist was the painter, architect and thinker Leonid Šejka. Other figures included the poetess Marija Čudina, painters Miro Glavurtić, Olja Ivanjicki, and Milić od Mačve. Šejka, who died in 1970, was a close friend of Danilo Kiš, and during the 1960s especially, Šejka and Kiš shared some aesthetic affinities, particularly the idea of reality as chaos, as a *đubrište*, a garbage dump, or a *skladište*, a storehouse, and artistic form as a seemingly random means to create order.[8] By the time of Kiš's death, in 1989, the rise of nationalist discourse had deeply divided the Medijala group, turning some of its members into fierce advocates and others into opponents of the new national era.

What makes a decisive discussion of the forms and meaning of Yugoslav postmodernism problematic is the relatively sudden end to the country's existence, which also implied the ending of an integrated Yugoslav literary space, and Kiš's untimely death only complicates the case further. By 1989 the debate about Kiš's work, especially about *Grobnica za Borisa Davidoviča* from 1975 (translated into English as *A Tomb for Boris Davidovič*, 1978) had enforced a distinction between advocates and opponents of postmodernism synonymous with either a cosmopolitan (multi-ethnic, Yugoslav) or a nationalist stance. Paradoxically, the war resulted not just in the implosion of the Yugoslav literary space, but in an explosion of its ideas, affecting writers and oeuvres all over Europe, the US and Canada. In its wake, authors such as David Albahari and Dubravka Ugrešić, both of a younger generation than Kiš, earned solid international reputations.

Kiš, who was to become known during the 1990s as 'the last Yugoslav writer', was certainly not the sole practitioner of a postmodern aesthetic in Yugoslav letters, although he was certainly the most influential one, and the only one of his generation with a lasting influence outside Yugoslavia. In the introduction to her selection of Kiš's essays in English translation, Susan Sontag writes in 1994, after her return from a besieged Sarajevo:

> *The death of Danilo Kiš on October 15, 1989, at the age of fifty-four, wrenchingly cut short one of the most important journeys in literature made*

> by any writer during the second half of the twentieth century [...] At the end
> of the century, which is the end of many things, literature, too, is under
> siege. The work of Danilo preserves the honor of literature.⁹

From the 1970s onwards, Kiš's work was widely translated, first into French and German, later into English. He still casts his shadow today over post-Yugoslav letters, influencing for instance the work of Aleksandar Hemon and Daša Drndić, who will be discussed later in this chapter. Echoes of Kiš's work can be found outside the literary realm of the former Yugoslavia, in authors as different as William T. Vollman, Edgardo Cozarinsky, and the late W.G. Sebald.

The bilingual son of a Montenegrin mother and an assimilated Hungarian Jew who disappeared in Auschwitz, between 1965 and 1971 Kiš published a trilogy on his family history, three novels that were extremely intertextual and meta-fictional, remarkable for their use of documents, either invented or genuine. Kiš himself visited France regularly from the late 1950s onwards, and settled there in 1979 when he felt he had to leave Belgrade after *A Tomb for Boris Davidovič*, stories about the Soviet Gulag, had caused a major scandal in Yugoslav letters. To us looking back now, the scandal appears to be one of the first open manifestations of aggressive nationalism, and the whole affair certainly explains why today the figure and work of Kiš are associated not only with anti-nationalism and cosmopolitanism, but also with postmodernist aesthetics as being politically subversive, i.e. anti-nationalist.¹⁰

In his 'Joycean exile' in Paris, Kiš became more and more self-conscious during the 1980s, and enjoyed a growing reputation in European literary circles. His stance toward postmodernism, in particular to Borges and to the *nouveau roman*, was ambivalent. Kiš praised them for their formal experiment, but criticized them for their blindness to what he considered the main task of twentieth-century literature: to re-tell the past incessantly, to re-narrativize it, especially the history of atrocities committed during the twentieth century in the name of totalitarian ideology, and to record the plight of its victims, outsiders mostly, individuals lost at the rim of history. In that respect, he deemed his own inventions in fiction, and those of some of his fellow Central European writers like the poet Czesław Miłosz or the novelist Péter Esterházy, more up to date and more relevant than, for instance, the renewal of the novel in France as a result of the *nouveau roman*.

The Reception of Kiš's Postmodernism: Unbearably Ambiguous?

What precisely were Kiš's inventions? How were they received and interpreted in his own, Yugoslav, literary milieu of the late 1960s and 1970s?

A Tomb for Boris Davidovič (1975) is a masterpiece of documentary fiction or, if one prefers, fictionalized documentary history.[11] The scandal following its publication is instructive because the very ambiguity of the narrative form was partly responsible for the offence caused. However, the full story behind what the critics found offensive remains partially obscure even today. Serge Shishkoff, who published an excellent account of the affair in 1987 (it lasted from 1975 until 1979), ascribes the opacity of its extremely obscure course to the specific literary culture of Tito's Yugoslavia, 'where nothing is what it seems to be, where there is more to everything than meets the eye, where more information is gleaned from what is not said than from what is, and where rumor, nurtured into an art form, is the chief source of information (and misinformation)'.[12]

If when reading Shishkoff's analysis one bears in mind the Yugoslav wars of the 1990s, and especially the conversion from pro-communism to pro-nationalism of much of Belgrade's literary establishment where the campaign against Kiš was conducted, the affair deserves perhaps less wit and more cynicism than Shishkoff allows. Vasa Mihajlovich in his 1994 prolegomenon to Shishkoff's article says it is 'an intelligent guess that [the affair] contributed to Kiš's early death from cancer in 1989'.[13] Also, as an example of a postmodernist literary artifact which caused political offence, the case seems highly instructive if we want to understand the entanglement of aesthetic form and ideology in the former Yugoslavia.

In 1978, three years after publication, Kiš was summoned to a Belgrade court to defend himself against charges of libel. This was not the real issue at stake, however. The affair started in 1975, a few months after the publication of *A Tomb for Boris Davidovič*, when Kiš was accused of plagiarism: he had allegedly copied the plots and many of the descriptions in the stories. The accusation was absurd – not that Kiš hadn't copied, but that he had done so openly, even stating some of his sources in footnotes, performing nothing more or less than the widespread practice of intertextual writing. His critics also failed to notice that the quotations were not verbatim but had been altered. Because the accusations were so absurd, Kiš was convinced that other literary and political motives lurked behind the farce. In 1978 he published an extensive defense of his postmodernist fiction, a collection of essays and polemics entitled *Čas Anatomije* (Lesson in Anatomy). From the accusers' articles as well as from Kiš's response, some of the motives behind the accusations, the grounds for the offence, as well as the role of Kiš's postmodernist aesthetics can readily be reconstructed.

A Tomb for Boris Davidovič consists of seven self-contained short stories, told by a dispassionate researcher, a kind of biographer, who reconstructs the lives of his protagonists. They participated in the Russian revolution from the very beginning, and all of them later fell victim to Stalin's purges. Although the stories present imaginary characters with fictitious names, most of the events which make up their lives are either historical or intertextual.

Now, it seems that the stories in *A Tomb for Boris Davidovič* caused offence first and foremost because of their criticism of Stalinism. Tito's Yugoslavia had been embroiled in an argument with Stalin ever since the dramatic events of 1948, but now it appeared that although Yugoslav communism itself was anti-Stalinist, criticism of some of the pillars supporting it, notably the myth of a heroic Russian revolution, was still taboo. That Kiš and his defenders identified their accusers as dogmatic communists is obvious from their allusions to the practices of the secret police and Zhdanov-like conduct.

Second, as formulated by one of the accusers – and this leads us right into the late 1980s and 1990s when the nationalist discourse became predominant on the cultural scene – it was suggested that artists who plagiarize do great harm to a nation's culture. In other words, by plagiarizing, Kiš had offended his own national culture. What the precise offence was against national, meaning Serbian, culture is hard to say in the opaque Yugoslav context of the 1970s although nationalism was undoubtedly a salient factor in the ideological landscape of that decade. Perhaps it was because Kiš had caused bad blood in the early 1970s with some vitriolic anti-nationalist essays published right after he finished his novel *Hourglass*.

What then was the precise role of aesthetic form? The Gulag stories show an evolution away from the complexity and painstaking texture of Kiš's earlier work, especially the novel *Hourglass*, which had much in common with the *nouveau roman*. Yet the narrative technique applied in those two works is very similar: in both cases contradictory generic markers enforce a double (both fictional and factual) reading pact.

If the narratives are so similar, the question becomes: why did *A Tomb for Boris Davidovič* arouse such a stir and *Hourglass* did not? With respect to the sensitivity of the thematic material, one could say that the effect was cumulative, that the affair was a consequence of Kiš's conscious oeuvre-building. The connection between the two texts as documents about victims of two different totalitarian systems was obvious, and Kiš never made any secret of his intention to connect the two. By adding Stalinism to the holocaust as a major crime, writing a historical version of Borges's *Universal History of Infamy*, Kiš had not only offended old apparatchiks but had violated a founding myth of Tito's Yugoslavia which claimed that the whole Yugoslav nation had collectively resisted fascism under the banner of communism. In a way, both the form and theme of the autobiographical trilogy made Kiš untouchable. Working in a literary culture where, as he writes in *A Lesson in Anatomy*, 'literature is still interpreted outside the text, and outside its context',[14] he wrote about victims of fascism and did so in such a meticulous way that those who might have felt offended by his focus on lives at the margins of official history could believe that incidents like the notorious 1942 pogrom in Novi Sad, which he described in *Early Sorrows*, was the doing of Hungarian fascists rather than of 'our own brethren'. If that did not confirm the Titoist myth about the Second World War, at least it caused no offence. Moreover, the autobiographical pact that permeates the whole trilogy and is confirmed by the letter from the father at the end of *Hourglass* made it clear that here was someone who was interested most of all in his own family history; even more so because he had himself been a child victim of the same political extremism that Titoist ideology had called 'fascism'.

That was not so in *A Tomb for Boris Davidovič*. There the narrator had not only opted for sensitive thematic material, putting the Gulag alongside the Nazi extermination camps, but he had narrativized it in an ambiguous way, on the one hand presenting characters with imaginary names and on the other hand, providing abundant proof, furnished by the narrator, that the biographies were highly plausible from a historical point of view. Kiš drew attention to that point in his defense. Contemplating the motives of his critics, he wrote:

> *What in the world does he (that is D.K.) have to do with all that when he was never in a concentration camp himself [...] So, they are saying that I 'changed states', meaning that I no longer know where I am living and what I am doing, so why do I not write other things and not the things about which I am writing, because when I was still working on my family trilogy, which was strange too, meaning, not 'ours', at least I wrote something that didn't have anything to do with us [...].*[15]

One can thus say that the Gulag stories in *A Tomb for Boris Davidovič* were the immediate cause of the polemic but that the attacks were implicitly directed against the trilogy. At stake was a combination of material with a historically sensitive theme and an ambivalent – postmodern – narrative form.

Such then was the ambiguity of Kiš's legacy when he died in Paris on 15 October 1989, less than a month before the fall of the Berlin wall and barely four months after Milošević's notorious speech in Kosovo marking the official conversion of the Serbian communist establishment into a nationalist one. Soon, Kiš became an icon of 'ex-Yugoslavs' and 'post-Yugoslavs', and his work and style were taken up by writers such as Dubravka Ugrešić. However, the times were changing, and while Kiš had always resisted the playfulness – actually a sort of 'non-commitment' – of postmodernism elsewhere, the challenge his successors faced was much more acute: how to write about the direct experience of war and expulsion?

Postmodernism Under Siege

Kiš's postmodernism had violated a convention that was not necessarily limited to the former Yugoslavia or East/Central Europe, which was that sensitive themes should be narrativized in testimonies, autobiography or memoir. More needs to be said about the 'documentary imperative', as it will lead us directly to the 1990s when the 'return of history' (to amend Fukuyama's phrase), the wars on Yugoslav soil, prompted literature to thoroughly re-evaluate its relation to reality, and when writers in the former Yugoslavia faced a sudden and dramatic return of reality.

As early as 1953, the Polish writer and poet Czesław Miłosz wrote in *Zniewolony umysł* (*The Captive Mind*, English translation 1953) that to experience history in East/Central Europe in the twentieth century 'surpassed the most daring and the most macabre imagination'.[16] One could list numerous examples of autobiographical and other factual writings that portray the historical experience of mainly Nazi and Stalinist terror as being unimaginable and sometimes even impossible to represent. In *Medaliony* (*Medaillons*, 1946), a literary report about the Nazi camps in Poland, Zofia Nałkowska remarks that one can stand reality 'only when it is not entirely known'.[17] Likewise, Karlo Štajner (whom Kiš knew personally and whose memoirs were a major source for *A Tomb for Boris Davidovič*) opens his account of his detention in the Soviet Gulag, *7000 Hiljadu Dana u Siberiji* (*7000 Days in Siberia*, 1972) by expressing his fear that in the eyes of many, his experiences will seem 'unlikely and tendentious'.[18] Both Nałkowska and Štajner attempted to describe historical facts and events as precisely as possible, and both authors took great pains to exclude fictional narration for it would undermine their intention to report accurately. That is what one can refer to as the 'documentary imperative': fiction about the Holocaust and the Gulag not based on personal experience had to be grounded in historical documents.[19]

In the remainder of this chapter, I shall discuss the work of two novelists and one poet, each of them confronted with the wars in the former Yugoslavia, and all of whom felt urged both to return to Kiš's legacy and to alter it, especially his deliberate transgression of the documentary imperative. I shall discuss their work as a continuation but at the same time a moving away from Yugoslav postmodernism as it was dominated by the towering figure of Kiš. Each of the three writers represents a different facet of the shattered and fragmented literary scene of the 1990s. Semezdin Mehmedinović comes closest to a classical form of exile whereby a poet continues to write in his native tongue;

yet his poetry is also a lucid reflection on his new surroundings, specifically the post-9/11 landscape of the US. Aleksandar Hemon, an Anglophone writer ever since his American debut, shuttles constantly between themes, forms and stories from his first language, Serbo-Croat (Bosnian), and themes and fashions dictated by his new surroundings where he lives in Chicago. Daša Drndić, finally, is a writer who after a short exile returned to Croatia, where her recent work zooms in on local, mostly urban themes, specifically the 'universal histories of infamy', of provincial towns like Rijeka and Gorizia.

Semezdin Mehmedinović from Sarajevo to Post-9/11 America

When the siege of Sarajevo began in May 1992, the poet Semezdin Mehmedinović (b. Kiseljak, near Tuzla, Bosnia, 1960), writing about the siege while under siege himself, initially reverted to the documentary imperative. The Serbian presence imposed very strict restrictions on physical movement and limited the poet's view to what he could see of his immediate surroundings:

> *First of all I want to say the following: for over a year already, as long as the war has been going on, I've been writing about my experiences in Sarajevo. I don't even dare to think about anything beyond this city – everything that isn't part of my own personal experience, is simply guesswork.*[20]

Indeed, those words recall older responses to writing under immediate danger or the threat of extinction. But while the older belief was that simply recording what was going on gave literature a basic, existentially meaningful task, writing in Sarajevo meant, for Mehmedinović, simply reproducing images of the horror in a world saturated with news. The outside world already knew: moreover, whereas it was too dangerous to look out of the window for fear of snipers, one could watch CNN news to see a neighboring area being shelled.

Suspicion about his own words describing his experiences under the siege gradually amounted to a suspicion of writing itself, and especially of metaphors – of each form of writing that describes things in different shapes from those in which they appear. Therefore, although it might be true that 'the war controls my sorrow',[21] as he wrote in a short essay entitled 'Gubitak' (Loss), he still had the option of trying to write directly about the catastrophe, using words that would keep him as close as possible to his everyday experience. Mehmedinović's concern was not just aesthetic, for it seemed motivated by fear that his language, instead of serving his intentions, would convey a different, unintended meaning and begin a life of its own – quite a risk in surroundings as politically charged as Sarajevo in the years 1992-1995.

Mehmedinović's meticulous writing resulted in *Sarajevo Blues* (*Sarajevo*

Blues, English translation 1998), a collection of reportage, poems and essays, a first version of which was published during the siege but outside the city, in Ljubljana, Slovenia. An extended version appeared in Zagreb, Croatia, in 1995. The English edition, translated by Ammiel Alcalay and published in 1998 by City Lights, San Francisco, did not fail to attract the attention of major critics. Some of them, like Paul Auster and Tomaž Šalamun, praised the work as an essential text about the Bosnian war, not only because it witnessed and recorded daily life under the Serbian siege, but also because it pondered the act itself of recording and bearing witness to the reality of the siege.

Crucially for a book conceived as close to reality's skin as one can get, Mehmedinović thoroughly edited and re-arranged the manuscript for the English edition.[22] It seemed that text and reality were different entities after all, in spite of the author's intention not to move away from his own experience. Almost a third of the initial poems and essays were removed, and more importantly, the order of the texts was thoroughly revised. Significantly, one of the last texts in the book was now one called 'Freedom', the one quoted above, written only a year after the beginning of the siege, while other texts, written later, were positioned before this devastating analysis of the poet's disillusionment with his own writing.

'Freedom' contains a reflection on the uses and ethics of writing about one's experience in a reality which contained, as Mehmedinović called it, 'a surplus of history'. He recalls passing an advertisement in a street in Sarajevo 'famous for its massacres'.[23] The advertisement showed a photo of skydivers who 'smile, conscious of the fact that they're flying'. But 'their smiles are almost hysterical [...] proof that every form of freedom is inevitably connected to risk', and 'even though their faces are clearly different, their individual fate is wiped out by the signature beneath the photo: *Produkt von Kodak*. What remains, is an ad for the photo itself [...]'. Immediately, Mehmedinović signals the significance of the image for his own 'documentary' writing: 'writing these sentences, I am writing an ad for the war'.[24]

Seventeen years after the publication of *A Tomb for Boris Davidovič*, at a time when the free world was living through the end of history and enjoying the 'post-political *Zeitgeist*' (again the words of political philosopher Chantal Mouffe), the Sarajevo siege confronted literature with a complicated challenge: how to use one's pen against the horrors of a war taking place in the here and now? How to write, after Kiš, in order to open up a new, critical register, which reflects the awareness that literature, the written word, does not function in isolation but in a dazzling, self-repeating maelstrom of images? *Sarajevo Blues* gave the diagnosis, but no answers.[25]

In 2002 Mehmedinović published a book of poetry which, although it gives no answers, does, I believe, point to a new way of writing. After he left Sarajevo with his wife and their son as political refugees in 1996 ('Exhausted by living under camp conditions' Alcalay 1998:118), he settled in the US, where he still lives today. In the week after 9/11, Mehmedinović made a journey by train through the US connecting all nine cities called Alexandria. In the resulting book of poems, *Devet Alexandrija* (*Nine Alexandrias*, English translation 2003), his first person poetic voice appeared as a traveler in the footsteps of the beatniks (perhaps due to his fortunate entrance into the US through City Lights, Ferlinghetti's publishing house, and not through the various Slavic departments in the US). But the voice speaking in these poems is also that of a stranger, a foreigner, someone on a poetic quest in American space that was politically highly charged in the week after 9/11. Once more, pressure was exerted upon him, as the world was now becoming polarized in terms of Islam vs. non-Islam. For someone fleeing from Sarajevo, a nightmare had come true: it seemed as if the local parochial, ethnic thinking which initiated the siege was now reproducing itself on the world stage.

While a considerable number of exiled writers from the former Yugoslavia modeled their exile after Kiš's,[26] Mehmedinović's poetry seems to dismiss this basically Central European model of literary exile. His work is highly critical of the postmodern, ironical view of identity which prevails in this strand of writing and the main representatives of which are Dubravka Ugreši and David Albahari. Mehmedinović claimed kinship with Kiš on a different level: Kiš served as an example because of 'the balance he achieved between form and *engagement*'.[27] What he admired were 'Kiš's sentences, the inherent vertigo, the feverish syntax which aligns itself with the central theme, the knowledge, sustained by persecution and destruction, that the ground under your feet can disappear at any moment'.[28]

So, the extremely self-critical spirit which urged him to rewrite *Sarajevo Blues* did not prevent Mehmedinović from writing about the new polarization after 9/11. On the contrary, although his own persona in the poems is still immersed in a postmodern play with non-identity, not unlike Jerzy Kosinski's novel *Steps* (1968), reality is approached from a deadly serious, analytical angle. Take for instance how the poem 'East and West' both dismantles the ideological connotation of a clash of civilizations, while at the same time positioning a multi-layered view of reality:

> *Interesting how primary words*
> *Square the circle of meaning every now and then*
> *[...]*
> *Right now, for instance, east and west,*

> *Invented so a body could orient itself*
> *By the stars in the desolate expanse,*
> *Mean more than maps*
> *Where Mecca's on the east side and*
> *Los Angeles on the west.*[29]

During the days following 11 September 2001, the political meaning of the words 'east' and 'west' became extremely powerful and highly charged. But in the poem they mean more than that. To be sure, it is not a naive return to a belief in the autonomy of poetic discourse. The poet's native tongue, Bosnian, is spoken on the historical borderline of Islam and Christianity, both Roman and Orthodox. For Mehmedinović, the words *istok* and *zapad*, 'east' and 'west', originate in the historical borderland of the Balkans. In its most extreme ideological use, Bosnian 'west' means an essentially Roman Catholic west; and the Bosnian 'east' is taken either as the essentially orthodox Christian east, or as an outpost of the Islamic Orient. Every time the connotation of the border between Islam and the Christianities, Orient and Occident, is imposed upon them, the words recall their own past of political use and abuse. They cannot be properly applied unless with caution.

Now in American space the Bosnian words east and west became fused both with the local historical meanings of east and west coast and with 'the Frontier', the historical westward movement of colonization, and with its global meaning – western space that is characteristically American, and eastern space that is defined by its Islamic center, Mecca. A triple perspective is opened up: three wars, the oldest being local, American: the extermination of native American culture referred to in another poem as 'an entire continent shrunk in dizzying implosion',[30] the violent ending of Yugoslavia, and the post 9/11 'War on Terror'. In a voice stripped of irony, Mehmedinović's poems take Kiš's history of infamy into the twenty-first century.

Aleksandar Hemon's Post-9/11 Return to Europe

Early in 1992 Aleksandar Hemon traveled to the US on a scholarship. Before he could return, the siege of his native city had begun, and he published his first novel in Bosnian in 1995, although he is now widely acclaimed as a writer in English, starting with *The Question of Bruno* (2000). His switching to English has prompted critics, always prone to hysteria, to compare Hemon's literary achievements with those of Vladimir Nabokov and Joseph Conrad. Exaggerated or not, here is a writer who explores new places to write fiction in between Europe and the US.[31]

Hemon's most recent novel, *The Lazarus Project* (2008), traces the whereabouts of Lazarus Averbuch, an immigrant to Chicago at the beginning of the twentieth century, who survived the notorious pogrom of 1903 in Kishinev which was part of the Russian empire at the time, only to be shot by the Chicago Chief of Police in 1908. The novel suggests the killing was prompted by xenophobia and anti-Semitism, and in both style and narrative technique the novel qualifies as historical meta-fiction[32] much in the manner of the work of a novelist like Doctorow. But in at least one respect the critics' eagerness to mention Conrad and especially Nabokov is not too far-fetched: it is first and foremost a novel which shuttles between America and East/Central Europe, between the US and Moldova and Bosnia. Echoes of *Pnin* and especially *Pale Fire* permeate the text.

Much about the novel qualifies as postmodern. First, the manner in which boundaries between fiction and non-fiction are blurred. Vladimir Brik, a writer of Bosnian origin who lives in Chicago, wants to write a novel on Lazarus Averbuch. Together with his friend, Rora, he travels to Kishinev and then to Bosnia, where Rora is killed by a petty thief, a robber-junkie. In alternating chapters we read about their journey and about Lazarus and his sister Olga. Also, squeezed between the chapters, historical photographs of Lazarus alternate with Rora's pictures taken during the journey. Rora's pictures have an anachronistic style and are difficult to distinguish from the genuine historical ones.

There are many more clues which enforce a 'meta-fictional' reading pact, and they situate the narrative both inside and outside the realm of fiction. To name but one: a cameo appearance by Bruno Schulz, the great Polish avant-garde writer and graphic artist, as a bartender in Chicago in 1908, who is a witness to Averbuch's fate.[33] The Jewish Schulz was killed in Drohobycz, by a Nazi officer, in 1942, and his death and Averbuch's are linked through fiction, connecting the anti-Semitism of Tsarist Russia and Nazi Germany, a gesture much in the spirit of Danilo Kiš.

There is also ample use of documents in the chapters dealing with Averbuch. Again, Kiš's *Tomb for Boris Davidovič* is never far away. A dispassionate narrator collects documents, witness statements, and is tempted to fictionalize Averbuch by presenting his consciousness, but always refrains from doing so. Such chapters cannot qualify as non-fiction because they are embedded in the fictional account of Vladimir Brik's attempts to write about Averbuch. Or can they? Again, a double reading pact seems to be in operation.

And yet I would argue that *The Lazarus Project* transgresses the limits of postmodern aesthetics, among other things by trying to overcome the genre-irony it has itself generated. Let me explain: while in *The Question of Bruno* and *Nowhere Man* (2002) fictional character Joseph Pronek meets his author Hemon in his own fictional realm (following the character Pnin's meeting

Nabokov in the novel *Pnin*), Vladimir Brik and Hemon are clearly separate identities, as are the photographers Rora and Velibor Božović. One belongs to fiction, the other to reality. Furthermore, Averbuch is in a sense more historical than are Kiš's fictionalized historical characters. Averbuch is identified as a historical character by his proper name, which Kiš was careful to remove from his Gulag stories. When the novel's ending suggests that Brik, at the end of his journey in Sarajevo, is now embarking on the story of Averbuch, a cyclic structure is completed in which, as in Mehmedinović's post-9/11 poetry, at least three 'histories of infamy' rotate: that of Averbuch, already a double story identifying anti-Semitism both in Kishinev and in Chicago, that of Bosnia and the Sarajevo siege, and that of the post-9/11 War on Terror waged from the US, to which the novel gives a US national pedigree of ethnic and racial thinking coupled with anxiety over immigration which dates right back to the xenophobia of the 1910s and 1920s.

Yet, reality and fiction, historical personae and the reasons why they persecuted or were subjected to persecution or racial violence are clearly distinguished. In a recent interview Hemon adopts a clear political stance:

> *But the xenophobic madness after 9/11 that entranced a large number of Americans (many of whom now wish to forget all that) was crushing to me – Bush and his cohorts brought out the worst in Americans, and we are all still reeling from that. The madness was very close in kind, if not in degree, to the rabid Serbian nationalism that resulted in the mass murder of Muslims in Bosnia. The government of this country committed – repeatedly, in full view of everyone – horrendous war crimes. Now we've moved on, and airports and highways will be named after the scum, and we are once again a proud nation.*[34]

But even though he expresses connections similar to those the novel suggests, between Europe and the US, past and present, between anti-Semitism at the beginning of the twentieth century, nationalism in the Bosnian war and xenophobia in the American War on Terror, we clearly know that we should distinguish between that voice and the polyphony of the novel.

A Fictional Look at Real Photographs: Daša Drndić

In his afterword to *The Lazarus Project*, Aleksandar Hemon expresses his indebtedness to the Chicago Historical Society, and to his friend the photographer Velibor Božović, 'whose mind and photography were indispensible and I must acknowledge that'.[35] Indispensible they were, too, Božović as second 'author' of this formidable piece of literary art, the Historical Society as the guardian angels of precisely one photograph of Averbuch. It is a harrowing sight: a policeman holding Averbuch's head, his eyelids half closed. As if Averbuch, already dead, can still be forced by the police to act according to their will.[36]

Indeed, the use of photographs seems to be a trademark of precisely the kind of late postmodernism which we are trying to identify here, as a genre, a style, and certainly as a sentiment. I submit that the precise way in which photographs are inserted into a literary text is a key to determining the relation between that literary work and reality. Let me once more return to Kiš, as his work, in this respect too, seems to have informed the work of Daša Drndić, the last author whom I wish to discuss in this context.

In 1965, in *Garden, Ashes*, his Proustian invocation of a childhood under the shadow of anti-Semitic persecution, Kiš had his narrator and alter ego Andreas Sam describe his mother's sewing machine, a Singer. Andreas goes to great lengths to catch his profound memories of the sewing machine and put them into words, but finally he has to resort to a picture of a Singer machine. Later, when he proves to be an unreliable narrator,[37] the fictional pact between reader and author is shattered, and the status of the story, fiction or autobiography, becomes ambiguous. I have never found direct proof, neither intertextual nor contextual, of any knowledge W.G. Sebald might have had of the work of Kiš, but Sebald's most ambitious and perhaps most obsessive novel, *Austerlitz*, seems unimaginable without Kiš's explorations of the distinctions between fact and fiction. Most especially, the well-known photograph of Jacques Austerlitz as a child, retrieved only after he had retraced his own biography to Prague, may be interpreted as Sebald's formal indebtedness to Kiš.

The photograph comes at a point in Sebald's novel when the reader is at a loss as to whether Austerlitz is a fictional character or not. An anonymous first-person narrator has opened up to us, through Sebald's peculiar quoting techniques, the mind and memories of Austerlitz, which would qualify as a fictional narrative technique. But is, or was, Austerlitz a historical character? If not, then who is the boy in the photograph? Sebald's photograph is historical in that it displays the real face of someone who has existed, some time, some place. But as we never find out whether Austerlitz truly existed, just as we also never find out the name of the first-person narrator who meets Austerlitz and presents his narrative to us, there is the very disturbing possibility that the picture represents someone whose identity is obscured by that of Austerlitz. Can it be that the melancholic placing of the picture into the novel hides the identity of someone whose name we shall never get to know? It is all the more relevant as the whole poetics of melancholy in Sebald is precisely about the imbalance of our cultural memory: we remember, yes, but that is futile compared to all those people whom we don't remember, who have forever vanished from history.

Such ambivalence is precisely the point of departure in Daša Drndić's 'documentary novel' *Sonnenschein (Sunshine,* English translation forthcoming with MacLehose Press in 2011). It is also what she leaves behind. Her text (not to be confused with István Szabo's 1999 film of the same title), full of references to the work of Danilo Kiš, tells two stories. One is that of Haya Tedeschi, a young Jewish woman from an assimilated family who has a relationship with an SS officer under the Nazi occupation. Still an infant, her son is taken away from her and ends up in the *Lebensborn* program. Her story is set in the city of Gorizia/Görz/Gorica, a divided city during the ensuing Cold War, a 'little Berlin'. The second story is that of her son himself, who finds out about his real identity only in the late 1990s and starts to search for his parents. The novel ends with his entering the room where his mother has been waiting for him for decades. We don't get to see how they meet, we only know that they will. The son, as someone who finds out his real identity only as an adult, is almost the mirror image of Sebald's Austerlitz. Almost, because his father was a notorious SS officer. Hence, his attitude toward his own past, to his own self-identity switches constantly between rage and melancholy, *engagement* and equanimity.

What is radically different about Drndić's novelistic poetics is that the text functions for only one part of the melancholic register which we have come to appreciate in Sebald. If we consider his *Austerlitz* as the *ne plus ultra*, the absolute climax and dead end of postmodernism,[38] then Drndić's novel points to at least one way out of the melancholy informed by the kind of literature which is aware that it will never be able to point to any reality other than its own.

Indeed, *Sonnenschein*, just like the fiction of Sebald, is full of historical documents and photographs. But *Sonnenschein* also looks for ways to preserve the ethical impetus of first-hand eyewitness testimonies and is morally outraged by the very subject matter it fictionalizes. Confusion as to the status of photographs and other documents is therefore out of the question. A good example is a photo from the album compiled by Haya's lover Kurt Franz, the notorious former camp commander of Treblinka. The caption says: 'Kurt Franz with Haya on a day out in the country, near Gorizia, May 1944' (my translation).[39] The photo, of course, shows only Kurt Franz. The fictional suggestion is that Haya was holding the camera. But we know she did not, for she did not exist in the historical world of Kurt Franz. *Sonnenschein*'s play in this respect bluntly uses historical documents and rewrites history, it cuts historical documents right out of their historical-narrative context and provides a new frame that we know to be fictional. Knowing that, the reader has to take sides; he or she must either accept or reject the technique.

A key passage in *Sonnenschein* is a 70-page(!)-long list of all the Italian-

Jewish victims of Nazi persecution. To be sure, the name of Primo Levi figures here, as do the names of the Bassani family. Why do we look for them, immediately? Because they are well known. The motto of the novel, repeated throughout the book, forces us to consider that 'there is a hidden story behind every name'. This awareness both urges and prevents us from reading the list. Even if we wanted to, it would be impossible, or would require enormous research and in fact would make a writer out of the reader, someone who is actively engaged in reanimating the past.

Drndić not only explores borders between past and present, but she looks for ways to blur aesthetic borders as well. Her reader does not just listen and is not just invited to mourn and reflect, her reader is called upon to actively remember or, rather, to actively and consciously interpret documents and their meaning for our assumptions about historical reality. In a recent public interview[40] she explained that her intention with the list was to urge readers to look for familiar names, names they recognized, and then, once they came across one, to rip out the page. Active remembering would then result in a physical void, an emptiness at the heart of the book. Alas, the author explained, readers still had too much respect for the moral value of books!

Conclusion

It is difficult to say whether post-Yugoslav literature has responded aptly to the challenges imposed upon its writers by war and mass expulsion. What is certain, I believe, is that from a post-9/11 perspective the texts which have been discussed here and which originate in the post-Yugoslav experience can be considered as the avant-garde of a much broader tendency to write literature directly informed by the new antagonisms of our time.

Engagement, commitment to political and moral issues, seems to have been inevitable for the writers discussed in this paper. Hemon applies postmodern narrative techniques, most notably meta-fictional ones, in order to link post-9/11 racist and nationalist tendencies in the US with historical Eastern European anti-Semitism, Balkan nationalism, and xenophobia in the US in the 1910s and 1920s. Mehmedinović, through poetic means such as analogy, attempts to deal with a new East-West divide he has encountered himself as an exile in post-9/11 America. Drndić, by contrast, keeps silent about the present, yet her vitriolic narrative about the Nazi Lebensborn project reminds us that history never ended, unlike what the euphoric autumn of 1989 seemed to announce.

Chapter 7

Norwegian Literature

The Return of the Narrative

Suze van der Poll

Introduction

Narrative, especially realist narrative, seems to hold a firm position within Norwegian literature. During the 1970s, literature in Norway was dominated by a socio-politically orientated realism, while in the early 1980s when postmodernism was gaining ground, several authors wished to distance themselves from 1970s political-realistic writing and in fact expressed their dislike of it. A number of them turned to what is often considered as realism's exact opposite, namely postmodernism. And they did so in various ways. Taking a closer look at Norwegian literature, however, we see that it is difficult to deny that for most Norwegian authors it was more important to indicate their wish to distance themselves from a kind of literature which in the early 1980s was considered old-fashioned, namely social realist prose, than it was to develop truly new poetics, as the critic Øystein Rottem stated in his history of Norwegian literature which appeared in 1998. As a result, in Norway realist narrative never became seriously threatened by postmodernism, which is reflected by the fact that most critics are reluctant to label a whole generation or literary period as 'postmodern'. At a conference on literary criticism held in Bergen in 2010, the theatre critic Knut Ove Arntzen called postmodernism in Norway a 'missing link'. But as European and American literature is and has long been an important point of reference for many contemporary authors, it would be naive to state that postmodernism did not have any influence at all. This chapter focuses mainly on late postmodernism in Norway, above all mapping the literary landscape in the aftermath of postmodernism.

Creating a Postmodern Poetics

While postmodernism was confirming its dominance over European literature, renewal was forthcoming in Norwegian literature of the 1980s. There, many established authors fell back on the same modernist tradition that had caused such a furor when they had made their debuts in the 1960s. They were members of the so-called *profilgruppa* which, as the Norwegian literary critic Heming Gujord noted, is related to American beat literature and to the so-called third-phase modernism in Denmark. *Profil* modernism was characterized by a concrete, minimalist narrative and radical formal experiments – notably in poetry – and was strongly reminiscent of the early twentieth-century European modernist tradition. Some critics even hold that the *profilgruppa* anticipated postmodernism.[1]

That form of modernism came to a halt when many an author from the *profilgruppa* joined the Norwegian communist party in the 1970s or supported left-wing politics. In line with their political stance, they started publishing realist novels with strong socio-political characters. However, after the failure of that political-mimetic literature, caused by the fact that many were bored with it, such authors returned to the modernism of their youth. The question raised by several critics, like Øystein Rottem and Idar Stegane, for example, is whether the literature which emerged in the 1980s should not bear a 'new modernist' stamp or 'late modernist' rather than 'postmodernist'.[2]

However, the early 1980s also saw the rise of a new and younger generation of authors making their literary debuts. Some of them, like Ole Robert Sunde, Karin Moe, Jan Kjærstad and Jon Fosse, wrote literature showing clear postmodern features. Intertextuality, for example, lies at the core of Sunde's literary project, as is clear from his novel *Den lange teksten* [*The Long Text*] which builds upon both Homer's *Odyssey* and Joyce's *Ulysses*.

Writing is explored in a different way by Karin Moe, one of the most radical formal innovators of her generation. Moe made her literary debut in 1980 with *Kjønnskrift* [*Sex Writing*] a collection of poems which clearly bears the marks of the so-called *écriture féminine*, in addition to which Moe plays with a hybrid form found in her later essays, short stories and novels. Obviously, postmodernism was not totally absent from Norwegian literature but, Fosse apart, the works of the writers mentioned here didn't find their way to the attention of the wider public, nor did they receive much notice from literary critics. Postmodern literature in Norway seems to be have been reserved for a rather small academic readership.

One of those who did develop an interest in the works of postmodern authors was the writer and critic Jan Kjærstad, who became one of the most prominent Norwegian standard-bearers for postmodern thought during the 1980s. Like Jon Fosse, Kjærstad formulated his poetics explicitly in a number of essays and lectures, and most of his reflections on postmodern literature were published several years later in a journal called *Bøk*, edited by Fosse and Kjærstad himself.

The journal appeared between 1993 and 1996 and contained one of the earliest and most important literary theoretical debates about postmodernism in Norway. The debate between the two authors is all the more interesting because Fosse had expressed his dislike of 'hard core' postmodernism as early as 1989, characterizing it as dull, while Kjærstad's dedication to postmodernism remained ostensibly unchanged.

Kjærstad made his debut in 1980, but unlike members of the *Profil-gruppa*, he did not fall back on the modernist movement from the 1960s. He even questioned whether modernism proper had ever reached Norway. His dedication to postmodernism did not result in a literature which turned its back upon society. This might be explained by the relatively late arrival of postmodernism in Norway, which means that Kjærstad could already take into account the criticism postmodern literature had provoked. He searched for a novel form which could be tied in with a global information society. He did not reject the grand narratives which were criticized by post-structuralism but wondered how both the novel form and the grand narratives (which he called myths, also containing the more trivial myths provided by film and television) could fit into modern literature. He never agreed with the relativistic notion that literature is unable to say anything about reality. On the contrary, he considered literature in all its manifestations to be a means of gaining a wider understanding of reality, and used its polymorphous nature to create a hybrid or even transgressive text form which he called 'novel'. An early example of his poetics is *Homo Falsus* (1984), a detective novel which not only points out that politics and social institutions are fictions, but even reveals mankind as fictional. The fact that Kjærstad holds on to the novel genre should not be much of a surprise as the novel is traditionally a bastard genre, which likes to flirt with what is considered trivial, and is especially suited to combining several models of reality.

Kjærstad's attempt to save the novel form by a combination of poetics and transgression has long been seen as an individual project. The more traditional realistic narratives published in the 1990s, however, show that Kjærstad's initiative found a following. Among those were both authors of the earlier *Profilgruppa* and younger writers who adopted varying textual forms as well as combining images and text in their novels in order to depict a multifaceted reality.

Not only Kjærstad's revaluation of the novel form, but also his renewed interest in plot was copied by others in the 1990s. Plot structure had long been crucial to the novel form but, together with the rejection of narrative, was undermined by post-structuralism. Kjærstad replaced the linear plot structure with a plot form that had clear connections to an eclectic matrix structure, inspired alike by Bach's compositions and quantum physics. The course of events is no longer structured along causal-logical or chronological lines, but by means of their connection to the subject, which for Kjærstad still serves as the centre of fiction despite all literary and philosophical attempts to kill it. That becomes most clear in Kjærstad's trilogy about Jonas Wergeland, a fictional TV celebrity named after the well-known romantic poet and nation builder Henrik Wergeland (1808-1845). In the trilogy, *Forføreren* (1993), *Eroberen* (1996) and *Oppdageren* (1999) [*The Seducer, The Conqueror, The Explorer*], eclecticism is used to renew the novel form. According to Kjærstad, new and arbitrary connections can provide a new coherence which thwarts relativism. Implicitly, Kjærstad responds to the reproach postmodern authors heard, that their efforts tended to decline to relativism.

Narrative in the 1990s and early 2000s: The Coalescence of Postmodernism and (Post?)Realism

The case of Kjærstad proves that postmodernism in Norway never seriously endangered the prominent position of realist narrative, and even postmodernism's anchor man incorporated narrative right from the start, a strategy which became more widespread in the 1990s. But postmodernism did reach Norwegian literature in a more latent way in the last decade of the twentieth century. In the mainstream novel, such postmodern features as self-reflection and the use of intertextuality were widely accepted literary means, and in the following section I shall trace the forms of narrative literature in the 1990s, a decade during which postmodernist and more realistic prose seemed to form an alliance. This we may call Norway's turn to a late postmodern literature. The border between the two formerly diametric opponents proved itself to be less clearly defined than might have been supposed previously.

Authors during the last decade of the twentieth century distanced themselves from what was called 'unworldly' postmodernist literature, but were reluctant to reject literary features like intertextuality, meta-fictionality and a fragmented plot structure, features pre-eminently associated with postmodern poetics. Those features were evidently a natural part of contemporary fiction.[3]

It has been argued that contemporary literature should be labeled as 'postmodern realist', postmodern because authors are reluctant to provide an overall view of reality, but simultaneously realist because literature's referential meaning is not wholly rejected.[4] We should think of it as 'realism' in a broader sense, since authors no longer confined themselves to the depiction of palpable, concrete and above all identifiable reality. Per Petterson tried to fill the gap between dreamed and 'actual' reality, and Jon Fosse, widely known for his plays, looked for a way to render the no-man's-land between life and death, by describing what happens just before birth and after death. His texts are therefore endowed with a Christian-mythical undertone, without affecting the realism of the text.

Despite the fact that it is tempting to apply a term like 'postmodern realism' to contemporary Norwegian prose, that kind of generalization disguises its kaleidoscopic character. The differences between Lars Saabye Christensen's epic bestseller *Halvbroren* [The Half-Brother] (2001), Per Petterson's psychological memory novels and a minimalist novel like *Det er Ales* [That is Ales] (2004) by Jon Fosse are enormous, even though all three of them focus on rendering the past.

Where Fosse, Petterson and Saabye Christensen largely retain fictional prose, there is a vast number of younger authors who want to render reality by explicitly crossing the border between fiction and fact, frequently using crossover and multi-media techniques. Although the phenomenon is not quite new, it is popular amongst young authors like Erlend Loe, Nikolaj Frobenius and Frank Lande. They all use narrators or protagonists who share the author's name, creating a kind of auto-fiction, a genre hybrid which undermines the difference between autobiography and fiction. Loe's *Naiv. Super* (1996) contains e-mails sent to Loe, and in *L*, about a fictional journey undertaken by Loe and his friends, are displayed a number of pictures of the travelers. The use of pictures, whether as pure illustration or as a means to represent parts of the history, has become relatively common, as Orhan Pamuk's *Istanbul*, W.G. Sebald's *Austerlitz* and the Danish author Claus Beck-Nielsen's *Claus Beck-Nielsen (1963-2001)* show. The use of pictures further challenges the relation between truth and fiction. The cover of Frobenius's *Teori og praksis* [*Theory and practice*] (2004) shows a picture of Frobenius as a six-year-old schoolboy and as a teenage punk, Frank Lande's *Frank Lande* (2006) has a cover which is a manipulated copy of one of Norway's national newspapers, containing pictures of Lande involved in several events described in the novel, illustrating the novel's plot as well as underlining the story's realistic effect. Lande simultaneously plays with the effect of reality by means of which, to use Foucault's words, a sort of second self is created, because narrator and author can never actually be identical, and furthermore the relationship between the two undergoes continuous change.[5]

Another author who plays with the autobiographical is the grand old man of Norwegian modern literature, Dag Solstad, whose career followed the typical path sketched above. He was a member of the *profilgruppa* in the 1960s, who joined the Norwegian communist party a decade later and became a writer of social realist novels. He too refused to eschew auto-referentiality, but in his novels it is always clearly combined with a performative strategy. Since the novel *16.07.41*, which is Solstad's date of birth, the author was more concerned with the process of writing itself.

Although the appearance of the author in fiction is far from new, this autobiographical turn in fiction seems to mark a re-emphasis of the fact that the subject, after being one of the main targets of post-structural and postmodern attacks and after being all but demolished, has regained its former central position in narrative. This turn-around can be seen as a response to such phenomena of modern media as internet blogs and reality TV, where the line between the intimate or private and the public is less clearly defined. It goes without saying that this complicates the post-structuralist idea of an autonomous text. Nikolaj Frobenius comments in a footnote on the title page in *Teori og praksis*: 'The fact is, that I can no longer be sure what has happened in the real world, and what is fictional. When I have to make a rough estimate I would say that 50%, may be even 60% of the writing has happened and is objectively verifiable.'[6]

Late Postmodernism

In order to give a more specific outline of contemporary Norwegian prose, in the following section we shall look more closely at the writings of three authors. All three of them are clearly indebted as much to a postmodern as to a long realist literary tradition, but the way they handle that legacy seems to differ widely.

Jon Fosse's Minimalist Narrative: Crossing Borders

Jon Fosse is an author who was called a postmodernist after his literary debut in 1983 with *Raudt, svart*, but who himself, in a later essay called 'Skrivarens nærver' ['The Presence of the Author'], considered postmodernism in its pure form to be a rather dull tradition. According to Fosse, the solution was to be found in a combined form of poetics, in a postmodernism that goes hand in hand with a realist tradition – which makes him a 'late-postmodernist' in the terms used in the introduction to this volume. In all the novels he has written since 1990, the tension between the meaningless and the meaningful seems to be the main object of interest, and he continuously crosses the borders between different literary genres, so creating genre hybrids. That can be explained partly by the fact that Fosse is not only a novelist and poet, but a writer of drama, children's literature and essays.

His later novels, those which came out after Fosse had started to write drama in the early 1990s, are clearly influenced by that genre, with clauses rendered as dramatic dialogues. The dramatic technique makes it possible to create the illusion of simultaneousness when past events are being described, which is exactly what Fosse intends: the past cannot be considered to be closed. That is clearly illustrated in Fosse's novel *Det er Ales* [*That is Ales*] (2004), in which the novel's main character Signe can't stop thinking about her husband Asle who disappeared in 1979 while fishing on the fjord during a storm. He wasn't the first to have died there, for a century before, his grandfather's brother, whose destiny Asle shares along with his name, drowned at the same spot. Asle disappeared just after Signe had moved with him into the house which has been owned by his family for more than a hundred years. Apart from the people living there, the house appears to be exactly the same as it ever was. Signe's life stands still, she never seems to leave the house, but sees the people who lived there before, even those she has never met. At that point then, Fosse has defied realism.

Plot in *Det er Ales*, which is largely based on Fosse's play *Ein sommarsdag* [*A Summer's Day*] (1998), is constructed in neither a linear nor a temporal way. On the contrary, Fosse places four time periods one on top of the other. The layers of time lack borders, so that characters can cross them with ease, and the only constant is the house and its surroundings. The story takes place in the desolate rural west of Norway, in a place seemingly untouched by the passage of time, a place indeed where almost all of Fosse's plays and novels are set. The importance of this focus on place is indicated immediately in the opening sentence, which reminds the reader of a stage direction: 'I see Signe lying on a sofa in the living room, looking at all the familiar things, the old table, the stove, the wood bin, the old paneling, the big window on the fjord side, she looks at it without seeing' (Fosse, 2004:5). By utilizing the spatial as a structural and combining factor, Fosse offers a solution to linguistic insufficiencies. The house 'archives' all its inhabitants' memories and so assumes a function more usually performed by the characters. Asle comments on it when he expresses his feeling that the walls seem to be telling him something, 'something which can't be rendered, but which just *is*, he thinks, and it is as if he touches a human being' (Fosse, 2004:39).

The focus on space enables Fosse to cancel out the causal and temporal, making everything seem to occur simultaneously, thus emphasizing the idea that the past isn't something completed, but lives on in what we call the present, and what is made topical in the act of memory. Events are repeated; Asle dies in the same way as his namesake, but the repetitions are not linked by any causal connection, giving the impression that Fosse means to render isolated, static memories, structurally organized by means other than chronology or cause.

Repetition marks the novel at a lower textual level, too. Words and sentences are repeated – almost mantra-like – creating a minimalist prose form apparently lacking referential meaning and more static than moving forwards towards any kind of denouement. Syntax is coordinated, and hierarchy is absent. The lack of hierarchy is reflected in the use of punctuation: full stops and capitals have been almost non-existent in Fosse's prose since the mid-1990s, apart from clauses and proper names. Fosse's use of punctuation thus underlines the fact that beginning and end cannot be made knowable, and that furthermore transitions are kept unmarked. *Det er Ales* contains only 50 full stops (the book has 79 pages). The absence of chapters and sections can be seen as part of the same, non-hierarchical structure. It is rather a flow of words, raising a number of existential questions (the novel counts 200 question marks), but implicitly acknowledging the impossibility of answering them. This might sound as a perfect example of a postmodern novel, but as the novel is permeated with the search for meaning, the novel serves rather as an example of the late postmodern combinational poetics.

Despite the fact that Fosse is regarded as unique because of his minimalist novels with their repetitive, plot-less structure which is so different from the narrative provided by other authors, I would argue that his texts illustrate many other facets as well, especially the search for a way to bridge the gap between past and present by removing the hindrance of a linear narrative and a focus on visualizing events and memories. The same thing distinguishes the novels of authors like Lars Saabye Christensen and Hanne Ørstavik. And, perhaps even more noteworthy, Fosse's texts illustrate the importance of the spatial or geographical in relation to identity issues, which in itself is not particularly new but was traditionally linked to the temporal, whereas the spatial clearly prevails in Fosse's novels. The same can be said of the novels of Hanne Ørstavik, Linn Ullmann and Per Petterson, and for that matter of Michel Houellebecq and W.G. Sebald. It is as if authors in the globalized society need to stress the importance of space in 'fixing' identity. In that, Fosse is an exemplary author.

Lars Saabye Christensen's Visualized Narrative: Incorporating the Writing Process

In Lars Saabye Christensen's novels, 'place' is as important as in Jon Fosse's, but it is first and foremost visibly reflected in the body. According to a number of critics, Saabye Christensen is one of the most significant writers of his generation, and on first acquaintance his novels seem to represent an opposite narrative form when compared to Fosse. Saabye Christensen does not set his stories in rural environments, but in post-war Oslo, where his teenage male protagonists are born and raised. His style is verbose rather than minimalist, and is full of jokes. Underneath, however, lurks the question of how to render reality, or rather the memory of the past in order to hold on to a kind of historical consciousness, thus going beyond postmodernism. The question dominates *Halvbroren* [*The Half-Brother*] most of all, Saabye Christensen's 650-page *magnum opus* from 2001. In *Halvbroren* the unfulfilled screenwriter Barnum Nilsen tries to render the complicated and mystical story of his family. He finally finds a way to do so: 'write images, not sounds' (2001:521). In contrast to Fosse, the narrator in Saabye Christensen's novel openly reflects upon the representational possibilities, and he thereby positions himself clearly in relation to postmodern thought.

The narrator interferes frequently, commenting not only on the events but on the writing process too, a technique generally thought of as an element of postmodernism. The narrator's reflections are simultaneously referential in that they visualize the writing of the novel and the presentation of the family history, thus becoming a realist trait, and it is precisely that figuration or visualization which is a fundamental component of the realist style. As Peter Brooks formulated in *Body Work*:

> *To know, in realism, is to see, and to represent is to describe. [...] Sight is the sense that represents the whole epistemological project; it is conceived to be the most objective and objectivizing of the senses, that which best allows an inspection of reality that produces truth.*[7]

The interest in the visual shown by many authors of contemporary fiction concerns not only representation itself but also the possibilities and confinements inherent in visualization. It would be hopelessly old-fashioned (for which read 'in the nineteenth century style') to suppose that visual perception produces or renders truth, and just as outdated is the thought that representation concerns only extra-textual reality. The result is that contemporary fiction both doubts the objectivity of visual perception and visualizes the process of representation itself, in a kind of cross-bonding between the postmodern and realist that, while it might seem a paradox, does indeed characterize large parts of contemporary Norwegian narrative. Paul Binding's review of *Halvbroren* in *The Guardian* where he praised the novel for its 'realism of presentation' is illustrative in every respect.[8]

In the following section I shall amplify how this 'realism of presentation' is created. In Saabye Christensen's novel, presentation is governed mainly by images. The narrator renders his family's story as a film script, thus making use of visual representation which concerns not only the simple form of the presentation. The structure is influenced more by images than by the linear progression of time. Like Fosse, Saabye Christensen uses a transgressive form, and both authors play with the tension between drama and film on the one hand and narrative prose on the other, and both replace the linear narrative by 'imagination'.

The narrator in *Halvbroren* intends to render his family's history, which starts in 1900 when Barnum Nilsen's grandfather disappears in the Greenland ice. He disappears just after writing a farewell letter to his pregnant fiancée, the silent movie actress Ellen Jebsen. The letter serves as a kind of genesis for the family, as it is read aloud time and again, so that even as a child Barnum knows it by heart. The part of the history which unfolded between 1900 and the narrator's birth in the early 1950s is rendered as a series of the memories of Ellen, her daughter Boletta and her granddaughter Vera. Barnum had probably heard their memories in his youth and renders them as if they were his own, although he points out several times that he himself didn't yet exist at the time. 'I feel someone close on my heels, because this isn't my story yet, I'm still absent, in the circle, in the warmth, and when I arrive in the story, in the ring, I'll probably be stuck to the magnetic details, like the kind of brake pad I used to be.'[9] The narrator thus constantly challenges the possibilities a first person narrator has, and acts as an auctorial narrator. He describes himself as a little God, stressing the novel's performative status.

In addition, Barnum himself is part of the story he tells, which implies that he is *seen* as well as operating as a viewer. Barnum is quite a notable person, as his half-brother Fred notices: 'Everybody knows who you are, Barnum' (2001: 411), referring to the fact that Barnum is an extremely small person, almost half a person. The focus upon the corporeal is of great importance to Saabye Christensen's narrative. As Peter Brooks stated in *Body Work*, the marked body serves as a traditional topos in literature, especially in realist literature, where it functions as a signifier of previous events. The body is therefore an excellent means to render events which precede or occur parallel to the actual plot. The corporeal is frequently made a theme in contemporary Norwegian prose, in which we often find deformed or mutable bodies. The title *Halvbroren* refers not only to the fact that Fred and Barnum appear to be half-brothers, it makes it more explicit that this is a novel about incomplete human beings whose bodily deficiencies illustrate psychological incompleteness.

The deformed body is constitutive not only for *Halvbroren* and the bold little protagonist in Saabye Christensen's *Herman* (1988). In most novels by Saabye Christensen, the protagonists suffer bodily deficiencies. Novels like Lars Ramslie's *Fatso* (2003) and Jonny Halberg's *Flommen* show that several younger authors are likewise influenced by modern society's preoccupation with the body. Their bodily deficiencies not only legitimate the characters' existence, they also serve as a means to visualize the main themes. Although illustrating different thematics, a similar focus on the body can be seen in Michel Houellebecq's and Arnon Grunberg's novels, where the body, or rather the story the body, tells us, functions as a 'little narrative'.

In *Halvbroren* all important characters suffer from bodily deficiencies. Barnum's father Arnold cut off his little finger when he was a child in order to escape the demands made by his domestic environment. Fisherman and farmers with their strong bodies were the norm, and Arnold was far from tall and strong. The fact that he had cut off his little finger already presages the immorality in his character. In *Peer Gynt* (1867), the well-known play by Saabye Christensen's famous predecessor Henrik Ibsen, another young man cuts off his little finger in order to avoid military service, a deed Ibsen considered highly immoral, but Ibsen's young man went on to use the rest of his life to clear his conscience, something which can't be said of Arnold. The hand serves as an important motif in *Halvbroren*, Fred's identity being revealed by a marked hand, too. Fred is born after his mother Vera is raped on liberation day by an unknown person – Vera saw only the rapist's hand; he was missing a finger.

Barnum himself is first and foremost a physically small man, given the nickname 'småen' [the little one]. The characteristic makes Barnum a noticeable person, but at the same time his lack of height means that he must view the world from a low vantage point, just like little Oscar in Günther Grass's *Die Blechtrommel* (1959). This physically low viewpoint further stresses the narrator's lack of overview. In addition, Barnum's eyelid droops, the effect of a brutal attack some years before, which means he can't control his glance. The sum of the hindrances clearly marks the representational act of the novel.

Corporal deficiencies not only legitimize the literary character's existence, they also fill a void in the verbal representation. In Saabye Christensen's novel, the void is conveyed by the silence the characters cloak themselves in, whether deliberate or unintentional. Barnum's father Arnold keeps silent because he doesn't want to reveal his identity – the many references to Knut Hamsun's prose make the reader wonder if Arnold is not simply a reincarnation of one of Hamsun's characters like Nagel from *Mysteries* (1892).

Clearly, the story of the family in *Halvbroren*, a family which consists solely of abject individuals, can't be rendered in a traditional way with a coherent, chronologically and causally structured plot. The memories which form the story's root are only rarely interconnected; they have their own logic, as Barnum puts it, and are often difficult to render. The narrator chooses to visualize them by using techniques more closely associated with film than with novels. That might sound paradoxical as *Halvbroren* never really becomes the film script Barnum wants it to be despite flirting with filmic imagery: it is, unmistakably, a novel.

The inherent dilemma forces the narrator to reflect constantly upon the question of which representational mode is most appropriate, thus combining a mimetic-referential narrative with a performative dimension which is hidden behind the writing process. A form of literature thus appears which reminds the reader of a kind of performance, a process in which the author, the work itself and the reader, as audience, are all involved.

Narrating Family Life: The Return of the Narrative

Even though the performative dimension and (transmedial) genre hybrids appear to be the main features of contemporary Norwegian prose, there is still a sizeable group of authors who stick to a more naive and schematic form of realist narrative than do Fosse, Saabye Christensen, Solstad and Frobenius. The published novels of Linn Ullmann, Trude Marstein, Per Petterson and Hanne Ørstavik are less meta-reflective when confronted with the problem of rendering the past. It is striking that those authors also use family relationships as the background for their main themes. Family has long been at the core of Norwegian fiction, a literary tradition many authors refer to by way of inter-textual remarks. But whereas nineteenth-century authors like Henrik Ibsen wanted to place socio-political issues on the agenda in order to change society, any such critical dimension is less clear and in some cases even absent from contemporary Norwegian fiction.

The focus on the individual in relation to family life, called by Øystein Rottem 'individets lille samfunn' [individual's little society],[10] seems to be more prevalent in Norwegian literature than in fiction from elsewhere in Europe. I'd like to argue that the thematization of family life in a seemingly realist way may be seen as an answer to the end of the 'grand narratives', as proclaimed in post-structuralist philosophy. Just like Saabye Christensen and Ramslie focussed on the body, these authors chose 'small narratives'. They thus take into account the postmodern criticism of traditional (i.e. realist) literature without accepting a denial of narrative as such, however fragmentary or introspective it may be.

In some cases the thematization of family and family matters leads to vast novels, like Karl Ove Knausgård's *Min Kamp* [My Battle] (2009-2010) which came out in six volumes of around 300 pages each, challenging the division between autobiography and fiction. It may be considered a provocative novel since Knausgård presents his intimate relations and family members with precision and under their own names, resulting in a number of his relatives publicly criticizing the work. Although the autobiographical is often the bedfellow of other authors, not all of them are so explicit about it. Especially female authors seem to be more reluctant to use their own names, thus more strongly stressing the fictional.

Restriction is the most striking characteristic of these novels. The focus on the family makes the world described in these novels rather small, restricted effectively to the subject or protagonist and his or her immediate surroundings. Restriction applies to the plot too, which is pared to the bone by authors like Petterson, Marstein and Ørstavik, the described setting is restricted, and the same can be said about time. Trude Marstein's *Ingenting å angre på* [*Nothing to Regret*] (2009) covers only 48 hours, Hanne Ørstaviks *Kjærlighet* [*Love*] (1997) just a single day.

The narrative choices authors make seem rather restricted, too. The narrator lacks an overview in the vast majority of cases, and whether operating through a first- or third-person narrator, thoughts and observations are rendered by stream-of-consciousness. Although most novels shift focus, as in the above-mentioned novels by Ørstavik and Marstein, the narrator never really achieves objectivity. Critics like Eivind Tjønneland have on a number of occasions criticized those authors for being far too narcissistic. Instead of taking an interest in socio-political matters, authors seem to turn their back upon them even though they write in a traditionally committed, realist style.[11] Their lack of interest can be questioned, however, as many writers do refer indirectly to socio-political problems, such as child abuse, for example, or eating disorders, but they are always rendered from an individual point of view without offering any generalized comment.

That is made clear in Hanne Ørstavik's *Kjærlighet*, a novel labeled as one of the central novels of the 1990s. A short work numbering only 111 pages, in Ørstavik's unadorned style it describes the everyday life of Vibeke, a single mother and community consultant who is more preoccupied with facades than with the care of her nine-year-old son Jon. The two of them have only recently moved to a small town in a desolate part of northern Norway, and the day described is the one before Jon's birthday. With constantly shifting focus, the novel describes the day as it is experienced individually by Jon and by Vibeke, without making the shifts explicit, which makes it unclear whose thoughts are being rendered.

Although their stories are told in parallel, they could not contrast more. It soon becomes clear that the relationship between mother and son is far from close as they each live their own lives. When they eat supper, Vibeke reads a magazine and is irritated by Jon's incessant blinking, a nervous tic. Jon has adapted quite quickly to his new environment: meeting a stranger he says: 'I'm fairly known here',[12] while Vibeke doesn't know where to go on a 'date' with a traveler. Jon makes genuine contact with people and dresses himself properly – it is winter and extremely cold, whereas Vibeke prefers to wear skirts and nylon stockings. She is insensitive in many ways, a narcissist to the core, stopping in front of every mirror she sees. She is more concerned with her looks than with the heating in her car not working. Her preoccupation with the exterior is noticeable in her professional life as well, where she is more interested in the form of things, in the covers of reports, than in their contents.

The story's setting illustrates the relationship between mother and son, as it takes place on a cold winter's day in the north of Norway. The houses in their village are built alongside a circular road, which connects with a main road heading either further north or back south. Living in the village, most people are caught in the circle. Jon and Vibeke leave home, return, and leave again. They are not only physically restricted, but psychologically too they are caught in their own thoughts, fantasies and dreams; they live a life imprisoned in themselves. Only the reader sees the picture: Jon's love for his mother, who in her self-absorption neglects her son. The lack of concern and love, the fact that they don't truly live together, stressed by the lack of dialogue and the dominance of interior monologues and the present tense, leads to a dramatic result in the end. When Jon comes home late at night, the front door is locked. Expecting Vibeke to turn up before long, Jon decides to wait for her outside, where he ultimately freezes to death.

Hanne Ørstavik's *Kjærlighet* is just one of many 'small' novels which problematize family life, where a traumatic event either gives rise to the narrative act or serves as the tragic result of the course of events. It is clear that such intimate and often dystopian portraits of family life lack a broader sociopolitical scope, but as they shed light on widespread problems within the sphere of the family, their meaning is not restricted to a Norwegian context. The postmodern heritage is less clearly marked in these novels than in the performative texts mentioned above, which reflect on the nature of narrative, such as Saabye Christensen's, Solstad's and Frobenius's *cum suis*. But the more traditional form of the realistic does not automatically result in an absolute view nor in absolute answers. They indicate by suggestion, just as Jon Fosse does. They do not refrain from representing 'the real', despite the fact that postmodernists have long questioned the possibility of doing so, pointing to the fact that the perception of reality is based first and foremost on linguistic structures. However complicated and extensive modern life may be, contemporary Norwegian authors try to lay hold of reality and represent it by rendering a multiple, 'de-hierarchicalized' view of it, where every individual view is as true as any other, even if they are mutually exclusive.

Conclusion

Like nearly all cultural and literary renewals, postmodernism reached Norway, geographically situated in a relatively desolate outskirt of Europe, at a rather late stage of its development. By the time Norwegian authors were influenced by postmodern thought, postmodernism was already being criticized for having lost contact with society. With a few exceptions most Norwegian postmodernists adopted a 'mild' form of postmodernism. They took into account self-reflection, intertextuality, the death of the so-called 'grand narratives', fragmentarity, but never really put aside the literary subject nor lost contact with society, something which is clearly reflected in Jan Kjærstad's novels.

In the 1990s postmodernist features were incorporated in a more realist narrative and could thus be called late-postmodernism. Although a number of authors still wrote a kind of naive realist prose, like for example Herbjørg Wassmo, postmodern thought was no longer seen as alien or opposite to realist narrative by many others. A focus on the process of writing could easily be mixed with realist fiction. In the course of the 1990s and the 2000s, a clear response to several characteristics of postmodern literature was visible, especially the denial of transparent meaning, of the subject and of the author as an individual. Rendering of real life became more important, which resulted in a vast increase in autobiographical fiction, auto-fiction, and in the use of transmediality as authors incorporated photographs, e-mails and so on to illustrate their story. As a reaction to the end of grand narratives, authors came up with various forms of small narrative, focusing on the individual, his body and family, telling stories which mattered. They did not claim to tell the truth about the outside world, but reflected just a small part of reality, often a complex part which was difficult to render. The difficulty of rendering traumatic events, for instance, was itself discussed in the narrative, and the solutions found were various, as shown by the novels of Jon Fosse, Lars Saabye Christensen, Dag Solstad, Per Petterson and Hanne Ørstavik.

Chapter 8

Flemish Literature

Questions of Commitment and Authenticity

Sven Vitse

Introduction

Since the 1980s postmodernism as a cultural phenomenon has been at the centre of an on-going, often vigorous debate among literary and cultural theorists. While some theorists, such as Linda Hutcheon and Mark Currie, continued to defend the critical impetus that poststructuralism and postmodernism gave to the field of literature and literary studies, others followed Fredric Jameson and Christopher Norris in their dismissal of postmodernism as a reflection of the ideological confusion in late capitalist society. To some, postmodernism has retained its subversive edge; to others, it has turned into a relativist position blocking a clear-sighted social critique.

Postmodern fiction in Flanders has never been an ultra-relativist, nihilistic affair, weighed down by the crushing load of irony. In the novels of Flanders's prominent postmodern writers – Peter Verhelst, Paul Verhaeghen and Pol Hoste – irony and ambiguity do not preclude worldly concerns and critical reflection on political and ideological history. Depending on one's literary preferences and philosophical convictions, one might consider Verhelst's and Verhaeghen's work deeply problematic, both aesthetically and ideologically, but there is no denying that these novels have a strong ethical dimension from a deconstructivist point of view. In exploring the issues of complexity, ambiguity and undecidability, these novels invite their readers to call into question their stances on contemporary society and history.

Even the work of Paul Mennes, a novelist usually associated with the nihilist *Generation X* style of postmodernism, cannot convincingly be accused of ultra-relativist and therefore reactionary irony. His most accomplished novel, *Soap* (1995), indeed reproduces the excesses of decadent consumerism – including everything from moronic conversations on crisps to gory sexual violence – but it is infused with a genuine longing for purification and escape from the nihilist hell of the 1990s.

Still, towards the turn of the century postmodernism had lost its lustre and its critical edge in the eyes of some Flemish observers. In this chapter I will discuss the critical reflection on postmodernism in Flanders, focusing on three novelists – Koen Peeters, David Nolens and Jeroen Theunissen. All three have tried to develop critical reflection on postmodernism in their literary production. I will start though with a brief overview of postmodernism in Flanders.

Postmodernism in Flemish fiction

In Flemish fiction postmodernism has always been associated with formal innovation and with poststructuralist conceptions of language and the self. Although the term 'postmodernism' did not gain currency in Flanders and the

Netherlands until the 1980s, it was used by some scholars to refer, in retrospect, to experimental fiction dating back to the 1950s and 1960s.

Anne Marie Musschoot, for instance, in her contribution to *A Literary History of the Low Countries* (2009, edited by Theo Hermans), argues that the concept of postmodernism can be convincingly applied to the wave of structural and linguistic innovation in Flemish literature in the 1960s inspired by the French *nouveau roman*. This would include the 'non-referential, 'absolute' writing'[1] by Ivo Michiels as well as the many-layered and highly self-reflexive novels by Daniël Robberechts and Paul de Wispelaere. Even the towering figures of post-war Flemish fiction, Louis Paul Boon (*Chapel Road*, 1953) and Hugo Claus (*Wonderment*, 1962), could in retrospect be considered early exponents of or precursors to postmodernism.[2]

The scope of postmodernism as a scholarly concept was significantly sharpened by Bart Vervaeck in his benchmark study of postmodernism in the Dutch and Flemish Novel,[3] although the concept in Vervaeck's use continued to refer primarily to formally challenging, self-reflexive fiction. His delimitation of postmodernist fiction excluded both the avant-garde writing from the 1960s (inspired by the French *nouveau roman* and by German/Austrian montage fiction) and so-called 'literary pop-art', a kind of nihilistic and highly ironical but formally conventional fiction influenced by American *Generation X* writers.

Vervaeck's body of works included novels by Flemish writers such as Koen Peeters, Peter Verhelst, Pol Hoste and Paul Verhaeghen, among a majority of Dutch writers including Willem Brakman, Louis Ferron, Atte Jongstra and Charlotte Mutsaers. Postmodern fiction, according to Vervaeck, is excessively metafictional and intertextual, effacing all traces of sources or origins, and debunks ideological truth-claims and received wisdom. This conception of postmodernism, which has been highly influential in Flanders, is compatible with a wide range of international, formally innovative postmodern fiction, including novels by Thomas Pynchon, E.L. Doctorow, Salman Rushdie, Julian Barnes or Christoph Ransmayr.

Although Vervaeck's study features both Dutch and Flemish writers, the earliest postmodern novels are to be found in the Netherlands, in the 1970s. The heyday of postmodernism in Dutch-language literature, in the Netherlands and Flanders alike, was between 1985 and 1995. An early example of postmodern fiction in Flanders is *Conversaties met K* (*Conversations with K*, 1988), the first novel by Koen Peeters (see section 'Koen Peeters'). In a more recent article,[4] however, Vervaeck observes that Flemish postmodern fiction continued to develop in the first decade of the twenty-first century, particularly in the work of Verhelst and Verhaeghen. At that point the Dutch literary climate had already become rather hostile to postmodernism. The examples of postmodernism in Flemish fiction I will be discussing in this section were all published in the 1990s and the early years of the twenty-first century.

It is interesting to see that, contrary to widely held assumptions about postmodernism as a cultural phenomenon, postmodernism in Flanders has always been firmly rooted in a tradition of critical thinking and writing. One of the most prominent spokesmen of postmodernism in Flemish literature, the poet and essayist Dirk van Bastelaere, aligned postmodernism with the poststructuralist critique of ideology and with critical branches of discourse theory. In a seminal poetical contribution to the literary journal *Yang*, 'Rifbouw' ('Reefbuilding'), he characteristically quoted a wealth of literary theorists, most notably Roland Barthes and Paul de Man, to depict postmodern poetry as discontinuous, non-linear, saturated with meaning while lacking a central signified.[5] Postmodern writing is committed to the critique of ideology, as it subverts self-contained philosophical beliefs, including the idea of historical progress.

Traces of political commitment in Flemish postmodern fiction are most clearly discernible in the novels of Pol Hoste. Devoted to the legacy of Daniël Robberechts, whose writings from the late 1960s onwards became increasingly critical of bourgeois society and its cultural infrastructure, Hoste never revoked his dismissal of free market ideology and the subjection of the field of literature to the laws of commerce. In his novels Hoste has always been concerned with the social position of the intellectual and the artist, stuck between his social commitment and his critical distance towards political and ideological institutions. In the past two decades he has developed a nomadic, somewhat playful style of writing, constructing not so much a linear narrative as a dazzling dissemination of voices, stories and fragments. Thematically, he has turned towards a critique of Europe's colonial and imperialist past.

High Key (1995), his novel most clearly indebted to postmodernism's witty meta-fiction, combines powerful cultural criticism with a heavily ironic style of narration. When a character discusses colonial violence in plain terms, the narrator responds ironically: 'Truly, this character is delirious!' In some cases the narrator openly demonstrates the artificial nature of his narration, exposing and undercutting the conventions of fiction. Irony in this novel may serve to underpin its political implications, although it may also achieve the opposite effect and call into question the validity of those implications. Irony, if applied carefully, *can* have its cake and eat it, too. Hoste seems to move away from ironic meta-fiction in his novels devoted to the history of Montréal, without, however, refraining from irony and humour altogether. In *Montréal* (2003) and *Een dag in maart* (*A Day in March*, 2006) the narrator comments on the eradication of the Canadian Indians' culture and history, while at the same time castigating Western culture and its debilitating exploitation of language for commercial purposes.[6]

In the work of Peter Verhelst, a modern art enthusiast, the critique of ideology is a much more complicated and ambiguous affair. Already in his early novels Verhelst showed a keen interest in unstable and self-destructive structures and an eagerness to apply the basic tenets of chaos theory to novel-writing. In more recent novels, especially *Tongkat* (1999, English translation 2003: *Tonguecat*) and his magnum opus *Zwerm* (*Swarm*, 2005), this fascination is played out against the backdrop of the political history of the twentieth century leading up to the 9/11 attacks.

Castigated in the literary journal *Yang* as decadent aestheticism,[8] *Tonguecat* nevertheless allows for an unsettling ethical reading from a postmodern point of view. The world of the novel is part Greek mythology, part the 'short' twentieth century, including references to the Second World War and to anti-capitalist terrorist gangs. The pivotal event in the story is the killing of Prometheus, the boy said to keep the fire burning, thus symbolizing mankind's utopian dreams. At that moment a fairy-like glacial age sets in, soon followed by an outburst of revolutionary and terrorist activity.

The political implications of *Tonguecat* – a novel on a par with the work of Kathy Acker – are at best ambiguous. The novel raises disturbing questions. Do we live in an age which has killed (utopian) hope? To what extent is leftist activism ideologically complicit with right-extremist chaos-mongering? *Tonguecat* is all the more interesting for its formal complexity: the story is told from the perspective of a number of different characters, but these versions do not seem to merge seamlessly into one consistent story. Subtle inconsistencies underscore the novel's deconstruction of closed systems.

The structure deconstructs itself – the same postmodern logic is at work on an extended scale in Verhelst's *Zwerm*, the most ambitious post-9/11 novel to emerge from Flanders so far. Verhelst sets up a structure of unremittingly recurring motives and images (such as the swarm, the virus or the injection), creating a network structure in which all elements of the plot and various subplots are interconnected in an unfathomable manner – a technique reminiscent of the work of Thomas Pynchon. This is arguably Flemish postmodernism at its most sophisticated and intellectually challenging. The plot defies recounting, but its many threads include references to major events in twentieth-century political history: the Holocaust, the war in Vietnam (or possibly Iraq?), the conflict between Israelis and Palestinians, etc. This is quite clearly a novel concerned with political reality, although it does not allow for anything like a clear-cut conclusion.[9]

As ambitious and far-reaching as *Zwerm* is *Omega minor* (2004, English translation 2007: *Omega Minor*[10]), the second and latest novel by the Flemish writer and neuropsychologist Paul Verhaeghen (who lives and works in the US). Verhaeghen made his first appearance in Dutch-language literature with the novel *Lichtenberg* (1994), a curious but compelling jumble of postmodern pastiche, twentieth-century physics, narrative twists and turns, and romantic sentimentalism. A novel scoring points for sheer fun and general weirdness. *Omega Minor* is a different story altogether: it is still fun and weird in its knack for erotic pastiche and baroque stylistic diversity, but at the same time it is an extremely serious descent into the dark pits of recent Western history.

Hailed by Flemish literary critics as an encyclopaedic masterpiece on a par with Thomas Pynchon's *Gravity's Rainbow*,[11] *Omega Minor* tells the story of Paul Andermans, a young postdoctoral researcher who meets an Auschwitz survivor in Berlin called Josef De Heer. The bigger part of the novel is devoted to De Heer's memoirs, ghost-written by Paul. A second important thread in the novel is the life-story of a Jewish Nobel Prize laureate who fled Nazi Germany as a child, only to become one of the architects of the atomic bomb. A novel about the Second World War, about European communism and the resurrection of Nazism in post-*Wende* Germany, *Omega Minor* is also a sincere contemplation of the notion of authenticity. As Paul eventually discovers, De Heer is not a Jewish victim after all, but a Nazi officer posing as an Auschwitz survivor to escape punishment. His memoirs are a patchwork of elements taken from real memoirs by holocaust survivors, such as Primo Levi. Are these fraudulent memoirs devoid of authenticity because they constitute a collage of other people's life stories, or can they just as well serve as a monument for the victims?

As this brief overview shows, postmodernism in Flemish fiction has generated formally innovative and ethically challenging novels, in keeping – although somewhat belatedly – with an international tradition of postmodern fiction. Hoste, Verhelst and Verhaeghen published some of their most accomplished novels in the first decade of the twenty-first century. By that time, however, critical objections against what some felt to be postmodernism's ironic and uncritical aestheticism had already been raised in Flemish literature. Those objections could be aimed at individual writers – e.g. Peter Verhelst – but also at the literary and philosophical notion of postmodernism in general.

Critical Reflections on Postmodernism

Around the turn of the century, objections against postmodernism were raised in the literary journal *Yang*. In the preface to the second issue of 2000, the editorial board renewed and rephrased its conception of literature. The previous decade had seen the development of so-called '*Yang* poetry', claiming an essentially postmodern poetics inspired by poststructuralist ideas on language and reality. In the new decade the editors of *Yang* declared that they had moved on: 'The "impossibility of representing reality in a poem" is not really our concern. That notion has by now become a platitude.'[12] They describe their position as 'beyond postmodernism'.[13]

Beyond postmodernism implies a turn to worldly concerns through postmodernism; not a defeatist return to pre-postmodernist or even pre-modernist notions of realism, not a renunciation of the tradition of literary experimentation which had informed *Yang* in previous years, but indeed a critical reappraisal of the principle of formal and linguistic innovation as a literary value in and of itself. '(I)t is clear that formal innovation even less than before is a guarantee for authentic experimentation.'[14] *Yang* questions the critical relevance of 'ostentatious formal tricks' if these are not rooted in 'a wayward experience of reality'.[15] Literature beyond postmodernism is still aware of problems of form and language, but 'above all it is "worldly"',[16] it does not evade everyday life nor the language of everyday life. It should no longer explicitly question mimesis, but use it and debunk it at the same time.

There is a strong sense that formal experimentation does not necessarily have to imply commitment. In the wake of Theodor W. Adorno's defense of autonomous literature, avant-garde writers in the 1960s and 1970s tended to believe that revolutionizing literary form was in and of itself an act of resistance and political commitment – a point made by Dirk van Hulle in an issue of *Yang* devoted to the literary experimentation in the 1960s.[17] Postmodernism still pays tribute to Adorno. Bart Vervaeck's analysis and interpretation of postmodern fiction, for instance, were strongly influenced by Adorno's poetics of negativity, a debt the author explicitly acknowledges. The novels he calls postmodern, 'say no to the typically market-related features of our social context'.[18]

It is this assumption the editors of *Yang* called into question. It seems that what they attacked was the premise of literature as an autonomous linguistic construct rather than postmodernism as such, although they quite clearly felt that postmodernism had become the latest installment in the history of literary autonomy. As Mark Reugebrink's introduction to the fourth issue of 2002 demonstrates, the critical reappraisal of formal innovation was not limited to postmodernism. *Yang*'s 'worldly turn' also involved reassessing its critical attitude towards avant-garde poetics. The poetical problem guiding the issue was that of 'return', of trying to find 'a way back to a reality that is (once again) inhabitable'.[19] It is an implicit plea for a literature which no longer uses the avant-garde critique of language and representation as an excuse to renounce reality altogether.

The critical questioning of postmodernism was not limited to *Yang*. In 2006 the literary journal *DW B* (*Dietsche Warande & Belfort*) followed suit with an issue tackling the concept of (postmodern) irony. The editors had no intention to forswear irony as a literary strategy altogether, even less to abandon the critical apparatus of postmodernism. However, given the journal's reputation ever since the 1990s as a stronghold for literary postmodernism, it was quite significant that *DW B* entered the debate on postmodernism with a thematic issue entitled 'Irony and beyond'. The main questions the editors wanted to address were the following.[20] Has irony in postmodern culture turned into a form of nihilistic sophistry, a rhetorical defense mechanism against genuine commitment? Or is irony still a viable and legitimate weapon against established ideas and Manichean demagoguery? There is no doubt that *DW B*'s editor-in-chief leans towards the second alternative. In his editorial, while castigating morally bankrupt relativism posing as irony, he maintains that irony is needed to deconstruct those discourses pretending to hold the absolute truth.

In 2008 *DW B* devoted an issue to political commitment in literature. The editors felt the need to answer the call for 'more reality' in literary fiction with a number of contributions reflecting on the artistic value and the desirability of literature dedicated to a social or political cause. The issue did not result in a clear-cut position in the on-going debate on literary autonomy, although the editors did discern 'a countermovement', aiming to 'exchange indifference for a creatively worded rebellion. What this literature achieves in the world is a different question altogether'.[21] This conclusion, quite clearly, does not indicate a wholehearted embrace of political commitment in literature, particularly in its more straightforwardly mimetic or explicit guises.

Moving Beyond Postmodernism? Three Case Studies

In the final part of the chapter I present the work of three Flemish novelists who have demonstrated a critical awareness of the limits of postmodernism and a longing to move beyond those limits in their literary fiction. I will be discussing recent novels by Koen Peeters (1959), David Nolens (1973) and Jeroen Theunissen (1977).

Going beyond postmodernism, however, does not imply rejecting postmodernism's cultural and philosophical heritage altogether. As the case of Koen Peeters shows, the critical reflection on postmodernism takes place *within* postmodernism. Peeters's literary work shows a growing concern for community-building and commitment to a social and political reality, but it is equally clear from his most recent novels that this concern is balanced by a postmodern questioning of notions such as authenticity, mimesis or genuine understanding. Moving beyond ironic detachment (understood as a lack of involvement) does not necessarily imply leaving postmodern irony (and its potential for debunking received wisdom) behind.

Contrary to Koen Peeters, whose first novel was published in 1988, both David Nolens and Jeroen Theunissen only started publishing novels in the twenty-first century. Born in the 1970s, they made their first appearances in a literary climate which had grown increasingly critical of postmodernism (although prominent postmodern novelists such as Verhelst and Verhaeghen published their major works in the first decade of the twenty-first century). Neither formally nor thematically did their early novels continue the trend of postmodern fiction as analysed by Vervaeck. These novels nevertheless demonstrated a keen awareness of the objections raised against postmodernism in the previous years. In that sense their literary work relates to the legacy of postmodernism. Quite paradoxically, Nolens's most recent novel is his most recognisably postmodern novel to date.

Koen Peeters

In 1988 Koen Peeters surprised the Flemish literary scene with the quirky novel *Conversaties met K* (*Conversations with K*, 1988), a novel indeed brimming with conversations on topics ranging from Belgian colonial history to the scientific status of the okapi. Written in a lucid, mildly ironic style and wittily making fun of the Western urge to classify and systematize, this was a postmodern novel *par excellence*. Peeters went on to publish a series of books – both collections of stories and novels – that were to make their way into the literature on Flemish postmodernism.

A general concern in Peeters's fiction is the validity of systems and structures: characters devise or detect systems, which then turn out to be the result of arbitrary decisions or paranoid sign-reading. Another major concern in this work is the status of our cultural heritage in a postmodern age which tends to experience history and heritage as a collection of random objects in a shop-window or pictures in a mail-order catalogue. How can society preserve its cultural heritage without falling for the illusion of authentic sources or original purity? Peeters managed to combine these philosophical issues in accomplished and highly entertaining works of fiction such as *Acacialaan* (*Acacia Avenue*, 2001) or *Mijnheer sjamaan* (*Mister Shaman*, 2004).

In his *Grote Europese roman* (*Great European Novel*, 2007),[22] an ironic allusion to the *great American novel*, Koen Peeters tackles the issue of European identity and citizenship. The protagonist, Robin, travels around Europe to attend meetings and conferences on marketing, advertising and public relations. Moving in and out of hotels, walking the streets of Europe's major cities in between generic business talks, he ponders the war traumas in European history and the future challenges for European integration. His is a world of empty catch-phrases, complacent business chatter and superficial acquaintances, clashing painfully with Robin's understated yearning for community and true companionship.

Against the backdrop of 9/11 and post-9/11 stress, the story unfolds of a slightly ageing young man, trying to rekindle a passionate but short-lived love fling from his student days, while being haunted by the war memories of his boss, a self-made man of Lithuanian-Jewish descent. His main concern is the problem of communication in a world in which 'all people will be brothers'[23] primarily refers to shared commercial interests and in which mutual understanding is both guaranteed and truncated by the lingua franca of the travelling salesman. At a conference in Luxembourg, Robin realises that economic integration implies a stifling reduction of diversity: 'there are hardly any differences between the attendants. We are so equanimous, so similar, we are empty and generic'.[24]

And yet, despite their apparent homogeneity, people do not seem to understand one another very well, no matter where they are from. Our language, so Robin thinks, is inherently deficient, although this does not kill the urge to communicate. 'Somewhere halfway between the misunderstandings we meet'.[25] On his travels through Europe, Robin collects interesting particularities about the languages he hears, but his notebook is more than a random patchwork, barely scratching the surface of things. It is his Great European Notebook, reaching for 'the suddenly emerging depth in superficial conversations with someone you hardly know'.[26] How do Europeans manage to understand one another? If we tend to resemble one another, will this improve our mutual understanding? Suppose 'in two thousand years we all speak the same language. Will we then understand one another?'[27]

This novel takes as its starting point the postmodern questioning of language and communication in a culture governed by commercial interests, but it moves beyond that skepticism in its only slightly ironic longing for community. The network of companies across Europe sharing a commercial interest is the free market simulacrum of 'one big family'.[28] European citizenship, according to Robin, involves more commitment than 'being friendly to one's fellow traveller'.[29] Europe is an idea, it is 'the thought of what it could be',[30] and this thought is founded on a common history of brutal violence, fascist and communist alike.

Koen Peeters's most recent work, *De bloemen* (*The Flowers*, 2009), is a genealogical novel: from the international, European scene, Peeters turns to the local. Inspired by his grandmother's letters and extensive conversations with his uncle, the narrator writes down the life story of his grandfather Louis

Peeters, a small-time merchant and shopkeeper, and his father René Peeters, a successful politician and member of parliament. As much as it is a story about the Peeters family, it is a homage to the 'Kempen', the area to the north of Antwerp where the narrator was born but which he left as a young man. The 'Kempen' used to be a rural and poverty-stricken part of Flanders, and although times have changed, its reputation as a breeding place for humble, hard-working and God-fearing people still lingers on in public memory.

As Uncle Jos confidently declares, the 'Kempenaars' are 'still stubborn and honest', they are 'friendly and good-humoured', they are 'obedient' and 'they know how to share'.[31] In the narrator's imagination, however, the 'Kempen' is a sleepy, petty bourgeois area which bears no traces of its struggle with its natural environment: 'all ditches have been straightened, on Saturdays men wash their cars in the drive, and never can a loud scream be heard in the landscape'.[32] As a result of the economic development of the area, God has disappeared over the years from the 'Kempen'. God can conquer all, except for wealth and prosperity, so it seems. In the final chapter the narrator, a non-believer himself, addresses God directly: 'Hey God, nowadays you don't live in the 'Kempen' anymore. (...) Everything is new and rich and fresh. They don't need you anymore'.[33]

De bloemen acknowledges its debt to postmodernism, as it self-consciously presents the family history as an artificial construction. The narrator copies his grandmother's letters but admits having slightly 'rewritten'[34] them and 'added'[35] one or two things. 'That is the least you can say,'[36] the uncle replies as he leafs through the manuscript. According to the narrator, a story grows naturally, like a tree, spurred on by an 'invisible core': 'the story is born, develops itself and tells itself'.[37] The past is artificially resuscitated, although it is not blotted out altogether. It lives on 'disguised in a new shape',[38] the uncle remarks.

The invisible core that spurs on the family history is arguably God himself, and it is precisely the presence of God in those lives that the narrator tries to grasp and make visible. To the generation of his grandparents in rural Flanders, God was not an abstract theological concept, he was 'merry and concrete: like one meets people on the market between the stalls, congenial and imperfect'.[39] God is always around, he is in 'persistency' and 'human freedom',[40] but he is also in every 'faulty design'.[41] He is on people's 'bedside cabinets' and 'sometimes he barks and yaps like a faraway dog'.[42] When Louis angrily addresses him after the tragic death of his daughter, he has the dignity to reply. God can 'lip-read'[43] and addresses people in their dialect form of the personal pronoun.

God's contribution to life is quite similar to that of the novelist or biographer: he fills the holes, 'the last gaps in the life-story'.[44] This is similar to what the narrator does in his manuscript, except that the narrator acknowledges the fictional nature of the narrative chain of 'causes and consequences', whereas God deals in 'single, just and righteous' causes.[45] This genealogical novel is imbued with mild irony and postmodern self-reflexivity, but the overall impression it leaves is one of sincerity and a genuine willingness to understand the lives of other people. The otherness of the past is accepted as a fact, the disappearance of God is not deplored as a loss – 'I don't need your kind of order or higher understanding',[46] the narrator assures the God of his ancestors. In the end, God is just a 'good story, not hampered by truth'.[47] And that is something the narrator in this novel can respect.

David Nolens

In the universe of David Nolens's fiction, the characters fall victim to seemingly irreparable monadic isolation. The disintegration of the self and the psychotic chasm separating the subject from everyday reality are the reverse side of the coin of postmodern subjectivity. Postmodern theory has deconstructed the liberal conception of the subject, it has convincingly questioned the social and psychological autonomy of the subject and its conscious control over the language it uses to express its thoughts and give meaning to its life. Although some have deplored it, many postmodern thinkers and writers have welcomed the possibilities for managing and manipulating the self as a story that this deconstruction opened up. In the life of Nolens's characters, this deconstruction has backfired. The nomadic subject has become a monadic subject, and this is understood as a turn for the worse.

In *Het kind* (*The Child*, 2005) the young couple Paul and Judith are the main victims of this phenomenon. 'The disease of their time also means that they have become individual to such an extent that they have become nobody.'[48] Somewhere along the line the psychological mechanism of identification failed, and these people are no longer able to identify with other people or even with a certain image of themselves. Paul experiences an overwhelming feeling of emptiness and cannot shake off the 'disgusting impression that he is a stimulant, that he is merely acting life. Everything about him is fake'.[49] He is the Lacanian subject in the flesh: his name is nothing but a signifier covering up a void. His name Paul 'doesn't speak to him'.[50]

Even though the emptiness inside him is terrifying, Paul's most heartfelt desire is to become nobody. On the one hand, he yearns for a 'destination', he yearns 'to be somebody in the eyes of others';[51] on the other, he wants to keep all options open and fears the prospect of becoming somebody in particular. This is why he enjoys the thought of having a baby so much: the unborn child 'is already alive, but it is not yet somebody'.[52] His sexual attraction to the corpulent and middle-aged Fien can also be explained by this desire not to be somebody (yet). Fien's body is a home that accommodates his special 'need to lie down once and for all in a soft and humid tissue',[53] a place that fits his emptiness perfectly well. At the age of fifty Paul unexpectedly succeeds in becoming somebody in the eyes of society. Quite ironically, he turns out to be a highly original collage artist. This late artistic calling suggests that despite the experience of emptiness and fragmentation there is still hope that art can give meaning to a shattered world.

David Nolens's novel *Stilte en melk voor iedereen* (*Silence and Milk for Everybody*, 2008)[54] is a very strange novel indeed, combining formally innovative and alienating techniques reminiscent of postmodernism with a scathing critique of postmodern nomadic thinking on the level of content. It is one of the most intriguing novels to emerge from Flanders in recent years, and it is certainly the most ambitious and experimental book by this young writer so far.

Formally, the novel has a three-level structure of embedment. The long first section is narrated by Sarah, a young woman who describes weird – and probably imaginary – therapeutic sessions during which she breastfeeds a whole range of people, including a famous singer, a high-ranking cleric and a nationalist politician. One page into the second section, the narrator reveals that he is actually Paul, Sarah's psychologically unstable husband. Paul admits having pretended to be Sarah, driven by his desire to be a woman and his deep love of his wife. The ultimate debunking, or so it seems, takes place in the third and final section, in which none other than the couple's psychiatrist confesses to be the true voice behind the two previous narrators. The world he describes, however, appears to harbour some of the characters taking part in Sarah's delusions. So who is inventing whose story in this paradoxical narrative circle?

On the one hand, *Stilte en melk voor iedereen* is littered with statements about the split nature of the subject and is pervaded by postmodern skepticism towards knowledge of the self and the other. As Sarah tells her husband: 'You never get to see yourself. Even "one" never gets to see oneself. Nobody ever gets to see himself'.[55] Quite clearly, Sarah does not believe in authenticity, 'being yourself', and she is reluctant to consider 'The return to authenticity' she reads about in an advert. 'Has anyone ever succeeded in being authentic? Has anyone ever succeeded in being himself?'[56]

On the other hand, there is a very strong sense of loss and emptiness in the lives of the main characters. The human condition in the early years of the twenty-first century is symbolized by the donut: 'The Western world is a donut. There's a hole in the middle. We no longer manage to fill it. Western man is a donut. There's a hole in the middle. We no longer manage to fill him.'[57] According to Sarah, people wander around in a spiritual desert, in desperate need of a firm intellectual and ideological grip. 'Nowadays there is a tendency to look for an ideology convulsively, as an anchorage in the storm of doubt. Everybody wants to go home. We don't survive as nomads.'[58] Postmodern nomadic thinking has left people vulnerable to the lure of nationalist and populist politics.

Jeroen Theunissen

The young and promising Flemish novelist Jeroen Theunissen was a member of *Yang*'s editorial board before that literary journal joined forces with *freespace Nieuwzuid* in the newly established journal *nY*. Although postmodernism is not an explicit reference in his fiction, Theunissen's work ties in with *Yang*'s plea for a socially committed literature beyond postmodernism. Perhaps it is more accurate to say: beyond a certain kind or image of postmodernism. *Yang* was particularly critical of a rather shallow type of postmodernism in which Lyotard's deconstruction of 'grand narratives' (*métarécits*) merges with the ultimately conservative 'post-ideological' and 'post-historical' denunciation of utopian thinking and radical politics. It explicitly wanted to move beyond that kind of postmodernism.

The narrator in Theunissen's novel-in-stories *Het einde* (*The End*, 2006) acknowledges the deadening weight of neoconservative politics in the social and cultural climate of the 1990s, the decade in which he reached adolescence. In the 1990s 'history according to Francis Fukuyama had ended, the wall had fallen, the red danger had passed, and capitalism's beatification was completed, happiness for all merely a matter of patience'.[59] The stifling political and philosophical climate of the 1990s' neoliberal monoculture sits uncomfortably with postmodernism's devotion to dissidence and subversion. This strain of (deconstructed) utopianism, a legacy of the 1960s, is revealed in Derrida's commitment to a 'non-messianic messianism' and Deleuze's celebration of the event. From the 1980s onwards, however, there has been a growing concern, voiced most notably by leftist cultural critics such as Fredric Jameson and Terry Eagleton, for deconstructive postmodernism's theoretical allegiance to obscurantist and relativist post-ideological thought. Be that as it may, it is this negative image of postmodernism which informs much of Theunissen's writing.

Both *Het einde* and *Een vorm van vermoeidheid* (*A Kind of Weariness*, 2008) investigate the possibilities and pitfalls of utopian thinking beyond postmodernism. 'The volunteer', the third and final story in *Het einde*, focuses on ecological activism. The protagonist Marc, a solitary 33-year-old virgin, unexpectedly leaves for Ecuador, to work as a volunteer in a preservation and ecotourism project run by an American ex-hippie. While never calling into doubt the validity of green activism and the sincerity of the activist, the story nevertheless invites a serious questioning of the green movement's philosophical grounds.

Clearly indebted to postmodernism is the deconstruction of authenticity and purity, philosophical notions that still inspire some of the westerners volunteering in Ecuador. A well-off middle-aged eco-tourist shatters this nostalgic longing for purity: 'Authenticity does not exist, and that's a good thing. The head-hunters no longer hunt heads, they have a website now. (...) The untrodden wilderness has beautiful paths and is accessible to everybody'.[60] Convincing as these words may sound, the character uttering them is perhaps less than credible: a carelessly consuming, heavily ironic intellectual who has renounced his youthful knack for anti-capitalist deep ecology and is no longer prepared to let his leftist leanings spoil his fun. The young activists, on the other hand, entertaining trendy apocalyptical thoughts, seem hampered in their commitment to Third World activism by emotional issues which drive them to parts of the world they do not really understand.

These are the odds which utopian thought beyond postmodernism is up against. Still the narrator refuses to wallow in apocalyptic despair: 'If need be I become religious. Willy-nilly I start to conceive utopias, imaginary and non-existing perfections'.[61] The protagonist in 'Joost Helder', the opening story of *Het einde*, struggles with this persistent feeling that something is amiss, that something has to change in his life. He longs for an extra dimension in life and walks the streets of his comfortable town waiting for that 'second, unimaginable town'[62] to open up. As a painter he specializes in *trompe-l'oeils* that create a sense of infinity: 'Breaking the bounds of the limited space of a room, people like that: break barriers, illusion of endlessness.'[63] His strong attraction to religious iconography results in a series of paintings – icons at first sight but also self-portraits – which according to one enthousiast reveal 'the religious through the eyes of the atheist artist'[64] and which he ends up destroying in a fit of rage.

The narrator is not a light-hearted relativist either. His main concern is his social position as a well-educated, vaguely leftist but post-utopian consumer in a prosperous community. 'Day after day I have to consume and throw away. I'm not an anarchist or Marxist or something like that. You don't hear me criticize our way of life, well yes, maybe a little, yes of course, but that's not the point.'[65] His wavering between resistance and easy-going acceptance of consumer society is symptomatic of young intellectuals coming of age in the post-ideological 1990s.

The theme of political activism in a self-complacent and self-indulgent bourgeois environment is further explored in the novel *Een vorm van vermoeid-*

heid. Horacio, a successful university lecturer in Spanish literature, abandons his wife and daughter for no apparent reason and without any notice and sets off on an improvised journey that brings him to Paris and eventually to Patagonia, in the south of Argentina. In Patagonia he teams up with a colourful coalition of indigenous and Western activists to fight the exploitation of the land by a multinational corporate group.

The main targets of critical reflection in this novel are ironic detachment and political cynicism. Horacio is a typical, decent-minded, cosmopolitan intellectual, who uses irony to disarm his romantic leanings and to fence off emotional involvement with the bigger problems in the world. He observes the world from a distance: 'Irony is important. (...) He is a man who likes to leave things untouched as much as possible.'[66] It is all the more puzzling what triggers his nervous breakdown and drives him to an act of random and unprovoked physical violence. 'He's never been a fighter. He has always been neutral, impartial and harmless.'[67]

When his wife and friends argue about Hugo Chávez and leftist politics in South America, he does not voice an opinion. Is there really no alternative to global capitalism, or are we witnessing a reawakening of genuine socialism that might spark off a new wave of anti-capitalist resistance? Horacio has 'no opinion',[68] and even after his seemingly cathartic journey through Patagonia, he keeps up this front of detachment. There are, however, alternatives to this attitude of non-involvement, to this suppression of commitment and utopian aspirations which may result, as Horacio's example shows, in outbursts of senseless violence. In Paris, Horacio meets a Danish student devoted to the philosophy of the event, a clear reference to the philosophy of Alain Badiou (which is conceived as a critique of postmodernism). According to this student, we need 'a new and powerful affirmative thinking'.[69] An unpredictable, inexplicable event might turn a cynic into an enthusiast: 'you are an apolitical creature, until a political consciousness, a political being-seized brings about a break in your life'.[70]

Is this what happens to Horacio? Is he seized by a political consciousness? There are no clear indications that he is. In *Een vorm van vermoeidheid* Jeroen Theunissen leaves open the question of whether or not political detachment can be overcome and whether the anti-capitalist struggle is a cause worthy of our unconditional involvement. At least this novel poses the question.

Conclusion

Postmodernism in Flemish fiction started in the late 1980s – although elements of postmodernism can be found in Flemish experimental fiction from the 1950s onwards – and flourished in the 1990s. It continued to develop in the early years of the twenty-first century. By that time, however, influential theorists such as Fredric Jameson and Christopher Norris had already voiced their objections against literary and philosophical postmodernism. By the time postmodernism in Flemish fiction reached its climax in Verhaeghen's *Omega minor* and Verhelst's *Zwerm*, the critical reflection on postmodernism in Flemish literature had already begun, particularly in the literary journal *Yang*.

In the first decade of the twenty-first century, a number of writers started to question (implicitly) the limits of postmodernism in their literary work. Koen Peeters, one of the poster boys of postmodernism in Flemish literature in the 1990s, can be seen to move beyond postmodernism's ironic detachment in two recent novels, although he does not renounce postmodernism altogether. David Nolens and Jeroen Theunissen only started publishing fiction in the first decade of the twenty-first century. Nolens experiments with narrative techniques reminiscent of postmodernism in his most recent novel, while criticizing postmodern conceptions of the world and the subject. Theunissen is critical of ironic detachment and explores the possibilities for political commitment in an age deeply influenced by postmodernism. It is hard to predict in what direction the literary work of these young novelists will develop, but it is quite safe to say that postmodern irony has had its day and that the questions of commitment and authenticity, although critically addressed, are back on the agenda.

Chapter 9
Polish Literature

Saving Men and Nations
Arent van Nieukerken

Introduction

Recently, a young literary scholar, just engaged by the Department of Philology of Warsaw University, complained to me about the necessity of giving 'boring' lectures on Derrida and other postmodernist grandees. She would have much preferred informing the students about the recent developments in Western literary history, such as 'new realism' and 'the return of fictionality'. It appears that in Poland a new generation of literary historians is about to hit on a new literary paradigm. This allows us to appreciate certain texts that were excluded from the previous paradigm (or, at least, marginalized by it). It is also an indication that during the two decennia after the fall of communism, Polish literature has moved much closer to Western literature in the eyes of many readers, a fact applauded by many and regretted by some.

Boundaries between literary periods are, of course, always arbitrary and fleeting. Literary historians should be firm nominalists, aware of the fact that systematic (structural) differences between literary phenomena do not immediately derive from literature, but are imposed by succeeding generations of literary historians according to a premeditated superstructure that regularly requires revaluation.

It would be easy to show that Polish literature developed in the second half of the twentieth century according to similar rhythms as in 'Western (i.e. West European and North American) Literature', even though this was not always clear to the general public; Poland (and other East European countries), like in the 'West', often yielded to the temptation of dividing world literature according to 'political' criteria (employing for instance the once popular paradigm of 'dissident literature'). However, when we put this ideological approach to the test of poetics, it becomes clear that the historical experience of occupation and totalitarian oppression did not alter the orientation of most Polish writers towards the same modernist literary models that were also adopted by Western European and American writers with their roots in the *Fin de Siècle*. This closeness of Polish literature to the 'West' was reinforced by the role of two authors living in exile. The poet and essayist Czesław Miłosz (1911-2004) played a major part in introducing Western-style modernism into Polish poetry by creating a context in which certain literary phenomena discarded by their contemporaries (like the oeuvre of the late romantic (or perhaps rather 'proto'-modernist) poet Cyprian Norwid [1821-1883][1]) appeared as a realization of the poetics of the 'objective correlate' (T.S. Eliot).

The second exiled writer, Witold Gombrowicz (1906-1969), initially had a more limited influence on Polish prose. It could be maintained though that his discovery of the dialectics of form,[2] the reason for becoming a writer with a worldwide reputation, derived from his rebellion against his own Polishness, perverting it from within.

Artistically, the Polish post-war literature did not lag behind Western literature. However, the same cannot be said about the efforts of Polish literary historians to describe the dynamics of the literary process. Developments that could easily be accounted for in the context of the Western modernism/postmodernism debate[3] were not integrated into a comprehensive structure encompassing the whole of the Polish twentieth-century literature. The inadequacy of the attempts by Polish literary historians at periodizing twentieth-century literature derived only partly from their conservatism. Even more important was a terminological coincidence. The term 'modernism' had already been employed to describe various literary phenomena around 1900.

This 'historical' Polish modernism was conceived of as a hybrid period, a reaction to the époque (1890-1918) in which decadent, symbolist, Parnassian and neo-romantic tendencies coexisted with the poetics of naturalism and Expressionism (after 1900). It appeared to be opposed to the poetics of the Avant-garde (Futurism and Constructivism) that started to make inroads into Polish literature only after 1918. Therefore, it is tempting to exclude this Fin de Siècle variety of modernism from the 'wider' Western modernism. However, one of the main representatives of modernism in the generally accepted, Western sense of the word, Czesław Miłosz, emphasizes in his famous *Poetical Treatise*, a private and somewhat ironical history of modern Polish poetry, that its (and his own) roots reach the Fin de Siècle: 'Our style, even if this may sound unpleasant, was born there.'[4]

Miłosz's preference for an 'impure', hybrid poetics (creating space for moral assessments) made him susceptible to certain aspects of 'postmodernism', particularly its rejection of 'purity'. On the other hand, the programmatic antagonism of postmodernism towards clear-cut standards of moral assessment by a real subject speaking on behalf of a community was obnoxious to him. Milosz himself was precisely such an authorative subject, even though he expressly repudiated the role of the national bard [*wieszcz*]. When he touches upon the post-modern human condition in his critical writings of the 1990s, he presents it as an attitude that should be overcome by sincerity and goodness.

The importance of Miłosz's attempts to grasp the dynamics of the history of modern Polish literature cannot be overestimated. His literary career spanned the largest part of the twentieth century, and as a critic Miłosz took a position towards almost all schools and currents of modern Polish literature, including modernism, postmodernism and its consequences. We will see that in the 1990s Miłosz, reviewing a novel by Tomek Tryzna, unearthed a current, which he called 'Postmodernism *à la polacca*'. It may be understood as realizing certain postmodern techniques that derive from 'mass literature' and pop art. However, this variety of postmodernism did not lose its grasp on the 'real' world. It rejects the poetics of self-referentiality (Miłosz expressly disappoves of postmodern labyrinths) and preserves the ethical relevance of literature (ultimately Tryzna's 'exemplary' novel *Miss Nobody* is about goodness). This makes 'Postmodernism *à la polacca*' very similar to what is called 'late postmodernism' in some of the contributions to the present volume. Furthermore, it seems to accomplish in prose what Miłosz himself aimed for as a poet: a simplicity and transparency that he achieved only in the 1990s, i.e. at the very moment when – as a literary critic – he discovered 'Postmodernism *à la polacca*'.

This chapter shall therefore devote a good deal of attention to Czesław Miłosz who, being already an octogenarian, demanded an anti-elitist literature, rejecting the intervention of 'gatekeepers'. He was certainly not the only writer of an older generation protesting against the insincere – in his opinion – experimental formalism of some of his contemporaries. His view was shared by his fellow poets Herbert and Szymborska. For that reason it would even be possible to construe a literary model establishing a certain congruence between the popularity of their poetry and the new prose of the 1990s (it is certainly not a matter of chance that translations of Szymborska's poems became bestsellers in some Western countries). Miłosz's critical stance and creative example will be of great help, both in the description of Polish postmodernism (1) and in the description of what came after (2). Three exemplary contemporary authors (3) will illustrate the state of Polish literature today.

Polish Postmodernism: The Making of

It should by this time be clear that describing the making of 'Polish' postmodernism is a rather complicated task since the meaning of the term is – as a antithesis – chronologically dependent on its thesis: 'Polish' modernism. However, this latter term was first employed in a 'Western' sense at a very late stage, more or less simultaneously with 'postmodernism'.

Previous to this revolution in literary periodization, Polish literary historians had ordered contemporary literature along extra-literary (historical) lines (the outbreak of the Second World War, the official adoption of socialist realism [1949], the 'Thaw' [1956], the overthrow of Communism [1989]) that, even though they may have had some impact on poetics and particularly the choice of subject matter, only interfered with the attempts of the literary historian to elaborate a more comprehensive image, showing twentieth-century Polish literature as a dynamic paradigm of similarities and oppositions (c.f. Ryszard Nycz[5]).

Starting from this point of view, Polish literary critics distinguished between diverse postmodern poetical strategies, employed by a number of older writers who suddenly were identified as postmodernists.[6] The textual peculiarities which classified authors like Stanisław Ignacy Witkiewicz and Bruno Schulz as members of one band (some of them would have been astonished to be lumped together) realize all the tenets and characteristics of postmodernism, according to the influential literary historian Włodzimierz Bolecki. On the other hand, attempts to interpret the texts of the above-mentioned authors as realizations of the post-modern human condition,[7] being the result of certain 'transformations within Western society', show an essential incompatibility of the post-modern sensibility (Bolecki characterizes it with a 'catch-word once invented by Carlos Fuentes: *nothing matters, anything goes*') with the almost always 'serious', not merely 'sincere', but often even 'obsessive' attitude of authors like Witkacy, Gombrowicz, Schulz, Bialoszewski, Konwicki, Różewicz, etc. According to Bolecki's succinct formula, 'postmodernism cultivates the artificial; Polish literature – if we like or not – is ruled by cultivating the authentic'.[8]

Epitomizing Bolecki's doubts, we could say that the adoption of postmodernism as a descriptive category of Polish post-war literature is unnecessary (or even harmful) because it emphasizes the formal perspective of 'laying bare the device', 'foregrounding the apparatus', whereas the authorial intention (its 'sincerity' or even 'moral pathos') is a central fact of modern Polish literature, apart from its degree of formal complication. Constructing a 'textual' space is not only a matter of artifice, but above all an existential act. The opposition between the constructive efforts of form and an intention 'underlying' it is a false one. An interesting example of this 'existential constructivism' is Gombrowicz's carefully constructed narrative texts and his purportedly autobiographical *Diary* that appear – at first glance – to represent a postmodernism that 'cultivates the artificial'. For that reason we should perhaps consider modifying Bolecki's distinction: the act of 'cultivating the artificial' should not be confused with rejecting authenticity in the sense of 'existential sincerity'. The antinomies embodied by these texts turn out to be unsolvable because, according to Gombrowicz, existence cannot be but 'artificial', being determined by form that is produced and/or modified by man himself, an 'eternal debutant' (Gombrowicz's own term) who never achieves maturity. Liberty is not a positive experience of the subject, but should be conceived of as indeterminacy, a pre-reflective state that 'happens' to me, but vanishes at the moment when I start to think or reflect upon it. Thus, the act of equating 'authentic' existence with liberty (in other words: indeterminacy) effaces the very condition it wishes to conjure up. Man's existence is 'authentically inauthentic', sincerely insincere. Its figure (or literary trace) is the irony of self-betrayal, which appears to be much more than a formal device.

From this perspective we can understand that the attempts of literary criticism to describe the distinctive features of the newest Polish literature (written after 1989) display much wavering and even incoherence. On the one hand, this literature is characterized by a 'gradual departure from myth-making in favour of displaying the conventionality of form, due to which *sincere* myth-making becomes impossible'.[9] On the other hand, a large part of this literature, particularly its prose, appears to feature historical, autobiographic experience.[10] These two strategies, the first ostentatiously postmodernist, the second pointing to a 'new' sincerity, seem to exclude each other. Klejnocki and Sosnowski neutralize this paradox: the autobiographic content turns out to be an 'existential alibi'.[11] The author communicates with the reader by means of conventions. This 'formalist' attitude, sincerely 'cultivating the artificial', mirrors the (postmodern) condition of man.

This formula, however, does not grasp the innovative character of the newest Polish prose, since it seems also to be an apt description of Gombrowicz's poetics of 'authentic inauthenticity' (a circumstance that confirms his status as a predecessor of postmodernism). The difference is that this new prose, though to a certain extent 'foregrounding the apparatus', achieves its aim in a less obtrusive manner than older postmodern Polish authors. It is stylistically relatively straightforward (in this respect it differs from Gombrowicz's grotesque autobiographical novel *Trans-Atlantic*) and certainly less ironic than the poetry of Miłosz and Herbert initially was. It would even be possible to read the prose of Stefan Chwin, Paweł Huelle, Andrzej Stasiuk, Olga Tokarczuk, etc. naively as engaging stories, but the 'expert' reader immediately notices that it is imbedded in the literary tradition, referring to realist models through a conscious neglect of the ontological and ethical antinomies of modernism: a 'double coding' that is often considered to be typically postmodernist.[12] Thus, it could be maintained that it 'foregrounds the not-foregrounding of the apparatus'.

The recent realism and preference for distinct narrative structures (the rebirth of fictionality) could be seen as a reaction to both Polish modernism and postmodernism that, in accordance with Polish usage, we should rather envisage as a radicalization of some modernist antinomies than as a literary époque in its own right.

Polish Late-Postmodernism

It would be a mistake to describe the new Polish prose of the 1990s *only* in terms of a revival of existential sincerity that had never been done away with.

Its more or less discrete 'foregrounding' of the conventionality of existence ('cultivating the artificial') must still be explained in the specifically Polish context of literature. In that perspective it is a means to change the course of history or, at least, to show individual man ways of saving his dignity in the face of totalitarian (fascist and communist) oppression without falling victim to the pressure of traditional Polish patriotism. These authors had to invent a poetics, in order find their own voice, that would be both artistically viable and sincere, on the one hand, and on the other could not be confused with the poetical constructions of sincerity (or perhaps rather authenticity) invented by Gombrowicz, Herbert and Czesław Miłosz who had all been exposed to totalitarianism. This proved to be a far from easy task since Herbert, Szymborska and particularly Miłosz adapted remarkably well to the changes that occurred in the literary paradigm of post-communist Poland.

The rise of 'late' postmodernism should not only be linked to literary facts, but also to sociological facts, the emergence of a Western-style press, the birth of a capitalist 'culture industry'. In the second half of the 1990s, the model of a readable and sincere literature (that should not be too elitist) was taken up by literary critics publishing in newspapers with a wider circulation or expressing their views on radio and television. At the same time the influence of 'specialist' literary periodicals dwindled into insignificance.[13] Literary criticism had to find a niche in the emerging media landscape if it wanted to survive. The essentially informal (based on 'hearsay') model of communication between the author and his readers that dominated in post-Stalinist Poland was gradually replaced by a model relying on marketing techniques.

Nevertheless, it would be a misunderstanding to attribute the establishment of a new realist paradigm of literary fiction solely to the forces of the market. It was in fact the outcome (accidental?) of the cooperation between the mass media and a few influential professional literary critics (sometimes even academic, like the already mentioned Jan Błoński). Czesław Miłosz's review of *Panna Nikt* is an excellent example of this alliance. Literary criticism, tacitly assuming that literature should mirror the rhythms of historical change, started to disapprove of the traditional Polish forms of political commitment in literature, even if they were not detrimental to aesthetic criteria (due to irony, Aesopian language, intertextuality). The non-committed, artistically sophisticated literature held its own, but its impact diminished, since literary critics, opposing it to the fresh literary phenomenon of mass literature, emphasized its elitist nature, requiring 'expert' readers. The space that emerged between politically non-committed, highbrow literature that had survived the fall of communism and mass literature was easily closed by novels like Tryzna's *Panna Nikt* and Paweł Huelle's *Weiser Davidek* that, due to their multilayered (double-coded) structure, allowed for both a naïve and expert reading.

This revived paradigm of realist fiction that should be equated with 'late postmodernism' – in my opinion – had been established by professional literary criticism during the period of 'anarchic' transition (1989-1996),[14] immediately following on the disintegration of communism and before the mass media imposed their own rules of communication by the creation of a new paradigm of literary communication, with the concept of a 'mainstream' literary public at the core of it. The literature of late-postmodernism, 'the return of the narrative' and 'new sincerity', appeared to match ideally the expectations and needs of this literary public. Simultaneously with this development, the position of the leading professional (mostly academic) literary critics changed. In the 'anarchic' period of transition, these critics had access to the mass media, due to their prestige in the preceding period of declining communism, more or less independent of the kind of literature they discussed (moreover their essays and reviews were often quite demanding for the non-expert). At the moment the consolidation of the mass media (including the main, often recently privatised publishing houses) as part of a market structure was finally accomplished, the literary critics had to adapt to new rules. The 'double-coded' literature of new realism, originally introduced by professional literary criticism as merely one option among a variety of possibilities to create an artistically satisfactory literature, became the norm and centre of a new paradigm.[15] The reviews appearing in the mass media usually merely stated the double-coded nature of this literature, without elaborating on it. Real analysis of these novels was 'banished' to the 'specialist' literary periodicals or even to academic criticism.

This change, in combination with the 'anxiety of influence' by which the efforts were thwarted of the poets publishing in the scandalizing periodical *BruLion*[16] to revitalize Polish poetry, could account for the gradual decline of Polish poetry (perceived as an elitist genre *par excellence*, resisting all attempts of double-coding) that has almost entirely vanished from the public consciousness (with the exception of some 'old masters' like Szymborska, Różewicz, Zagajewski and of course Czesław Miłosz).

Three Polish authors
The Anti-Postmodernism of Zbigniew Herbert

Referring in a poetical letter to this deliberate linguistic asceticism, Herbert presented the ethical poetry of his generation as opposed to the poetry of the 'great shamans' Rilke and Eliot:

> *Not much, Richard will remain truly not much*
> *From the poetry of this mad century definitely Rilke Eliot*
> *A few other noble shamans that knew the secret*
> *Of incantation words a form resistant to the action of time without which*
> *There cannot be a sentence worth remembering and language is like sand*
> *[...]*[17]

Paradoxically, but not unexpectedly, these very phrases, equating poetry with beauty and joy ('so little joy – daughter of the gods in our poems, Richard') that appear to be impossible in an époque of 'sweat tears blood' are often quoted by literary critics as an example of the art of speaking beautifully (*'bene dicendi'*). A poem (even though it is called a 'letter') that denies being a successful artefact may seem autotelic in a very specific sense. The sincerity of the speaker (who, in this case, is identical to the author) is not put into doubt, but his utterances, apparently showing the impossibility of escaping irony as a force by which man's existence is determined, still seem typical of the modernist plight (his sincerity expressly derives from his renunciation of beauty).

Herbert has hit here on an antinomy very similar to Gombrowicz's form that is at the same time a constructive device ('cultivating the artificial') and an existential experience. If we accept that real communication between the author and the reader (or, more generally, between subjects) presupposes immediacy, sincerity can only be the result of a self-defeating quest that – by the way – sacrifices poetical beauty (created by form as a 'constructive' device). This is, of course, the very thing Herbert wants to deny in his poetical 'letter' (addressed to a fellow poet). However, he would prefer to show the illusiveness of the modernist plight directly, without taking recourse to irony as a constructive device. The poem fails to accomplish this task.

Herbert's poetical development in the 1980s and 1990s could be described in terms of a tentative reduction of elements complicating the relationship between the author and the reader, in order to speak out both sincerely and directly. Already in the 1970s he had created a persona ('Mister Cogito') that may not be completely identifiable with his own biography, but certainly presents a worldview of clearcut ethical categories that could be shared by him as an Eastern (or Central) European intellectual. After Jaruzelski's imposition of the State of War (1981), Herbert continued to employ the persona of Mister Cogito in some of his poems, but the extent and variety of his opinions seemed to have shrunk, and the distance between the persona and the author had diminished considerably. In other words: Mister Cogito had become a specifically *Polish* intellectual, expressing his solidarity with his nation, combating foreign oppression and exposing internal treason. In the famous title poem of his volume *Report from the Besieged City*, the author speaks simply as a chronicler, considering it his duty to give an account of the siege of the City that could still be understood as representing the values of Western culture, but became increasingly reminiscent of Poland and its tragic history. It must be said that this kind of ethical poetry was much admired in the Western world, but many Polish critics regretted the gradual loss of poetical ambiguity. The positive attitude of Western critics to this poetry (Seamus Heaney called *Report from the Besieged City* a poem that 'will always belong in the annals of patriotic Polish verse'[18]) could be explained by their nostalgia for a pre-modernist authenticity. This 'pre-modernism' explains to a certain extent the discomfort of their Polish counterparts, who thought of Poland as an inalienable part of Western civilization, sharing in the complications and antinomies of modernity, even though it had been overwhelmed by totalitarianism (temporarily).

These critics probably expected that after the overthrow of Communism, Herbert would return to his ironies, but in his last volumes (*Rovigo, Epilog burzy*) he actually reduced the complications of his poetry even further. Many of his poems could be read as confessions, reminiscences or admonitions of a speaker that seemed to be identical to the 'real' Herbert. Particularly his right-wing political opinions caused offence among critics who did not fail to point out that this love of political moralizing was expressed in naïve, regressive poetical forms (Herbert even started to rhyme).

From a different point of view, this can be understood as an anti-[post]modernist attitude, preferring existential sincerity as the 'cultivation of the authentic' to the perfection of the poem as a multilayered artefact (in other words: 'cultivation of the artificial', in which case existential sincerity would only be thinkable as Gombrowicz's 'inauthentic authenticity'). The same goes for Herbert's refusal to treat the poetical idiom as a 'special' language and for his deliberate quest for simple words allowing identification with the community of Polish readers.[19] Also rather unpostmodernist is the combination with the almost psychosomatic presence of an increasingly discouraged subject, attached to a weakening body, allowing for the post-*Wende* poetry of Herbert to be called a picture of the 'silent face of a diseased person'.[20] This formula seems to be an apt characterization of much of Herbert's poetry from the 1990s.

A consequent postmodernist could, of course, invert (or rather pervert) the argument, arguing that this simplicity is nonetheless an example of foregrounding: that is, of a not-foregrounded artificiality (as seems to be the case in 'late' postmodernism). However, it seems that Herbert's poetry of the suffering body and decaying mind is a more convincing realization of an anti-postmodernist strategy than the 'young poetry' of *Bru-Lion*. The poets of this poetical movement were fond of provocations, but failed to overcome the ethically motivated antinomies of Polish modernism. Their adoption of a postmodernist exuberance and playfulness did not entirely harmonize with their craving for an authenticity that would be impervious to ethical commitment in the sense of belonging to a 'national' community. Poets like Marcin Świetlicki, who attempted to [re]-construct poetry as the utterance (confession) of a 'private' subject, still could not evade the necessity of including previous traditions (particularly 'ironical moralism') as self-denying textual perspectives.[21] Their poems express the imperative of a new beginning, but fail to accomplish the task they set themselves.

Czesław Miłosz

Postmodernism has been often criticized because it denies the idea of being as the presence of something real to which the human self can gain access, even though it fails to exhaust all meanings of this 'object'. From this point of view we could explain the internal dynamics of Miłosz's oeuvre starting from his volume of wartime poems *Ocalenie* ('Redemption') as an attempt to overcome ontological relativism. Miłosz wanted to re-establish the substantiality of the world which could only be achieved by restoring the integrity of the human self as an ideally all-inclusive field of 'real presences'.[22]

According to him, art should represent the world as a surface consisting of 'real presences' that can be adequately grasped due to the ability of the human senses. Of course, man's sensual perceptions do not exhaust the presence that they grasp, but man's efforts of representation suffice (particularly if he is endowed with a poetical sensibility) to convince other people of the reality of the described presences.

However, as Miłosz wished to re-present reality 'as it is', he also had to come to terms with the specific historical situation of modern man who was deeply imbued with epistemological subjectivism. In order to represent being 'as it truly is', the reader must look at it from the perspective of an author sympathizing with a naively realist mentality (taking sensual impressions 'substantially'). The poem itself should make it clear to the reader that the author does not accept the modern sensibility (according to Miłosz 'nihilistic' and 'self-destructive'). A return to realism as the re-presentation of a substantial world could only be achieved by a poetics of irony, based on a tension between the speaker of the poem and the authorial instance. It follows that irony, structurally complicating and enriching the artefact that becomes a labyrinth of layers that mirror each other, is not a purpose in itself (in this respect Miłosz was certainly a conscious critic of literary [post]-modernism, in spite of his adoption of some [post]-modernist devices). It is a necessary evil that should be overcome:

> *But it is a fact that ironical poetry began with me during the war. It is hard in the twentieth century to do without irony, the grotesque, the burlesque – these are the instruments of our age. Writers as tragic as Beckett employ the technique of slapstick, in this way a contact with our époque is established. This is a peculiar irony, since – for instance – the poems of Oscar Miłosz written before the First World War are packed with auto-irony, but of a different sort: an amazingly romantic irony. We cannot to do without it, but all depends on the purpose irony serves. There is something evil in irony itself, a peculiar fear of showing oneself. But it may be used for good purposes. Let's say,* The World *(a naïve poem), written during the war, is a work of pure irony, but of a sort very remote from what we call sarcasm.*[23]

It seems these post-modern devices appealed to Milosz as a means to invert T.S. Eliot's brand of modernism, to turn it 'inside out'. He attempts to overcome the self-enclosedness of the modernist poem. There seems to be no reason why the text should have distinct boundaries. In fact, it can be infinitely enriched with new elements. This 'open text' is 'enjoyed' (with reference to Roland Barthes's *'plaisir du texte'*) in accordance with certain aesthetical criteria that change, depending on the individual expectations and needs of the reader (or, indeed, author setting himself up as a provisional centre of a labyrinthine world).

In the 1980s Miłosz adopted this 'open' form that from the point of view of post-modernism (one-sidedly formal) appeared to be existentially 'indifferent'. However, in Miłosz's case (c.f. 'A Separate Notebook' ['Osobny zeszyt'], 'Chronicles' ['Kroniki']) the possibility of the juxtaposition of many styles, the incorporation of diverse elements of the world and the presentation of many narrative lines have a relevance that could almost be called religious. They serve the aim of representing being as infinite growth under the condition of temporality that is responsible for the passing of individual existence. Poetry (in other words: the poem conceived of as a 'grand book' of existence) attempts to redeem the fleetingness of living forms by recapturing them in their variety and diversity.

Notwithstanding the artistic success of his existentially relevant realizations of the post-modernist open form, Miłosz was not entirely satisfied with this poetical model, precisely because it could be easily confused with ordinary postmodernist aesthetics. In the 1990s (in the volumes: *Dalsze okolice* [Farther Regions], *Na brzegu rzeki* [On the Border of the River], *To* [That], *Druga przestrzeń* [A Second Space]) he returned to smaller poems that speak immediately about limited 'chunks' of the 'real' world. The author does not hide behind a poetical persona and tries to avoid all irony. If a poem foregrounds its apparatus, it does so by referring *directly* to literary tradition. It avoids 'lay[ing] bare its artificiality' by the creation of a form that alludes to the pre-modernist literary tradition with the intention of showing the impossibility of reviving it. A poetical letter is simply a means of addressing a friend whose sincerity (and goodness), being relevant to other people, can be expressed without self-protective irony,[24] and not a meta-text that by its very form convinces the reader that the self cannot overcome its self-enclosedness. In his poetical letter to the author of the once famous 'Howl', the speaker, i.e. Miłosz himself, becomes aware of a hitherto unknown feature of his self by grasping it as 'otherness' compared with Ginsberg's stance: 'Accept this homage of one who was so different, but served the same unnamed cause.'[25] This revival of a poetics of a pre-reflective, 'spontaneous' community attempts to prove that the poet can be sincere, even though he remains entangled in the ontological and existential antinomies of [post]modernity. From a formal point of view, this realization of an immediately expressed sincerity could be compared with 'The Return of the Narrative' in prose because of its 'first-order narrative base'[26] ('here and now' I speak to you).

This sincerity is enforced by the construction of the speaker whose point of view seems to be identical to that of the author. He can speak about the world in a variety of modes, lyrical, didactical, reflective, moral, etc. In the existentially relevant, post-modern, long poem, these different modes of speaking were 'mixed' and needed justifying from the eschatological perspective. Taken by themselves, time, space, and personality seemed unreal shadows (men, being imprisoned in this unsubstantial realm, crave redemption). An excellent example of the transition towards a 'late postmodern model' of poetry (that could be equated with a 'new realism'– as Miłosz suggested in his essay about Tomek Tryzna's novel *Panna Nikt*) appears to be another poem from the volume of verse *On the Border of the River*. In 'Realism' (a title that is not ironical, but should be taken at face value) the author suggests that 'we' (by employing the first person plural he potentially includes into the community of his poem the whole of humanity) can enjoy Dutch seventeenth-century art, even though the 'true' ontological nature of the world of objects represented by it does not cease to be a secret:

> [...] *We agree*
> *That these probably existing trees behind the window*
> *Only feign woodness and greenness,*
> *And that language is defeated by bundles of molecules.*
> *But it is here: bread, a tin plate,*
> *A lemon half peeled, nuts and bread*
> *Endure, and that so strongly that it is hard not to believe.*[27]

The point is that language as a human medium (in other words: intersubjective, 'communal') *cannot be but* an adequate means of 'describing' the world. It accomplishes this task in a manner *differing* from other arts (particularly painting) or science, but this does not compromise the veracity of linguistic descriptions. Of course, they do not exhaust the object that they attempt to represent. Many of its properties cannot be grasped by (verbal) language and are only revealed by pictorial art or by science. Therefore, the value of literature (poetry, prose) as an instrument of the individual to reach out for the 'external' world (this possibility is proof in itself that existence can only be understood as self-transcendence) depends on the ability of the author to understand and express his position in the world. What he grasps is by definition *real* (unless he consciously misrepresents his experience of 'being-in-the-world'), but not *absolute*. Thus, his representations must be understood as existential acts that allow independently existing objects 'to show themselves'.[28]

Tomek Tryzna

It is hardly surprising that Miłosz looked forward to finding traces of his own realist turn in the Polish literature of the 1990s. We have seen that the 'new realism' conceived by Miłosz is based on the possibility of an alliance between truth and goodness. Descriptions are supposed to reflect the reality they describe (they should not engage in epistemological discussions, even when this is achieved by strictly poetical devices). Author, speaker, protagonists, etc. should be constructed in a way enabling us to relate these instances *directly* (irony is forbidden) to a 'real' world of moral choices and assessments.

Miłosz perceived these qualities in Tomek Tryzna's novel *Panna Nikt* ('*Miss Nobody*') that had been written in 1988, a year before the overthrow of Communism. Initially, the novel had been hardly noticed by the literary critics, but due to Milosz's review (1994, published in the literary supplement of Poland's leading newspaper, the *Gazeta Wyborcza*), it became a bestseller and was subsequently translated into most European languages. It tells the story of the poor girl Marysia who wants to become friends with two girls from a better, modish milieu (Kasia represents the 'artistic' way of life and Ewa stands for the lure of wealth) and dreams about a life in the rich West. Under the influence of these girls, Marysia's uncomplicated and frank character is gradually corrupted (she even chooses a 'cooler' sounding name: 'Majka'), and she turns into a cynical and calculating person. Then she accidentally discovers that their friendship for her is insincere and that she is ridiculed and manipulated by them. Marysia realizes that she has betrayed her true self and commits suicide. Commenting on this story, Miłosz drew attention to the realist descriptions mirroring the reality of Poland during the last years of communism.

The rather simple plot of the story (told from Marysia's point of view) serves a moral purpose, exposing cruelty as the cause of unhappiness. This feature of Tryzna's novel recalls Rorty's opinion that there exist 'books which help us become less cruel' that should be distinguished from 'books that help us to become autonomous'[29] (more particularly, *Panna Nikt* could be classified as a book 'about the ways in which particular sorts of people are cruel to other particular sorts of people'[30]). The construction of the narrative leaves no room for irony. The distance between Marysia, the main protagonist, and the author has been minimized. Miłosz concludes that 'Tomek Tryzna must be a good person',[31] but we need not know anything about him in order to appreciate the story and its (didactic?) intentions. *Panna Nikt* could be simply read as an entertaining (even though disturbing) story. Its existential import (Miłosz was not alone in calling it a morality) derives directly from its rhetorical effectiveness. Nevertheless, he is aware of the allegorical potential of the story. Marysia's plight could be read as a metaphor of Poland, a poor relative at the dining table of the rich Western countries, at the same time tempted and rebuffed. This impression may not be an 'objective' fact, but merely a subjective state of mind. Yet, this possibility does not diminish its moral significance.

Curiously, Miłosz characterizes Tryzna's book as 'the first truly postmodernist Polish novel'. This may, at first sight, seem surprising in view of his unflattering criticism of Western postmodernist poetry and prose. Umberto Eco is, for instance, presented as a mere craftsman who possesses the ability 'to mould sensational pseudo-detective romances out of very incoherent materials'. To this postmodernism of 'anything goes' Miłosz opposes *Panna Nikt* as the first literary specimen of 'a postmodernism *alla polacca*' that remains very much concerned with historical circumstances and the hopes and fears of society.[32] Thus, it would seem that Tryzna's novel, being the first harbinger of a new current in Polish literature (represented by the prose of Andrzej Stasiuk, Paweł Huelle, Olga Tokarczuk and Andrzej Bart), could be called *latepostmodernist*.

According to literary criticism, the discrete double-codedness of *Panna Nikt* did not impair the impression of sincerity aroused by the sufferings of Marysia. Tryzna's literary debut luckily evaded the accusation of 'coldness' that was (and is) often levelled at the carefully 'constructed' novels of Olga Tokarczuk. From the point of view of Tryzna's subsequent novels (*Idź kochaj* [Go and love, 2002], *Blady Niko* [Pale Niko, 2010]), it could, in fact, be maintained that his realism deepened. Double-codedness was rejected in favour of the possibility of an autobiographic reading, identifying the adventures of a boy [*Idź kochaj*] and a teenager [*Blady Niko*] growing up in a gloomy provincial town with Tryzna's own experience. The ambiguity in these novels does not derive from the construction of the story, but simply reflects the state of mind of an 'innocent' child, not understanding what happens around him, or a still immature youth, unable to distinguish between dream and reality. With regard to such almost pre-modernist psychological realism, the very idea of 'foregrounding the not-foregrounding' seems to lose its sense. Again (as in the case of the late Herbert and the late Miłosz) the reader arrives at the conclusion that both the modernist and postmodernist ironies were the result of [self]-deception. Not surprisingly, expert critics often complain about the lack of intellectual ambition and artistry of Tryzna's unambiguously realist prose that cannot be interpreted as the ultimate stage of an individual poetical development (as in the case of Miłosz and Herbert) but is simply there, mirroring an objective world.

Conclusion

A literature that 'saves men and nations' [Miłosz] (albeit not always in the 'grand romantic manner') can still be realized, if we only wish it. Polish literature has shown on many occasions since 1989 that authors (particularly poets) can speak out on matters of vital importance for the whole community through the medium of literature.

Miłosz and Szymborska wrote (from a 'liberal' point of view) a number of poems about recent events from Polish politics that were printed in the leading Polish newspaper *Gazeta Wyborcza*. Szymborska's poem about the attack on the World Trade Center was published in the same newspaper. Noble Prize winners are of course always privileged objects of public attention, but there are other examples of poetry aspiring to 'save men and nations' attaining the honor of appearing in the mass media. Such as the poem written by the 'right-wing' (in the Polish context such terms should be used with caution) poet, essayist and literary historian Jarosław Marek Rymkiewicz immediately after the tragic death of the Polish president Lech Kaczyński (19 April 2010) in an aircraft crash near Katyń,[33] a poem in which he attempted to construct the uniqueness of the Polish role (always requiring 'pathos') in European history. Its 'antiquated', rhyming form (c.f. the later poetry of Herbert), devoid of all ironic intentions, seems to be an example of intertextuality serving sincerity. Moreover, its very form could be conceived of as the expression of a fundamental disagreement with Szymborska's and Miłosz's anti-romantic idea of Polishness. This poem, contrasting the 'liberal' Poland 'that wants to please the world' with the Poland that is 'clothed in our blood as a banner/ the mysterious wound of our holy ancestors' and indirectly appealing to Jarosław Kaczyński to stand for the presidency, was published in the 'conservative' newspaper *Rzeczpospolita*[34] and provoked heated debates.

Should we from this typically Polish phenomenon of public poetry infer that Polish literature is not 'Western' after all? At first sight it seems difficult to avoid this conclusion, but I personally think that it points rather to a fresh development that goes beyond the boundaries of one national literature. 'Late' postmodernism, being the ultimate product of the highly individualized Western society, allows us to speak sincerely about the plight of the individual man. However, pulling down the walls between the individual self and the world with its other selves is tantamount to the rebirth of communities of common interests and goals. Thus, literature retrieves its ancient task of 'saving men and nations'.

Chapter 10

German Literature

The Dialectics of Readability

Ewout van der Knaap

Introduction

In a German review of *Extremely Loud and Incredibly Close*, the critic refers to Jonathan Safran Foer as a 'postmodern reconciler' who uses the heritage of the postmodern without the critical power of writers like Pynchon or Vonnegut. According to the critic, the novel enables catharsis in spite of its postmodern profile: in the end the reader will feel 'very postmodern and nevertheless healed somehow'.[1] This review outlines the expectations of many German readers: novels should contribute to morality with a bearable lightness. Time and again German critics have insisted upon this code, which derives from divergent discussions regarding the social functionality of literature. The expectations reveal how much readers long for clarification in postmodern times in which a univocal and comprehensive centre is perceived as lost. The ethical turn in German literature has had a clear impact on discussions related to matters of representation.

Scholars assigned several literary works to postmodernism after it had been introduced in Germany in 1968. Reflections of the postmodern mode were mostly the concern of the academic domain. Notions of what has been called postmodern or postmodernist did not loom large in German criticism and self-reflection, or so it would seem. They were in fact present as an undercurrent in many debates. Prevailing comments of both writers and critics were related to features of pop culture and readability on the one hand, and the need for ethics, reflection and clarification of matters of cultural identity on the other hand. The legacy of postmodernist patterns in German literature appears to be manifold.

By now, the aesthetic impulses of what has been called postmodern seem to have been accepted, despite the skepticism towards the bluntness of the notion itself.[2] Several studies have uncovered the scattered postmodern tendencies, mechanisms, and strategies, revealing undercurrents of avant-garde, countercultural, poststructural and aesthetic postmodern writing.[3] Even if there is no true consensus to be found, a pragmatic approach invites the conclusion that the denominator of postmodern techniques, both from the writer's and the reader's perspective, refers to a *homo ludens* who is not attached to tight concepts or styles in the first place. Generally, American postmodern fiction was critically acclaimed in the FRG because of the combination of innovation and readability.[4] In the GDR, the influence of postmodern American fiction in the 1980s was inevitably more ideological. Since institutionalized aesthetics caused intense conflicts, writers used postmodern aesthetics to undermine the hegemonic ideas of the state. This led only marginally to radical positions, though.[5]

Recent controversies are signs of the reshuffling of positions in the literary field since reunification. In Germany, the dichotomy between high and low literature – between literature for the elite and for the masses, between serious and popular – dates back to the end of the eighteenth century.[6] The persistence of this dichotomy indicates that this tradition is deeply rooted in German culture. Discussions about literature since the 1960s arise from the discovery of different audiences. Many discussions can be viewed as the finalization of trying to merge these concepts whenever possible. Yet the self-consciousness of different groups does not contribute to acceptance of this pluralism. The controversy between autonomous and engaged attitudes also complicates the matter.

First, I will provide a brief history of the discourse about postmodernity and postmodernism in German literature, then unfold some aspects of the heritage of the postmodern profile in German literature in which discussions about relevance prevail, and finally zoom in on three authors born in three different decades. In doing so, the focus will shift from West to East (Brussig), and include Austrian authors (Handke, Menasse).

A Brief History of the German Postmodern Debate

It is tempting to radically reduce both the story and the critique of postmodern phenomena in Germany to the years 1968, 1980, 1987 and 1998.

The era of postmodern concepts in Germany started as early as 1968. The prevailing view was that intellectuals should also engage with territory outside of the literary battlefields. This diagnosis coincided with Lesley Fiedler's conclusion in 1968, in Freiburg im Breisgau, that the birth of postmodern literature implies the integration of elite and pop culture. That year of 1968 has become symbolic for the student protest movement, the creativity of countercultures and generational conflicts in a country that was striving for democracy and suffering from a Nazi past. Fiedler's plea for the subversive power of trivial elements and the entertainment factor in literature was only accepted by a handful of young authors. Others insisted on the need for political commitment in literature against the background of coming to terms with the past. The suspicion that the playful postmodernists were repeating the fascist pattern of bashing elite culture can be understood in the perspective of this deeply felt belief that Germans had to relate to their recent history. In this view, Fiedler's concept gave away the power of literature to the culture industry – which made postmodernism potentially fascist. Nonetheless, postmodern aesthetics were also approached positively, for example, by focusing on their emancipatory potential.[7] All in all, Fiedler's diagnosis that a threshold to a new juncture had been crossed was widely accepted. Other fruits of the discussion included the convictions that the dominance of literary critics had to be broken, that a powerful anti-authoritarian literature must be pursued, and that literature must respond to the aesthetic law of autonomy.

Scrutinizing the phenomenon called postmodernity in 1980, Jürgen Habermas, as a gatekeeper and major representative of German philosophy, denied that the age of modernity had come to a close. He revealed his fear of neo-conservatives and claimed that the project of enlightenment had not yet ceased. During the 1980s, the debate about postmodernism had reached a climax, which was also sparked by Habermas's lecture: 'Is modernity as passé as postmoderns assert? Or is the many voiced call for postmodernity itself nothing but phony?'[8] Given his position in the debate about postmodernity and its sequel, and his status as a representative of the Frankfurt School, it would be justified to call him a godfather. It is no coincidence that the philosopher's sharpest words were uttered on the occasion of a celebration for Theodor W. Adorno. A slight resistance to globalism and cosmopolitism can be found in positions that stress the German literary and philosophical framework. In the end, Habermas's intervention was not in vain, as demonstrated by the literary prose that succeeded in combining the ethical aims of the German tradition of enlightenment with concepts of postmodernism. The emergence of an ethical postmodern trend in literature was the synthesis of a true dialectical process, and the best result Habermas and others who insisted upon the indispensability of the German responsibility to reflect on the past could have hoped for.

It is imperative to emphasize that the claim of the leaders of the Frankfurt School that 'barbarism is the flipside of Enlightenment and Modernity' continued to be a source of inspiration;[9] to Horkheimer and Adorno, the culture industry was part of Modernity. This inherence made it seem nonsensical to speak of something beyond Modernity. It also needs to be underlined that the concept of 'modernism' rarely appears in German culture, whereas the rough periodizing concept of 'die Moderne' (Modernity) is widely used. Hence the emergence of the term 'die Postmoderne' (Postmodernity). Habermas seems to adhere to Adorno's position that a separation between 'Moderne' and 'Modernismus' is inadequate,[10] and mostly speaks of the 'postmodern', which seems to have been influential in the German discourse on postmodern phenomena.

In spite of the strong opposition, two book publications by Wolfgang Welsch successfully defended postmodernity for a German readership at the end of the 1980s.[11] Furthermore, in his defense of postmodern writing in 1987, Hanns-Josef Ortheil concludes that 'with a considerable delay', 'postmodern versions' of literature had entered German literature. He claims that this trend will increase, that it will be 'the literature of the future': 'It will set the decisive standards that will later indicate the criteria of the new style (the style of our era). This is becoming visible already'.[12] Ortheil refers to three 'masterpieces of postmodern attitude': Wolfgang Hildesheimer's novel *Marbot* (1981), Gerold Späth's *Commedia* (1980) and Klaus Hoffer's *Bei den Bieresch* (two volumes, 1979, 1983). These authors represent three countries – FRG, Switzerland and Austria. Hildesheimer in his 1976 lecture 'The End of Fiction' (originally in English) proclaimed that narrative was no longer adequate as a representational mode for facing human disasters.[13] Späth's novel was republished in 2001.[14] In an aside, Ortheil refers to Hoffer's poetological lecture[15] by clarifying that Hoffer, who is a translator of Vonnegut, Carver, Gordimer and Conrad, is also a profound reader of Kafka. When the *Bieresch* volumes were republished in one volume in 2007, it was again received with critical acclaim. 'It has rarely happened that German postmodern literature presented itself more staggeringly and entertainingly.'[16]

In 1998 an issue of the influential magazine *Merkur* proclaimed the end of postmodernity,[17] culminating in an article that stated that postmodern thought could neither compete with nor improve modern concepts.[18] The editors of *Merkur* noted that many 'postmodern revisions, variations and substitutions of the modern in our awareness and daily life are obvious nowadays'.[19] The articles reveal a 'de-dramatization' and claim that 'important oppositions' used in the binary battle of modern versus postmodern are not new at all, but sprang from earlier periods. The lesson of the 'skepticism' of postmodern features has been learned.[20] In their contribution to the *Merkur* volume, Alan Sokal and Jean Bricmont ask what will follow the postmodern movement. They mention two possibilities: either there will be 'a relapse in a form of dogmatism, mysticism or religious fundamentalism', which would mean a total loss of the Age of Reason, or intellectuals would either refrain from fundamentally criticizing the status quo for ten to twenty years, or give up their political *engagement* totally.[21] The controversy continued in the weekly *Die Zeit*. After a critic had called postmodernity a 'fatalistic yuppie theory',[22] a literary scholar defended the concept of the postmodern.[24]

Looking for Authenticity, Relevance, and Germany's Next Top Novel

Clearly, discussions about and the success of several postmodern(ized) novels have paved the way for the revival of narration. Recent German literature has produced worldwide bestsellers and caused debates on the relevance of literature against the background of discussions (old and new) about depoliticized aestheticism. In the era of post-unification, the war in former Yugoslavia, and global terrorism, German critics were inclined to avoid concepts that might support nihilism or political non-commitment. The paradox inherent in the term postmodern is 'to say the least, unpopular',[24] but the fact that postmodern patterns are rampant after unification is striking. The postmodern mode seemed to fit an engaged attitude, corresponding to the postcolonial discourse. Contrary to the idea that contemporary German writers have avoided participating in social matters, several German writers have written about global issues, such as civil wars.[25]

Looking back, the 1990s constitute the most intense period of discussion possibilities for German contemporary fiction. Several critics have attacked the state of German fiction from the West. One viewpoint was that German culture had been dominated by the left-liberal consensus that prioritized moral concerns rather than aesthetic concerns, and that contemporary fiction lacked quality.[26] In 1989 the critic Frank Schirrmacher lamented the provinciality of German fiction, he complained that epigones were spoiling the freshness of literature.[27] On the eve of unification in 1990, Schirrmacher wrote a 'Farewell to the literature of the Federal Republic' in which he expounded on the founding myth that was defended by the old guard with cultural power.[28]

Younger critics were also disappointed by West German literature. In an article in 1991, Maxim Biller provocatively claimed that the new generation's total biographical inexperience, combined with their lack of adventures and conflicts, had made German literature unexciting.[29] Later he accused contemporary German writers of having a slouchy attitude, for showing little interest in the relevance of literature, for being candidates for compromise and 'system opportunists' seeking 'total affirmation' and making themselves 'intellectually comfortable'. Biller mentions two positive exceptions, Christian Kracht's *Faserland* (1995) and Feridun Zaimoğlu's *Abschaum. Die wahre Geschichte des Ertan Ongun* (1997).[30] Similarly, in 1992 Matthias Altenburg fulminated against irrelevant, self-referential literature, mentioning Thomas Hettche and Thorsten Becker (without referring to their postmodern concepts). In Altenburg's view, texts ought to be 'as good as films and thousands of times better than television'; he yearned for authors who did not hide behind profundity, and who could write realistically without forgetting the classic modernists (Joyce, Beckett, Musil, Celine). Altenburg's source of inspiration is American literature, but he also points to German authors who seem to have been forgotten after initially being met with praise: 'Undine Gruenter, Johannes Jansen, Patrick Roth, Peter Wawerzinek, Klaus Modick'.[31]

In response to this criticism, the trend called New Readability represented the hope that by standing up against the competition of the global market, after the crisis in creativity as well as in marketability, German literature will matter and be read again. A volume published in 1996 with the subtitle 'Neues Erzählen' coined the usage of 'Neue Lesbarkeit' used by some scholars.[32]

Clearly, new texts marked a shift in mentality and broke away from anti-narrative resentment.[33] A new generation was apparently supplanting Grass and his generation,[34] as well as non-bestselling representatives of self-referential literature. Of course, intermediate positions have also been defended, for instance in the claim that the alleged crisis existed only in an imitation of Anglo-American trends or in opting for autonomous writing.[35o]

The case of Daniel Kehlmann's *Die Vermessung der Welt* (2005, *Measuring the World*), a novel that has been hailed for its readability, is indicative of the fact that this issue continued in the new millennium. In Kehlmann's novel, the life stories of two groundbreaking eighteenth-century scientists comically converge. Staged as a fake interview and a sham battle, Kehlmann held public lectures in 2007. Kehlmann ironically demands that the interviewer not play 'postmodern games, [because] that has gone out of fashion'.[36] Furthermore, he thinks the interviewer should avoid 'postmodern meta-leaps'.[37] Kehlmann confesses: 'To me, literature has always been the most fascinating when it defaces rules of reality rather than those of syntax.'[38] In his view *Die Vermessung der Welt* demonstrates playfulness with regard to the genre of biography and to narrative. The only terms he uses are 'surrealism' for his phantasmagoria, and 'realism' for the narrative as such. Kehlmann is known to be inspired by Spanish magic realism.

Another case touches upon a trend which shows that elements of pop culture have become part of the German literary market. In that sense the literary system has been postmodernized. In January 2010, the German media created a hype about the 17-year-old Helene Hagemann who had shown her own media savvy by producing a trailer on YouTube for her novel *Axolotl Roadkill*, in which children are shown to be part of a decadent generation that is itself a phenomenon of an affluent society. Critics responded to the directness and harshness with which Hagemann wrote about the life (nightlife) of experimental Bohemian teenagers as a perverted result of society's achievements.[39] Both the hype and the phenomenon were criticized. What has been called the restless tendency to deal with literature along the lines of 'Germany's Next Top Novel'[40] is also common to hypes, which means that many novels will remain unnoticed.

In addition to new trends, a notable continuity can be found. Most striking is the continuation in the post-unification era of two pillars that constitute the German cultural identity.[41] One pillar is the Holocaust. Writers of the younger generation also devote themselves to Holocaust narratives, although they use different modes.[42] Documentary fiction rules, but was very quickly questioned and even lampooned. Klaus Modick, one of the authors who is inspired by postmodernism, uncovers in *Bestseller* (2006) how easily editors, the book market and readers can be deceived if a writer fictionalizes the Holocaust and conforms to the hype of family stories and histories. His novel tells the story of a writer who almost becomes successful by inventing an 'authentic' story that he passes on to a young woman deemed attractive enough to achieve success. In the guise of a *roman à clef*, Modick's mutation of postmodern patterns is a satire on his own oeuvre as well as on trends and mechanisms in the literary market. Modick's character criticizes a publisher for previously being a 'prototype of the literary opposition against cultural industry' and now encouraging books in Hollywood-style.[43]

The second pillar of German national identity builds on the economic miracle that had been heavily discussed from 1968 onwards in novels by Chotjewitz, Brinkmann, Heißenbüttel and Ortheil. These novels represent a typical German kind of postmodernism which recycles modernist writing and also focuses on national identity,[44] being reluctant to fully commit to postmodern horizons.[45] In the 1990s, especially in originally Western novels, protagonists reveal their consumerism and hedonism, while the authors note that they have been fully inspired by mass media.[46] This current within pop literature seems to be the result of postmodern bourgeois society; the narratives are less focused on narrative than on reflecting the cultural archive of their generation. Literature has become a machine that archives discourses and is not a weapon that demands changes, although it opposes leftist cultural hegemony. Representatives of the so-called pop literature – apart from uncovering consumerism and hedonism – reveal patriotic pride, in contrast to the generation before that criticized the aura of prosperity that resulted from the economic revival.

The non-fiction book *Generation Golf* is an example of this new literature. It portrays the fun generation that is associated with pop literature.[47] However, the phenomenon of listmania is not restricted to those who grew up in the FRG. Several writers who grew up in the GDR also reflect their childhood by enumerating what their occupations and possessions were.[48] The poetics of enumeration seems to contribute to both the personal and the collective cultural identity process: only through explicitly naming it can the other (East/West) be comprehended.

Moreover, authors like Wladimir Kaminer have found a niche for telling straightforward stories of, e.g. his childhood in Russia, or of life in Berlin or Germany in general.[49] The *Lesebühnen* (reading stages) also demonstrate a non-elitist literary approach and an ironic way of dealing with everyday life.[50] The stages close the gaps between literature and bars, between production and distribution, between high and low culture. These stage texts are written for instant effect. The writers of pop literature and those who represent *Lesebühnen* illustrate a playful and cool, almost unambitious way of integrating kitsch, commonplace, and elements and genres of pop culture.

The loudness of trends could easily eclipse other developments in the aftermath of unification and following the ostracism of postmodern writing. Several writers have focused on repositioning the self since unification, thus connecting to the trend in other literatures to return to the subject.[51] In *Die Überfliegerin* (2002) by Angela Krauß, born in the GDR, the protagonist tries to cope with the new coordinates by zooming in on details, by observing and absorbing them, to understand herself better as well.[52] In lectures, Krauß meditated on the need to integrate the world:

> *Will our lives continue to be intelligible to us and will we still be able to interpret them? Will we be able to recognize a continuous life story within them? Can we be sure [...] that we can prevent our own life from falling apart, by repeatedly recounting our own life story, as if it were a serialized novel? An impulse to do so appears almost by itself. [...] Asking myself who is in charge takes me down a path that leads me to tell my own life story, as well as a literary narrative.*[53]

Krauß's position is similar to that of the novelist Andreas Maier, who wrote a dissertation on Thomas Bernhard's prose. He pointed to his need to focus on his own position, to make the self possible: 'If I want to be honest, then I must try to explain why everything inside me always occurs in confusion, and why I have always viewed talking in a confused manner as the truth of human speech, especially in my own case.'[54]

Maier's statement echoes his response to the debate that four of his colleagues launched in 2005.[55] Martin R. Dean, Thomas Hettche, Matthias Politycki and Michael Schindhelm argued the necessity of a 'Relevant Realism' as opposed to dominant 'solipsistic self-examinations':[56]

> *Expel the epigones of the family novel, and the murmuring invokers of the imperfect to their places on the margins. [...] We are too young to let our experiences burn up in the stuffy cathedrals of self-referential literature. At the same time, we are too old to be taken in by the popularist concept of reality, as the younger generation has been, with their motto of pseudo-spontaneity. 'Pop literature' is dead, as is the attempt to describe problems by infantilizing society. [...]*
>
> *[...] our aim [is] a relevant narration, we believe that nowadays the novel must raise social questions: it must take on the problems of the present which have been forgotten or made taboo; it must cover difficult areas – whether local or global – and present them authentically. We are calling for*

more relevance not simply due to our age, but also due to the eeriness present in the world. The task of the novel is then to maintain and extend the world's habitability. If this is to be done, the writer must adopt a recognizable position which uses an aesthetic medium to substantiate moral values. [...]

Instead of living on the shoulders of giants, we live on the fragmented ruins of giants. But those who have now turned towards a post-modern game of 'anything goes' should realize that this game remains – as it has always been – deadly serious. Narration is the moralist's way of hiding his intentions and is practiced with the pathos of those who not only indulge in telling stories, but also feel that they are no longer obliged to observe society from the midst of their generation from an aesthetic point of view, which has always also been a moral one. [...]

[The moral attitude of Relevant Realism is] the constant scrutiny of our dying world and the struggle for new utopias. If we are to overcome the rampant cultural cannibalism, then – even as long-standing left-wing liberals – we may well have to switch the way we think to a direction that would otherwise be considered conservative. In this way even a writer of our own generation would once again be in the place he has been avoiding with good reason for many years, but which he must no longer shun. He must return to the focal point of social discourse: a place where it is necessary to not only scrutinize and stylistically elaborate on reality, but to take sides. What we need now more than anything else is intolerance.

The manifesto was countered: to Juli Zeh, their definition of 'relevance' was unclear; Hans-Ulrich Treichel claimed that all novelists are realists, no matter which style they use; and most briefly Uwe Tellkamp added fuel to the rejection by replying that the only task of writers is to write 'good books' – 'The rest is irrelevant'.[57] It could be that the heritage of Adorno still checkmates aesthetic positions, at least those of the establishment: 'the function of art in the totally functional world is its lack of functionality'.[58] The response to the manifesto was limited, as though these young white male writers shared the last convulsions of a merely polemical dichotomy. Deservedly, the topos of relevance demands clarification.

In 2009, for an exhibition in the Tate Gallery, a manifesto was launched that once again proclaimed that 'postmodernism is dead'. The manifesto accompanies 'the emergence of a global altermodernity':

> *The times seem propitious for the recomposition of a modernity in the present, reconfigured according to the specific context within which we live – crucially in the age of globalisation – understood in its economic, political and cultural aspects: an altermodernity.*

Der Spiegel paid attention to the exhibition and its concept. According to the British curator Lizzie Carey-Thomas, 'altermodernism is the return to activity', whereas 'postmodernism is always a reaction to the changes in the world'.[60]

> *The artist becomes 'homo viator', the prototype of the contemporary traveler whose passage through signs and formats refers to a contemporary experience of mobility, travel and transpassing. This evolution can be seen in the way works are made: a new type of form is appearing, the journey-form, made of lines drawn both in space and time, materializing trajectories rather than destinations. The form of the work expresses a course or a wandering rather than a fixed space-time.*[61]

On another level the manifesto verges on what the manifesto of Relevant Realism strove for. Altermodernism seems to be focused on societal relevance as much as some young German authors are. This could mean that altermodernism in literature is a fusion of postmodernist concepts and *engagement*. The following three miniature cases will help to clarify positions beyond postmodern writing.

German Literature Beyond Postmodernism

Obviously, trend-watching is part of criticism. In 2005 the following phenomena were spotted in German literature in an article: 'meditative realism', 'new modesty and sincerity', 'new plainness', 'neo-mysticism', 'neo-conservative backlash'.[62] Although the 'cult of sincerity' had been criticized by the historical avant-garde,[63] at the beginning of the twenty-first century, the re-evaluation of the achievements of Western capitalist society was highly dominated by stressing sincerity as a moral codex for conquering the economic crisis.[64] Analogous to this, the German literary field seemed to rediscover strategies of sincerity. For example, in a speech Ralf Rothmann referred to the inner compass he follows in his writing. He used the occasion to make some remarks about the private sphere in times of political tension after 9/11.[65] This position, demarcating the line between the writer as a storyteller and the writer as a speaker, makes clear how literature can be viewed as a sanctuary in which to develop ideas without thinking of the direct political impact.

Thomas Brussig: From Wild to Mild Postmodernism

Thomas Brussig has put the lachrymose behavior of many fellow former GDR civilians behind him, undermined the discourse and collective myth of the East Germans as heroes of history, and attacked the literary system. For this he created an anti-hero (anti-heroes can be found in large numbers in post-GDR literature) in his burlesque and satirical novel *Helden wie wir* (1995).[66] The sexually frustrated Klaus Uhltzscht tells his life story to a journalist of *The New York Times* as if it were a psychoanalytical session. In Brussig's obscene-picaresque anti-Bildungsroman, the perverted protagonist who becomes an official Stasi-employee demythologizes the heroic courage of 'the people' and the collapse of the Berlin wall that, according to Klaus, only fell because he dropped his trousers. Brussig finally sacrifices Christa Wolf, who epitomized literature of the GDR, in a matricide. She had already been the cause and target of an ideological controversy amongst critics after the unification process. A 1991 volume with documents about the debate on her moral position, the role of intellectuals, and their aesthetics of political persuasion was a milestone in the debate on writership.[67] In the last chapter of *Helden wie wir*, Brussig denounces Wolf's utopian belief in the GDR, mocks her style, and notes the lack of eroticism in her novel *Der geteilte Himmel* (1963) – although it only suits Klaus that it is not a suggestive book. Because his member has swollen disproportionately due to an infection, he cannot afford to get an erection. In contrast to the erection of the wall in Wolf's book, not much later his erect penis will contribute to the opening of the wall. This grotesque chapter is provocatively titled 'Der geheilte Pimmel' ('The Healed Pecker'): a semantic permutation of *Der geteilte Himmel*, a scurrilous settlement of an angry young (and witty, white heterosexual) man with an older generation and a modern, canonized classic. In a sense, Klaus appears to be a true motherfucker when he humiliates Wolf and penetrates the wall. In contrast to Wolf's socialist heroine, Brussig's anti-hero does not comply with the GDR standards of socialist realism; similarly, Klaus fails to satisfy the general human ideal to be mild to others. *Helden wie wir* sheds a carnivalesque light on historical truth, clearly inspired by Günter Grass's *Die Blechtrommel* (*The Tin Drum*, 1959), but also by Philip Roth's novel *Portnoy's Complaint* (1969).[68]

Of course, the postmodern mode seemed to fit the requirement of writing about the GDR; it was appropriate for the mental stance. Even though German counterhistorical novels had already been canonized before 1989 (Christa Wolf's *Kassandra* – 1983, Hans Joachim Schädlich's *Tallhover* – 1986), postmodern thinking fuelled the aesthetic possibility of looking back in astonishment at the change that occurred in 1989 in the political climate, and the possibility of exploring the contingency of that change. Writers who have defended cultural pluralism and demanded the right to unravel positions from below have thus shown how important the lessons of postmodernism have been.

Brussig's narration *Am kürzeren Ende der Sonnenallee* (1999), an adaptation of his screenplay for the film *Sonnenallee* (1999), is a good example of pop literature and a choice for readability. His mild story about East Berlin teenagers in the 1970s in a street that was bisected by the Wall contains numerous absurd situations from daily life, such as a non-functional multifunctional table or the rituals and dangers of secretly listening to music from the West. The superficiality fits the sitcom elements the tale uses, but also contributes to the readability and lightness. It seemed as if Brussig aimed to reassure the Germans, so that they could face the past without tension. *Sonnenallee* supplied the need for nostalgia. After the rapid and successful unification, many citizens yearned for aspects of the lost world. 'Ostalgie' appeared to be a response to assimilation pressure and the consumer society, although it was commercialized rapidly. The partially cultivated longing for rituals and products of the GDR became well known via the film *Goodbye Lenin* (2003). 'Ostalgie' proved to be a healing concept for former GDR civilians when it was seen as a parody of GDR-socialist ideology.

However, the gunshot that nearly kills a teenager in the novel (he is saved by a record of the Rolling Stones he had just bought illegally) is a reminder of the danger that was part of a happy childhood in the GDR. Brussig concludes that a white veil of nostalgia covers memories, which conceals their sharp outlines.[69] Axiomatically, Brussig alleges: 'When one wishes to capture what happened in the past, one should not succumb to memories.'[70] Published in the midst of a booming memory culture, Brussig implies that people are entitled to their view but should not confuse that with the Grand Narrative. My interpretation does not fit the poppy structure of the tale, but on the other hand, Brussig's empathic concluding lines hardly match the tendency of his story.

In a meditation on (post)modern literature, Moritz Baßler expressed his surprise that text procedures of realism had endured the classical modern literature ('high modernism' some would call it). Only 'in the shape of the fantastic' would there be a 'postmodern return of realism' in German literature.[71] In my view, the case of Brussig's monumental novel *Wie es leuchtet* (2004), which zooms in on life shortly after the fall of the Berlin wall, reveals that Balzacian realism is still possible.[72] However, critics disapproved of the great quantity of characters and thought the 'ponderous' 'waxworks show' lacked a central storyline and depth and was too ambitious, considering it was also partly a *roman à clef*.[73] The conclusion that 'one reads it with pleasure to the end' yet one is not gripped by the novel[74] is a verdict that is the result of an intercultural gap: the incapacity of West German critics to read literature about Germany in the midst of transition from a position that recognized the transitional nature of the critical moment and location. The verdict does not do justice to the human aspects of the characters, nor to the irony or the complexity of 1989/1990. For example, when Brussig presents a young woman who left the GDR, he implicitly raises the question of how a former GDR citizen can be irritated by the confrontation with the throngs of strangers from the East in West Berlin. The attitude of this student of ethnology (!) can be typified as auto-xenophobia.

Before writing *Wie es leuchtet,* Brussig co-wrote the screenplay for the film-epic *Heimat 3* (2004) by Edgar Reitz. It may have been this experience that culminated in the parataxical construction and wide panorama of *Wie es leuchtet.* Clearly, Brussig's aim was to portray a society undergoing change, and the stories he tells are a mix of reportage and the grotesque. The number of stories seemed to kill the potential enthusiasm of critics, who probably identified him as a writer of the burlesque and were disappointed by the realist mode. The question of why this mode was chosen was hardly raised. After *Helden wie wir,* Brussig is less primarily focused on identifying national meta-narratives as constructs and on questioning national assumptions. It is true that his writing has become less postmodern; Brussig's transformation process saw him exchange a wild attitude for a mild postmodern attitude, and develop a tendency toward documentary realism. The composition and scope of *Wie es leuchtet* differ from Ingo Schulze's *Simple Storys* [sic] (1998), which were successful due to the manner in which the protagonists were connected in 29 stories.[75] Schulze was inspired by Robert Altman's seminal film *Short Cuts* (1993). In contrast to Schulze, Brussig opted for long and drawn-out stories, thus indicating the complexity of a turbulent period.

Peter Handke: Between Subjectivity and Relevance

Peter Handke's attack on the older generation of the Gruppe 47 in 1966 was a turning point in literary history. He claimed that it had failed to use the subversive potential of language. As Handke's case demonstrates, some writers partly retired from the postmodern mode at an early stage. His story, *Die Angst des Tormanns beim Elfmeter* (*The Goalie's Anxiety at the Penalty Kick,* 1970), can be regarded as 'the beginning of an attempt to recuperate the realist narrative',[76] after which he became highly introspective. By contrast, Handke's screenplay for Wim Wenders's film *Falsche Bewegung* (*Wrong Move,* 1974) can be viewed as a postmodern text that reframes Johann Wolfgang Goethe's canonical Bildungsroman *Wilhelm Meister.*[77] In the 1970s the non-rationalist phase of New Subjectivity had revealed the need of writers to undertake a quest for identity within a stressful and dogmatic society, to recover from the growing pains of the student movement. This *habitus* of striving for personal authenticity and genuineness is of course revealed in ego-documents that exclude postmodern concepts. Prioritizing indulgence in navel-gazing above carrying on with the project of social liberation might be regarded as regression on the part of those who were close to achieving a changed world order. The poetics of enumeration used by the young generation after unification differs starkly from the slowness of Handke's nostalgic meditation on the aura of the jukebox as an element of early youth culture. His book *Versuch über die Jukebox*, most tellingly, was published in the year of Germany's unification.[78]

On the occasion of the publication of his novel *Die Niemandsbucht* (1994, *My Year in the No-Man's-Bay*), Handke was interviewed by journalists from *Der Spiegel*.[79] Referring to the success of the novel, which seems to be an ode to living in the country, the interviewers interpreted the success as a turning point: 'That could mean that the era in which literature always had to be factual, honest, enlightening or political, is coming to an end.'[80] Handke responded as follows: 'Yes, the situation we are in offers chances. We can really start anew – not postmodern but in the sense of a new modernity. We have the chance to be universal without all these ideologies.'[81] Asked to clarify what he meant, Handke replied: 'Dot, dot, dot'. In answer to the question of what will be different for him regarding the end of the great ideological confrontation, Handke said: 'First, we can be relieved that the communist utopia has fallen apart in this way. Temporarily relieved.'[82] In the interview Handke stresses he never belonged to the protest generation, he claims that at an early stage he was already the stereotype of the enemy of the protest generation.

It should not surprise us that Handke shakes off any ideological stance, as the turn to subjectivity (often accompanied with pathos and mannerism) occurred early. The subtitle of his novel, *Ein Märchen aus den neuen Zeiten* (*A Fairytale From the New Times*), sounds utopian and is almost a claim to post-postmodernity. Furthermore, it recalls the subtitle of E.T.H. Hoffmann's *Der goldne Topf* (1814): *Ein Märchen aus der neuen Zeit*. In fact, Handke evokes a world in the near future of 1997 in which a civil war is taking place in Germany. This reference is eerie, not least because Handke expected that a civil war could help to balance Germany, but also because in the second half of the 1990s, Handke was heavily criticized for defending the position of Serbia in the civil war.[83] Because he did not represent German positions of cultural identity, Handke's *engagement* was not supported.

The 'authentic decade' came to an end in 1980, when self-referentiality had also become a standard in German literature. A case in point is that Lionel Trilling's lectures *Sincerity and Authenticity* (1972) were published in German in 1980 under the title 'The End of Sincerity'.[84] Of course, expectations and demands were high when history altered its course, and readers began to long for literature that was in step with the times.

Robert Menasse: A Playful Synthesis of Realism

The works of the Jewish-Austrian writer Robert Menasse often challenge Austrian society. Nevertheless, Menasse, who is known for his erudite playfulness and ironic wit, is clearly a writer of import in the German literary field as well. A brief inspection of his work might help to put into perspective the idea that German literature has radically abandoned dominant narrative positions. In his essays as well as in his novels, Menasse seems to strategically use postmodern aesthetic modes to dissociate himself from postmodernity.[85] Most evident is his entertaining way of reshuffling both Hegel's vocabulary and philosophy in the *Trilogy of the Breakdown of Spirit* (*Trilogie der Entgeisterung*, an allusion to *Phenomenology of Spirit*), which culminated in the essay *Phänomenologie der Entgeisterung*. He wrote this appendix to the trilogy for the protagonist Leo Singer in part two, *Selige Zeiten, brüchige Welt* (1991). Singer is a man who reads Hegel to pieces and bears a most striking resemblance to Georg Lukács. Literature thus becomes reality as the book that could have been written by Singer now exists. Singer has to acknowledge that striving for totality and the absolute, as Hegel did, has become impossible. Menasse points out in the preface to *Phänomenologie der Entgeisterung* that the continuation of Hegel's work entails a trajectory from 'absolute knowledge to the modern [!] disparate "anything goes" (= a formal democratic euphemism for its truth: "nothing comes")', which is a history of disappearing knowledge.[86] Before, in 1990, Menasse had nominated postmodern consciousness in the sense of 'posthistoire';[87] in his Hegel-transformation he points out that reality is a 'varnish of unity' and that 'history – and the future too – has come to an end. Design prescribes consciousness'.[88] In Menasse's view, the shortcoming of postmodern literature is that it does not seem to care about 'meaning' and 'synthesis' in spite of all the quotations, paraphrases and eclecticism.[89] When Menasse integrates texts by Gustave Flaubert, Gottfried Keller and Laurence Sterne, as well as Grimm's fairytale 'Hans in Luck' into *Selige Zeiten, brüchige Welt*, the intertextual playfulness gains some depth through the poetological reflections that carry the trilogy. And when he restages the goalie Bloch from Handke's story *The Goalie's Anxiety at the Penalty Kick*, he mixes the philosophers Bloch, Hegel and Karl May.[90]

It is important that Menasse explicitly defends Lukács as having been misunderstood, and that he not only strives for detailed realism or photorealism, but also for what I would call filtered realism: literature in which ideas and impressions are interpreted. Time and again Menasse has stressed his attachment to the idea of realism in the tradition of Lukács, which also means that he aims to be socially relevant for his contemporaries.[91] This combination of realism with postmodern aesthetics can be found in his latest works.

Menasse's predilection for catchy titles emerges from his shrewd 'lectures on the critique of delightenment' ('Abklärung' in opposition to 'Aufklärung').[92] His stories 'from the end of postwar order' (*Ich kann jeder sagen. Erzählungen vom Ende der Nachkriegsordnung*, 2009) deliberately carry a pompous subtitle that also marks Menasse's preoccupation with discussions on modernity. In contrast to this, the title insists on the autonomy of the self that is always related to the collective. The first story (title: 'Beginnen') repeats the problem of telling a story by beginning anew repeatedly. The first-person narrator interrupts his story 'Romantische Irrtümer' by revising what has been said and disclosing that an answer had not been given. Menasse's final story 'Schluss machen' satirizes literary criticism and speaks of the over-appreciation of first sentences in novels.[93] These examples should suffice to illustrate that Menasse is a child of postmodern writing.

The title of his entertaining novel *Don Juan de la Mancha* (2007) stresses the amalgamation of two founding figures of European culture (Don Juan and Don Quichote)[94] This is a warning to the reader, who on the first page will be confronted with a protagonist suffering from the invitation to have anal sex after his penis has had chili pepper rubbed into it. Is this tasteless, merely a provocation, or a satire on the pornification of people's love lives? Nathan, the protagonist, tells his psychologist about his love life. A portrait emerges of a generation in times of sexual liberation. What interests me here are the explicit narratological markers. Menasse stresses in this novel that jokes are being told: all of Nathan's mother's suitors die shortly after their last visit, Nathan's divorced parents die almost at the same time, an editor's name resembles the name of an Austrian soccer player, Nathan takes an extended bath in artificial amniotic fluid, and at first he refuses to talk about his wife so instead claims that she died.[95] This playfulness as well as the quest for purification seem to be a mixture of a postmodern attitude and an effort to obtain epistemological clarity.

His novel *Die Vertreibung aus der Hölle* (2001, *Expulsion from Hell*) also reveals the joy of storytelling. Menasse counterpoints and mirrors two storylines, those of the life stories of Samuel Manasseh ben Israel and of Viktor Avranel, the latter of whom is preparing for a lecture on the teacher of Spinoza.[96] By means of historiographic meta-fiction, Menasse juxtaposes the persecution of the Jews in the seventeenth century and the aftermath of the Holocaust in the 1970s. Avranel shocks his former classmates and teachers at a reunion by uncovering the Nazi background of the teachers. Although it is a malicious practical joke (Avranel's funniness is repeatedly stressed), his announcement works, and the reunion ends. Also here, by foregrounding contingency, Menasse plays with the postmodern frame and oscillates between traditions.

In the novel *Sinnliche Gewißheit* (1988), Menasse had speculated that today, one could write 'at best a Rückentwicklungsroman': 'a reversed Entwicklungsroman'.[97] The iconographic image of Walter Benjamin's angel of history is reversed in the novel when it faces the future.[98] At the centre of the Frankfurt School, Menasse's 2005 lectures, *Die Zerstörung der Welt als Wille und Vorstellung*, provocatively engaged in discussions about social reality and claimed that the 'project of modernity has become history'; that the traditional idea of 'engagement' has become obsolete, as has been shown in 'postfascist modernity'; that after 9/11 (2001) the only message can be that the individual is the 'creator of life reality'; only the individual can be socially relevant and change the world order; that novelists can only repeatedly tell their 'Rückentwicklungsromans' anew if they are to be 'socially necessary'.[99] Maybe it is in this sense that Menasse's novels should be understood, as well as his remark in his essay about 'the country without qualities', which claimed that Austrians had failed to acknowledge the relevance to Austrian society of Christoph Ransmayr's meta-historical novel *Die letzte Welt* (1988).[100]

Conclusion

Very soon after unification, a debate on realism aroused attention. The fact that light tones and humor had become elements of German literature and that pop literature had become part of the establishment had been noticed. Several novels, some of which have been mentioned here, arrived in postmodern shape after the debate about postmodern issues seemed to have come to an end.[101] Postmodern modes are not dominant today, unless in an adapted and mutated form. These modes proved to be fruitful for dealing with entities other generations had explored and also fitted the refresher course writers from the former GDR took when dealing with the past. In recent German literature, different postmodern patterns can be found, ranging from an ethical twist to a means of counterhistory. Global issues have been addressed in literature, issues of cultural identity are being reframed, and trends toward being authentic or even relevant have become visible. The renaissance of readability reinforced the basics of storytelling, but it also countered more complex narrative structures, whereas several highly readable novels do not avoid complexity. It is delusional to think that proportions of postmodern writing within the German literary field are quantifiable. The ethical attitude seems to be dominant, much of it originating in German traditions. In addition to this, a noncommittal attitude can be observed in the trend of pop literature that has its genesis in postmodern discussions of bridging the gap between high and low culture.

Part II
The Transatlantic Connection

Chapter 11
Spanish and Spanish American Literature

Memory, Evil and the Rhetorics of Authenticity

Brigitte Adriaensen & Maarten Steenmeijer

Introduction

No other writer from the Spanish-speaking world has been more closely identified with postmodernism than Jorge Luis Borges. We will begin this article by taking a closer look at the received idea of Borges as a postmodern master *pur sang* – an author who exposed language's referential capacity to represent reality as illusory – and by showing that another Borges can be appreciated in the contemporary critical discourse: a writer whose epistemological ideas of language and literature do not exclude political and historical dimensions. Subsequently, we will focus on two writers whose latest novels have been acclaimed by the international press as the most innovative literary projects from the Spanish-speaking world in the new century. The first one is *Your Face Tomorrow* (2002, 2004, 2007; English translation: *Your Face Tomorrow*, 2005, 2006, 2009) by Javier Marías (Spain, 1951), which 'may very well be the first authentic literary masterpiece of the 21st century'.[1] The second one is *2666* (2004; English translation: *2666*, 2008) by Roberto Bolaño (Chili, 1953-2003), who has 'posthumously risen [...] to the summit of modern fiction'[2]. How does Marías's work and that of Bolaño relate to (late) postmodernism? That is the main question we will try to answer in the other two parts of this article.

Borges and Postmodern Fiction

'I am an invention of Roger Caillois'.[3] With this witty remark, Jorge Luis Borges (1899-1986) referred to the far-reaching consequences of the French intellectual, writer and translator's successful efforts to introduce the Argentine writer's work in France. During the World War II period, Caillois had found refuge in Buenos Aires, where he became acquainted with Borges. Back in France, he founded La Croix du Sud, a pioneering series of Latin American literature published by Gallimard. The first volume was *Fictions*, the French version of the short story volume *Ficciones* (1944), published in 1951. With *Fictions*, Borges was introduced 'au grand public' in France,[4] and very soon, the literary elite came to appreciate him as a highly original writer. From France, the news spread gradually to other central parts of the world republic of letters (Italy, Germany, the United States) and, from there, to other countries. In each of them, Borges was introduced through vernacular versions of *Ficciones*.

Before he was introduced in France, Borges had been highly appreciated in certain literary circles of Argentina (especially by the writers and intellectuals associated with the important cosmopolitan cultural review *Sur*). However, in the 1950s his presumed elitism made him a polemical figure in other literary circles, dominated by the Sartrian dogma of political *engagement*.[5] In the preceding decades Borges had profiled himself as the writer of a wide variety of genres and styles. Starting off around 1920 as a radical avant-garde writer, he soon turned to a mythical kind of locally oriented poetry (*criollismo*). In the 1930s Borges had not yet fulfilled the expectations he had raised as a promising young and gifted author, and had to make a living by writing hundreds of articles and reviews for the women's magazine *El Hogar* and other periodicals. It was only at the end of this decade, after a nearly fatal accident, that he had the idea of writing the stories of *Ficciones*.

It was this writer – this 'invention of Roger Caillois', that is to say, the 'European' Borges – who would make history as the patriarch of postmodernism and, as such, would become one of the most, if not the most, important innovative and influential writer of the second half of the twentieth century. In the words of Douwe Fokkema:

> *It can be argued that Postmodernism is the first literary code that originated in America and influenced European literature, with the possibility that the writer who contributed more than anyone else to the invention and acceptance of the new code is Jorge Luis Borges.*[6]

In 1967, when the literary-critical concept of postmodernism was not yet *en vogue*, John Barth had already published a pivotal essay written out of admiration for Jorge Luis Borges, whom he hailed as the pioneering writer of 'the literature of exhaustion' or, as Barth later preferred to call it for reasons of clarity, 'the literature of replenishment'. This new, groundbreaking literature confronted the exhaustion of high modernism and, employing it against itself, created a new, vital literature that came to be known as postmodernist.

Ficciones, then, forged the dominant idea of Borges in the Western world: a writer who mocked the established philosophical, religious, scientific and literary concepts and theories of reality and human existence, revealing them to be mere fictions or text. A writer who, not surprisingly, was hardly read as an Argentine writer but embraced as a European or universal writer who paved the way for the non-referential phase of postmodernism in which texts hardly allow meaning beyond themselves:

> *The stories in* Ficciones *[...] are extraordinary game systems in which philosophies, cosmologies, our various* Weltbilder, *are unmasked as rule-bound constructs of the fantastic, which is to say, playing mind. And fantasies are shown to function as systematic constructs springing from the play impulse toward order. The creation of systems that order a world is a gratuitous form of play, and, as such, all are equally worthy of interest. Or, conversely, as the narrator of 'Pierre Menard, Author of the* Quijote,*'*

> *somewhat cynically notes, there is no exercise of the intellect which is not, in the final analysis, useless.*[7]

This understanding of Borges as a postmodern author might be associated with the second current of postmodernism, which holds that 'ultimately language is doomed to self-reflexivity and that because it cannot reflect the world, language paradoxically must constitute whatever we take to be reality'.[8] As we pointed out, such a postmodern reading and celebration of Borges contrasts with the polemics his work had raised in Argentina, where writers in the vein of French existentialism found his lack of political *engagement* problematic. The importance of a political dimension in literature and the resistance against a kind of playful, gratuitous and non-referential postmodernist literature were considerable in most Latin-American countries where dictatorships were in power and *engagement* was a matter of life and death in the 1960s, 1970s and 1980s. This explains why the European interpretation of Borges and the second current of postmodernism hardly took root among Latin American scholars.

Not surprisingly, then, the third current of postmodernism, which according to Hans Bertens appeared in the 1980s and stressed the power conflicts involved in representation, could count on a much warmer welcome. Although the implications of importing a concept like 'postmodernism' into Latin America gave way to heated debates[9] since some critics saw its Western provenance as a new move of intellectual imperialism, the postmodern readings of Foucault's theories fitted perfectly into the ongoing debates in Latin America, focusing on the idea that

> *in the absence of representation it matters more than ever who has authored, or who controls, any given representation. If representations do not represent the world, they must represent something else, and in so doing they will inevitably be political, always emerging within a time- and place-bound ideological framework. The emphasis, in other words, is on power.*[10]

From the 1990s on, the political dimension of his work and its historical embedding were increasingly acknowledged by prestigious critics like Beatriz Sarlo or Daniel Balderston.[11] Not only the connection of his work with the specific Argentine political, historical and cultural context was stressed more often, also from a postcolonial perspective Borges began to be acclaimed, due to 'El escritor argentino y la tradición' ('The Argentine Writer and Tradition'). In this lecture, which was given in the early 1950s and would become one of his classic essays, Borges had proposed a strategy for peripheral writers in words that turned out to sum up the spirit of what came to be known as postmodernism:

'I believe that we Argentines, we South Americans in general (...), can handle all European themes, handle them without superstition, with an irreverence which can have, and already does have, fortunate consequences.'[12] In short, Borges was acclaimed as an author from the margins who wrote against the grain, that is, against the literary norms imposed by the hegemonic centre.[13]

In conclusion, the conception of Borges as a cosmopolitan and apolitical, intellectual writer – still en vogue in European literary circles – has been questioned by the idea of Borges as a writer aware of his discursive position in the margins of the world republic of letters. The tension between both interpretations reflects the evolution that took place between the second and the third current of postmodernism as defined by Hans Bertens.

In recent discussions on postmodernism, however, this twofold discussion on literature as an ironic, playful and disengaged medium on the one hand, and as a discursive tool with a political and ideological dimension on the other, has been rendered even more complex by the introduction of a new dimension, the so-called rhetorics of sincerity. This entails another turn in fiction that has been advanced by Ernst van Alphen and Mieke Bal as a salient aspect of the latest current in postmodernism: 'In the larger public-cultural field, one can also think of all of the denunciations of 'postmodern irony' that have marked public discourse (at least in the West) over the past two decades, denunciations that tend to valorize the authentic and the sincere over political intelligence and rhetorical sophistication.'[14] In other words, the rhetorics of sincerity denounce overtly postmodern irony and valorize authenticity as the supreme expression of the self. As Ernst van Alphen and Mieke Bal suggest, this new turn might be thought of as an essentially Occidental phenomenon.[15]

The following sections will show how the œuvres of Javier Marías and Roberto Bolaño take up the rhetorics of sincerity in very different ways. The next section situates Marías's prose in the historical context of Spanish literature and postmodernism. Subsequently, it is argued that in his latest novels, Marías sets literature apart as an authentic medium of knowledge and memory. In the last section, the similarities and differences between Bolaño's and Borges's conceptions of literary discourse and its relation with evil will be discussed in the light of postmodernism. Much more than Borges's short stories, Bolaño's novels engage explicitly with the political and historical context of the twentieth century, especially with the memory of violent practices during the Chilean dictatorship. Although the focus on the relationship between literature and memory might suggest a strong parallelism with Javier Marías's work, in Bolaño's fiction the use of irony insistently underlines the idea that authentic and sincere discourses in literature are, in fact, rhetorical constructions.

Javier Marías and the Strange Power of Fiction

Javier Marías belongs to a generation that was born and raised during the dictatorship of General Franco after the victory of the Nationalists that had decided the Spanish Civil War (1936-1939). Franco was very eager to represent his struggle for power as a crusade, propagating nationalism, patriotism and Catholicism as the pillars of 'true Spain', which he liked to label as 'the spiritual bastion of the Western World'. Despising communism and freemasonry above all, in fact he execrated everything that he considered to be in conflict with his very rigid notion of Spain. Franco's biased, authoritarian and anachronistic ideas and values and, more importantly, his insistence on identification of these particular ideas with the concept of Spain had an enormous impact on Marías's generation. They came to associate everything Spanish with repression and backwardness, including Spanish literature and, in particular, the social critical novel that dominated the literary system in the 1950s and 1960s. In spite of being very critical of the Franco regime, this kind of literature was nevertheless looked down upon as simple, obsolete, rigid; that is, vintage Spanish.

The reverse of this anti-Spanish attitude was an enormous curiosity and a very high esteem for cultural productions from abroad. Modernity – democracy, freedom, cosmopolitism, creativity – was to be found on the other side of the Pyrenees (Western Europe) and on the other side of the ocean (in the United States and, as far as creativity was concerned, in Spanish America). Bridges, therefore, were in great demand. In this respect, the activities of publisher Carlos Barral can hardly be overestimated. In the early 1960s he successfully tried to place/restore the Spanish literary system in an international context, creating a network of publishers during the legendary Formentor meetings, named after the peninsula on the north-eastern tip of Mallorca and the legendary hotel with the same name where they took place. Prominent publishers, literary critics and writers from all over the world gathered in Hotel Formentor to discuss literature and business, making plans for joint projects such as international prizes and publications.

Barral's literary sensibility matched his business instinct and his ambitions. This combination was essential for the success of his efforts to introduce la nueva novela hispanoamericana (the new Spanish-American novel) onto the Spanish market. The Spanish-American catalogue initiated by Barral for publishing house Seix Barral played a decisive role in enabling the famous *boom* of the 1960s and 1970s that put Spanish-American literature on the map. The activities of literary agent Carmen Balcells, nicknamed the 'Mamá Grande' of the boom, were equally groundbreaking.

Barral and Balcells were pioneers in creating a high-quality literary infrastructure that turned Barcelona into the literary capital of the Spanish-speaking world in the 1960s.[16] The Spanish-American literature benefited greatly from these developments. Barcelona became the gateway to the international success, recognition and prestige of the new Spanish-American novel. Shifting from modernism to postmodernism,[17] the authors of the *nueva novela* would make history with novels like Carlos Fuentes's *La muerte de Artemio Cruz* (1962, English translation 1964: *The Death of Artemio Cruz*), Julio Cortázar's *Rayuela* (1963, English translation 1966: *Hopscotch*) and Gabriel García Márquez's *Cien años de soledad* (1967, English translation 1970: *One Hundred Years of Solitude*), which have been analyzed and canonized in pivotal studies of postmodernism in literature such as Allen Thiher's *Words in Reflection* (1984), Brian McHale's *Postmodernist Fiction* (1987) and Linda Hutcheon's *A Poetics of Postmodernism* (1988). As can be deduced from the varied theoretical and thematic perspectives of these studies – modern language theories, ontological issues and historiographic metafiction, respectively – the *nueva novela* offered an exceptionally rich and original set of signifying potentialities.

The discovery of the *nueva novela hispanoamericana* was a revelation for Spanish writers which was as frustrating as it was stimulating, although it should be added that Luis Martín-Santos's iconoclastic novel *Tiempo de silencio* (1961, English translation 1964: *Time of Silence*) also played a decisive role. Reading South American writers like Julio Cortázar, Mario Vargas Llosa, García Márquez, Guillermo Cabrera Infante and – the acknowledged master of all of these writers[18] –Jorge Luis Borges, leading Spanish authors like Juan Goytisolo realised how poor their own literature was at that time and that writing from the periphery was not incompatible with generating an innovative, vital vein of postmodernist literature that could conquer a strong position in the centre of the world republic of letters. Couldn't and shouldn't this be done in Spain as well? Wasn't it time for the new Spanish novel?

Indeed, in the early 1970s publishing houses Planeta and Barral launched *la nueva novela española*. However, it soon became clear that the attempt to compete with *la nueva novela hispanoamericana* was an embarrassing fiasco. Spanish writers tended to demean themselves by producing poor emulations of prestigious Spanish American novels or to lose themselves in sterile linguistic experiments. Be that as it may, with *la nueva novela española* postmodernism definitely took root in Spanish narrative prose,[19] though this was only acknowledged from the 1980s on, when postmodernism was accepted as a serious critical concept[20] after the connotation of being alien and frivolous had been shaken off.[21]

In this insecure climate of frustration, curiosity and ambition, Javier Marías cut his literary teeth and wrote his first novels. Except for the language in which they were written, they had nothing to do with Spain. This was

Marías's radical way of making it clear that he did not want to be a Spanish writer like Miguel Delibes or Camilo José Cela, and that, as Carlos Barral remarked at the presentation of Marías's debut novel *Los dominios del lobo* [1971, The Dominions of the Wolf], he wanted to *desprovincianizar* (deregionalize) Spanish literature. Marías's techniques and devices could be categorized as playful postmodernist and bring to mind Borges's fictional recounting of the lives of legendary criminals in *Historia universal de la infamia* (1935, English translation 1972: *A Universal History of Infamy*).[22] Marías's intentions, though, transcended the frivolous. On the basis of the 85 American movies of the 1930s, 1940s, and 1950s that the young Marías had seen in Paris in the summer of 1969, he wrote these 'wittily recounted and entertaining tales of gangster rivalry, femmes fatales, racketeering, corruption, double-crossing, blackmail and murder, prisoners and hidden treasures, greed and sex, and friendship and love'.[23] In *Travesía del horizonte* [Crossing of the Horizon, 1973], his second novel, the setting, characters and models (exclusively literary in this case) were also all foreign.

More than once, Marías has characterized his first novels (as well as the ambitious translations he made in these years) as exercises, as a literary training, as a way to find his literary voice and to tune and refine it. In fact, it was only after he had published *Todas las almas* (1989, English translation 1992: *All Souls*), his sixth novel, that Marías felt that he had found this 'true' voice. And indeed, all the following novels are first-person narratives that share a very similar tone and style.

The 'mature' novels of Javier Marías are full of passages dominated by narratological and rhetorical techniques and devices that are at the core of 'high' postmodernism. Problematizing or obscuring the ontological boundary between reality and fiction is, perhaps, the most obvious one. A paradigmatic case in point would be the indefinite status of the narrator of *Negra espalda del tiempo* (1998, English translation 2001: *Dark Back of Time*). Similar to what Borges did in his pivotal text 'Borges and I', Marías makes it almost impossible to determine the ontological status of the narrator. Actually, *Negra espalda del tiempo*'s narrator has the same name as the author, but even if all that he says about himself and his family is true (which seems to be the case), it would be impossible to consider the two of them identical, if only for the indeterminacy of the 'genre' in which the author framed this text by labelling it a 'false novel'. To make matters even more complicated, the narrator of *Todas las almas* (the novel that generated, so to speak, *Negra espalda del tiempo*, which elaborates on the ontological confusion in the real world and, in particular, in the writer's life, generated by the episodes and characters of *Todas las almas*) has been identified with the author, although Marías himself has not ceased to insist on the sovereignty of the novel's voice, underlining the differences between his character and himself.

Caricature, farce and parody are other prominent examples of postmodernist strategies in Marías's novels. An evident case is the detailed and often hilarious representation of official (Spanish) authorities, such as 'el Único' (the One and Only) in *Mañana en la batalla piensa en mí* (1994, English translation 1996: *Tomorrow in the Battle Think on Me*) (allegedly, King Juan Carlos of Spain), dictator Franco in *Negra espalda del tiempo* and diplomat Rafael de la Garza in *Tu rostro mañana*.

It would, however, be reductive to label Javier Marías as a postmodernist author solely on the basis of these kinds of prototypical postmodernist techniques, as Karen Berg did in *Javier Marías's Postmodern Praxis. Humor and Interplay between Reality and Fiction in His Novels and Essays* (2008). In our opinion, it is more fruitful to focus on what we see as the most salient and idiosyncratic element of Marías's novels: the first-person voices that monopolize its discourse. What they have in common is their tireless attempts to penetrate reality, to try to understand human existence and behaviour, scrutinizing and interpreting the smallest details exhaustively, and to express a particular kind of 'estar en el mundo' (being in the world). Marías's narrators channel and elaborate on their perceptions and impressions in arguments that digress and fork in the form of suspicions, suppositions, conjectures, inquiries, deductions, calibrations or speculations that emphasize one of the most pertinent and repeated affirmations in *Tu rostro mañana*, Marías's latest, most voluminous and most ambitious novel: 'life is not recountable'.[24] This speculative attitude goes hand in hand with a hyper-conscience of the narrator's own mental activities and the concomitant epistemological processes. Seen from this perspective, Marías's novels seem to be closely related to modernist fiction, which, in Brian McHale's definition,

> *deploys strategies which engage and foreground questions such as (...):*
> *'How can I interpret this world of which I am a part? And what am I in it?' Other typical modernist questions might be added: What is there to be known?; Who knows it?; How do they know it, and with what degree of certainty?; How is knowledge transmitted from one knower to another, and with what degree of reliability?; How does the object of knowledge change as it passes from knower to knower?; What are the limits of the knowable? And so on.*[25]

Paradoxically, though, the tentative spirit that is so essential in Marías's discourse doesn't exclude an apodictic tone, abounding in categorical affirmations such as 'no one ever seems to have enough of anything, no one is ever contented, no one ever stops'[26] and 'everything is always being usurped, always becoming more imprecise, more oblique and fictitious and often incomprehensible, words and customs and reactions'.[27] And paradoxically, this apodictic style undermines itself with categorical affirmations that express a deep scepticism towards language, which is more akin to postmodernism than to modernism, such as 'language can't reproduce events and shouldn't attempt to'[28] and 'almost all our phrases are in fact metaphorical, language is only an approximation, an attempt, a detour'.[29]

Language deforms the facts of life and manipulates human behaviour. Language betrays us, and it betrays reality. Why, then, say anything? Why recount? Why write a novel over fifteen hundred pages long like *Tu rostro mañana* if its narrator ominously starts off telling himself (and us) that 'one should never tell anyone anything'?[30] In the case of *Todas las almas, Corazón tan blanco* (1992, English translation 1995: *A Heart So White*) and *Mañana en la batalla piensa en mí* the answer combines a deterministic dimension with a personal one: for unreliable, manipulating and threatening as it is, language imposes itself on the narrators. Whether they like it or not, they need language to cope with reality, to make some sense of the world and, in particular, of the past.

In *Negra espalda del tiempo* and especially in *Tu rostro mañana* these dimensions are accompanied by important social, historical and ethical dimensions that link Marías's novels with the cardinal memory debate that impressively entered Spain's public arena in the course of the last decade. Civilians came to defy *el pacto del olvido* (the pact of silence), successfully propagated during and after the *Transición*, the period around Franco's death when Spain became a democracy without bloodshed thanks to arduous but, in the end, fruitful negotiations between moderate representatives of the Franco regime and left-wing bigwigs. Many Spaniards defended the human need and the moral obligation to remember the recent past (Civil War, dictatorship, *Transición*), to honour the victims decried by Franco and ignored during the first decades of democracy, and to cope with the traces of trauma in contemporary society. Literature played a pioneering role in stimulating and sophisticating this debate. A celebrated case in point is *Soldados de Salamina* (2001, English translation 2003: *Soldiers of Salamis*), Javier Cercas's immensely successful novel which not only rehabilitated an anonymous republican soldier buried in oblivion but also the leading fascist politician and writer Rafael Sánchez Mazas. Another conspicuous element of *Soldados de Salamina* is that it foregrounds literature as a privileged medium to cope with the past. This is also the case with *Tu rostro mañana*, as we shall see in more detail below. But unlike Cercas, Marías does not aim at the reconciliation of adversaries. A striking example of his position is the ferocious way he denounces the two men who, in the aftermath of the Spanish Civil War, falsely accused Marías's father (the prominent philosopher Julián Marías) of collaborating with the Russian communist regime. He was sentenced to death, a verdict that was eventually changed into imprisonment and a ban from teaching in Spain.

Juan Deza, the literary replica of Julián Marías in *Tu rostro mañana*, is not eager to articulate this traumatic episode of his life. He does, however, pass some dreadful stories from the Civil War period on to his son. A similar mediating role is played by Peter Wheeler, a character very closely based on Peter Russell, the eminent Hispanist and Lusitanist who Javier Marías befriended during his teaching years in Oxford. Wheeler is Jaime Deza's other 'father of memory', so to speak, who conveys stories about World War II and who suggests that Jaime – an 'interpreter of life', who is able to 'see' how people will act in uncommon situations – should work for the British Secret Service. There he meets Bertram Tupra, who becomes his third father or master and who, unlike Juan Deza and Peter Wheeler, turns out to be a very violent man and, significantly, does not talk about his past.

Tupra, on the one hand, confronts Jaime Deza with real and present violence and, in the end, with the real, present and unexpected violence within himself; Juan Deza and Peter Wheeler, on the other, pass the *memory* of violence on to him, making him the heir of recollections that are both individual (they concern specific people) and collective (Spanish Civil War; World War II). If not redeeming, in *Tu rostro mañana* memory, apart from being an existential need, has become a moral duty. But why should literature be privileged as a medium for memory? In *Sobre la dificultad de contar* (2008, *About the Difficulty of Telling*), the speech Marías held on the occasion of his entrance into the Real Academia Española, the Spanish writer brings up various factors that explain the 'strange power' of fiction. The most evident one is that fiction gives people the opportunity to identify with other lives or to get an idea of the lives they wanted to live but could not or did not dare to. More importantly in our case, Marías emphasizes the longevity of fictional characters, as will perhaps (or perhaps not, as Marías ironically adds) be the case with the literary replica of his father in *Tu rostro mañana*. The third point made by Marías is that what is told in fiction is fixed forever and ever, and cannot and will not be told in any other way:

> (...) in spite of the absurdity of his labour (...), the inventing novelist is the only one authorized to tell completely, in contrast with (...) chroniclers, historians, biographers, autobiographers, memorialists, diary writers, witnesses and other skilled narrators doomed to fail. Sometimes we need to

> know something entirely, to fix it in memory without the risk of rectification. We need something sometimes to be told from beginning to end and irreversibly (...). Without possible corrections nor additions nor suppressions nor refutations nor emendations.³¹

Marías's high esteem of literature as a superb medium of knowledge and memory is similar to Borges's understanding of literature. Through Borges's paradigmatic scepticism and irony with respect to our ways of knowing (or trying to know) the world and our existence shine a serene longing for or even belief in a transcendental world of archetypes, of everlasting presences, of characters and episodes that repeat themselves eternally. Language, then, does not necessarily alienate us from reality. Language can, in the case of literature (and, in particular, in the case of poetry), connect us with a reality that transcends our time and place.³² As Borges wrote in the prologue to *El otro, el mismo* (1964, *The Self and the Other*), the book of poetry he loved the most, in poetry we are made of time, which is our substance, and time is something we can share.³³ As we have seen, even a founding postmodernist like Borges did not exclude relationships between language and reality. It is important to stress, however, that Marías's late-postmodernist reality is more concrete and explicit.

It is tempting to link Borges's idea of (literary) time with the time referred to by the late Juan Benet (the only Spanish writer of the post war period repeatedly recognized as a mentor by Marías) in a quote that pops up in *Negra espalda del tiempo* and that is insistently repeated in *Tu rostro mañana*: '(...) it seems to me that time is the only dimension in which the living and the dead can talk to each other and communicate, the only dimension they have in common'.³⁴ In fact, literary discourse is privileged as a tool and medium of memory. Literature makes memory possible or, even more so, enables us to connect with the past and the deceased, an idea that is presented as ontologically authentic and morally exemplary. In this respect, Marías's fiction is a far cry from postmodernist irony.

Roberto Bolaño and the Universal History of Evil

In contrast to Javier Marías, who ended up in his hometown Madrid after prolonged stays in Venice and the UK, Roberto Bolaño left Chile at the age of 15 and would only sporadically return to his home country. In 1968 his parents took him to Mexico, where he attended high school for one year and then decided he had better things to do. From that moment on, he would combine writing with all kinds of small jobs that would provide him with a living – at times with extreme difficulty. In August 1973, charmed and fascinated by Allende's socialist regime, Bolaño returned to Chile, only to be surprised one month later by the military coup of Pinochet. After spending eight days in jail, he went back to Mexico in January 1974. In 1977 he left the Latin American continent and headed for Europe. He finally settled in Blanes, on the outskirts of Barcelona, where he remained until his death in 2003.

In a certain sense, the migrating lifestyle of Bolaño is reflected in his novels, which alternately take place in Chile, Mexico, Spain and other European countries. For instance, three of his early novels, by some critics considered a trilogy – *Estrella distante* (1996, English translation: *Distant Star*, 2004), *La literatura nazi en América* (1996, English translation: *Nazi Literature in the Americas*, 2008) and *Nocturno de Chile* (2000, English translation: *By Night in Chile*, 2003) – are closely related to the experience of evil and the position of artists during the Cono Sur dictatorships, the Chilean in particular. On the other hand, novels like *Los detectives salvajes* (1998, English translation *The Savage Detectives*, 2007) or *Amuleto* (1999, English translation: *Amulet*, 2006) are protagonized by fragments of Mexican history, such as the famous massacre at Tlatelolco in 1968. Bolaño's last novel, *2666*, has been designated a 'planetarian novel'[35] since Russian, European, Mexican and Chilean history appear alternately, while its characters – most of them literary critics, writers or journalists – turn out to be as nomadic as the author himself.

Each of these novels, and the same might be said about Bolaño's short stories and poetry, engages in a continuous dialogue with the various literary traditions in which the characters are placed. Not only is Bolaño's œuvre marked by a very intense intertextual dialogue with the work of Borges, Cortázar, Nicanor Parra, Enrique Lihn, Kafka, Enrique Vila-Matas and many other authors, it also continuously reflects – often in a very ironic and sometimes even cynical way – on the position of art in relation to its particular political and historical context.

Therefore, it is very difficult to pin Bolaño down to one single nationality or national literature. Unlike Borges, who also had a nomadic youth but always considered himself an Argentine, Bolaño never kept a very intense or nostalgic bond with Chile. As his fellow writer Juan Villoro recalls: 'He wouldn't stand for even the mildest criticism of Mexico (the last word he wrote, the word that concludes the novel *2666*, was precisely '*México*'), any more than he would tolerate a good word about Chile'.[36] Bolaño preferred his condition as a Latin American or transatlantic writer,[37] and refused systematically the label of 'exiled author', arguing that '[f]or the real writer, his only homeland is his library, a library that might be located in bookshelves or in his memory'.[38]

Despite this difference in attitude, the priority given to literature as the real homeland of the author evidently brings to mind Borgesian poetics, where fiction always stands in a privileged position compared to the ungraspable, and often even boring, reality. One might say that the problematic relationship between literature, or art in general, and reality is a key issue in both Borges's and Bolaño's work, which is also proper to postmodernism. The former's opposition to realism is well known: his stories stress the necessarily mediated nature of all our knowledge. Intertextuality, pastiche and irony are frequently used as strategies to underscore the inaccessibility of reality. The same might be said about Bolaño, who consistently plays with the confusing boundaries between literature and reality by placing mostly fictitious artistic characters at the centre of his stories and making them comment assiduously on the potentials and limits of art. Moreover, the philosophical and ethical issues lying at the core of their narratives are often approached through a playful perspective. In Bolaño's case, however, the game is less innocent than in Borges's stories: the constant reflections on evil and the representation of evil in art give the irony and laughter that resound in Bolaño's novels a sinister and cruel echo, which makes them rather different from Borges's sometimes perturbing but never horrifying stories.

Although Bolaño affirmed the importance of Borges to all of his work on various occasions,[39] this influence is most obvious in one of his early books, *La literatura nazi en América* (1996). Following in the footsteps of the Borges of *Historia universal de la infamia* (1935), Bolaño gives us a short overview of the life and works of a series of imagined characters that are all related to the concept of 'infamy', the abject or the horrible. The idea of a fictitious biography continuously blurs the distinction between reality and fiction in a postmodernist way, leaving the reader in doubt about the historical background of what is exposed. In *Historia universal de la infamia,* Borges followed the example of Marcel Schwob's *Vies imaginaires* (1896). He defined his labour in the prologue of the 1954 edition: '[These stories] are the irresponsible game of a shy young man who dared not write stories and so amused himself by falsifying and distorting (without any aesthetic justification whatever) the tales of others.'[40] The amusing volume includes the story of various murderers, slave dealers, pirates and swindlers from remote centuries and countries who systematically make use of violence in order to obtain more economic benefits or power.

In a similar way, Bolaño invents the lives of thirty different characters, subdivided into different categories like 'Itinerant Heroes or the Fragility of Mirrors' or 'Magicians, Mercenaries and Miserable Creatures', although there are some remarkable differences. In the first place, all of them are writers, and not ordinary bandits or criminals like in Borges's case. Secondly, these writers are not cruel in a direct way, in the sense that most of them did not commit violent acts themselves. Instead, they are all implicated in Nazi or fascist ideology through their artistic activities. Bolaño describes their affinity with Hitler's regime (like the poetess Luz Mendiluce who is extremely proud of a picture of herself as a child on Hitler's knee), their collaboration with South American dictatorial regimes or their own exalted tributes (poems, novels, discourses) to these regimes. This preoccupation with the position of art towards evil, its possible complicity with it, are in fact central issues in all of Bolaño's prose, which shows very clearly that he cannot possibly be qualified as a postmodern apolitical writer or as a representative of playful, gratuitous and non-referential postmodern literature associated with what Hans Bertens called the second current of postmodernism.[41]

This brings us to the third difference: Borges's 'universal' stories are much less engaged with Latin American history than Bolaño's horrifying and obviously very verisimilar biographies. While Borges plays with the stories of some legendary characters which might be familiar to the reader, like the Western hero Billy the Kid, for example, Bolaño treads on much more delicate ground, infected by the painful and traumatic memory of dictatorship. This renders his writings far more sinister.

His prose is also perceived as sinister because of the playful and, in a sense, irreverent way of dealing with the traumatic past. As Celina Manzoni explains,[42] *La literatura nazi en América* might be read as a parodic response to the established post-dictatorial novel, in which the horrors of the dictatorships in Chile or Argentina are represented in a rather traumatic and serious tone. In fact, *La literatura nazi en América* gave rise to much controversy in Latin America, precisely because of the defying, ironic tone in which Bolaño establishes his imaginary fascist literary network, playing with historical veracity, always a delicate issue when history's injuries are far from being healed. And just like Borges, who added a long list of sources at the end of *Historia universal de la infamia*, the enumeration of fascist publishing houses, magazines and the exhaustive bibliographical references of the characters in the epilogue of *La literatura nazi en América* give a verisimilar status to these imaginary biographies.

Yet *La literatura nazi en América*'s playful overtone progressively loses ground and disappears completely in the last chapter, where the life and work of Alberto Ruiz Taggle is described from the perspective of the first-person narrator named Bolaño. Apart from being a member of Pinochet's military forces, Ruiz Taggle is a fascist avant-garde poet whose art performances are described in detail. As a pilot, for example, he writes sinister poems in the air with the exhaust fumes of the airplanes he commands, representing a kind of homage to death. Another one of his works consists of an installation of pictures of the mutilated, tortured, raped bodies of the women he captured and murdered as a member of the DINA, the Chilean intelligence forces. The argument of this chapter is further elaborated on in *Estrella distante*, Bolaño's next novel that, according to the narrator of the prologue, is the product of a joint writing project: by the author himself and by a certain 'Arturo B'. This is a recurrent character in *Estrella distante* and other novels of Bolaño, where he functions as the alter ego of the author himself:

> *So we took that final chapter and shut ourselves up for a month and a half in my house in Blanes, where, guided by his dreams and nightmares, we composed the present novel. My role was limited to preparing refreshments, consulting a few books, and discussing the reuse of numerous paragraphs with Arturo and the increasingly animated ghost of Pierre Menard.*[43]

The allusion to Pierre Menard refers to Borges's short story 'Pierre Menard, Author of the Quixote' (1944), in which Menard decides to reproduce *Don Quixote* literally, producing a completely different text. In the case of *Estrella distante*, Bolaño portrays himself as his own Pierre Menard, rewriting his prose with the help of one of his closest characters.

The postmodern, Borgesean imprint in Bolaño's work is undeniable: apart from the evident intertextual references, there is the common aspect of the continuous reflection on the role of art and literature in the representation of reality. Although at first sight Bolaño sticks to the political context of Latin American dictatorship in both novels, they simultaneously offer a more Borgesian reflection on the universality of evil and infamy. As Celina Manzoni states referring to *La literatura nazi en América*:

> *The parodic accumulation of the biographies of characters that are identified in a diffuse quality of nazi writers [...] can be read as a way of conjuration, but also might seem to reveal a conviction on the inevitability of the repetition, the recurrence in distinct times and places of an ideological and esthetical will signified by irrationality, violence, intolerance and the common places of nationalism whose most flagrant clichés are unraveled.*[44]

This preoccupation with the recurrence of violence, irrationality and intolerance in distinct times and spaces becomes all the more obvious in Bolaño's posthumous novel *2666*. In this totalizing novel, not only different continents (Russia, Europe and the Americas) are conjoined, but also different times (the Russian Revolution, the Second World War, the end of the twentieth century, the mysterious future date 2666) and different experiences of evil (Stalin's purges, the Holocaust, the Chilean dictatorship, the atrocious murders of women in Ciudad Juárez). The position of literature with respect to evil is, again, a tricky one: four European literary critics in search of Benno von Archimboldi – a pseudonym for the German author Hans Reiter to whom they dedicated almost a lifetime of research – are confronted with extreme violence. Sometimes they reveal themselves unexpectedly as violent subjects, for example when they knock out a London taxi driver without any apparent motive, but on other occasions they seem to be completely unaware of or perhaps insensitive to the dramatic violence that surrounds them, immersed as they are in their literary quest.

The fourth and largest part of the novel, 'The Part about the Crimes', consists of an endless description of the hundred and ten corpses of young women that are found in the rubbish dump in the imaginary town of Santa Teresa. This town can easily be identified with Ciudad Juárez, the Mexican city located at the border with the US where at least four hundred women – most of them working as cheap labour in the textile factories – have been killed since 1993. Adopting the form of police reports, the novel seems to distance itself from more sensational fictionalizations of these atrocities as they were fashioned by authors of crime novels and cheap Hollywood movies.[45] In other words, the playful, but nonetheless sinister game of *La literatura nazi en América* gives way to a dry and sometimes boring enumeration of crimes in *2666*, characterized by the distant language of administrative police reports. According to Marco Kunz, in his

> *almost endless enumeration of atrocities, Bolaño avoids all suspense, keeping himself from exploiting the murders to entertain the reader. Actually, Bolaño submits reality to a very superficial fictionalization, because it is evident that many characters, despite having different names, are inspired in identifiable models [...].*[46]

One could argue, then, that *2666*, just like *La literatura nazi en América*, blurs the limits between literature and history in a postmodernist way, although it does so in the opposite direction: while *La literatura nazi in America* is characterised by its extreme fictionalization, inventing a network of crime in order to better imagine the perverse logic of dictatorship, *2666* departs from one of the most extreme examples of violence in the twentieth century, almost renouncing fiction through the adaptation of the unembellished prose of police reports. However, it would be reductive to say that part four of *2666* is nothing more than an appeal to realism, an authentic testimony of horror and a renunciation of fiction. In fact, even in this part the unreliable narrator that is so characteristic of the previous parts of this novel and Bolaño's other work pops up regularly. In the following example, his comment on the smile of the policemen when they find the body of another dead woman might suggest some complicity on their part, although this remains implicit: '[Michelle Requejo's] hands were tied behind her back and a little later someone noticed that the rope was knotted the same way as the rope that had bound Estrella Ruiz Sandoval, which made some policemen smile'.[47]

This passage brings to mind the comparison that Juan Villoro made between Bolaño's narrator and a hunter who continuously misleads you and makes you fall into one trap after another.[48] That is especially true for part four of 2666: although the murderer(s) of Ciudad Juárez were never found by the Mexican police, and despite the fact that Bolaño refrains from designating one single perpetrator as well, it does not keep the narrator from laying multiple false trails that insinuate complicities and untold stories. Ellipsis and digression, two of Bolaño's preferred style figures that can be linked with the oblique discourse of irony, are operative as well in this part of the novel and incite the reader incessantly to try and reconstruct the scene of the crime. Without success, though, for time and time again, he finds himself in an impasse.

Although the reader does not receive any definitive answer concerning the multiple questions the killings raise, the link between art and evil is again clearly implied, since the main suspect of the murderers in Santa Teresa – Klaus Haas – turns out to be the uncle of the mysterious writer Hans Reiter. As Peter Elmore correctly observes, 'a strange solidarity connects the person of the novelist [Hans Reiter] with that of the murderer [Klaus Haas], drawing in this way an analogy between the narrative corpus and the *corpus delicti*'.[49] This unspoken association shows once more that Bolaño's fiction is very much engaged with the relationship between art and evil. Once again, crime and literature are related, although in 2666 the specific form of this relationship is more mysterious and enigmatic than it was in novels like *Distant Star*.

In conclusion, we might say that the dialogue of Bolaño's prose with the recent political and historical context of Latin America is more radical than in the case of Borges. The thorough reflection on the power (perverse) behind literature (fascist) in Bolaño's narrative is characteristic of the third current within postmodernism, in which the issue of representation can no longer be dissociated from power mechanisms.[50]

His predilection for unreliability and irony underlines the complicity of literature with fascism, highlighting its most obscure dimensions and recalling its untrustworthy character. Therefore, it would be hard to recognize what Ernst Van Alphen and Mieke Bal called a rhetorics of sincerity in his work: Bolaño's unreliable narrators make us reflect continuously on political complicity and the dangers of apparently innocent, authentic and sincere artistic expression, emphasizing rhetorics rather than sincerity in literary discourse.

Chapter 12

American Literature

A New Aesthetic of Sincerity, Reality and Community

Allard den Dulk

Introduction

As we have seen in the previous chapters, many of the European debates refer to the reconsideration of literary postmodernism that has recently taken place in American fiction. Therefore, this chapter will outline the most important developments in contemporary US literature.

From the first half of the 1990s onward, a growing number of American writers of a 'younger' generation (born, mainly, in the 1960s and 1970s) started to express their discontent with the detached self-reflectivity and endless irony that had come to pervade American fiction during the preceding decades, and American culture in general. Self-reflectivity and irony are hallmarks of postmodernism, its favoured instruments of unmasking. But more and more writers criticised these instruments, and came to regard postmodernism as a 'blind alley'. In response to this perceived 'dead end of postmodernism', these writers placed new emphasis on the idea that communication and searching for new sources of meaning are the most important purposes of fiction. This development is increasingly recognized as an 'aesthetic sea change' in American literature.[1]

The terms most frequently used to label this development are 'post-postmodernism' and 'new sincerity'. Although I am reluctant to adopt these terms *outright*,[2] I will employ them sporadically, for practical reasons, as they are widely used when discussing the subject at hand. Far more important than a terminology discussion, is mapping out the common aesthetics of these works. In my opinion, it is on the basis of their shared philosophical dimension that these works can be said to form a new trend in American fiction. Although other writers have also been associated with it,[3] this chapter will focus on David Foster Wallace (1962-2008) and, to a lesser extent, on Dave Eggers (1970-) and Jonathan Safran Foer (1977-), because their work is the most representative of this new literary trend and the philosophical dimension that underlies it.

This dimension consists of two parts: on the one hand a critique of postmodernism, and on the other hand the outlines of a new aesthetic, striving to overcome the problematic aspects of postmodernism. First, with regard to the critical part: this critique is in fact levelled at two different forms of postmodernism that can be distinguished in American fiction, namely postmodernist 'meta-fiction' and postmodernist 'minimalism',[4] which I will describe in section 1. Section 2 will focus on the critique of postmodernist irony, formulated mainly in the works of Wallace and Eggers. Finally, in section 3, I arrive at the second part of the shared philosophical dimension of the works of Wallace, Eggers and Foer: there, I will give some outlines of the new 'aesthetic' that has taken shape in these works.

American Postmodernism

It is notoriously difficult – if not impossible – to provide a comprehensive definition of postmodernism. In this section I will, therefore, limit myself to describing two important trends in American literary fiction that are commonly regarded as 'postmodernist' and that are criticized as such, implicitly and explicitly, in the works of Wallace, Eggers and Foer, namely: the postmodernist 'meta-fiction' of mainly the 1960s and 1970s, and the postmodernist 'minimalism' of mainly the 1980s and first half of the 1990s. These two literary trends also seem to represent the two senses in which the term postmodernism is most often employed: on the one hand, a 'theoretical' postmodernism, signifying a more 'academic' problematization and subversion of beliefs considered to be central to 'modernist' thought, or Western thought in general; and on the other hand, a 'popular' postmodernism, referring to a broader, societal situation, namely the widely shared perception of reality as having become uncertain and devoid of value (this distinction is similar to the one drawn by Thomas Vaessens in chapter 3, between 'intellectual' and 'playful' postmodernism). I do think, however, that there is a clear connection between these two 'forms' of postmodernism. I will elaborate on this below.

Meta-fiction

The literary trend labelled as postmodernist meta-fiction is strongly related to French postmodernist philosophy, especially to Jacques Derrida's (1930–2004) philosophy of deconstruction.[5] In both postmodernist meta-fiction and deconstruction the impossibility of connecting language to reality leads to the conclusion that language must fail. Deconstruction can be said to take aim at the ideal of 'presence': all Western philosophy, according to Derrida, strives to reach a fundamental level where truth and meaning are fully *present*. However, this ideal of expressing essences in perfect, pure definitions is an illusion, an impossible dream, says Derrida. Similarly, the main target of postmodernist meta-fiction is the notion of 'reality'. Unfortunately, I cannot further elaborate on this similarity here.[6] In what follows, I will focus purely on postmodernist meta-fiction.

First of all, what does the term 'meta-fiction' mean? Patricia Waugh defines it as follows: '*Meta-fiction* is a term given to fictional writing which self-consciously and systematically draws attention to its status as an artefact.'[7] In itself, this literary technique is as old as literature itself. But in certain texts, mainly from the American 1960s and 1970s, the use of such techniques became so prominent that the term 'meta-fiction' also came to designate these texts as a specific literary trend or genre, namely *postmodernist* meta-fiction.[8] At the same time it is important to keep in mind that these works do more than employ meta-fictional techniques. To label this literary trend 'meta-fiction' is a *pars pro toto*, symbolic of its larger postmodernist project of unveiling artificiality and problematizing reality.

This trend in American literature is closely connected with the sociocultural transformation of that time. What, as Raymond Federman writes, the new 'self-reflexive fiction' that rose during the 1960s tried to do, was 'to render concrete and even visual in its language, in its syntax, in its typography and topology, the disorder, the chaos, the violence, the incongruity, but also the energy and vitality, of American reality'. For these writers the notion of 'reality' as something apparent and unequivocal had become problematic. Prompted by the circumstances of their time, they came to speak of the 'mess of reality' or the 'unreality of reality', to quote Federman again.[9] They regard reality as constructed, artificial fake.[10]

The *meta*-fictional character of their works follows from this problematization. As Waugh writes: 'for meta-fictional writers the most fundamental assumption is that composing a novel is basically no different from composing or constructing one's "reality"'.[11] According to these writers, fiction is based on maintaining the illusion of 'reality'. Postmodernist meta-fictional writing, by 'reflecting' on itself – that is: by showing how it is structured, how it has come into being – *pierces* this illusionary reality by revealing the 'artificiality' that underlies a piece of fiction: 'it systematically disturbs the air of reality by foregrounding the ontological structure of texts and of fictional worlds,' writes Brian McHale.[12] Meta-fictional texts do so, for example, by letting the authorial voice intrude into the narrative and declare the fictionality of the story. Or by using excessively difficult language to describe simple events, or by using strange lay-out, thereby stressing the linguistic or material character of the story. By showing how fiction works, these authors want to make clear that, similarly, the reality we live in is turned into an orderly whole by omitting inevitable elements of disorder and lack of clarity. In other words, reality is fictionalized in order to become how we expect it to be.

The most important manifestation of this literary trend is the work of American author John Barth (1930-).[13] The stories of Barth's *Lost in the Funhouse* (1968) are thematically connected by their meta-fictional intention, summarized by the authorial voice in the story 'Title': 'to acknowledge what I'm doing while I'm doing it is exactly the point'.[14] Waugh writes about the radical meta-fictionality of Barth's text: 'almost every sentence is undermined and exposed as fictional'.[15] Stan Fogel and Gordon Slethaug note that '*Lost in the Funhouse* [...] engages the means of fiction almost at the expense of content'.[16] Barth had already expounded the ideas underlying this radical 'aesthetic' in the essay 'The Literature of Exhaustion' (1967).[17] In the essay, Barth's main contention seems to be that literary means no longer succeed in expressing the world and what the writer wants to say about that world. Therefore, the only remaining option for fiction writers, according to Barth, is to turn this exhaustion 'against itself' by portraying the exhaustion of literary means and, by doing so, still make new literary works.[18] Or, as the essay's central thought is summarized in *Lost in the Funhouse*: 'To turn ultimacy against itself to make something new and valid, the essence whereof would be the impossibility of making something new.'[19]

The reflexive-ironic nature of postmodernist meta-fiction is clear: its essential operation is a constant ironic self-distancing through the self-conscious unveiling of its own structures. The assumptions behind this project are idealistic, aimed at liberation.[20] However, the ('post-postmodernist') critique of this form of fiction denounces the fact that its reflexive-ironic unmasking has no end, and that, as an *end in itself*, solely concerned with the endless uncovering of its own structures, it cannot realize anything new to replace what it has unmasked. Therefore, postmodernist meta-fiction can be seen as leading, ultimately, to 'scepticism' and 'solipsism' (terms that Wallace uses in his critique of literary postmodernism).[21] That is: it is regarded as leading to a felt inability to express *anything* truthful about reality, except for its absence, its *un*reality, its fictionality. This 'scepticism' is seen as tied in with the 'solipsistic' effect of postmodernist meta-fiction: constant ironic distancing from my own words and actions requires constant self-consciousness, turning my own thoughts into the sole place where meaning is decided. However, just as I am unable to describe the reality outside me, I am equally incapable of giving a 'real', pure description of my interior life.[22] As a result, postmodernist meta-fiction is seen by critics as withering away into noncommittal introversion.

Minimalism

Gradually, these potentially 'scepticistic' and 'solipsistic' aspects of postmodernism became visible in a broader, 'popular' outlook on reality as well. Robert McLaughlin writes: 'postmodernism's main qualities, irony and self-referentiality, percolated into the culture at large'.[23] What was described 'academically' during the 1960s and 1970s becomes, in a narrowed-down version, a widely held 'intuitive' perception of daily reality in the 1980s. As truths are increasingly said to be 'provisional' and values to be 'relative', the frameworks that Western individuals formerly used to navigate reality become uncertain and do not provide direction any longer for a future that comes to look increasingly hopeless.

These developments are reflected in American literature by what can be regarded as a subsequent 'wave' of postmodernist fiction: a trend of 'minimalist realism' that portrays the bleak futureless present of a world where irony has unmasked every claim to intrinsic value. Elizabeth Young explains that, compared to the writers of meta-fiction, the authors of these minimalist works 'have a very different engagement with postmodernism'. Young: 'Their fiction arises directly out of their own observations and experiences of postmodern culture, from out of the streets with no name; they are reporting from within a lived reality, not dissecting its constituents from the academic perimeters.'[24]

But, *as* in postmodernist meta-fiction, there is a sense of turning a felt 'ultimacy' against itself, only this time an ultimacy experienced in daily life.[25] The lived reality of postmodern culture is characterized by the absence of clear, objective criteria by which to choose from the endless possibilities that have become available to us. Subjective preference is the only recognized decider that remains. This can easily lead to consumer hedonism, each individual *solely* concerned with the continuous satisfaction of his needs. The internalizing of the presumed 'lessons' of postmodernist irony leads to what can be labelled as 'nihilism': the conviction that nothing has intrinsic value, that no choice has superior value over other options (the feeling that 'anything goes'). Accordingly, for the minimalist fiction of the 1980s the only thing left to express is exactly this: an American reality saturated by the conviction that nothing has value. And the best way to do this: through extremely 'flat', minimalist writing, terse prose offering present tense descriptions, often from a first-person perspective, of events and conversations of which the content, the value has flattened as well: a rape or a murder is described in the same style and tone as someone's new car. James Annesley summarizes:

> *Their novels are predominantly urban in focus and concerned with the relationship between the individual and consumer culture. Instead of [...] dense plots, elaborate styles and political subjects [...], [these fictions] prefer blank, atonal perspectives and fragile, glassy visions. [...] [They are] preoccupied with 'sex, death and subversion'.*[26]

Bret Easton Ellis (1964-) is generally considered to be the most important representative of this literary trend.[27] Julian Murphet writes: 'If we call Ellis a 'postmodern' author, we probably mean this above all; this flattening and erasure of the texture of his world, manifest above all in the flatness and affectlessness of his prose style'.[28] Ellis's 1991 novel *American Psycho* offers the most extreme and consistent elaboration of this fixed style and subject matter.[29] Its first-person narrator, Patrick Bateman – an investment banker who is also a bloodthirsty psychopath – is the embodiment of total irony, and the extreme consequence of consumer hedonism. Bateman accepts neither responsibility nor limitation for his actions: *everything* should be possible. The violent acts he commits are the most obvious example of this. Some critics have classified Bateman as 'illiterate', as a character too 'stupid' to be ironic, arguing that 'Bateman cannot fathom irony because he has no layers, no sense of depth'.[30] But it is exactly *because* of irony that Bateman has no layers (he himself suspects that this 'levelling' took place during his time at Harvard).[31] Bateman has ironically distanced himself from every content and is, as a result, merely interested in appearance: 'Surface, surface, surface was all that anyone found meaning in... this was civilization as I saw it, colossal and jagged...' he says in *American Psycho*.[32]

Although some critics regard the novel as a triumphant indictment of this attitude, Wallace and others see *American Psycho* as operating on the basis of the same total irony of which it portrays the extreme escalation.[33] For the only way in which the novel can be said to 'critique' its main character, and therefore the life view that he symbolizes, is by constant ironic distancing. The novel offers no outer perspective that can function as an alternative to the life view that is ironized: there is, in the words of Murphet, no 'possibility of offering even the outline of another vision'.[34] Young writes: 'It is as if, having articulated the affectlessness and shallowness that so obsesses him [Ellis] lacks the imagination with which to create anything other. He can only go deeper into surfaces and this he does'.[35] For Wallace and others, *American Psycho* does not just portray but *embody* the scepticistic and solipsistic aspects of popular postmodernism – the erasure of all value, the flattening of the world, the unreality of other 'selves'.

Criticizing Postmodernist Irony: A Comparison with Kierkegaard

The preceding section has shown that irony plays an all-important role in both postmodernist meta-fiction and postmodernist minimalism. It is this role of irony that bears the brunt of the critique levelled, as part of a newly emerging aesthetic, against these two preceding schools of fiction. A large part of the attention given to this new literary trend has been fixed on its critical stance towards irony, formulated most explicitly in the works of Wallace and Eggers. However, this critique has often been misinterpreted: some commentators have read it as a call to abolish irony completely, while others have thought the comments on irony to be meant ironically.[36]

In this section I will, therefore, provide a theoretical framework for the interpretation of this irony critique, by viewing it in the light of the critique formulated by the Danish philosopher Søren Kierkegaard (1813-1855). Kierkegaard is generally considered to be one of the most important irony theorists in Western philosophy;[37] and Wallace, in my correspondence with him in 2006, wrote: 'I too believe that most of the problems of what might be called "the tyranny of irony" in today's West can be explained almost perfectly in terms of Kierkegaard's distinction between the aesthetic and the ethical life'.[38]

The views of Kierkegaard, Wallace and Eggers show a striking resemblance on five crucial aspects: (1) their critique is concerned with irony as an attitude towards existence, not as just a verbal strategy; (2) they agree that irony can initially have a liberating effect; but (3) that things go wrong when irony becomes permanent and automated (Kierkegaard calls this the 'aesthetic' attitude); (4) that liberation from this empty, aimless form of irony cannot be achieved through the ironizing of irony (i.e. meta-irony); (5) liberation from irony is only possible through (what Kierkegaard calls) a 'leap', by 'ethically' choosing one's own freedom, by choosing the responsibility to give shape and meaning to that freedom. Here, I will only elaborate on the third point.[39]

Kierkegaard, Wallace and Eggers do not criticize irony *in general*: they are critical, specifically, of irony as a permanent, automated attitude. Initially, irony has a liberating effect: through irony the individual, realizing that he does not coincide with (for example) the structures within which he was raised, obtains a *negative* freedom (a freedom-from). As such, irony constitutes, for Kierkegaard, an indispensable step towards freely choosing a personal interpretation of one's moral life (that is: a *positive* freedom, a freedom-to). But Kierkegaard's 'aesthete' turns irony into a *permanent* attitude, using it to avoid all commitment, all responsibility, in order to retain his negative freedom. In *The Concept of Irony*, Kierkegaard writes: 'In irony, the subject is continually retreating, talking every phenomenon out of its reality in order to save itself – that is, in order to preserve itself in negative independence of everything'.[40]

This 'total irony', or 'infinite absolute negativity' as Kierkegaard also calls it, is similar to the postmodernist irony Wallace and Eggers criticize.[41] Just like Kierkegaard, Wallace writes that irony should not become an end in itself, subsequently quoting Lewis Hyde: 'Irony has only emergency use. Carried over time, it is the voice of the trapped who have come to enjoy their cage'. Wallace himself adds:

> *This is because irony, entertaining as it is, serves an almost exclusively negative function. It's critical and destructive, a ground-clearing. Surely this is the way our postmodern fathers saw it. But irony's singularly unuseful when it comes to constructing anything to replace the hypocrisies it debunks.*[42]

Nothing has been replaced: no new values have been formulated after the ground-clearing. Instead, postmodernist irony has, according to Wallace, become an automatism ground into the culture, no longer serving as a means to *expose* hypocrisy, but rather as an *instrument* of hypocrisy and cynicism, used 'largely unconscious [...] [,] as a mechanism for avoiding some really thorny issues'.[43] Thus, postmodernist irony is tied in with 'the contemporary mood of jaded weltschmerz, self-mocking materialism, blank indifference', and is the cause of 'great despair and stasis' within contemporary Western culture, writes Wallace.[44] As we read in *Infinite Jest*: 'We are shown how to fashion masks of ennui and jaded irony at a young age [...]. And then it's stuck there, the weary cynicism that saves us from gooey sentiment and unsophisticated naïveté.'[45]

Eggers agrees with Wallace's critique of this automated, cynical form of irony: 'it's just worthless, totally vacant and empty and terrible. And it's pure attitude without anything to back it up. [...] I'm on the same page with [Wallace] in a lot of ways'.[46] In their novels, Wallace and Eggers often describe characters that employ this form of irony. In *Infinite Jest*, for example, many characters are addicts, hiding their anxiety and the emptiness of their existence behind 'the coyly sincere, ironic, self-presenting fortifications they'd had to construct in order to carry on Out There, under the ceaseless neon bottle'.[47] Kierkegaard offers a similar description of the aesthete, who 'holds existence at bay by the most subtle of all deceptions, by thinking. He has thought everything possible, and yet he has not existed at all'.[48] In Eggers's *A Heartbreaking Work of Staggering Genius*, the critique of the ironic attitude is at its clearest in the passages about *Might Magazine*. Eggers describes the growing cynicism amongst the editorial staff of *Might* as follows:

> *We begin a pattern of almost immediate opinion-reversal and self-devouring. Whatever the prevailing thinking, especially our own, we contradict it. We change our minds about Wendy Kopp, the young go-getter we heralded in the first issue, and her much-celebrated Teach for America. Where we originally praised her gumption and her organization's goals – to bring young, enthusiastic, well-educated teachers into underprivileged schools for two years – now in a 6,000-word piece that dominates the second issue, we fault the nonprofit for attempting to solve inner-city problems, largely black problems, with white upper-middle-class college-educated solutions. 'Paternalistic condescension', we say. 'Enlightened self-interest', we sigh.*[49]

This passage summarizes how total irony makes commitment impossible. Every position, every ideal has a flip side that can be exposed. Therefore, the ironic stance of 'immediate opinion-reversal', i.e. to be 'positionless', is the only 'safe' stance.

In the course of the book, Eggers shows how the editors grow more and more frustrated with their own cynicism:

> *Work becomes ever more depressing, routine [...]. It is any day at all when I am at my desk, working on a spread debunking raves, one in a long line of contrarian articles pointing out the falsity of most things the world believes in, holds dear. We have debunked a version of the Bible written for black kids. We have debunked the student loan program. We debunk the idea of college in general, and marriage, and makeup, and the Grateful Dead – it is our job to point out all this artifice, everywhere.*[50]

In the end, the magazine loses out to general frustration. The editorial staff realize that their ironic efforts have led to nothing. They have exposed 'falsity' and 'artificiality' everywhere, but have offered no alternatives instead. Now they stand empty-handed: 'all this – what had it all been? It had been something to do, some small, small point to make, and the point was made, in a small way'.[51] Passages like the ones above clearly illustrate the futility of total irony. Eggers himself writes: '*Might*, and its ironic contents, were included in the book simply so that they could be knocked down and picked apart.'[52] (Note that this is not the same as *being ironic* about irony; such an equation would rely on the overly simplistic reading of irony as covering all instances of 'not saying what you mean' or 'saying what you do not mean' – a reading that would, in fact, render all fiction ironic.)

But how to rid oneself of this 'tyrannizing' form of irony? The literary execution of what Kierkegaard calls the 'leap' towards the ethical can be said to form the heart of the new aesthetic that is the subject of the next section.

A New Aesthetic: Wallace, Eggers and Foer

David Foster Wallace is generally regarded as the most important representative of the recent reconsideration of postmodernism in American fiction. In Wallace's writing the engagement with the problems of postmodernist literature and culture, and with the need to move beyond them, is constantly present.[53] Wallace's non-fictional texts provide an analysis of the problems as well as possible solutions, elements of which can also be recognized in his fictional writings. Wallace clearly wants fiction to 'forge ahead', carrying with it the valuable lessons of postmodernism but overcoming its problems.[54]

Wallace's example of a new direction in American literary fiction has inspired many novelists to explore similar paths in their own writing. Dave Eggers and Jonathan Safran Foer are the two best-known examples of this.[55] As many critics have noted[56], the works of Eggers and Foer clearly exhibit the influence of the newly developing aesthetic: they show us a – for lack of a better word – 'intuitive' adaptation of many of Wallace's ideas (whereas in Wallace's work we witness the full 'labour', the struggle to arrive at these ideas).[57] Eggers's and Foer's worldwide success in a sense signifies the 'success' of the new aesthetic, and has given Wallace's ideas a far wider exposure than they perhaps would have gotten solely through his own, more 'difficult' fiction.

Accordingly, I regard the work of Wallace, Eggers and Foer as the three most determinative instances of this recent literary trend. In the following subsections I will analyse their shared aesthetic by taking together the works of these authors and discerning therein three important common themes (because the thematic 'family resemblances' between these works make it possible to speak of a new 'trend' to start with): first of all, a desire for sincerity as a basic attitude needed to overcome the dead end of postmodernism; secondly, a desire to provide our experience of reality with a sense of value and urgency; and thirdly, a desire for community, for dialogue (including between writer and reader).

Sincerity

Here, desiring 'sincerity' means, first of all, countering the total irony that has left the postmodern individual feeling fragmented, in a state of scepticism and solipsism. In response to these problems, the novels of Wallace, Eggers and Foer lay (renewed) emphasis – on the level of the 'story world' as well as on the level of the novel as a whole, as a text – on the importance of openness, trust and vulnerability, which together can be labelled as a desire for sincerity.[58] In these novels, sincerity serves as a basic attitude that enables the individual (and the novel) to attribute meaning and value to his actions (again), and to his relations with others. Those two aspects (featured in the next subsections) are made possible by a 'basic' sincerity, and in turn, these aspects bring about the further realization of that sincerity.

For example, in Eggers's second book, *You Shall Know Our Velocity* (2002), the first-person narrator states: 'I wanted agreement now, I wanted synthesis and the plain truth – without the formalities of debate. There was nothing left to debate, no heated discussion that seemed to progress toward any healing solution.'[59] In Foer's second novel, *Extremely Loud & Incredibly Close* (2005), the main character, nine-year-old Oskar Schell, keeps thinking up 'inventions' that symbolize a desire for sincerity. For example: 'What if the water that came out of the shower was treated with a chemical [...], so that your skin changed color according to your mood? [...] Everyone could know what everyone else felt, and we could be more careful with each other.'[60] In Wallace's *Infinite Jest*, Mario Incandenza serves as the sincere 'alternative' for the novel's mass of cynical, depressed characters. When we read that 'Mario doesn't seem to resemble much of anyone', at first that might seem to refer purely to his physical appearance, as Mario was born severely deformed ('He had to be more or less scraped out, [...] like the meat of an oyster').[61] But Mario's 'not resembling' quickly turns out to refer, more fundamentally, to his sincerity, his utter lack of cynicism, distinguishing him from all other characters.[62] As a 'regulative' example of sincerity, Mario prefigures the development of the two main characters of the novel (Mario's younger brother Hal Incandenza and addict Don Gately), which runs from constantly hiding behind the 'empty mask' of irony,[63] becoming increasingly depressed, to the willingness to place trust in oneself and in the others to whom this self is shown: 'the trajectory of their transformation is one of restoring personal agency by turning the self inside-out rather than suppressing it beneath deliberate artifice,' writes Catherine Nichols.[64]

It is on the level of the novel as a whole that Eggers urges readers of *A Heartbreaking Work of Staggering Genius* (in response, by the way, to hearing 'a few people tell it, this entire book, or most of it, was/is ironic') to: 'trust your eyes, trust your ears, trust your art'.[65] Wallace's short story 'Octet', from *Brief Interviews with Hideous Men* (1999), emphasizes a similar idea: that literature, to uphold its claim that it is about something important and meaningful, requires trust (between writer and reader): 'you'd have to be 100% honest. Meaning not just sincere but almost naked. Worse than naked – more like unarmed. Defenseless'. This stance has the following implications:

> *It's going to make you look fundamentally lost and confused and frightened and unsure about whether to trust even your most fundamental intuitions about urgency and sameness and whether people deep inside experience things in anything like the same way you do... more like a reader, in other words, down here quivering in the mud of the trench with the rest of us, instead of a Writer, whom we imagine to be clean and dry and radiant of command presence and unwavering conviction as he coordinates the whole campaign back at some gleaming abstract Olympian HQ.*
> *So decide.*[66]

This passage connects the desire for sincerity to providing the experience of reality with meaning *and* to the importance of community.

Reality
Literary postmodernism poses a problem for the meaningful connection of fiction to social reality: because reality is judged to be always 'unreal', it has to

be self-consciously exposed as such when portrayed in literature, and the only remaining value or meaning that such literary portrayals seem to be able to express is that of unmasking. One of the desires that connects the works under review is what McLaughlin describes as 'a desire to reconnect language to the social sphere, or, to put it another way, to reenergize literature's social mission, its ability to intervene in the social world, to have an impact on actual people and the actual social institutions in which they live their lives'.[67]

Wallace agrees with postmodernist meta-fictionalists that contemporary Western reality is diverse and confusing. But for him, fiction cannot limit itself to revealing 'artificiality' and 'unreality', because the conclusion that 'all experience can be deconstructed and reconfigured [...] is about as "liberating" as a bad acid trip'.[68] It can make us lose sight of what it means 'to be a real human being',[69] as has happened to many characters in *Infinite Jest*: '[Everyone] finds stuff that's really real[, stuff about heartbreak and people you loved dying and U.S. woe,] uncomfortable and they get embarrassed. It's like there's some rule that real stuff can only get mentioned if everybody rolls their eyes or laughs in a way that isn't happy.'[70] According to Wallace, good fiction should counter this development and 'dramatize the fact that we still *are* human beings, now'.[71]

The novels of Wallace, Eggers and Foer have been 'accused' by some commentators of being typically postmodernist in their portrayal of reality, because their novels show us fragmented characters in a confusing world, and because they seem to employ typical 'postmodern hardware', such as footnotes, an abundance of information and characters (who sometimes provide *conflicting* information), self-conscious narrative, and pop references. However, in their rush to reach such conclusions, these commentators pass over the possibility that similar means can have a different significance for a different literary generation, and can also be used to different ends. As was mentioned above, some aspects of postmodernism have become part of popular postmodern culture and, therefore, part of everyday reality. So, a certain amount of fragmentation, mediation and self-consciousness in a contemporary novel is, in the words of Wallace, 'just plain realistic'. The same goes for pop references, says Wallace: 'the belief that pop images are basically just mimetic devices is one of the attitudes that separates most U.S. fiction writers under c. 40 from the writerly generation that precedes us, reviews us and designs our grad-school curricula'.[72] For these younger writers, who grew up with postmodernism, all these things are part of a reality of which, in their opinion, *certain aspects* have become problematic.[73] But while describing these problems and exploring possible ways to overcome them, a 'realistic' description of the reality that forms the backdrop to these problems imports techniques that were previously deemed subversive, but are no longer considered to be so by this new literary generation.

For example, some of the works of Eggers and Foer use photographs and strange typography, not to expose the *un*reality of the story, but rather as unproblematic 'depictions' of the fictional reality described. So, all these things are not typical 'postmodern pyrotechnics'[74] but rather, as Nicolas Confessore aptly describes, 'characteristics of a certain generational vernacular, whose sources are widely recognized' – Confessore mentions, among others, 'six hours of television a day, advertising metastasized to every cranny of life', etc. – 'but whose real purpose is just as widely misunderstood'. This is not a language of 'disengagement', he says, but 're-engagement'.[75]

To offer another example: Wallace's *Infinite Jest* has more than 300 characters. In postmodernist meta-fictional novels, the use of an abundance of perspectives, coupled with contradictory information, aims to effect an 'overload' that constantly puts the reader off the track, pointing out to her that she is reading something fictional. In *Infinite Jest*, on the other hand, the abundance of information and characters – all portrayed empathetically, and with a caring attention to detail – draws the reader *into* the story world, and convinces her of its reality. Wallace's fictions make clear that what they speak of is 'real' pain, 'real' confusion; they speak about 'real' life. As Frank Louis Cioffi writes about Wallace's fiction: 'actuality and artwork have fully merged [...]; the artwork affects [the reader] in the same way as do "real" objects; it has a truth that deeply stirs [her]. It is in fact not art, but life'.[76] Wallace's works show plurality and confusion, not as aspects of an 'unreality' that has to be exposed, but as part of a reality that has to be lived – this is what a new type of fiction should help us see, according to Wallace.[77]

The desire to engage with 'lived' problems is a concern of these novels as a whole, as well as a concern of the characters in these novels. In Eggers's *You Shall Know Our Velocity*, for example, we read: 'Every second we could have done something and we were waiting. We too were waiting. We were standing, blinking, waiting. We were thinking of things to do with our hands while we waited. Everyone was waiting.'[78] And in *A Heartbreaking Work of Staggering Genius*: '*to feel urgency* – because this part of us craves purpose. *Give me something to do!* it yells. *For Christ's sake, tell me what to fucking do!* And when you know, when you've been given this, Oh, you feel at peace. It feels so good, and you do not ever want to go back'.[79] This concern to engage with what is real, with what is urgent, clearly forms an important preoccupation of these novels.

Community

But how does one judge what is urgent, which concerns are 'real'? If my preoccupation with certain issues is legitimized purely by the fact that I *think* they are real, that I *think* they are urgent, how do I avoid self-congratulating solipsism? The works of Wallace, Eggers and Foer portray postmodernist reality as a lonely experience, with every individual thrown back upon his own considerations, disconnected from every subject-transcending order that can help attribute meaning to experience and to choice. In reaction to this, the desire to reconnect with others is an important theme in these works. In *A Heartbreaking Work of Staggering Genius*, for example, we encounter the idea of forming a 'lattice', a community ending postmodern loneliness:

> *The lattice is the connective tissue. The lattice is everyone else [...] People who have everything in common no matter where they're from, all these people know all the same things and truly hope for the same things, it's undeniable that they do, and if we can bring everyone to grab a part of the other, like an arm at the socket, everyone holding another's arm at the socket, and if we can get everyone to, instead of ripping this arm from the socket, instead hold to it, tight, and thus strengthening [...] So people, the connections between people, the people you know, become a sort of lattice, and the more people [...], the wider and stronger the lattice.*[80]

In *Infinite Jest* Hal Incandenza describes a similar 'community' and 'need for a *we*': 'the point is togetherness [...] The suffering unites us'. Large parts of the novel, especially the sections on the workings of 'Addicts Anonymous' (AA), elaborate on this need and portray the potentially healing effects of community: 'Empathy, in Boston AA, is called Identification. [...] [Identifying] isn't very hard to do, here. Because if you sit up front and listen hard, all the speakers' stories of decline and fall and surrender are basically alike, and like your own.'[81] AA shows its members that they are not alone, that they have all deluded themselves with similar forms of solipsism and scepticism. This realization, so at odds with those delusions they had both cursed and cherished, is an important step towards finding hope and meaning again.[82]

Community is also a theme in the relationships these novels set up between author and reader. I already mentioned that the aim of these works is not to constantly push the reader out of the story, as is often the case in postmodernist meta-fiction, but rather the other way around: to draw the reader in. They all treat fiction as a dialogue between writer and reader. Kevin Mattson writes about Eggers's work: 'Crack open a copy of *A Heartbreaking Work of Staggering Genius* and early on you get a sense of how this young writer is struggling to bring readers into a two-way, communicative relationship.' To that, Mattson adds: 'Some might think these examples nothing more than gimmicks. Nonetheless, they represent Eggers's hope to draw the reader into the act of communication.'[83] For example, the introduction to Eggers's first book states that one of the reasons for writing the book lay in 'The Search for Support, a Sense of Community, If You Will, in One's Peers, in Those One's Age'. Further on, the need for reader participation is formulated as follows: 'I need community, I need feedback, I need love, connection, give-and-take.'[84]

In Foer's *Everything is Illuminated*, we read: 'With our writing, we are reminding each other of things. We are making one story, yes?' And: 'We are talking now, Jonathan, together, and not apart. We are with each other, working on the same story, and I am certain that you can also feel it'.[85] These passages are part of letters written by one narrating character to another, but they also seem to address the reader. Foer himself states in an interview: 'Writing is not something like singing in the shower; it is not even like singing on a podium. For me, it's more like singing together, around a camp fire or something.'[86] And he adds: 'For me, a book is not a success if the reader doesn't become a sort of co-author [...]: it is very important for me that the reader has the idea that it's her book as well.' In another interview, Foer says: 'I write because I want to end my loneliness. Books make people less alone. That, before and after everything else, is what books do. They show us that conversations are possible across distances.'[87]

Similarly, according to Wallace,

> *a piece of fiction is a conversation. There's a relationship set up between the reader and the writer [...]. Somebody at least for a moment feels about something or sees something the way that I do. [...] I feel human and unalone and that I'm in a deep, significant conversation with another consciousness.*[88]

For Wallace, the purpose of fiction is to 'reaffirm the idea of art being a living transaction between humans', to establish 'a relationship between the writer's consciousness and [the reader's], and that in order for it to be anything like a real full human relationship, [the reader]'s going to have to put in her share of the linguistic work'.[89] As mentioned above, *Infinite Jest* forces the reader to 'put in work' in many ways, resulting in a story world that for the reader becomes all the more 'credible'. Marshall Boswell writes that in doing that 'linguistic work', writer and reader 'become a community where meaning is made'.[90]

Conclusion

This is what the new 'aesthetic' in the novels of Wallace, Eggers and Foer aims at: to provide our contemporary experience of reality with meaning and urgency, and, realizing that this is an inherently social process (meaning cannot be made by the individual alone; it requires others, a community), to try and do so through a conversation with the reader. Sincerity is necessarily implied as the underlying attitude, because an *insincere engagement* with reality and/or with the other would undermine the whole process of meaning-making.

However, whether this whole process is deemed successful, in part or in whole, or even deemed to be sincere in the first place depends largely on the reader. For if sincerity is understood here as implying (at least) the absence of total irony, then who determines whether it is absent? According to Linda Hutcheon, 'irony happens because what could be called 'discursive communities' already exist and provide the context for both the deployment and attribution of irony'. Hutcheon explains: 'for most [theorists], it is irony itself that is said to *create* that relationship. I want to [...] argue instead that it is the community that comes first and that, in fact, *enables* irony to happen'. So, whether an utterance is deemed to be ironic (or sincere, for that matter), depends on the social environment within which that utterance is performed – and in some communities, irony can become the standard 'dialect', expected in all utterances.[91]

The automated, omnipresent form of irony that the works of Wallace, Eggers and Foer criticize in contemporary postmodern culture is exactly such a standard 'dialect'. However, the formulation of that critique perhaps indicates that the 'climate' is changing. But old habits die hard. Therefore, whether the new 'aesthetic' of these works is judged to be sincere and successful depends on the reader. To quote the closing sentence, already cited above, from one of Wallace's stories:

'So decide.'[92]

Notes

Introduction

1 Bertens & Fokkema (eds.) 1997.
2 See, *e.g.* Frow 1997:13-63 and Green 2005:1-18.
3 In this Introduction the term 'Western (world)' broadly refers to all the nations which are European, or greatly influenced by European languages, traditions and culture (including e.g. the US).
4 Cf. Suleiman 1997:55.
5 Hutcheon 1988:178.
6 Kang cited in Hoberek 2007:233.
7 Humm 1998:111.
8 Green 2005:19-24.
9 See Crews 2001 and http://www.elswhere.org/pomo/.
10 Arnold 1882:4.
11 London 2001. See for a critical statement about the link between the end of postmodernism and 9/11: Fish 2001.
12 Rothstein 2001.
13 Rosenblatt 2001.
14 Amis 2008:5, 11-2.
15 Jensen 2005.
16 Martin Amis in *The Guardian* 18-9-2001 (Amis 2008:5).
17 Slattery 2001.
18 McEwan 2005:124. See also p.77 and p.146.
19 See, *e.g.* Watman 2005; Miller 2005; Van der Pol 2005.
20 See, *e.g.* Bertens 1996:103-105.
21 Sokal & Bricmont 1998 and 2003.
22 Furedi 2004.
23 Those literary conditions are themselves subsumed and shaped within broad existing conditions that have much to do with global terrorism, the rise of neoliberalims, urgent problem-solving needs such as global warming, rising religious fundamentalisms, the exhaustion of postmodern insights by marketeers...
24 Vaessens 2009:16.
25 McCaffery 1993:148.
26 Bewes 1997:2.
27 Rorty wrote about the postmodern 'ironist', who 'is not in the business of supplying himself and his fellow ironists with a method, a platform, or a rationale. He is just doing the same thing that all ironists do – attempting autonomy. He is trying to get out from under inherited contingencies and make his own contingencies, get out from under an old final vocabulary and fashion one which will be his own (Rorty 1989:97).
28 Grunberg cited in Vaessens 2010:318.
29 Hutcheon 1998.

30 Foster 1996.
31 Ebert 1991:291.
32 Cf. Eagleton 1996 and McDonald 2007:138-9.
33 Ignatieff 1997.
34 See chapter 10 (Ewout van der Knaap).
35 Bourriaud 2009.
36 Gibson 1999:6-9. Gibson adresses the work of Nussbaum and Rorty, which he calles 'rather pre-structuralist'. Rorty (1996) does indeed refer to liberal humanists such as Arnold, Leavis, T.S. Eliot, Frank Kermode and Harold Bloom in a very positive sense.
37 Egan 2009.
38 Adams in a BBC4 interview, 24-5-2010. URL: http://news.bbc.co.uk/today/hi/today/newsid_8700000/8700144.stm.
39 Shields 2010.
40 See chapter 7 (Suze van der Poll).
41 According to Green (2005:11) writer's block is a typical late-postmodern theme for this reason.
42 Burke 2010 & Booth 1988.
43 Kiberd 2009.
44 Finkielkraut 2009 & 2010.
45 See chapter 1 (Ellen Rutten).

Chapter 1 – Russian Literature

1 Prigov 1996:222.
2 Petrus Antonius Hoogeboom, 'Untitled', card in card collection *Graduation Exhibition Gerrit Rietveld Academie Beeldende Kunst / Fine Arts 2009* (Amsterdam: Artists, 2009).
3 Citation from talk by Willem Bongers, at '(Laat-)postmodernisme revisited', discussion session at Poetry Centre Perdu, Amsterdam, 18 September 2009.
4 Among others, I am thinking of the following sources, which all focus primarily on Western European and American cultures: Toth and Brooks 2007; Turner 1995; Scharg 1997; Harris 1996; López and Potter 2001; Rebein 2001; Stierstorfer 2003; *Twentieth-Century Literature* 2007; Eshelman 2008; Timmer 2010.
5 This poem, as well as other *Militsaner* poems by Prigov, can be read online: the *Russian Virtual Library* hosts his cycle 'Apofeoz militsanera' (1978) on www.rvb.ru/np/publication/01text/ 33/03prigov.htm#cycle1. The spelling 'Poliseman' reflects a conscious typo in the Russian original: mimicking colloquial speech, Prigov writes *militsaner* rather than *militsioner*.
6 An example of a particularly influential (and extensive) recent discussion of Russian postmodernism is Mark Lipovetsky's *Paralogii* (Lipovetsky 2008). For an English summary of the contents, see ibid.:834-36.

7 Helpful discussions of Russian postmodernism include Kuznetsov 1997; Lipovetsky 1999; Skoropanova 2004; and Epstein et al. 1999.
8 Among other analyses, an insightful exploration of Russian versus non-Russian notions of postmodernism is provided in Menzel 2001:328-35.
9 See on this distinguishing feature of Russian postmodernism also Skoropanova 2004:71.
10 Ibid.:356.
11 On this, see also – apart from Skoropanova – Lipovetsky (1999: 233), who claims that Russian postmodernism is 'first and foremost, a question of Russian culture's identity'; and Brown 1993:169.
12 Summarizing an often-proclaimed view on postmodernism, Lipovetsky calls the 'reaction to the inevitability of living through a historical trauma' the '"basic" cultural function of postmodern discourse' in general, and of Russian postmodern literature in particular (Lipovetsky 2008: 530). I have defended this position, zooming in on the writer Vladimir Sorokin, in Rutten 2009.
13 For a history of the introduction of the term 'postmodernism' in Russia, see Menzel 2001:306-307. The term occurred in Russian critical – especially art-historical – debate from 1983 onwards, but it only gained 'popularity and broad resonance', in Menzel's words, when it was picked up by literary critics in 1990-91 (Ibid.:307).
14 My italics. The conference in question, held in Moscow, was called 'Postmodernism and Us' ('Postmodernizm i my') – a title which alludes to an idea that was popular in early-1990s Russia, but which has been modified and criticized in later analyses: that postmodernism 'came to Russia (us)' as a preconceived, ready-made 'Western' philosophical concept.
15 On Moscow Conceptualism and its relation to postmodernism, see, for instance, Backstein and De Baere 2005, or Epstein 1999.
16 Among other publications, see Leiderman and Lipovetsky 1993; Aizenberg 1994; Epstein 1996; Kuritsyn 1997; and Kibirov 2001:349, 356, 395.
17 My information is based on a recounting of the event by Max Frei (the pen name of writer Svetlana Martynchik) on the online creative platform *Teneta* on April 10, 2000 (www.teneta.ru/archive-chat-2000/Apr10.html).
18 I agree with analyses of contemporary cultural trends which criticize the inelegant term 'post-postmodernism'; but for lack of a more precise alternative and given its prominent role in the discourse at stake, I nevertheless opt for this umbrella term here.
19 See, for instance, Man'kovskaia 1998 and 2000:307-328; the conclusion of Kuritsyn 2000; and reproductions of Epstein's essays on 'post-postmodernism' and the end of postmodernism in Epstein 2000 and 2005. For sources in English, see Lipovetsky 1999:244-247, and 2008:834-36; and Epstein et al. 1999:423-469.
20 See, for instance, Shneidman 1995:205; Weststeijn 1999, and the latter's farewell lecture, Amsterdam, October 2008 (unpublished). Eshelman's *Performatism, or the End of Postmodernism* (2008) discusses 'post-postmodern' trends as an transnational paradigm, but with a special eye for Russian cinema and visual art.

21 Part of the reason for Epstein's popularity among American writer-bloggers lies, no doubt, in the availability of his texts on 'post-postmodernity' online (on www.focusing.org/apm_papers/epstein.html, for instance, or on www.emory.edu/INTELNET/e.pm.erofeev.html). For representative reactions, see 'The New Sincerity as a Response to Postmodernism', a 2005 post by the American-Canadian poet Neil Aitken (blog.boxcarpoetry.com/?p=67); or, for a more recent example, 'Reading the Song', an entry posted in 2010 by the poet-cum-writer Wythe Marschall (chronolect.com/archives/590).

22 Among others, see Mezhieva and Konradova 2006:10-11; Skoropanova 2004:528; or Iu. Ivanov's 'Art Styles'–a course description for the Higher School of Economics, State University of Saint Petersburg, 2006, which can be read online on vorona.hse.ru/.../O_Стили%20в%2искусстве_сı,экı_юИ_н.doc.

23 For a transnational perspective, see Van Alphen et al. 2009; for the US, the UK and France, Korthals Altes 2001 and 2008; on the US and the Netherlands, see Vaessens 2009; for the US see also Den Dulk 2004 and 2004.1; for China, Chung and Jacobi 2007; for Germany, Kirchmaier 2001; and for Indonesia, Sarjono and Mooij 2006:9.

24 Yurchak 2008.

25 The search tool I use to browse Russian blogs is the Russian search engine Yandex (blogs.yandex.ru).

26 Their contributors sometimes reject the trend ('new sincerity is invented by inept critics and poets') or laud it ('this is the answer to postmodernism') – but most often, they discuss it as an indispensable, if problematic, element of the contemporary literary culture. Among many others, examples include Naratov 1998; Kostiukov 2000; Kukulin 2002; Ulanov 2002; Davydov 2005; Vezhlian 2009; Kaspe 2009; Kulle undated. An openly critical or derogatory view is expressed, among others, in Ivanova 2007; explicitly positive interpretations resound in, for instance, Ivanova 1998:12-13; and Bondarenko 2002.

27 Yurchak 2008.

28 Mikhail Epstein, 'Katalog novykh poezii', 'Novaia sentimental'nost'. Timur Kibirov i drugie', and 'Proto-, ili konets postmodernizma', in Epstein 2000:138-141, 274-295; Boym 1994:102; Lipovetsky 1999:247, and 2008:575ff.

29 Mikhail Epstein, 'Conclusion. On the Place of Postmodernism in Postmodernity', in Epstein et al. 1999:456-468, available online on www.emory.edu/INTELNET/e.pm.conclusion.html.

30 Ibid.

31 For an example of such a reading, see Mitrenina 2003.

32 Epstein et al. 1999:456-468.

33 Ibid.:457.

34 Weststeijn 1998:277.

35 I am referring to Vladimir Pomerantsev's essay 'On Sincerity in Literature' ('Ob iskrennosti v literature'), published in the journal *Novyi mir* in 1953. For an overview of the discussions which Pomerantsev's essay set in motion see, among others, Gibian 1960:7ff.; Brown 1982:193-94.

36 For an overview of Prigov's artistic output, see Dobrenko et al. 2010:711-770.

37 Prigov 1992:102.

38 For some samples, surf to http://www.youtube.com/watch?v=q_-l2h5mNYs&feature=related or http://www.youtube.com/watch?v=npRiTk6Bn6c&feature=related. Examples of Prigov adopting alternate identities also appear on his personal websites www.prigov.com and www.prigov.ru (under 'performances' and 'photos'); but they do not necessarily refer to Soviet stereotypes and clichés.

39 The literary historian Ol'ga Bogdanova cites several commentators who voice this view in an extensive analysis of the poet's work and reception in Bogdanova 2004:454-87. Some readers disagreed with it from the start (Andrei Zorin is a good example), however, and the view of Prigov as a more 'serious' poet than previously acknowledged became common coin after his death in 2007; the revised view permeates a thematic section devoted to his work and life by the journal *Novoe literaturnoe obozrenie* (no. 87, 2007, available online on http://magazines.russ.ru/nlo/2007/87/) and in a recent monograph on his work (Dobrenko et al. 2010). For this newer view, see also Alexei Yurchak's general conclusion that, in non-conformist late-Soviet art, 'cynicism and sincerity were always linked' (Yurchak 2008:257n2, and 2006:249ff.).

40 As said, the theoretical language of postmodernism was little known in pre-1990s Russia. In retrospect, Prigov has even defined his pleas for a New Sincerity as a step that marked his transition from Moscow Conceptualism *to* postmodernism. He saw it as a marker of a postmodern, rather than 'post-postmodern' phase in his career (see Prigov and Shapovalov 2003: 13-14). By opposing a longing for sincerity to the all-pervading irony of which others accuse him, he does pave the way for later 'anti-postmodern' discussions of sincerity, however.

41 In introductions to his own collections, Prigov already protested against overly ironic and relativistic readings of his poetry in the early 1970s. For examples, see Prigov 1996: 8-11.

42 Dmitrii Aleksandrovich Prigov, Mikhail Epstein, 'Popytka ne byt' identifitsiirovannym', in Dobrenko et al. 2010:69.

43 Ibid.

44 Prigov 1996:222.

45 As far as I have been able to establish, the phrase does not occur in most literary-artistic cultures until the (late) 1990s. When first gaining currency in the US, in the second half of the 1980s, the denominator 'new sincerity' was used solely for a loosely connected group of music bands from Austin, Texas, which protested against the ironicism of punk rock and New Wave (thus, an essay on Austin rock bands published in 1986 was called 'The New Sincerity'; for a reprint, see Corcoran 2005).

46 Prigov 1996:297.

47 Ibid.:300.

48 Ibid.:301.

49 Prigov 2005.

50 flippi754, post dated March 3, 2009, online on flippi754.livejournal.com/151341.html.

51 Alex Blagg, post dated November 4, 2005, online on http://blaggblogg.blogspot.com/2005/11/new-sincerity.html.

52 For a comprehensive interview with Medvedev on his political views and activities, see Tsvetkov 2009.

53 Ibid.

54 Medvedev 2008. The Russian original appeared a year earlier as 'Literatura budet proverena: individual'nyi proekt i 'novaia emotsional'nost'' in Medvedev's collection of essays *Reaktsiia voobshche* (Medvedev 2007).

55 Ibid.

56 Ibid.

57 All citations ibid.

58 I do outline a more comprehensive overview of sincerity rhetorics in post-Soviet Russia in the forthcoming monograph *Post-Soviet Sincerity: A Cultural History*.

59 Lipovetsky 2008:575.

60 Ibid.:591; italics original.

61 Yurchak 2008:257.

62 Ibid.:276.

63 Ibid.

64 Among others, see on this trend Markovits 2008:82. According to Lipovetsky, in a 'Russian analogy' to 9/11, the 1999 bombings of apartments in Moscow and Volgodonsk triggered a Russian shift from postmodern to late postmodern culture; other critics envision the same shift as a Russian turn to 'post-postmodern' thinking (see Lipovetsky 2008:470ff).

65 Etkind 2009:654; Marsh 2007:13.

66 Etind 2004.

67 Van Alphen et al. 2009:1.

Chapter 2 – British Literature

1 Larkin 1974:6-7.

2 Leavis 1948:18.

3 Homi K. Bhabha, *The Location of Culture*, p. 328.

4 Rushdie 1988:156.

5 Rushdie 1992:20.

6 Dominic Head, *The State of the Novel: Britain and Beyond* (Oxford: Wiley-Blackwell, 2008), p. 32.

7 See Brian McHale, *Postmodernist Fiction* (London: Routledge, 1999), p. 10-11.

8 Richard Bradford, *The Novel Now: contemporary British fiction* (Oxford: Blackwell, 2007), p. 67.

9 David Shields, *Reality Hunger: A Manifesto* (London: Hamish Hamilton, 2010), p. 3.

10 Ibid.:5.

11 Ian McEwan in 'Journeys without Maps: An Interview with Ian McEwan' in *Ian McEwan:*

Contemporary Critical Perspectives, edited by Sebastian Groes (London and New York: Cotoniuum, 2009), p. 131.

12 Ian McEwan, *Saturday* (London: Jonathan Cape, 2005), p. 168.

13 J.G. Ballard, 'Introduction', *Crash* (London: Vintage, 1995), p. 4. Originally published in 1973 by Jonathan Cape.

14 Mark Currie, *About Time* (Edinburgh: Edinburgh University Press, 2007), pp. 130-31.

15 Alistair Cormack, 'Postmodernism and the Ethics of Fiction in *Atonement*', in *Ian McEwan: Contemporary Critical Perspectives* (London and New York: Continuum, 2009), p. 82.

16 Zadie Smith, *White Teeth* (London: Hamish Hamilton, 2000), p. 459.

17 Zadie Smith in an interview on the website of her publisher, Random House: http://www.randomhouse.com/boldtype/0700/smith/interview.html [accessed 3 June 2008].

18 See Lorna Sage, *Women in the House of Fiction* (Basingstoke: Macmillan, 1992), pp. 72-113.

19 Zadie Smith, *White Teeth* (London: Hamish Milton, 2000), p. 23.

20 Pilar Cuder-Domínguez, 'Ethnic Cartographies of London in Bernardine Evaristo and Zadie Smith', *European Journal of English Studies* 8(2), 2004:173-88, p. 188.

21 Bruce King, *The Oxford English Literary History: The Internationalization of English Literature*, Vol. 13 (Oxford: Oxford University Press, 2005; first published 2004), pp. 289-90.

22 Smith, *White Teeth*, 465-6.

23 Zadie Smith, *Changing My Mind* (London, Hamish Hamilton: 2009), p. 71.

24 Smith *Mind*, 73.

25 Smith, *Mind*, 93.

26 Tom McCarthy, *Remainder* (2006), p. 5. First published by Metronome Press, Paris, in 2005.

27 McCarthy, *Remainder*, 62.

28 Tom McCarthy, *C* (London: Jonathan Cape, 2010), p. 23.

Chapter 3 – Dutch Literature

1 http://www.arnongrunberg.com/blog/1567-censor (blog posting, October 2, 2010).

2 I use the term 'liberal humanism' to denote the ruling assumptions, values and meanings of mainstream literary theory until the late 1960s: literature is timeless; literature contains its own meaning; the text will reveal constants and universal truths for each of us; the purpose of literature is the enrichment of life; content stems from form; a literary work is 'sincere'. See, e.g. Barry 2002, Bertens 2001:6-9 and Waugh 2006:245-55.

3 See Hutcheon 1988:178.

4 See, e.g. Jameson 1984, who argued that the late capitalist cultural logic of postmodernism had ruined the normative values of modernism (and that this is not necessarily a good thing), or Rorty 1989, who analysed the drawing apart of postmodern theorists and the general public and who posed the question if and how politics and ethics are still possible after the postmodern rejection of concepts such as 'truth' or 'foundation'.

5 I will focus on the Dutch situation, leaving Belgian literature written in Dutch aside: the

idea of postmodernism has a different history in Belgium, and therefore the reconsideration of its legacy by Flemish authors (such as Pol Hoste, Koen Peeters or David Nolens) has taken a different shape. See, e.g. Vervaeck 2007 and chapter 8 in this volume (Sven Vitse).

6 The exception that proves the rule is Carel Peeters, the only critic in Dutch newspapers who thought it was worthwhile to parry postmodernism's criticism of liberal humanism. None of his colleagues reacted to this essay. See Ruiter 1997; Overstijns 1996:15-42; Heynders 1997:220-1 and Vaessens 2009:55-6.

7 The first review (available in the comprehensive digital database of Dutch literary criticism in newspapers: LiteRom, http://www.knipselkranten.nl/literom) in which the word 'postmodernism' is used to characterize a Dutch work of literature appeared on 12 May 1983 (Geerts 1983).

8 The first essays on postmodernism by Dutch literature scholars in the Netherlands are: Mertens 1988; Van Alphen 1985 and 1989; Beekman 1989 and 1991. Some subsequent publications include Van den Akker 1993; Vaessens & Joosten 2003.

9 Mertens in Ligtvoet & Van Nieuwenborgh 1993:120. Free translation: Recently the concept of 'Postmodernism' also took root in the Netherlands. It is significant that it provoked a response amongst literary journalists in particular and that it – like any buzzword – rapidly suffered from semantic inflation.

10 Ebert (1991:292) distinguishes between the floating signifiers of playful text-based postmodernism and forms of postmodernism that mobilize resistance. Ebert: 'Ludic postmodernism finds its articulation in the disappearance of the transcendental signified, as in such writers as Derrida, Lyotard and Baudrillard, for whom reality is a theatre of "simulation" marked by the free play of images, disembodied signifiers and the heterogeneity of difference'. The concept of 'play' is vital in postmodernism and is not superficial.

11 While it is true that this notion has become one of the landmarks in the debate on postmodernism, it should nevertheless be noted that a general relativist stance, a juggling with genre conventions, a blurring of boundaries between high and low culture, and a hypertrophy of intertextual or intermedial references may but does not necessarily lead to, or indicate, an 'anything goes'. In fact, there are several contributions to the debate on postmodernism that critically discuss such an uncritical equalization (cf., e.g. Welsch 1993).

12 Zwagerman 1987:20-50.

13 Ibid. and Van Peteghem 2003:151.

14 See Bultinck 2009.

15 See, e.g. Steinz 2004:401. Some Dutch 'playful postmodernists' include Joost Niemöller, the writing duo Martin Bril and Dirk van Weelden and the poets who came to be known as 'De Zestigers', e.g. J. Bernlef and K. Schippers.

16 Vervaeck 1999:14; Ruiter & Smulders 1996:288.

17 Vervaeck 1999:47.

18 Willem Brakman, Gerrit Krol, Louis Ferron and Charlotte Mutsaers (in her early work) are among Dutch 'intellectualist postmodernists'.

19 The debates are discussed extensively in Vaessens 2009 and 2002.
20 In the Dutch debate this criticism was expressed by journalists such as Michaël Zeeman and Carel Peters, and by academics such as Maarten Doorman. See Vaessens 2009:220.
21 Compagnon 2000:136. Free translation: Literature has become a marginal area, a peripheral appendix of culture; it has disappeared from social discourse. See also Marx 2005.
22 Van Heydebrand & Winko 2008:224.
23 Van Dijk 2008.
24 De Vries 2010:35.
25 Vullings 2007.
26 Peters 1990.
27 Peeters 1990. Cf. Osstyn 1990 and Mertens 1990.
28 Vervaeck 1999:12.
29 See Gielis 2007:170 and Rovers 2008:3.
30 Cloostermans 2008.
31 Lamoree 2007.
32 Luis 2007.
33 Februari 2007:61.
34 Ibid.:86.
35 Bauman 1998.
36 Cf. Vaessens 2009:168-75.
37 Februari 2009:147.
38 Ibid.:207.
39 Februari 2007:30.
40 Ibid.:30-1.
41 Februari 2004:209.
42 Van Erkelens 1994. Cf. Matthijsse 1998 and Gerbrandy 2001.
43 Van Kempen 1989.
44 Heumakers 1989. Cf. Meijsing 1989.
45 See, e.g. Zwagerman 1987:135.
46 Hoogervorst 1994; Oosterwaal 1993.
47 Zwagerman 1994:258-9.
48 Zwagerman 1997:63.
49 Ibid.:30.
50 Ibid.:126;55.
51 Zwagerman in an interview (Schutte 1997): both characters are 'two nightmare-like versions of myself'.
52 Vaessens 2009:125-50.
53 See for Zwagerman's essays on this topic, e.g. Zwagerman 2003:27-35; 2003:114; 2006 and 2006a:117. Since the 1950s 'the connection between literature and social life is lost,' said Zwagerman in an interview (Zwart 1989): 'literature is a pastime for the well-to-do middle

class'. Zwagerman wants to see this changed. See for a reflection on writer's block novels, the position of the writer and postmodernism Green 2005.

54 Zwagerman 1994:179.

55 Adriaens 1997.

56 See, e.g. Peeters 2001 ('Grunberg is the laughing stock of postmodernism'); Zwier 1994 and Bakker 1998.

57 See, e.g. Grunberg 2004:334: 'I do not believe anything'.

58 Coupland 1991:69.

59 Grunberg's early work was judged as fundamentally ironical and free of true *engagement*. See, e.g. Werkman 1998 and Hoomans 2003.

60 Blom 2007.

61 Yasha (=Grunberg) in VPRO-gids, 6 December 1999.

62 Grunberg 2007:12. Grunberg's attitude to irony is ambivalent (cf. Eggers and other New Sincerity writers). He had been brought up a postmodernist; deconstruction had become second nature to him. He tries to overcome his own initial cynicism without falling back upon a naïve, non-ironical (pre-postmodern) attitude.

63 Groenewegen 2004:81.

64 See, e.g. Cloostermans 2008.

65 The reports have been brought together in Grunberg 2009. Of Grunberg's recent novels, only the non-representative novel The Jewish Messiah (2004) is available in English translation (2008): this novel was rightly characterized by a Dutch reviewer as a thoroughly ironic book in which 'ideals are just a cover for selfish desires' (Wallet 2005:4-10).

66 Grunberg 2008:637.

67 Van Dijk 2010:50-1.

68 't Hart 2008. Cf. Schut 2008; Ruyters 2008.

69 Grunberg 2009:25.

70 Grunberg 2001.

71 Grunberg 2009:23.

72 R.V., 'De mensheid zij geprezen: Arnon Grunberg zoekt een redelijk wezen', Humo, 30 April 2001.

73 http://www.arnongrunberg.com/blog/1567-censor (blog posting, 2 October 2010).

74 Grunberg 1996.

75 See Van Dijk 2009.

76 Zeeman 2001.

77 See Vaessens 2009.

Chapter 4 – Italian Literature

1 Cf. Vaessens 2009:16.

2 Cf. Foster 2001:226: 'We can [...] make value judgments that, in Nietzschean terms, are not

only reactive but active – and, in non-Nietzschean terms, not only distinctive but useful. Otherwise critical theory may come to deserve the bad name with which it is often branded today'.

3 Ricciardi 2011:15.
4 Calvino 1983.
5 Wu Ming 2009.
6 See for instance Wren-Owens: 'In a period in which the early practitioners of *impegno* reject committed writing in the face of political and literary challenges, Sciascia and Tabucchi demonstrate a real belief in the power of writing (and especially literature) to engage with contemporary society' (2007:188).
7 Cf. in the Netherlands an interview with Heijne 2010a.
8 See, e.g. Lanslots 1999.
9 Cf. Jansen 2005.
10 Chirumbolo & Moroni 2010:12.
11 Luperini 1984:15.
12 Cf. Petrella 2006:139, who argues that the cultural concept of 'double coding' has been essential for American postmodernism, but in Italy is represented by just a few examples, among which *The Name of the Rose*.
13 Wu Ming 2009:24. All translations from Italian are mine.
14 Cf. Van Stralen's analysis of neo-Marxism's criticism of the postmodern worldview: 'The major criticism of the postmodern mental attitude is that it is necessary to adopt an external point of view with regard to a juncture primarily in order to make a rational analysis of the situation to be able subsequently to undertake actions as a result of this investigation. According to neo-Marxists, both elements are lacking within postmodern philosophy' (2005:215).
15 Ceserani in a 2010 article, goes into alternatives for the concept of postmodernism, of which 'reflexive modernization' dates back from 1994 (Ceserani 2010:11; Beck, Giddens and Lash 1994).
16 Ceserani 1997:135.
17 Pasolini 1975.
18 Antonello 2001:46.
19 Casadei 2007:7.
20 Wu Ming 2009:125-26.
21 Wu Ming 2009:44-45. Their analysis of transmedia storytelling is based on Jenkins 2006.
22 Wu Ming 2009:14-15.
23 Casadei 2007:11. For an analysis and introduction to NIE's intentions and outcomes, see *Journal of Romance Studies*' special issue edited by Boscolo (2010).
24 Cf. La Porta's 'pamphlet' against the success of Italian crime fiction, 'Contro il Nuovo Giallo Italiano (e se avessimo trovato il genere a noi congeniale?)' (2006).
25 This self-critical version of national character, according to Patriarca is typical for the concept of Italian national identity and often becomes a means 'to shift the blame from concrete actors and precise responsibilities on to that timeless factor: the eternal Italian character' (2010:11).
26 Cf. Carravetta 2009.

27 Casadei 2007:40.
28 Vasta 2009.
29 Casadei 2007:14.
30 Wu Ming 2009:19.
31 Virno and Hardt 1996:4.
32 Luperini 2005:20.
33 Baricco 2001:61.
34 Portoghesi 1983:11-12.
35 Cf. Hutcheon in *A poetics of Postmodernism*: 'postmodern architecture seems to me to be paradigmatic of our seeming urgent need, in both artistic theory and practice, to investigate the relation of ideology and power to all of our present discursive structures, and it is for this reason that I will be using it as my model throughout this study' (1988:36).
36 Voce in Barilli 2005:272. See also Jansen 2010c. A *Gruppo 93* anthology was edited by Petrella in 2010.
37 Stellardi 2009:89.
38 Cf. Agamben 1998 and Esposito 2008.
39 According to Antonello & Mussgnug, 'Global co-dependency and the horizontal proliferation of networks force us to think in systemic and no longer in dialectical terms' (2009:6-7).
40 Cf. Revelli in Virno & Hardt: 'Change, proteiformity, and speed – the grand myths of modernity – have to all intents and purposes become the attributes of capital' (1997:115).
41 De Michele 2010:68.
42 De Michele 2010:72.
43 Petrella 2006:147.
44 Petrella 2006:148.
45 Antonello & Mussgnug 2009:3.
46 Antonello & Mussgnug 2009:10-11.
47 Donnarumma 2008:34.
48 Donnarumma 2008:54.
49 Wu Ming 2009:69.
50 Timmer argues that what distinguishes this new generation of American authors is 'the emphatic expression of feelings and sentiments, a drive towards inter-subjective connection and communication, and also a sense of "presence" and "sameness"' (2008:10).
51 Genna 2006: '*Troppi paradisi* is absolutely the first example of *postmodernism* in Italy since many years'.
52 Wu Ming 2009:41. See also Boscolo: 'A UNO is a novel that [...] produces testimony from local documents [...]. However, contrary to reportage, the specificity of these 'narrative objects' [...] lies in the 'narrative translation' they operate on the documents, that is, the way documents are fused into the story and turned into fiction' (2010:3).
53 Cf. Ricciardi 2011:183-85.
54 Palumbo Mosca 2009:320; 322.

55 Ceserani 2009:44.
56 Cf. Petrella 2006:144.
57 Tabucchi 2006:126.
58 Jansen 2009:58.
59 Foster 2001:207.
60 Critchley 2007:10.
61 Critchley 2007:132.
62 Critchley 2007:120: 'An ethical politics flows from our constitutive powerlessness in the face of the other'.
63 Tabucchi 2009:171.
64 Barilli 2000:XVII.
65 Baricco 1993; 2002. Also his collected newspaper columns (Baricco 1995 and Baricco 1998) are examples of cultural criticism.
66 Cf. Giulio Ferroni's annihilating critique of the *I barbari* essay which he defines a brilliant example of 'neosaggistica metapostmoderna', of neo metapostmodern essayism (2006:11).
67 Baricco 2010:51.
68 Baricco 2010:50.
69 Ferroni 2006:31. Also Bas Heijne comes back on his initial enthusiasm and underlines that as long as we feel a lack of depth, there must be something like depth (2010b).
70 Scalfari 2010:277: 'Ours was a melancholic generation [...] conditioned by existential guilt complexes'.
71 Scalfari 2010b.
72 Magris 2009:66.
73 Scurati 2006.
74 Cf. Jansen 2010b.
75 McNeill 2009:160.
76 Cf. Pellegrini 2009.
77 Calabrese 2005:52-53.
78 McKenzie Wark 2007, cit. in Wu Ming 2009:53.
79 Wu Ming 2009:53.
80 His work possesses, according to La Porta, 'a unique expressive mixture made out of literary and cinematographic horror, B-rate Italian comedy, American movies for television, images drawn from commercial ads, and a few good readings of canonical authors' (2001:61).
81 Rajewsky 2003:294-333.
82 Covacich 2005:134.

Chapter 5 – French Literature

1 Viart (in Viart & Blanckeman 2005) treats Echenoz in a chapter called 'Le roman impassible' stating that impassivity is the main characteristic of his novels.

2 Robbe-Grillet (1963) and Sarraute (1956) refer to Proust's *In search of lost time* and explain that they have been inspired by this novel because Proust breaks with the conventions of the realistic novel.

3 Robbe-Grillet 1984:27.

4 Viart & Blanckeman 2005:18. In my study *Le roman transgressif contemporain. De Bret Easton Ellis à Michel Houellebecq* (Van Wesemael 2011) I examine this neo-realism in contemporary French literature, and like Viart and Blanckeman I come to the conclusion that the contemporary novel is often a hybrid form in which realism and postmodernism converge.

5 Houellebecq 2004:189.

6 Clément (2004) develops this idea that Houllebecq's novels have some characteristics in common with the nineteenth-century naturalist experimental novel.

7 Houellebecq 2003:181.

8 Docherty (1983:14) states: 'Description is the establishment of attitude in the 'position' of character and reader. But in many recent novels we witness either a loss of individuation in characters, or their anonymity. Rather than being clearly delineated centers around which we can orient ourselves and our attitudes, they become fragmentary or evanescent. The stability of 'character' is replaced with the more mobile 'subject'; in some cases, instead of characters, we seem to have fragmentary 'instants of subjectivity' none of which seem to be related to each other, and none of which seem ever to develop into a more stable Self'.

9 See Van Wesemael 2005, chapter 'Le complexe de castration'.

10 Van Wesemael 2005, the chapter on Houellebecq's satiric approach to the utopian novel.

11 Houellebecq 2006:44.

12 See for instance Houppermans 2008, chapter 2, 'Territoires et trajets', in which the author explains that the French novelist constantly uses techniques from popular genres like the detective novel and the biography.

13 Houellebecq 2006:26.

14 Houellebecq 2005:142.

15 Demonpion (2005) argues in the same manner.

16 Lipovetsky 1992 :195.

17 Ibid.:38.

18 Houellebecq 2000:349.

19 Vaessens 2009. See also chapter 3 in this volume.

20 Houellebecq 2006:12.

21 Bessière (2006) also investigates the relationship between the contemporary postmodern novel and the neo-realist novel and concludes that they have still a lot in common.

22 Claudel 2005:159.

23 Claudel 2005:24-25.

24 Claudel 2005:170.

25 Claudel 2005:180.

26 Claudel 2005:35.

27 Claudel 2005:119.
28 Claudel 2005:180.
29 Claudel 2005:67.
30 Claudel 2005:27.
31 Claudel 2005:26.
32 Claudel 2005:104.
33 Claudel 2005:86-87.
34 Claudel 2005:79.
35 Claudel 2005:9.
36 Claudel 2005:10.
37 Houellebecq 2005:10.

Chapter 6 – Post-Yugoslav Literature

1 Tode 2004:40.
2 See Andrew Wachtel 2006 for a discussion of various (literary, economical, political) consequences of the end of communism for writers in Central and Eastern Europe.
3 Pleşu 2004:106.
4 In a short review of Mihai Sebastian's *Diary 1935-1944*, which caused a heated debate in Romanian literary life when it was first published in the 1990s, the celebrated novelist Norman Manea writes: 'At the time, he [Sebastian] was losing his best Christian friends to fanaticism (Mircea Eliade and E.M. Cioran, among them) and living with the impending danger of deportation and death, questioning the moments of ease that his provisional freedom allowed him.' *Common Knowledge* 9.1 (2003) 161. While someone like Sebastianu can be classed as a cosmopolitan writer, the post-1989 era also revived right-wing writers. The case of the Transylvanian-Hungarian writer Albert Wass is discussed in Neubauer 2009: '[...] the works of Wass have experienced an incredible boom, whose Hungarian repercussions far exceed the better-known resurrection of Sándor Márai's writing. [...] Wass has become the darling, something of an emblem, of right-wing chauvinists and anti-Semites' (569).
5 Stefanovski 2004:25.
6 Péter Esterházy's *Harmonia Caelestis* and its sequel, *Revised Edition*, are a case in point. Soon after *Harmonia Caelestis* was published in 2000, unknown documents about the author's father were discovered in the archives of the Hungarian Secret Police. It turned out that Esterházy's father had worked for over twenty years as an informant for the Secret Police, dutifully providing them with information about the former Hungarian aristocracy and much more. The discovery prompted Esterházy to write a sequel to his autobiographical novel, *Revised Edition - Supplement to Harmonia Caelestis*. The revised edition presents his father's reports to the Secret Police in red ink. It also gives Esterházy's own response to them.
7 Cultural life in Yugoslavia came to enjoy the full potential of its position between the Western and the Eastern bloc from the second half of the 1960s. Examples could include the

GORGONA group of artists (see Nena Dimitrijevi 2002) or the BITEF theater festival, founded in 1967, which hosted Robert Wilson in its early years, while at the same time receiving avant-gardists from countries from the Communist bloc. This more or less coincided with the arrival of postmodernism. Conceptual art thrived especially – Marina Abramović, Braco Dimitijević, Sanja Iveković.

8 See Urban 1997 for a detailed discussion of the metaphor of reality as a 'random storehouse'.

9 Sontag 1995:xiii.

10 Of course there is no absolute relationship between a writer's formal and aesthetic affinities and his political affiliation. The case of Milorad Pavić, an outspoken practitioner of postmodern writing and a ferocious nationalist, is discussed in Wachtel 1997:210-219.

11 Elsewhere I have referred to the genre as 'fictionalized biography', or, following Philippe Lejeune's distinctions between factual and fictional modes of reading, as a 'contradictory text', as it urges the reader to approach the stories both as fiction and as documented history. See: Snel 2004.

12 Shishkoff 1987:342.

13 Mihalovich 1994:169.

14 Kiš 1995:30.

15 Kiš 1995:20.

16 Milosz 1990:87.

17 Nalkowska 1970:34.

18 Štajner 1981:7.

19 The phenomenon is restricted neither to East/Central Europe nor to the pre-1989 era. An apt illustration is the case of Binjamin Wilkomirski, alias Bruno Doesseker. In 1995 he published early childhood memories, *Bruchstücke*, in which he reconstructs his time in a Nazi extermination camp. The 'memories' were exposed as a figment of his imagination. Already the amount of literature written on the subject confirms how crucial the documentary imperative still is, and how much it directs our perception of texts and their genre. See for instance: Susan Suleiman, 'Problems of Memory and Factuality in recent Holocaust Memoirs' in *Poetics Today*, 21:3, p.543-559.

20 Mehmedinović 1998:84.

21 Mehmedinović 1998:1.

22 In an e-mail exchange I conducted with the author while preparing a selection of his work for Dutch translation, Mehmedinović stated explicitly about the American edition: 'This is Sarajevo Blues'.

23 Mehmedinović 2002:86.

24 Mehmedinović 2002:87.

25 A similar analysis can be found in Jean Baudrillard's essay 'Pas de pitié pour Sarajevo'. His question was: what's the logic behind diplomatic negotiations when the European Union lacks a fundamental readiness to intervene in the Bosnian war? 'The strongest objection to

the offensive led by guilty consciences, and as displayed in such happenings as the one in Strasbourg, is that it perpetuates the image of the alleged weakness of European policies, and the image of Europe's conscience supposedly torn by its own powerlessness. It hereby covers up entirely what is really going on, by granting this reality the benefit of spiritual doubt.' Mehmedinović did not stop writing entirely, but he kept silent between 1995 and 2002; and he has been silent ever since 2002. See: Baudrillard 1993.

26 See: Snel in Neubauer and Török 2009.
27 Snel 2005:87.
28 Snel 2005:87.
29 Mehmedinović 2002:11.
30 Mehmedinović 2002:18.
31 Tempting, and I suppose very relevant, would be a comparison of Hemon with other recent American fiction dealing with 'returns to Europe', like Daniel Mendelsohn's non-fictional *The Lost: A Search for Six of the Six Million* (2006) or Jonathan Safran Foer's autofictional *Everything is Illuminated* (2002). I propose that Hemon is different in at least one respect; unlike Safran Foer and Mendelsohn, his is a return to a continent that is still part of direct, personal experience, visible, for instance, in multilingual competences: the character Brik of course speaks Bosnian and even, through his family history, a little Ukrainian. Hemon himself, who stresses in his biography the mixed Serbo-Ukrainian roots of his Bosnian family, lives a double linguistic existence, writing fiction in English and a column in Bosnian in the weekly DANI.
32 See for instance Hutcheon 1987.
33 Hemon 2008:58.
34 http://www.thedailybeast.com/blogs-and-stories/2009-05-14/way-out-of-sarajevo/full/ consulted on 18 March 2010, 10:49.
35 Hemon 2008:293.
36 Hemon 2008:52.
37 Snel 2004:392-396.
38 For a fascinating critique of the sometimes extremely cerebral praise for Sebald, see De Roder 2005.
39 Drndić 2007:136.
40 Historian Frank van Vree conducted the interview in Amsterdam, in Academic Debate Center SPUI25 on 15 February 2010.

Chapter 7 – Norwegian Literature

1 Cf. Stegane 1994:652. Gujord 1998.
2 Rottem 2004, Stegane 1994.
3 An interesting response to postmodernism is the way in which authors like Hanne Ørstavik, Lars Saabye Christensen, Nikolaj Frobenius and Dag Solstad in the first decade of the twenty-first century have renewed intertextuality. Several of their novels, perhaps most

clearly put forward in *Modellen* [*The Model*] (2005) by Lars Saabye Christensen, seem to transgress intertextuality, as they are modelled after canonical Norwegian texts. *Modellen* is a modern version of Henrik Ibsens play *Vildanden* [*The Wild Duck*] (1884). Therefore, not only is the originality of the texts being challenged, but that kind of imitation challenges the romantic view of the artist himself and the status of literature as a whole.

4 Cf. Fluck 1992:85.
5 Cf. Foucault 1977:129.
6 Frobenius 2004.
7 Brooks 1993:88, 96.
8 Binding 2003.
9 Christensen 2001:83.
10 Rottem 2004a.
11 Cf. Tjønneland 1999.
12 Ørstavik 1997:73.

Chapter 8 – Flemish Literature

1 Musschoot 2009:616.
2 Musschoot 1994.
3 Vervaeck 1999.
4 Vervaeck 2007:164.
5 Van Bastelaere 1990.
6 For a detailed discussion of irony and commitment in *High Key* and *Montréal*, see Vitse 2003.
7 Verhelst 2003.
8 Bultinck 2000. Patrick Peeters (2000) characterised the novel as an example of 'aesthetical postmodernism', implying an opposition between aesthetical and ethical postmodernism. For an alternative reading of *Tongkat*, see Vaessens 2001.
9 Curiously, the two most interesting reviews of *Zwerm* were radically opposed in their appreciation of the novel. Jeroen Theunissen (2006a) considered the novel to be 'totalitarian', whereas according to Bart Vervaeck (2006) the novel offers a disturbing critique of the excesses of capitalism.
10 Verhaeghen 2007.
11 One of those critics was *Yang* editor Bert Bultinck (2004).
12 Buelens et.al. 2000:153.
13 Ibid.:152.
14 Ibid.:151.
15 Ibid.:151.
16 Ibid.:153.
17 Van Hulle 2002:233.
18 Vervaeck 1999:15.

19 Reugebrink 2002:551.
20 Adriaensen, De Coster & Sintobin 2006.
21 Bassant & Snoekx 2008:569.
22 Bart Vervaeck (2009) analyses this novel as an example of contemporary historical fiction in Dutch literature, in an article which also discusses *Zwerm* by Peter Verhelst and *Omega minor* by Paul Verhaeghen. According to Vervaeck these are postmodern novels which have clearly moved beyond relativism.
23 Peeters 2007:161.
24 Ibid.:109.
25 Ibid.:162.
26 Ibid.:135.
27 Ibid.:153.
28 Ibid.:145.
29 Ibid.:89.
30 Ibid.:119.
31 Peeters 2009:43.
32 Ibid.:43.
33 Ibid.:225.
34 Ibid.:94.
35 Ibid.:111.
36 Ibid.:111.
37 Ibid.:112.
38 Ibid.:112.
39 Ibid.:225.
40 Ibid.:76.
41 Ibid.:77.
42 Ibid.:77.
43 Ibid.:46.
44 Ibid.:104.
45 Ibid.:104.
46 Ibid.:228.
47 Ibid.:230.
48 Nolens 2005:30.
49 Ibid.:35.
50 Ibid.:35.
51 Ibid.:75.
52 Ibid.:65.
53 Ibid.:88.
54 For a discussion of both *Stilte en melk voor iedereen* and *Een vorm van vermoeidheid* by Jeroen Theunissen, see Vitse 2009.

55 Nolens 2008:12.
56 Ibid.:15.
57 Ibid.:39.
58 Ibid.:54.
59 Theunissen 2006b:263.
60 Ibid.:234.
61 Ibid.:266.
62 Ibid.:76.
63 Ibid.:42.
64 Ibid.:84.
65 Ibid.:75.
66 Theunissen 2008:9.
67 Ibid.:56.
68 Ibid.:21.
69 Ibid.:132.
70 Ibid.:134.

Chapter 9 – Polish Literature

1 As a precursor of modernism, Norwid could be compared to the English poet Gerard Manley Hopkins, who was also overlooked by his contemporaries.

2 According to Gombrowicz, man is never at home with himself, because his existence is determined by conventions produced by other men. However, these forms are – in their turn – modified by his reaction to them, e.g. by his producing an 'anti-form' that should not be understood as a creation *ex nihilo*, as it remains negatively dependent on the forms of the world in which man has been 'thrown' (Heidegger's *Geworfenheit*). Due to this particular brand of 'existentialism', Gombrowicz appears to be firmly rooted in the postwar 'Western' literature.

3 Zdzisław Łapiński who popularised postmodernism in Poland in a seminal article, published in the academic literary periodical *Teksty Drugie* ('Postmodernism – what it is and why?'), noted – wishing expressly to evade all determinist notions about postmodernism as the product of a post-industrialist society – that the precursors of postmodernism (he mentions Borges, Becket, Gombrowicz and Nabokov) came from 'backward', rural, 'patriarchal', 'catholic' areas (Łapiński 1993:76-77).

4 Miłosz 2003:177.

5 Nycz 2000:166.

6 The Polish literary historian Włodzimierz Bolecki mentions the following 'candidates for representing Polish postmodernism': 'Stanisław Ignacy Witkiewicz, Witold Gombrowicz, Bruno Schulz, Aleksander Wat, Leopold Buczkowski, Teodor Parnicki, Jerzy Andrzejewski, Tadeusz Konwicki, Miron Białoszewski, Tadeusz Różewicz, Piotr Wojciechowski, Adam Zagajewski, Andrzej Bart, and this list could certainly be made longer'. Bolecki 1999:29.

7 Ryszard Nycz distinguishes between three different uses of the term 'postmodernism'. The first one designates a 'cultural époque', following on modernity, that started in the 1960s. The second use refers to a particular *Zeitgeist* and lifestyle, Lyotard's 'postmodern condition', that affected not only cultural phenomena but also politics and the economy. The third variety of postmodernism describes distinct artistic phenomena that are conceived of as being a 'critical continuation' of modernism in art and literature. In many cases it is far from easy to distinguish between these uses. However, the most frequently quoted authorities in the Polish modernism/postmodernism debate (Lyotard, Habermas, Rorty, Baudrillard, Jameson, Geertz, Vattimo) represent the first and second uses of the term (Nycz 2000:162-166).

8 However, it could be argued that the opposition between artificiality and authenticity is a false one. According to Ryszard, the postmodernist paradigm could bring some order in the ostensibly erratic development of the post-war Polish literature if we accept that it 'connotates not only *post-avant-gardism* (criticizing the illusiveness of literature's complete autonomy) but also *post-realism* (criticizing the illusiveness of mimesis as directly mirroring reality)'. Nycz 2000:191. From this point of view Czesław Miłosz could be classified as a postrealist.

9 Klejnocki & Sosnowski 1996:111.

10 Ibid.:111.

11 Ibid.:112.

12 The concept of double-coding with regard to a novel representing non-elitist literature was already employed before the fall of communism. The influential academic critic Jan Błoński published a review of Paweł Huelle's novel *Weiser Davidek* in 1987 in which he pointed to the possibility of reading it on many levels: as a 'novel of manners', a 'political parable', or even 'an allegory of the return of the Messiah' [Przemysław Czapliński, *Powrót centrali* (The Return of the Headquarter). Kraków, 2007, p. 105]. Czapliński himself draws attention to the fact that Huelle constructed *Weiser Davidek* as a detective story, 'in order to show different attitudes towards a mystery' (Czapliński 2007:198). During the 1990s the detective story ceased to be a subliterary genre. Particularly the novels of Marek Krajewski, set in the still German Breslau [Wrocław] and combining elements of the detective story with the thriller, appear to be an excellent example of double coding.

13 This process of change has been analysed in detail by Przemysław Czapliński in his seminal study, *The Return of the Headquarter Literature in the New Reality* ('Powrót centrali literature w nowej rzeczywisto ci', Kraków, 2007). The subsequent sections could not have been written without his research.

14 Cf. Czapliński 2007:111.

15 Ibid.:190-200.

16 In fact, this reaction started a few years before the fall of communism [1989]. The first issues of *Bru-Lion* appeared illegally, beyond the control of censorship [since 1986].

17 Herbert 1992:31.

18 Heaney 1988:69.

19 Cf. Czapliński & Śliwiński 1999:115.

20 Cf. Pietrych, 2007:135. Pietrych uses this formula to describe the later poetry of Herbert's younger contemporary Stanisław Barańczak.
21 On the antinomies of the poetry of *Bru-Lion* cf. Czapliński & Śliwiński 2000:284-319.
22 Steiner 1989.
23 Gorczyńska 1992:49.
24 Cf. 'Allen, good man, great poet of a murderous age, insisting on madness you achieved wisdom' (Miłosz 1994:30).
25 Miłosz 1994:32.
26 'First-order poems [...] have a first-person, narrative base [...] second-order poems reflect on that first-order plane'. Vendler 1988:75 .
27 Miłosz 1994:25.
28 Cf. 'I would say that the cognizability or non-cognizability of the external world in relation to our mind is pushed into the background, since only the act of submission and identifying (with the Dutch still-life) really matters, contrasting with the imagination that starts from the "I"' (Miłosz 1997:118). Miłosz's stance is almost the exact opposite of Gombrowicz's conviction that existence 'cannot be but artificial'. Yet, the fact that they arrive at different conclusions remains without consequences for the 'existential sincerity' of their attempts to grasp man's 'being-in-the-world'.
29 Rorty 1989:141.
30 Miłosz 1997:141.
31 Ibid. 154.
32 Ibid. 154.
33 The forest of Katyń was one of Stalin's 'killing fields' where in June 1940 thousands of Polish officers that had been taken prisoner in September 1939 were murdered by the Soviet security forces.
34 http://www.rp.pl/artykul/464644_Rymki__Do_Jaroslawa_Kaczynskiego.html

Chapter 10 – German Literature

1 Dietz 2005. All translations are mine, unless otherwise indicated. I owe thanks to Alana Gillespie for editing the manuscript.
2 Krause 2007.
3 See Harbers 2000.
4 Ruiter 1991, ch. 2.
5 Cf. Berendse 2000:233-256. Lewis 2000:257-286.
6 See Bürger, Bürger & Schulte-Sasse (eds.) 1982.
7 Luckscheiter 2002:32-46.
8 Habermas 1988:178-192, 178. For the context of postmodern writing and cultural identity, cf. Haak 2006, 55-86, and Kunne 2005.
9 Früchtl 2007:14.

10 Habermas 1988:178-192, 179. Cf. Adorno 1990:43-47.

11 Welsch 1987; Welsch (ed.) 1988.

12 Ortheil 1987. Interestingly, it is visible before Manfred Frank published his book in 1986.

13 Hildesheimer 1991:125-140. On the highly reserved and stern reception of this lecture, see Braese et al. (eds.) 1998:331-349.

14 Späth 2001.

15 Hoffer 1986.

16 Hillgruber 2007.

17 *Merkur. Deutsche Zeitschrift für europäisches Denken.* Eds. Karl Heinz Bohrer & Kurt Scheel. Vol. 52, no. 594/595, September/October 1998.

18 Müller, 1998:975-981.

19 Merkur. Deutsche Zeitschrift für europäisches Denken. Eds. Karl Heinz Bohrer & Kurt Scheel. Vol. 52, no. 594/595, September/October 1998, 755.

20 Merkur. Deutsche Zeitschrift für europäisches Denken. Eds. Karl Heinz Bohrer & Kurt Scheel. Vol. 52, no. 594/595, September/October 1998, 755-756.

21 Sokal & Bricmont, 1998:929-943, 943.

22 Assheuer 1998.

23 Lützeler 1998, http://www.zeit.de/1998/41/199841.postmod.2_.xml.

24 Wittstock (ed.) 1994:7.

25 Lützeler 2010.

26 Bohrer 1998:137-150.

27 Schirrmacher 1989. Cited in Moritz & Köhler (eds.) 1998:15-17.

28 Schirrmacher 1990.

29 Biller 1998:62-71.

30 Biller 2000:47-49.

31 Altenburg 1992:310, 311, 313. Reprinted in Moritz & Köhler (eds.) 1998:72-85.

32 Hielscher 1996.

33 Cf. Hielscher 2001:65-71.

34 Cf. Hage 1999:244-254.

35 Politycki 2004:133-140. Stolz 2004:111-126. For more examples see Taberner 2005:1-32.

36 Kehlmann 2007:6.

37 Kehlmann 2007:12.

38 Kehlmann 2007:15.

39 Hagemann 2010.

40 Hielscher 2010.

41 Cf. Giesen 1993.

42 Cf. Herrmann 2010, cf. Süselbeck 2009:53-68.

43 Modick 2006:68.

44 See dissertation (Utrecht) by Robert Haak on German postmodernism and cultural identity, forthcoming 2011.

45 Cf. Lamberechts 2000:59-77.
46 Baßler 2002.
47 Illies 2000.
48 See Hein 2003, Tetzlaff 2004.
49 To name a few: Wladimir Kaminer, *Russendisko*. München: Manhattan 2000, Wladimir Kaminer, *Schönhauser Allee*. München: Manhattan 2001, Wladimir Kaminer, *Mein deutsches Dschungelbuch*. München: Manhattan 2003. His site www.russendisko.de demonstrates his business sense.
50 See Kaminer, (ed.) 2001.
51 See Timmer 2010.
52 Krauß 2002.
53 Krauß 2004:76/77. Translated at my request by Tim Jack (Berlin).
54 Maier 2006:114. Translated at my request by Tim Jack.
55 Maier 2005. Translated at my request by Tim Jack.
56 Dean, Hettche, Politycki & Schindhelm 2005. http://www.zeit.de/2005/26/Debatte_1. Translated at my request by Tim Jack.
57 Maier 2005. http://www.zeit.de/2005/26/Debatte_2
58 Adorno 1990:475.
59 http://www.tate.org.uk/britain/exhibitions/altermodern, by Nicolas Bourriaud. See the Introduction to this volume.
60 Haaf, 2009, http://www.spiegel.de/kultur/gesellschaft/0,1518,612839,00.html
61 http://www.tate.org.uk/britain/exhibitions/altermodern
62 Von Festenburg 2005:72-74.
63 Lethen 1994:150. See Serner 1981.
64 See Engler 2009.
65 Rothmann 2008:28-36.
66 Brussig 1996.
67 Anz (ed.) 1991.
68 Cf. Gebauer 2002:222-240.
69 Brussig 1999:157.
70 Brussig 1999:156.
71 Baßler 2007:435-450, 436, 448.
72 Brussig 2004.
73 Pilz 2004.
74 Luedke 2004.
75 Schulze 1998.
76 MacCormick 1991:124.
77 MacCormick 1975.
78 Handke 1990.
79 *Die Niemandsbucht. Ein Märchen aus den neuen Zeiten*. Frankfurt am Main: Suhrkamp 1994.

80 Hage & Schreiber 1994:171.
81 Hage & Schreiber 1994:170.
82 Hage & Schreiber 1994:171.
83 The critics directed their criticism at *Eine winterliche Reise zu den Flüssen Donau, Save, Morawa und Drina oder Gerechtigkeit für Serbien*. Frankfurt am Main: Suhrkamp 1996. *Sommerlicher Nachtrag zu einer winterlichen Reise*. Frankfurt am Main: Suhrkamp 1996.
84 Trilling 1980.
85 See Holler 2003:148.
86 Menasse 1995:8.
87 Menasse 1990:166-174, 170, 172, 173.
88 Menasse 1995:83.
89 Neuber 1995.
90 Holler 2003:235-236.
91 Holler 2003:138-142.
92 Menasse 2009.
93 Menasse 2009a:139.
94 Menasse 2007.
95 Menasse 2007:194-197, 105, 203, 243.
96 Menasse 2001.
97 Menasse 1988:214-215.
98 Menasse, 1988:209.
99 Menasse 2006:24, 30, 27, 142, 128-129.
100 Menasse 1992:127-128.
101 For other novels see Lützeler 2005.

Chapter 11 – Spanish and Spanish American Literature

1 Lasdun 2010.
2 *The New York Times* 3-12-2008.
3 *Le Monde* 21-8-1965.
4 Molloy 1972:207.
5 For more details, see Sorensen 2007:136-139.
6 Fokkema 1984:38.
7 Thiher 1984:160.
8 Bertens 1997:5.
9 Cf. Larsen 1990.
10 Bertens 1997:6.
11 According to Sarlo, 'the defense by Borges of a rationalist fantastic literature is a response to what in the thirties was considered an irrational excursion by the Occident: fascism, the concrete shape of communism, the disorder of the democracy of the masses,

whose plebeian aspect was experienced by Borges with the same dislike as antiliberal authoritarianism' (Sarlo 2007:93, our translation). See also Balderston 1993.

12 Borges 1981:218.

13 Cf. Aizenberg 2002.

14 Van Alphen and Bal 2009:2.

15 It might be useful to emphasize that the authors do not believe that sincerity should be bound up with a traditional and naïve view of subjectivity, and for that reason they propose to focus on the theatricality or rhetoric of sincerity, its performative dimension (2009:3). In other words, the stress on sincerity and authenticity should not be approached in a naïve way: the *rhetorics* of sincerity is still a form of discourse, a rhetorical tool that is nothing but another shift in the struggle for power. Cf. also the contributions of Thomas Vaessens (chapter 3) and Ellen Rutten (chapter 1) in this volume.

16 Casanova 2004:246.

17 Steenmeijer 2009:286-329.

18 Steenmeijer 1996.

19 In Spanish poetry, postmodernism was established with the publication of José María Castellet's anthology *Nueve novísimos poetas españoles* (1970).

20 Gonzalo Navajas 1987 was a pioneering publication.

21 Lozano Mijares 2010:183-184.

22 Javier Marías (1951) has never concealed his literary preferences, as is illustrated by the many articles and essays that he has published about Henry James, James Joyce, William Faulkner, Vladimir Nabokov, Juan Benet, Thomas Bernhard and other writers who intrigue him. Remarkably enough, Marías has never written a monographic article or essay about Borges, with the exception of a short portrait based on two pictures of the Argentine writer (Marías 1997). Dispersed in prologues, articles and essays, though, there are a handful of references to Borges that reveal Marias's interest in the Argentine writer as an ingenious storyteller, an original theorist of translation and an at times rather poor translator.

23 Grohmann 2005:150.

24 Marías 2006:135.

25 McHale 1987:9. It would not be irrelevant to add that modernist kingpins such as Proust, James, Faulkner and Musil are quite frequently mentioned as interpretive frames of Marías's novels in the numerous reviews published in Spanish and, even more so, in non-Spanish newspapers and magazines.

26 Marías 2006:4.

27 Marías 2006:186.

28 Marías 2001:7.

29 Marías 2006:243.

30 Marías 2005:3.

31 Marías 2008:37-38. Our translation.

32 See Steenmeijer 2009a for an analysis of Marías's novels from this perspective.
33 Borges 2005:73.
34 Marías 2006:205.
35 Corral 2006:50.
36 Villoro 2010:14.
37 Corral 2006:47.
38 Bolaño 2004b:43. Our translation.
39 Cf. for example 'Borges y los cuervos', 'Borges y Paracelso', 'El bibliotecario valiente', in Bolaño 2004b.
40 Borges 1975:12.
41 Bertens 1997:5.
42 Manzoni 2002:18. Our translation.
43 Bolaño 2004a:6.
44 Manzoni 2002:21. Our translation.
45 Kunz 2008 offers a detailed analysis of the fictionalization (films, novels, documentaries) of the crimes in Ciudad Juárez.
46 Kunz 2008:147.
47 Bolaño 2008b:495.
48 Villoro 2010:9.
49 Elmore 2008:261. Our translation.
50 Bertens 1997:6.

Chapter 12 – American Literature

1 Scott 2000:40; McLaughlin 2004:55.
2 Although a certain desire for sincerity (in response to postmodernist irony and cynicism) does seem to be present in many of the works in question, 'sincerity' is not their only and often not even their main theme (cf. section 3). Furthermore, where the notion of 'sincerity' does figure in these works, it is treated as a complicated notion and not as some simple form of naïveté which is readily achieved (the term 'new sincerity', in my opinion, does not fully communicate this complicatedness). The term 'post-postmodernism' in turn provides us with an ugly label that carries forth the terminological unclarity that already surrounds the definitions of 'modernism' and 'postmodernism'. Moreover, the prefix 'post-' suggests too strongly a state of already 'being beyond' or 'having left behind' something, whereas in the case of this new literary movement, it seems just as much a case of *finding a new way* of coping with the *same* thing, in this case postmodern culture.
3 In addition to the mentioned writers, some recurring names are (in alphabetical order): Michael Chabon, Mark Danielewski, Jonathan Franzen, A.M. Homes, Nicole Krauss, Jonathan Lethem, Rick Moody, Richard Powers and William Vollmann. Oft-mentioned British writers are Nick Hornby and Zadie Smith.

4 Annesley 2009:132; Boswell 2003:66,70,78,103,207; Max 2009:52; McCaffery 1993:144; Wallace 1988. Other terms used to label this wave of postmodernist literature are: 'Brat Pack', 'Blank Generation', 'Punk Fiction', 'Blank Fiction' (cf. Annesley 1998; Young & Caveney 1993:iii).
5 I would like to emphasize that I am referring here to the notion of deconstruction as it was interpreted mainly in the US, based on Derrida's earlier, highly language-focused writings – and not taking into account, for example, the so-called 'ethical turn' of Derrida's later works.
6 For a further elaboration of this comparison between Derrida's philosophy of deconstruction and Barth's meta-fictional writing, see: den Dulk 2011.
7 Waugh 1984:2.
8 Ibid.:5.
9 Federman 1988:1146, 1156.
10 Cf. Waugh 1984:6-7.
11 Ibid.:24.
12 McHale 1987:221.
13 Cf. Worthington 2001:114; Fogel & Slethaug 1990:1.
14 Barth 1988:111.
15 Waugh 1984:95.
16 Fogel & Slethaug 1990:4.
17 Cf. Harris 1983:1; McConnell 1977:xxvi.
18 Barth 1984:71-73.
19 Barth 1988:109.
20 Cf. Wallace 2002:65-66.
21 Wallace 1990:221,236.
22 Cf. Timmer 2010.
23 McLaughlin 2004:64.
24 Young 1993a:14
25 Bran Nichol calls it 'fiction of the "postmodern condition" [...] [that] deals head on with the "death of affect" in contemporary society' (Nichol 2009:183, 197).
26 Annesley 1998:2.
27 Other prominent members are Jay McInerney and Tama Janowitz.
28 Murphet 2002:20.
29 Young 1993c:93.
30 Blazer 2002; Suglia 2004.
31 Ellis 1991:362.
32 Ibid.:360.
33 Cf. McCaffery 1993:130-132.
34 Murphet 2002:20.
35 Young 1993b:41.
36 For example, some reviewers of Eggers's 2000 debut, the autobiographical novel *A Heartbreaking Work of Staggering Genius* – in which Eggers describes how, within three months of

each other, both his parents die of cancer, whereupon he becomes responsible for the upbringing of his eight-year-old brother – claimed that the whole book should be read ironically, even the evidently 'sentimental' (in their opinion) description of the death of Eggers's parents. Similar comments were made about Wallace's 'conversion' to sincerity. Cf. Holland 2006:218,220; Hultkrans 1997; Korthals Altes 2008.

37 Marshall Boswell has also noted the relevance of Kierkegaard's philosophy in relation to Wallace's writing (Boswell 2003:138).

38 Letter from David Foster Wallace to Allard den Dulk, d.d. 20th of March 2006.

39 For a further elaboration of this comparison between Kierkegaard's irony critique and that of Wallace and Eggers, see den Dulk 2008.

40 Kierkegaard 1989:257.

41 Ibid.:254.

42 Wallace 2002:67.

43 Wiley 1997.

44 Wallace 2002:63, 49.

45 Wallace 1996:694.

46 Interview Allard den Dulk with Dave Eggers, d.d. 23rd of May 2006.

47 Wallace 1996:369.

48 Boswell 2003:138.

49 Eggers 2001a:240-241.

50 Ibid.:304.

51 Ibid.:417.

52 Eggers 2001b:35.

53 Other writers, like Richard Powers and William Vollmann, have also been widely credited for their innovative fiction, which has often been compared to that of Wallace (cf. Leclair 1996). But in their writing the problems of postmodernist literature and culture are less present and less clear than in Wallace's.

54 Scott 2000:40. Instead of wanting fiction to move 'back' in some way (to a more traditional, perhaps more 'realistic' mode of writing), as can sometimes seem to be the case with (for example) Jonathan Franzen (cf. Franzen 2002; McLaughlin 2004:55, 63).

55 Some Wallace fans would probably scoff at the idea that the work of their literary hero is equated with that of Eggers and Foer. And perhaps these fans are right, in the sense that the work of Eggers and Foer is not quite of the same *literary level* as Wallace's.

56 Cf. Annesley 2009:132; Boswell 2003:19; Burn 2003:76; Burn 2008; Kakutani 2000b; Mattson 2002:81; Myers 2005:115; Timmer 2010:11; Weber 2008.

57 This is probably an important part of its esteemed literary quality, compared to the work by Eggers and Foer.

58 In 1993, Wallace announced this aesthetic 'sea change' in the following words: 'The next real literary "rebels" in this country might well emerge as some weird bunch of anti-rebels, born oglers who dare somehow to back away from ironic watching, who have the childish gall actually to en-

dorse and instantiate single-entendre principles. Who treat of plain and old untrendy human troubles and emotions in U.S. life with reverence and conviction. Who eschew self-consciousness and hip fatigue. [...] The new rebels might be artists willing to risk the yawn, the rolled eyes, the cool smile, the nudged ribs, the parody of gifted ironists, the "Oh how banal". To risk accusations of sentimentality, melodrama. Of overcredulity, of softness'. (Wallace 2002:81-82)

59 Eggers 2002:27.

60 Foer 2005:163.

61 Wallace 1996:101, 312.

62 Cf.: Mario feels good when visiting the halfway house near his home, 'because it's very real; people are crying and making noise and getting less unhappy, and once he heard somebody say *God* with a straight face and nobody looked at them or looked down or smiled in any sort of way where you could tell they were worried inside' (Ibid.:591).

63 Ibid.:695.

64 Nichols 2001:13.

65 Eggers 2001b:33, 34.

66 Wallace 1999:131, 136.

67 To this, McLaughlin adds that the emphasis in the works of these writers 'is less on self-conscious wordplay and the violation of narrative conventions and more on representing the world we all more or less share. Yet in presenting that world, this new fiction nevertheless has to show that it's a world that we know through language and layers of representation: language, narrative, and the processes of representation are the only means we have to experience and know the world, ourselves, and our possibilities for being human' (McLaughlin 2004:55, 66-67).

68 Wallace 2002:65.

69 McCaffery 1993:131.

70 Wallace 1996:592.

71 McCaffery 1993:131.

72 Wallace 2002:43. Also, in an interview, Wallace stated: 'I'm always stumped when critics regard references to popular culture in serious fiction as some sort of avantgarde stratagem. In terms of the world I live in and try to write about, it's inescapable. Avoiding any reference to the pop would mean either being retrograde about what's "permissible" in serious art or else writing about some other world' (McCaffery 1993:148).

73 Cf. the fact that Hal (like almost all characters in the novels of Wallace, Eggers and Foer) 'is *already framed* by prevailing cultural thought in the story-world [...] [and] is struggling to break out and has to find other, alternative ways of conceptualizing what it means to be human' (Timmer 2010:30-31).

74 Kakutani 2000a.

75 Confessore 2000:86.

76 Cioffi 2000:175.

77 Cf. Wallace 2009:5, 3-4, 8, 131-133.

78 Eggers 2002:297.
79 Eggers 2001b:46.
80 Eggers 2001a:211.
81 Wallace 1996:114, 345.
82 Cf.: 'And so this unites them, nervously, this tentative assemblage of possible glimmers of something like hope, this grudging move towards maybe acknowledging that this unromantic, unhip, clichéd AA thing – so unlikely and unpromising, so much the inverse of what they'd come too much to love – might really be able to keep the lover's toothy maw at bay' (Wallace 1996:350).
83 Mattson 2002:76.
84 Eggers 2001a:xxxvii, 237.
85 Foer 2002:144, 214.
86 Kamphuis 2005:28. 'Schrijven is niet zoiets als zingen onder de douche; het is zelfs niet als zingen op een podium. Voor mij is het eerder iets als samen zingen, rond een kampvuur of zo. Een boek is voor mij niet geslaagd als de lezer niet een soort co-auteur wordt [...]: het is voor mij enorm belangrijk dat de lezer het idee heeft dat het zijn boek is' [my translation, AdD].
87 Solomon 2005.
88 Miller 1996.
89 McCaffery 1993:138, 142.
90 Boswell 2003:121.
91 Hutcheon 1995:18, 89, 91.
92 Wallace 1999:136.

Bibliography

Introduction

Amis, M. (2008), *The Second Plane. September 11: 2001-2007*. Toronto, Vintage Books, 2008.

Bourriaud, N. (2009), 'Altermodern Manifesto. Postmodernism is Death'. http://www.tate.org.uk/britain/exhibitions/altermodern/manifesto.shtm.

Bertens, H. & D. Fokkema (eds) (1997), *International Postmodernism. Theory and Literary Practice*. Amsterdam/Philadelphia, John Benjamins, 1997.

Bertens, H. (1996), 'Out of Left Field: The Politics of the Postmodern'. In: G. Hoffmann & A. Hornung (eds), *Ethics and Aesthetics. The Moral Turn of Postmodernism*. Heidelberg, Winter, 1996, p.97-113.

Bewes, T. (1997), *Cynicism and Postmodernity*. London, Verso, 1997.

Booth, W.C. (1988), *The Company We Keep: An Ethics of Fiction*. Berkeley, University of California Press, 1988.

Burke, K. (2010), *Equipment for Living. The Literary Reviews of Kenneth Burke*. Edited by N.A. Rivers & R.P. Weber. Anderson, SC, Parlor Press, 2010.

Crews, F. (2001), *Postmodern Pooh*. New York, North Point Press, 2001.

Eagleton, T. (1996), *The Illusions of Postmodernism*. Oxford, Blackwell, 1996.

Ebert, T. (1991), 'Writing in the Political: Resistance (Post)modernism'. In: *Legal Studies Forum* 15-4, 1991, p.291-304.

Egan, T. (2009), 'After the Deluge'. In: *The New York Times Book Review*, 13-8-2009.

Finkielkraut, A. (2009), *Un Coeur Intelligent. Lectures*. Paris, Stock/Flammarion, 2009.

Finkielkraut, A. (2010), *Een intelligent hart. Hoe romans je helpen in het leven*. Amsterdam, Contact, 2010.

Fish, S. (2001), 'Condemnation Without Absolutes'. In: *The New York Times* 15-10-2001.

Foster, H. (1996), *The Return of the Real. The Avant-Garde at the Turn of the Century*. MA, MIT Press, 1996.

Furedi, F. (2004), *Where Have All the Intellectuals Gone? Confronting 21st Century Philistinism*. London/New York, Contiuum, 2004.

Gibson, A. (1999), *Postmodernity, Ethics and the Novel. From Leavis to Levinas*. London, Routledge, 1999.

Green, J. (2005), *Late Postmodernism. American Fiction at the Millennium*. New York, Palgrave, 2005

Hoberek, A. (2007), 'Introduction: After Postmodernism'. In: *Twentieth-Century Literature* 53-3, 2007, p.233-247.

Humm, M. (1998), 'The Business of a 'New Arty': Woolf, Potter and Postmodernism'. In: J. Simons & K. Fullbrook, *Writing: a Womens Business. Women, Writing and the Marketplace*. Manchester, Manchester University Press, 1998, p.111-125.

Hutcheon, L. (1988), *A Poetics of Postmodernism. History, Theory, Fiction*. New York/Londen, Routledge, 1988.

Hutcheon, L. (1994), *Irony's Edge. The Theory and Politics of Irony*. London/ New York, Routledge, 1994.

Hutcheon, L. (1998), 'Irony, Nostalgia, and the Postmodern.' *English Library, Criticism and Theory Resources*. http://www.library.utoronto.ca/utel/ criticism/hutchinp.html.

Ignatieff, M. (1997), 'The Decline and Fall of the Public Intellectual'. In: *Queens Quarterly* 104-3, 1997, p.395-403.

Jensen, S. (2005), 'De invasie van de huiskamer. Ian McEwan en het belang van gewoon geluk'. In: *NRC Handelsblad* 24-6-2005.

Kiberd, D. (2009), *Ulysses and Us. The Art of Everyday Living*. London, Faber and Faber, 2009.

McAffery, L. (1993), 'An Interview with David Foster Wallace'. In: *Review of Contemporary Fiction* 13-2, 1993, p.127-150.

McDonald, R. (2007), *The Death of the Critic*. London/New York, Continuum, 2007.

Miller, G. (2005), 'Saturday, Bloody Saturday'. In: *The San Diego Union-Tribune* 20-3-2005.

Pol, B. van der (2005), '222 keer niet van hetzelfde'. In: *De Volkskrant* 20-5-2005.

Rorty, R. (1989), *Contingency, Irony, and Solidarity*. Cambridge, Cambridge University Press, 1989.

Rosenblatt, R. (2001), 'The Age of Irony Comes to an End'. In: *Time* 16-9-2001.

Rothstein, E. (2001), 'Connections. Attacks on Challenge the Perspectives of Postmodern True Believers'. In: *The New York Times* 22-9-2001.

Shields, D. (2010), *Reality Hunger. A Manifesto*. London, Hamish Hamilton, 2010.

Slattery, L. (2001), 'Wake Up and Smell the Cordite'. In: *The Australian* 24-10-2001.

Sokal, A. & J. Bricmont (1998), *Fashionable Nonsense. Postmodern Intellectuals' Abuse of Science*. New York, Picador, 1998.

Sokal, A. & J. Bricmont (2003), *Intellectual Impostures. Postmodern Philosophers' Abuse of Science*. London, Profile Books, 2003 (2nd ed.).

Suleiman, S.R. (1997), 'The Politics of Postmodernism after the Wall (or, What Do We Do When the 'Ethnic Cleansing' Starts?)'. In: Bertens & Fokkema (eds) 1997, p.51-64.

Vaessens, T. (2009), *De revanche van de roman. Literatuur, autoriteit en engagement*. Nijmegen, Vantllt, 2009 (2nd ed.)

Vaessens, T. (2010), 'Realiteitshonger. Arnon Grunberg en de (non-)fictie'. In: *TNTL* 126, 2010, p.306-326.

Watman, M. (2005), 'Ignorant Armies Clash by Night'. In: *New Criterion* 1-5-2005.

Zeeman, M. (2001), 'Hoe de feiten de verbeelding perverteerden'. In: *De Volkskrant* 14-9-2001.

Chapter 1 – Russian Literature

Aizenberg, M. (1994), 'Vozmozhnost' vyskazyvaniia'. In: *Znamia*, 6, 1994, online on www.vavilon.ru/texts/aizenberg/aizenberg6-1.html.

Backstein, J. & B. De Baere (2005), *Angels of History: Conceptualism and its Influence*. Brussels, Europalia, 2005.

Bogdanova, O. (2004), *Postmodernizm v kontekste sovremennoi russkoi literatury (60-90-e gody XX veka – nachalo XXI veka*. Filologicheskii fakul'tet S.-Peterburgskogo gosudarstvennogo universiteta, 2004.

Bondarenko, M. (2002), 'Roman V. Sorokina 'Led': siuzhet-attraktsion – ideologiia – novaia iskrennost' – kataficheskaia dekonstruktsiia'. In: *Literaturnyi dnevnik* May, 2002, online on www.vavilon.ru/diary/ 020518.html.

Boym, S. (1994), *Common Places: Mythologies of Everyday Life in Russia*. Cambridge, MA, Harvard University Press, 1994.

Brown, D. (1993), *The Last Years of Soviet Russian Literature*. Cambridge, Cambridge University Press, 1993.

Brown, E. (1982), *Russian Literature Since the Revolution*. Cambridge, MA, Harvard University Press, 1982.

Chung, Y. & T. Jacobi (2007), 'In Search of a New Sincerity? Contemporary Art from China'. Workshop for Tate Modern, 21-04-2007, announcement online on www.tate.org.uk/liverpool/eventseducation/courseswork shops/9154.htm.

Corcoran, M. (2005), 'The New Sincerity: in the Eighties'. In: *All Over the Map: True Heroes of Music*. Austin, TX, University of Texas Press, 2005, p.150-57.

Davydov, D. (2005), 'Dmitrii Vodennikov, Svetlana Lin. Vkusnyi obed dlia ravnodushnykh koshek'. In: *Kriticheskaia* 2, 2005, online on magazines.russ.ru/km/2005/2/dd19-pr.html.

Den Dulk, A. (2004.1), "New Sincerity': Beyond the Postmodern Stalemate, Towards Community and Commitment. Existentialist Engagement in the Work of Young Contemporary Artists' (forthcoming, project information online on www.narcis.info/research/RecordID/OND 1327285/Language/nl/;jsessionid=m05g9q07eod).

Dobrenko, E., M. Lipovetsky, I. Kukulin & M. Maiofis (2010), *Nekanonicheskii klassik: Dmitrii Aleksandrovich Prigov (1940-2007)*. Moscow, NLO, 2010.

Dulk, A. den (2004), *Over de drempel. Voorbij de postmoderne impasse naar een zelfbewust engagement. De literaire zoektocht van Dave Eggers vergeleken met het denken van Friedrich Nietzche en Albert Camus*. The Hague, Allard den Dulk, 2004.

Epstein, M. (1996), 'Proto-, ili konets postmodernizma'. In: *Znamia* 3, 1996, p.196-209.

Epstein, M. (2000), *Postmodern v Rossii: literatura i teoriia*. Moscow, R. Elinin, 2000.

Epstein, M. (2005), *Postmodern v russkoi literature*. Moscow, Vysshaia shkola, 2005.

Epstein, M., A. Genis & S. Vladiv-Glover (eds.) (1999), *Russian Postmodernism: New Perspectives on Post-Soviet Culture*. New York, Berghahn, 1999.

Epstein, M. (1999), 'Introduction'. In: Epstein et al., *Russian Postmodernism*.

Eshelman, R. (2008), *Performatism or the End of Postmodernism*. Aurora, CO, Davies Group, 2008.

Etkind, A. (2004), 'Hard and Soft in Cultural Memory: Political Mourning in and '. In: *Grey Room* 16, 2004, p.36-59.

Etkind, A. (2009), 'Stories of the Undead in the Land of the Unburied: Magical Historicism in Contemporary Russian Fiction'. In: *Slavic Review* 68-3, 2009, online on www.memoryatwar.org/publications-list/magical-historicism.pdf.

Gibian, G. (1960), *Interval of Freedom: Soviet Literature During the Thaw*. Minneapolis, University of Minnesota Press, 1960.

Harris, W. (ed.) (1996), *Beyond Poststructuralism: The Speculations of Theory and the Experience of Reading*. University Park, PA, Penn State University Press, 1996.

Ivanova, E. (2007), 'Molodaia poeziia v poiskakh zhivogo slova'. *Kontinent* 133, 2007, p.419-430.

Ivanova, N. (1998), contributions to the round-table discussion 'Literatura poslednego desiatiletiia i perspektivy'. In: *Voprosy literatury* 2, 1998, p.3-83.

Kaspe, I. (2009), 'Govorit tot, kto govorit 'ia': vmesto epiloga'. In: *Novoe literaturnoe obozrenie*, 96, 2009, online on magazines.russ.ru/nlo/ 2009/96/ka28-pr.html.

Kibirov, T. (2001), '*Kto kuda – a ia v Rossiiu...*' Moscow, Vremia, 2001.

Kirchmaier, V. (2001), 'Die Verdichtung der Sinne'. Curatorial announcement exhibition Der Tod, Tiefbunker am Blochplatz, Berlin, 2001, online on www.mais-de.de/Mais-flash.html.

Korthals Altes, L. (2001), *'Blessedly post-ironic'? Enkele tendensen in de hedendaagse literatuur en literatuurwetenschap*. Groningen, E.J. Korthals Altes, 2001.

Korthals Altes, L. (2008), 'Sincerity, Reliability and Other Ironies – Notes on Dave Eggers' *A Heartbreaking Work of Staggering Genius*'. In: E. D'hoker & G. Martens (eds.), *Narrative Unreliability in the Twentieth-Century First-Person Novel*. Berlin, Walter de Gruyter, 2008, p.107-128.

Kostiukov, L. (2000), 'Postoronnie soobrazheniia'. In: *Druzhba narodov*, 6, 2000, 210-215.

Kukulin, I. (2002), 'Every trend makes a brand'. In: *Novoe literaturnoe obozrenie*, 56, 2002, online on magazines.russ.ru/nlo/2002/ 56/kuk1.html.

Kulle, V. ''Novaia iskrennost'' po-ital'ianski'. In: *Novyi mir: biblioteka zhurnala novyi mir*, year not indicated, online on magazines.russ.ru/novyi_mi/ redkol/kulle/dop/article/ ono.html.

Kuritsyn, V. (1997), 'Vremia mnozhit' pristavki. K poniatiiu postpostmodernizma'. In : *Oktiabr'* 7, 1997, p.178-83.

Kuritsyn, V. (2000), *Russkii literaturnyi postmodernizm*, online on www.guelman.ru/slava/postmod/9.html.

Kuznetsov, S. (1997), 'Postmodernism in Russia'. In: H. Bertens and D. Fokkema (eds.), *International Postmodernism: Theory and Literary Practice*. Amsterdam, Benjamins, 1992-1996, p.451-463.

Leiderman, N. & M. Lipovetsky (1993), 'Zhizn' posle smerti, ili novye svedeniia o realizme'. In: *Novyi mir* 7, 1993, online on magazines.russ.ru/novyi_mi/1993/7/litkrit.html.

Lipovetsky, M. (1999), *Russian Postmodernist Fiction: Dialogue With Chaos*. Armonk, NY, M.E. Sharpe, 1999.

Lipovetsky, M. (2008), *Paralogii: transformatsii (post)modernistskogo diskursa v kul'ture 1920-2000-x godov*. Moscow, Novoe literaturnoe obozrenie, 2008.

López, J. & G. Potter (eds.) (2001), *After Postmodernism: An Introduction to Critical Realism*. New York, Athlone, 2001.

Man'kovskaia, N. (1998), *Ot modernizma k postpostmodernizmu via postmodernizm*. Moscow, Kollazh, 1998.

Man'kovskaia, N. (2000), *Estetika postmodernizma*. Saint Petersburg, Aleteia, 2000.

Markovits, E. (2008), *The Politics of Sincerity. Plato, Frank Speech, and Democratic Judgment*. University Park, PE, Pennsylvania State University Press, 2008.

Marsh, R. (2007), *Literature, History and Identity in Post-Soviet Russia, 1991-2006*. Oxford, Peter Lang, 2007.

Medvedev, K. (2007), *Reaktsiia voobshche*. Moscow, Kirill Medvedev, 2007.

Medvedev, K. (2008), 'The Writer in Russia'. In: *Dissent*, Fall, 2008, online on www.dissentmagazine.org/article/?article=1293.

Menzel, B. (2001), *Bürgerkrieg um Worte: die russische Literaturkritik der Perestrojka*. Köln, Böhlau, 2001.

Mezhieva, M. & N. Konradova (2006), *Okno v mir: sovremennaia russkaia literatura*. Moscow, Russkii iazyk, 2006.

Mitrenina, M. (2003), 'Netneizm i traditsionnaia kul'tura'. In: *Russkii zhurnal*, 24-03-2003, online on old.russ.ru/netcult/20030324_ mitrenina-pr.html.

Natarov, E. (1998), 'Timur Kibirov. Obzor kritiki'. In: *Literaturnoe obozrenie* 1, 1998, p.38-40.

Prigov, D. & S. Shapovalov (2003), *Portretnaia galereiia*. Moscow, NLO, 2003.

Prigov, D. (1992), 'What More Is There To Say?' In: K. Johnson, S.M. Ashby (eds.), *Third Wave: The New Russian Poetry*. Ann Arbor, MI, Michigan University Press, 1992, p.101-103.

Prigov, D. (1996), *Sbornik preduvedomlenii k raznoobraznym veshcham*. Moscow, Ad Marginem, 1996.

Prigov, D. (2005),'Iskrennost' – vot shto nam vsego dorozhe'. In: *Polit.ru* 12-08-2005, online on www.polit.ru/author/2005/08/27/prigov1208 2005.html.

Rebein, R. (2001), *Hicks, Tribes, and Dirty Realists: American Fiction After Postmodernism*. Kentucky, TX, Kentucky University Press, 2001.

Rutten, E. (2009), 'Art as Therapy. Sorokin's Strifle with the Soviet Trauma Across Media'. In: *Russian Literature* 65-4, 2009, p.539-559.

Sarjono, A. & M. Mooij (eds.) (2006), *Poetry and Sincerity. International Poetry Festival Indonesia 2006*. Jakarta, Cipta, 2006.

Scharg, C. (1997), *The Self after Postmodernity*. New Haven, CT, Yale University Press, 1997.

Shneidman, N. (1995), *Russian Literature 1988-1994: The End of an Era*. Toronto, Univerity of Toronto Press, 1995.

Skoropanova, I. (2004), *Russkaia postmodernistskaia literatura*. Moscow, Flinta/Nauka, 2004.

Stierstorfer, K. (ed.) (2003), *Beyond Postmodernism: Reassessments in Literature, Theory, and Culture*. Berlin, De Gruyter, 2003.

Timmer, N. (2010), *Do You Feel It Too? The Post-Postmodern Syndrome in American Fiction at the Turn of the Millennium*. Amsterdam, Rodopi, 2010.

Toth, J. & N. Brooks (eds.) (2007), *The Mourning After: Attending the Wake of Postmodernism*. Amsterdam, Rodopi, 2007.

Tsvetkov, A. (2009), 'Kirill Medvedev: 'Intellektual – ne privilegiia!''. In: *Rabkor.ru* 31-07-2009, online on www.rabkor.ru/interview/3612.html.

Turner, T. (1995), *City as Landscape: A Post Post-Modern View of Design and Planning*. London, Taylor & Francis, 1995.

Twentieth-Century Literature (2007), Special edition: 'After Postmodernism'. In: *Twentieth-Century Literature*, Fall, 2007, online on findarticles.com/p/articles/mi_m0403/is_3_53/ai_n24944809/pg_1?tag=artBody;col1.

Ulanov, A. (2002), 'Sny o chem-to bol'shom'. In: *Druzhba narodov* 2, 2002, online on magazines.russ.ru/druzhba/2002/2/ulan.html.

Vaessens, T. (2009), *De revanche van de roman. Literatuur, autoriteit en engagement*. Nijmegen, Vantilt, 2009.

Van Alphen, E., M. Bal & C. Smith (eds.) (2009), *The Rhetoric of Sincerity*. Stanford, CA, Stanford University Press, 2009.

Vezhlian, E. (2009), 'Pamiat' momentam'. In: *Novyi mir*, 7, 2009, online on magazines.russ.ru/novyi_mir/2009/7/ve16.html.

Weststeijn, W. (1998), 'Timur Kibirov'. In: J. Andrew and R. Reid (eds.), *Neo-Formalist Papers*. Amsterdam, Rodopi, 1998, p.269-280.

Weststeijn, W. (1999), 'After Postmodernism'. In W. Weststeijn (ed.), *Dutch Contributions to the Twelfth International Congress of Slavists*. Amsterdam, Rodopi, 1999, p.211-224.

Yurchak, A. (2006), *Everything Was Forever, Until It Was No More: The Last Soviet Generation*. Princeton, Princeton University Press, 2006.

Yurchak, A. (2008), 'Post-Post-Communist Sincerity. Pioneers, Cosmonauts, and Other Soviet Heroes Born Today'. In: Th. Lahusen and P. Solomon Jr. (eds.), *What is Soviet Now? Identities, Legacies, Memories*. Berlin, LIT Verlag, 2008, p.257-77.

Chapter 2 – British Literature

Ballard, J.G. (1973), *Crash*. London, Vintage, 1995. First published by Jonathan Cape in 1973.

Currie, M. (2007), *About Time*. Edinburgh, Edinburgh University Press, 2007.

Head, D. (2008), *The State of the Novel: Britain and Beyond*. Oxford, Wiley-Blackwell, 2008.

Groes, S. (ed.) (2009), *Ian McEwan: Contemporary Critical Perspectives*. London and New York, Continuum, 2009.

Leavis, F.R. (1948), *The Great Tradition*. London, Chatto & Windus, 1948.

Larkin, P. (1974), 'High Windows'. In *High Windows*. London, Faber, 1974.

McCarthy, T. (2006), *Remainder*. London, Jonathan Cape, 2006.

McCarthy, T. (2010), *C*. London, Jonathan Cape, 2010.

McEwan, I. (2005), *Saturday*. London, Jonathan Cape, 2005.

McHale, B. (1999), *Postmodernist Fiction*. London, Routledge, 1999.

Rushdie, S. (1992), *Imaginary Homelands*. London, Granta, 1992.

Sage, L. (2010), *Women in the House of Fiction*. Basingstoke, Macmillan, 1992.

Shields, D. (2010), *Reality Hunger: A Manifesto*. London, Hamish Hamilton, 2010. First published in the United States of America by Alfred A Knopf, 2010.

Smith, Z. (2000), *White Teeth*. London, Hamish Hamilton, 2000.

Smith, Z. (2009), *Changing My Mind*. London, Hamish Hamilton, 2009.

Chapter 3 – Dutch Literature

Adriaens, M. (1997), 'Dit is mijn eerste boek dat helemaal bij daglicht geschreven is'. In: *De standaard* 11-9-1997.

Akker, W.J. van den (1993), 'A Mad Hatter's Tupperware Party. Postmodern Tendencies in American and Dutch Poetry'. In: J.P. Snapper & T. Schannon (eds.), *The Berkeley Conference on Dutch Literature 1991*. Lanham etc. 1993, p.171-195.

Alphen, E. van (1985), 'Een kind droomt zich af'. In: *Forum der letteren* 26-1, 1985, p.20-32.

Alphen, E. van (1989), 'Naar een theorie van het postmodernisme'. In: *Forum der Letteren* 30-1-1989, p.21-37.

Bakker, J.H. (1998), 'Arnon Grunberg zoekt de grens van het spel'. In: *Haarlems dagblad* 17-3-1998.

Barry, P. (2002), *Beginning Theory: an Introduction to Literary and Cultural Theory*. Manchester, Manchester University Press, 2002.

Bauman, Z. (1998), *Globalization. The Human Consequences*. Cambridge, Polity, 1998.

Beekman, K. (1989), 'De strategie van het postmodernismedebat'. In: *Spektator* 18-5, 1989, p.343-346.

Beekman, K. (1991), 'Een proeve van postmoderne parodie en pastiche'. In: *Forum der Letteren* 32-2, 1991, p.81-89.

Bertens, H. (2001), *Literary Theory: the Basics*. London/New York, Routledge, 2001.

Blom, O. (2007), 'Mailen met Arnon Grunberg'. In: *Trouw* 29-12-2007.

Bultinck, B. (2009), 'Ik had wel hevige reacties verwacht maar niet dát'. In: *De morgen* 15-4-2009.

Cloostermans, M. (2008), 'Eenvoudig en ongevaarlijk'. In: *De standaard*, 7-2-2008.

Cloostermans, M. (2008a), 'Waarom zou je het goede aanbidden?' In: *De standaard* 3-10-2008.

Compagnon, A. (2000). 'Après la littérature'. In: *Le débat. Histoire, politique, société* 110, 2000, p.136-153.

Coupland, D. (1991), *Generation X. Tales for an Accelerated Culture*. New York, St. Martins Press, 1991.

Dijk, Y. van (2008), 'Vaarwel vrijblijvendheid. De Nederlandse literatuur betreedt het post-ironische tijdperk'. In: *NRC Handelsblad* 29-8-2008.

Dijk, Y. van (2010), 'Arnon Grunberg, de uitverkoren auteur'. In: Y. van Dijk e.a. (red), *Jan Campert-stichting Jaarboek 2009*. Den Haag, Jan Campert-stichting, 2010, p.50-73.

Ebert, T. (1991), 'Writing in the Political: Resistance (Post)modernism'. In: *Legal Studies Forum* 15-4, 1991, p.291-304.

Erkelens, R. van (1994), 'Toch liever een pitbull'. In: *De Groene Amsterdammer* 26-10-1994.

Februari, M. (2004), *Park welgelegen. Notities over morele verwarring.* Amsterdam, 2004.

Februari, M. (2007), *De literaire kring.* Amsterdam, Querido, 2007.

Februari, M. (2007a), 'Schrijven met open raam'. In: *De Groene Amsterdammer* 19-10-2007, p.30-31.

Geerts, L. (1983), 'Jaap Goedegebuure over Jeroen Brouwers of een kletsmeier over een praatgenie'. In: *De nieuwe* 12-5-1983.

Gerbrandy, P. (2001), 'Klare taal om in te bijten'. In: *de Volkskrant* 20-7-2001.

Gielis, S. (2007), 'Vlees noch vis. Marjolijn Februari's literaire spiraal'. In: *Ons erfdeel* 2007-3, p.169-171.

Green, J. (2005), *Late Postmodernism. American Fiction at the Millennium.* New York, Palgrave, 2005.

Groenewegen, H. (2004), 'Overleven als schuld en boete. Over Arnon Grunberg'. In: Hilberdink, K. (red.), *Jan Campertprijzen 2004.* Nijmegen, Vantilt, 2004, p.74-85.

Grunberg, A. (1996), 'Waarom ik de menselijke soort wil schaden'. In: *NRC Handelsblad* 19-7-1996.

Grunberg, A. (2001), *De mensheid zij geprezen. Lof der Zotheid 2001.* Amsterdam, Athenaeum, Polak & Van Gennep, 2001.

Grunberg, A. (2004), *Grunberg rond de wereld.* Amsterdam, Nijgh & Van Ditmar, 2004.

Grunberg, A. (2007), *Over Joodse en andere paranoia. Kellendonklezing 2007.* Nijmegen, Valkhofpress, 2007.

Grunberg, A. (2008), *Onze oom. Roman.* Amsterdam, Lebowski, 2008.

Grunberg, A. (2009), *Kamermeisjes & soldaten. Arnon Grunberg onder de mensen.* Amsterdam, Nijgh & Van Ditmar, 2009.

Hart, K. 't (2008), 'O, o, o, wat is ie slecht'. In: *De Groene Amsterdammer* 3-10-2008.

Heumakers, A. (1989), 'Het cynische ziektebeeld van de postmoderne cultuur'. In: *de Volkskrant* 12-5-1989.

Heydebrand, R. van & S. Winko (2008), 'The Qualities of literature. A Concept of Literary Evaluation in Pluralistic Societies'. In: W. van Peer (ed.), *The Quality of Literature. Linguistic Studies in Literary Evaluation.* Amsterdam/Philadelphia, John Benjamins, 2008, p.223-240.

Heynders, O. (1997), 'Poststructuralisme in de Nederlandse literatuur- en architectuurkritiek: een vergelijking'. In: *Tijdschrift voor literatuurwetenschap* 2-3, 1997, p.218-230.

Hoogervorst, I. (1994), '*De buitenvrouw*, roman over multiculturele samenleving'. In: *De Telegraaf* 14-10-1994.

Hutcheon, L. (1988), *A Poetics of Postmodernism. History, Theory, Fiction.* New York/London, Routledge, 1988.

Jameson, F. (1984), 'Postmodernism, or The Cultural Logic of Late Capitalism', *New Left Review* 146, 1984.

Kempen, Y. van (1989), 'Zeker weten'. In: *De Groene Amsterdammer* 19-7-1989.

Lamoree, J. (2007), 'Ik stop alles in mijn werk en raak daardoor uitgeput. Een gesprek met Marjolijn Februari'. In: *Het Parool* 22-3-2007.

Ligtvoet, F. & M. van Nieuwenborgh (Hrsg.) (1993), *Die niederländische und die flämische Literatur der Gegenwart*. München [etc.], Hanser, 1993.

Luis, J. (2007), 'De literaire kring'. In: *Opzij* 1-4-2007.

Marx, W. (2005), *L'adieu à la littérature. Histoire d'une dévalorisation XVIIIe-XXe siècle*. Parijs, Seuill, 2005.

Matthijsse, A. (1998), 'Altijd in contact met de tijdgeest'. In: *Haagsche Courant* 30-10-1998.

Meijsing, D. (1989), 'Modern leven. De snelle, jonge mensen van Joost Zwagerman'. In: *Elsevier* 13-5-1989.

Mertens, A. (1988), 'Postmodern Elements in Postwar Dutch Fiction'. In T. D'haen & H. Bertens, *Postmodern fiction in Europe and the America's*. Amsterdam, Amsterdam University Press, 1988.

Mertens, A. (1990), 'Een tikkeltje te koket misschien? M. Februari is niet voor één gat te vangen'. In: *De groene Amsterammer* 14-2-1990.

Oosterwaal, J. (1993), 'Een grotesk gevoel van machteloosheid'. In: *De Morgen* 16-10-1993.

Osstyn, K. (1990), 'Ergens gelezen'. In: *De standaard* 9-6-1990.

Overstijns, J. (1996), 'Van realism naar postmodernisme (en weer terug?). *Advocaat van de hanen van A.F.Th. van der Heijden in een postmodernistisch perspectief*'. In: *Spiegel der letteren* 38-1, 1996, p.15-42.

Peeters, C. (1990), 'Loodzware luchtigheid. Een postmoderne rapsodie van M. Februari'. In: *Vrij Nederland* 10-2-1990.

Peeters, C. (2001), 'Mefisto Grunberg'. In: *Vrij Nederland* 28-4-2001.

Peteghem, L. van (2003), 'Standplaats Zwagerman. Van de eclectische kruisbestuiving of: een tomeloze diversiteit'. In E. Lettringa (red.), *Standplaats Zwagerman*. Amsterdam, De Arbeiderspers, 2003, p.147-155.

Peters, A. (1990), 'Dat men mij postmodern noemt, vind ik droevig'. In: *Vrij Nederland* 10-3-1990.

R.V. (2001), 'De mensheid zij geprezen: Arnon Grunberg zoekt een redelijk wezen'. In: *Humo* 30-4-2001.

Rosenblatt, R. (2001), 'The Age of Irony Comes to an End'. In: *Time* 16-9-2001.

Rovers, D. (2008), 'Wie gemein ich bin! Over de auteur die zijn eigen lezer wordt'. In: *De witte raaf* 131, 2008, p.1-3.

Ruiter, F. & W. Smulders (1996), *Literatuur en moderniteit in Nederland 1840-1990*. Amsterdam/Antwerpen, De Arbeiderspers, 1996.

Ruiter, F. (1997), 'Postmodernism in the German- and Dutch-Speaking Countries'. In: H. Bertens & D. Fokkema (eds.), *International Postmodernism: Theory and Literary Practice*. Amsterdam/Philadelphia, John Benjamins, 1997, p.359-373.

Ruyters, J. (2008), 'Een liefdesverklaring aan hemelbestormers'. In: *Trouw* 19-1-2008.

Schut, L. (2008), 'Over leger en dood'. In: *De telegraaf* 10-10-2008.

Schutte, X. (1997), 'Een ware fabel'. In: *De Groene Amsterdammer* 27-8-1997.

Slattery, L. (2001), 'Wake Up and Smell the Cordite'. In: *The Australian* 24-10-2001.

Steinz, P. (2004), *Lezen etcetera. Gids voor de wereldliteratuur*. Amsterdam, Prometheus/NRC Handelsblad, 2004.

Vaessens, T. (2002), 'Een weg door het korenveld. Het Nederlandse poëziedebat sinds Maximaal'. In: *Nederlandse letterkunde* 7-4, 2002, p.343-372.

Vaessens, T. (2009), *De revanche van de roman. Literatuur, autoriteit en engagement*. Nijmegen, Vantilt, 2009 (2nd ed.).

Vaessens, T. & J. Joosten (2003), *Postmoderne poëzie in Nederland en Vlaanderen*. Nijmegen, Vantilt, 2003.

Vervaeck, B. (1999), *Het postmodernisme in de Nederlandse en Vlaamse roman*. Brussel/Nijmegen, VUB Press/Vantilt, 1999.

Vervaeck, B. (2007), 'De kleine Postmodernsky: ontwikkelingen in de (verhalen over de) postmoderne roman'. In: E. Brems e.a. (ed.), *Achter de verhalen. Over de Nederlandse literatuur van de twintigste eeuw*. Leuven, Peeters, 2007.

Vries, J. de (2010), 'Top-21'. In: *De groene Amsterdammer* 4-3-2010, p.34-35.

Vullings, J. (2007), 'Wie P.C. Hooft zegt, zegt penose. Over vervlakking, verwarring en verwachting in de nieuwe Nederlandse letteren'. In: *De gids* 170-12, 2007, p.1159-1170.

Wallet, B. (2005), 'Is het tijd voor ernst? Over het probleem van distantie en engagement in de moderne cultuur'. In: *Wapenfelt. Christelijk perspectief op geloof en cultuur* 55-1, 2005, p.4-10.

Waugh, P. (ed.) (2006), *Literary Theory and Criticism. An Oxford Guide*. Oxford/New York, Oxford University Press, 2006.

Zeeman, M. (2001), 'Hoe de feiten de verbeelding perverteerden'. In: *De Volkskrant* 14-9-2001.

Zwagerman, J. (1987), 'De tijdgeest en het geheim van de zeven schoenendozen'. In: *Haagse post* 18-4-1987, p.20-50.

Zwagerman, J. (1987a), 'Drie liefdesbrieven'. In: *Maatstaf* 35-11/12, 1987, p.124-139.

Zwagerman, J. (1994), *De buitenvrouw*. Amsterdam, De Arbeiderspers, 1994.

Zwagerman, J. (1997), *Chaos en rumoer*. Amsterdam, De Arbeiderspers, 1997.

Zwagerman, J. (2003), *Het vijfde seizoen*. Amsterdam, De Arbeiderspers, 2003.

Zwagerman, J. (2006), *Tegen de literaire quarantaine. Kellendonklezing 2006*. Nijmegen, Valkhofpress, 2006.

Zwagerman, J. (2006a), *Transito*. Amsterdam, De Arbeiderspers, 2006.

Zwier, G.J. (1994), 'Aan lager wal'. In: *Leeuwarder courant* 29-7-1994.

Chapter 4 – Italian Literature

Agamben, G. (1998), *Homo Sacer. Sovereign Power and Bare Life*. Stanford, Stanford UP, 1998.

Ammaniti, N. (1996), *Fango*. Milano, Mondadori, 1996.

Ammaniti, N. (1998), *L'ultimo capodanno*. Milano, Mondadori, 1998.

Ammaniti, N. (2009), *Che la festa cominci*. Torino, Einaudi, 2009.

Antonello, P. (2001), 'Cannibalizing the Avant-Garde'. In: S. Lucamante (ed.), *Italian Pulp Fiction. The New Narrative of the Giovani Cannibali Writers*. Madison, Farleigh Dickinson, 2001, p.38-56.

Baetens J., J. de Bloois, A. Masschelein & G. Verstraete (2009), *Culturele studies. Theorie in de praktijk*. Nijmegen, Vantilt, 2009.

Baricco, A. (1993), *L'anima di Hegel e le mucche del Wisconsin*. Milano, Garzanti, 1993.

Baricco, A. (1995), *Barnum. Cronache dal Grande Show*. Milano, Feltrinelli, 1995.

Baricco, A. (1998), *Barnum 2. Altre cronache dal Grande Show*. Milano, Feltrinelli, 1998.

Baricco, A. (2002), *Next. Piccolo libro sulla globalizzazione e sul mondo che verrà*. Milano, Feltrinelli, 2002.

Baricco, A. (2006), *I barbari. Saggio sulla mutazione*. Milano, Feltrinelli, 2008.

Baricco, A. (2010), '2026. La vittoria dei barbari'. *La Repubblica*, 26-08-2010, p.49-51.

Barilli R. (2000), *È arrivata la terza ondata*. Torino, Testo & Immagine, 2000.

Barilli R., et al. (eds.) (2005), *Il gruppo 63 quarant'anni dopo*. Bologna, Pendragon, 2005.

Beck, U., A. Giddens & S. Lash (1994), *Reflexive Modernization: Politics, Tradition and Aesthetics in the Modern Social Order*. Stanford, Stanford University Press, 1994.

Berman, M. (1982), *All That is Solid Melts into Air: The Experience of Modernity*. New York, Simon & Schuster, 1982.

Boscolo, C. (2010), 'Editor's introduction'. In: *Journal of Romance Studies* 10-1, 2010, p.1-6.

Calabrese, S. (2005), *www.letteratura.global. Il romanzo dopo il postmoderno*. Torino, Einaudi, 2005.

Calvino, I. (1983), 'The Written and the Unwritten World'. In: *The New York Review of Books* 12-5-1983, p.38-39.

Carravetta, P. (2009), *Del postmoderno. Critica e cultura in America all'alba del Duemila*. Milano, Bompiani, 2009.

Casadei, A. (2007), *Stile e tradizione nel romanzo italiano contemporaneo*. Bologna, Il Mulino, 2007.

Ceserani, R. (1994), 'Modernity and Postmodernity: a Cultural Change Seen from the Italian Perspective'. In *Italica* 3, 1994, p.369-384.

Ceserani, R. (1997), *Raccontare il postmoderno*. Torino, Bollati Boringhieri, 1997.

Ceserani, R. (2009), 'Intellettuali liquidi o in liquidazione?'. In: Antonello & Mussgnug 2009, p.13-47.

Ceserani, R. (2010), 'Qualche considerazione sulla modernità liquida'. In: *La modernità letteraria* 3, 2010, p.11-25.

Chirumbolo, P. & M. Moroni (2010), "Literature and the Arts in the 1960s: An Introduction". In: P. Chirumbolo, M. Moroni & L. Somigli (eds.), *Neoavanguardia. Italian Experimental Literature and Arts in the 1960s*. Toronto, Toronto UP, 2010, p.3-18.

Covacich, M. (2005), *Fiona*, Torino, Einaudi, 2005.

Critchley, S. (2007), *Infinitely Demanding. Ethics of commitment, politics of resistance*. London/New York, Verso, 2007.

De Michele, G. (2010), 'Afferare Proteo. Dire l'indicibile nel paese dei misteri'. In: M. Jansen & Y. Khamal (eds.), *Memoria in noir. Un'indagine pluridisciplinare*. Bruxelles-Bern, PIE Peter Lang, 2010, p. 67-73.

Donnarumma, R. (2008), 'Nuovi realismi e persistenze postmoderne: narratori italiani di oggi'. In: *Allegoria* 57, 2008, p.26-53.

Donnarumma R. & G. Policastro (eds.) (2008), 'Ritorno alla realtà? Otto interviste a narratori italiani'. In: *Allegoria* 57, 2008, p.9-25.

Esposito R. (2008), *Bios: Biopolitics and Philosophy*. University of Minnesota Press, 2008.

Ferroni, G. (2006), 'Profondità di superficie'. In: Ferroni 2006, p.9-31.

Ferroni, G. et al. (eds.) (2006), *Sul banco dei cattivi. A proposito di Baricco e di altri scrittori alla moda*. Roma, Donzelli, 2006.

Foster, H. (2001), *The Return of the Real. The Avant-Garde at the End of the Century*. Massachusetts/London, MIT Press, 2001.

Genna, G. (2006), 'Walter Siti: Troppi paradisi'. In: *Carmilla on line*, 21-08-2006, http://www.carmillaonline.com/archives/2006/08/001898.html.

Heijne, B. (2010a), 'Diepgang is een optische illusie'. In: *NRC-Handelsblad* 25-6-2010.

Heijne, B. (2010b), 'X-Factor Jaap wordt geil van sushi'. In: *NRC-Handelsblad* 30-10-2010.

Hutcheon, L. (1988), *A poetics of Postmodernism*. New York, Routledge, 1988.

Jameson, F. (1989), *Il postmoderno o la logica culturale del tardo capitalismo*. Milano, Garzanti, 1989.

Jansen, M. (2002), *Il dibattito sul postmoderno in Italia. In bilico tra dialettica e ambiguità*. Firenze, Franco Cesati editore, 2002.

Jansen, M. (2005), '"Il vero spettacolo è un altro": lo slittamento della cronaca secondo Baricco e Veronesi', in Martine Bovo-Romoeuf & Stefania Ricciardi, *Frammenti d'Italia. Le forme narrative della non-fiction 1990-2005*. Firenze, Franco Cesati, 2005, p.89-103.

Jansen, M. (2009), 'Has Postmodernism Ended? Dialectics Revisited (Luperini, Belpoliti, Tabucchi)'. In: Antonello & Mussgnug 2009, p.49-60.

Jansen, M. (2010a), 'Reconstructing the "Bond" of Labour Through Stories of Precarietà: Storytelling According to Beppe Grillo, Aldo Nove, and Ascanio Celestini'. In: *Romance Studies* 28-3, 2010, p.194-205.

Jansen, M. (2010b), 'Laboratory NIE: mutations in progress'. In: *Journal of Romance Studies* 10-1, 2010, p.97-109.

Jansen, M. (2010c). 'Neoavanguardia and postmodernism: oscillations between innovation and tradition from 1963 to 2003'. In Chirumbolo 2010, p.38-73.

Jenkins, H. (2006), *Convergence Culture. Where Old and New Media Collide*. New York/London, New York University Press, 2006.

La Porta, F. (1995), *La nuova narrativa italiana. Travestimenti e stili di fine secolo*. Torino, Bollati Boringhieri, 1995.

La Porta, F. (2001), 'The Horror Picture Show and the Very Real Horrors: About the Italian Pulp'. In: Lucamante 2001, p.57-75.

La Porta, F. (2005), 'Introduzione/ Inleiding'. In: *Kort Italiaans. Verhalen van hedendaagse Italiaanse schrijvers*. Amsterdam, Wereldbibliotheek, 2005, p.8-17.

La Porta, F. (2006), 'Contro il Nuovo Giallo Italiano'. In: Ferroni 2006, p.55-75.

La Porta, F. & M. Sinibaldi (1984). 'Ultime leve. Un questionario ai giovani scrittori italiani'. In: *Linea d'ombra* 8, 1984, p.91-96.

Lanslots, I. (1999), 'Alessandro Baricco's infinite tales'. In: *Spunti e Ricerche*, 1999, p.47-57.

Luperini, R. (1984), 'Statuto del "letterario scritto"'. In: *Alfabeta* 60, 1984, p.15.

Luperini, R. (2005), *La fine del postmoderno*. Napoli, Guida, 2005.

Magris, C. (2009), 'Debate on Europe'. In: H. Hendrix (ed.), *Literature, Law and Europe*. Utrecht, Igitur Utrecht publishing & archiving services, 2009, p.61-80.

McHale, B. (1987), *Postmodernist Fiction*. London, Routledge, 1987.

McKenzie Wark, K. (2007), *Gamer Theory*. Harvard, Harvard UP, 2007.

McNeill, D. (2009), 'Putting Sincerity to Work. Acquiescence and Refusal in Post-Fordist Art'. In: E. Van Alphen, M. Bal & C. Smith (eds.), *The Rhetoric of Sincerity*. Stanford, Stanford UP, 2009, p.157-173.

Palumbo Mosca, R. (2009), 'Prima e dopo *Gomorra*: *non-fiction novel* e impegno'. In: Antonello & Mussgnug 2009, p.305-326.

Pasolini, P.P. (1975), *Scritti corsari*. Milano, Garzanti, 1975.

Patriarca, S. (2010), *Italian Vices. Nation and Character from the Risorgimento to the Republic*. Cambridge, Cambridge UP, 2010.

Pellegrini, F. (2009), 'Conversazione con Niccolò Ammaniti'. In: Bonsaver, G., M. McLaughlin & F. Pellegrini (eds.), *Sinergie narrative. Cinema e letteratura nell'Italia contemporanea*. Firenze, Franco Cesati, 2009, p.281-293.

Petrella, A. (2006), 'Dal postmoderno al romanzo epico. Linee per la letteratura italiana dell'ultimo Novecento'. In: *Allegoria* 52-53, 2006, p.134-148.

Petrella, A. (ed.) (2010), *Gruppo 93, l'antologia poetica*. Arezzo, Zona, 2010.

Rajewsky, I. (2003), *Intermediales Erzählen in der Italienische Literatur der Postmoderne*. Tübingen, Gunter Narr, 2003.

Revelli, M. (1997), 'Worker Identity in the Factory Desert'. In Virno & Hardt 1997, p.115-22.

Ricciardi, S. (2010), 'Desiderio di realtà o realtà del desiderio? L'umanità catodica in *Troppi paradisi* di Walter Siti'. In: *Cahiers d'études italiennes*, 11, 2010, p.125-35.

Ricciardi, S. (2011) *Gli artifici della Non-Fiction. La messinscena narrativa in Albinati, Franchini, Veronesi*. Massa, Transeuropa, 2011.

Saviano, R. (2006), *Gomorra*. Milano, Mondadori, 2006.

Scalfari, E. (2010a), *Per l'alto mare aperto. La modernità e il pensiero danzante*. Torino, Einaudi, 2010.

Scalfari, E. (2010b), 'La lingua ignota dei barbari. Risposta alla profezia di Baricco'. In: *La Repubblica*, 2-9-2010.

Scurati, A. (2006), *La letteratura dell'inesperienza*. Milano, Bompiani, 2006.

Siti, W. (2006), *Troppi paradisi*. Torino: Einaudi, 2006.

Stellardi, G. (2009), '*Pensiero debole*, Nihilism and Ethics, or How Strong is Weakness?'. In: Antonello & Mussgnug 2009, p.83-98.

Tabucchi, A. (1985), *Piccoli equivoci senza importanza*. Milano, Feltrinelli, 1985.

Tabucchi, A. (1994), *Sostiene Pereira*. Milano, Feltrinelli, 1994.

Tabucchi, A. (2006), *L'oca al passo. Notizie dal buio che stiamo attraversando*. Milano, Feltrinelli, 2006.

Tabucchi, A. (2009), *Il tempo invecchia in fretta. Nove storie*. Milano, Feltrinelli, 2009.

Timmer, N. (2008). *'Do You Feel it Too?' The Post-Postmodern Syndrome in American Fiction at the Turn of the Millennium*. PhD thesis, Utrecht University, 2008.

Van den Bossche, B. (2010). 'Epics & Ethics. Il NIE e la responsabilità della letteratura'. In: *La libellula* 1, 2010, http://www.lalibellulaitalianistica.it/blog/?page_id=662#_edn29.

Van Stralen, H. (2005), *Choices and Conflicts. Essays on Literature and Existentialism*. Bern, Peter Lang, 2005.

Vasta, G. (2009),'Cosa raccontano i giovani scrittori'. In: *La Repubblica*, 10-06-2009.

Vattimo, G. (1989), *La società trasparente*. Milano, Garzanti, 1989.

Virno, P. & M. Hardt (eds.) (1997), *Radical Thought in Italy: A Potential Politics*. Minneapolis, University of Minnesota Press, 1997.

Wren-Owens, E. (2007), *Postmodern Ethics*. Newcastle, Cambridge Scholars Publishing, 2007.

Wu Ming (2009), *New Italian Epic. Letteratura, sguardo obliquo, ritorno al futuro*. Torino, Einaudi, 2009.

Chapter 5 – French Literature

Bessière, J. (2006), *Qu'est-il arrivé aux écrivains français? D'Alain Robbe-Grillet à Jonathan littell*. Loverval, Labor, 2006.

Claudel, P. (2005), *Grey Souls*. London, Phoenix, 2005.

Clément, M. & S. van Wesemael (2007), *Michel Houellebecq sous la loupe*. Amsterdam, Rodopi, 2007.

Clément, M. (2000), *Michel Houellebecq, Sperme et Sang*. Paris, L'Harmattan, 2004.

Demonpion, D. (2005), *Michel Houellebecq en fait* Paris, Maren Sell Éditeurs, 2005.

Docherty, T. (1983), *Reading (Absent) Character*. Oxford, Oxford Univeristy Press, 1983.

Houellebecq, M. (2000), *Atomised*. London, Heinemann, 2000.

Houellebecq, M. (2003), *Platform*. London, Vintage, 2003.

Houellebecq, M. (2004), *De koude revolutie*. Amsterdam, De Arbeiderspers, 2004.

Houellebecq, M. (2005), *The Possibility of an Island*. London, Weidenfeld & Nicholson, 2005.

Houellebecq, M. (2006), *Whatever*. London, Serpent's Tail, 2006.

Houppermans, S. (2008), *Jean Echenoz*. Paris, Bordas, 2008.

Lipovetsky, G. (1992), *Le Crépuscule du devoir*. Paris, Gallimard, 1992.

Robbe-Grillet, A. (1984), *Le miroir qui revient*. Paris, Minuit, 1984.

Robbe-Grillet. A. (1963), *Pour un nouveau roman*. Paris, Minuit, 1963.

Sarraute, N. (1956), *L'ère du soupçon*. Paris, Gallimard, 1956.

Viart, D. & B. Blanckeman (2005), *La littérature française au présent. Héritage, modernité, mutations*. Paris, Bordas, 2005.

Wesemael, S. van (2004), *Michel Houellebecq*. Amsterdam, Rodopi, 2004.

Wesemael, S. van (2005), *Michel Houellebecq. Le plaisir du texte*. Paris, L'Harmattan, 2005.

Chapter 6 – Post-Yugoslav Literature

Baudrillard, J. (1993), 'No Pity for Sarajevo'. http://www.egs.edu/faculty/jean-baudrillard/articles/no-reprieve-for-sarajevo/ [Assessed at 10-10-2010].

De Roder, J. (2005), 'De valse identiteit van W.G. Sebald? Enkele bedenkingen bij een heiligverklaring'. In: *Armada* 40, 2005, p.74-84.

Dimitrijević, N. (2002), 'Gorgona: Art as a Way of Existence.' In: L. Hoptman & T. Pospiszyl *Primary Documents. A Sourcebook for Eastern and Central European Art since the 1950s*. New York, The Museum of Modern Art, 2002, p.124-140, 2002.

Drndić, D. (2007), *Sonnenschein*. Zagreb, Fraktura, 2007.

Hemon, A. (2008), *The Lazarus Project*. New York, Riverhead Books, 2008.

Hutcheon, L. (1987), 'The Politics of Postmodernism: Parody and History.' In: *Cultural Critique*, No. 5, Winter, 1986-1987, p.179-207.

Kiš, D. (1975), *Grobnica za Borisa Davidovi a: Sedam Poglavlja Jedne Zajedni ke Povesti*. Beograd, BIGZ, 1995.

Kiš, D. (1978), as *Anatomije*. Beograd, BIGZ, 1995.

Kiš, D. (1978). *A Tomb for Boris Davidovich*. Trans. Duška Miki -Mitchell. New York, Harcourt Brace Jovanovich, 1978.

Mehmedinović, S. (1995), *Sarajevo Blues*. Zagreb, Durieux, 1995.

Mehmedinović, S. (1998), *Sarajevo Blues*. Trans. Ammiel Alcalay. San Francisco, City Light Books, 1998.

Mehmedinović, S. (2002), *Devet Aleksandrija*. Zagreb, Durieux, 2002.

Mehmedinović, S. (2003), *Nine Alexandrias*. Trans. Ammiel Alcalay. San Francisco, City Light Books, 2003.

Mihailovich, V. (1994), 'Faction or Fiction *A Tomb for Boris Davidovi* : the literary affair.' *The Review of Contemporary Fiction* 14-1, 1994. p.169-173.

Milosz, C. (1953), *The Captive Mind*. New York, Vintage Books, 1990.

Mouffe, C. (2005), *On the Political*. London, Routledge, 2005.

Nałkowska, Z. (1946), *Medaliony*. Warszawa, Czytelnik, 1970.

Neubauer, J. (2009), 'Albert Wass: Rebirth and Apotheosis of a Transylvanian-Hungarian Writer.' In: Török and Neubauer, *The Exile and Return of Writers from East-Central Europe*. Berlin, Walter de Gruyter, 2009, p.538-597.

Pleşu, A. (2004), 'We are the Past of Europe'. In: *Alter Ego. Twenty Confronting Views on the European Experience*. Amsterdam, Amsterdam University Press, 2004, p.103-108.

Shishkoff, S. (1987), 'Košava in a Coffee Pot. Or: A Dissection of a Literary Cause Célèbre.' *Cross Currents. A Yearbook of Central European Culture 6*, 1987, p.341-371.

Snel, G. (2004), 'Gardens of the Mind, Places for Doubt: Fictionalized Autobiography in East-Central Europe'. In: M. Cornis-Pope & J. Neubauer (ed.) *History of the literary cultures in East-Central Europe*. Amsterdam, Benjamins, 2004, p.375-386.

Snel, G. (2005), 'Over Semezdin Mehmedinović.' In Mehmedinović, Semezdin *Deze deur is geen uitgang*. Amsterdam, Atlas, 2005, p.118-125.

Snel, G. (ed.) (2004a), *Alter Ego. Twenty Confronting Views on the European Experience*. Amsterdam, Amsterdam University Press, 2004.

Sontag, S. (ed.) (1995), *Homo Poeticus. Danilo Kiš. Essays and Interviews*. New York, Farrar Straus Giroux, 1995.

Štajner, K. (1972), *7000 Dana U Siberiji*. Zagreb, Globus, 1981 (2nd Ed).

Stefanovski, G. (2004), 'A Tale from the Wild East'. In: *Alter Ego. Twenty Confronting Views on the European Experience*. Amsterdam, Amsterdam University Press, 2004, p.21-28.

Tode, E. (2004), 'Ego with Alter Ego'. In: G. Snel (ed.) *Alter Ego. Twenty Confronting Views on the European Experience*. Amsterdam, Amsterdam University Press, 2004, p.35-42.

Urban, P. (1997), *Leonid Šejka. Alchemie* Hamburg, Material Verlag, 1997.

Wachtel, A. (1997), *Making a Nation, Breaking a Nation. Literature and Cultural Politics in Yugoslavia*. Stanford, Stanford University Press, 1997.

Wachtel, A. (2006), *Remaining Relevant After Communism. The Role of the Writer in Eastern-Europe*. Chicago, Chicago University Press, 2006.

Chapter 7 – Norwegian Literature

Beck-Nielsen, C. (2003), *Claus Beck-Nielsen (1963-2001). En biografi*. Copenhagen, Gyldendal, 2003.

Beyer, H. og E. (1974), *Norsk litteraturhistorie bind II. Fra Wergeland til Vinje*. Oslo, Aschehoug, 1974.

Beyer, E. (1995), *Norges litteraturhistorie bind III. Fra Ibsen til Garborg*. Oslo, Cappelen, 1995.

Binding, P. (2003), 'Life's a circus'. In *The Guardian* 24-05-2003.

Brooks, P. (1993), *Body Work. Objects of Desire in Modern Narrative*. Massachusetts, Harvard University Press, 1993.

Christensen, L.S. (1988), *Herman*. Oslo, Cappelen, 1988.

Christensen, L.S. (2001), *Halvbroren*. Oslo, Cappelen, 2001.

Christensen, L.S. (2003), *Maskeblomstfamilien*. Oslo, Cappelen, 2003.

Fluck, W. (1992), 'Surface and Depth, Postmodernism and Neo-Realist Fiction.' In: K. Versluys (ed.), *Neo-Realism in Contemporary American Fiction. Postmodern Studies 5*. Amsterdam & Atlanta, Rodopi, 1992, p.65-85.

Fosse, J. (1983), *Raudt, svart*. Oslo, Det Norske Samlaget, 1983.

Fosse, J. (1989), *Naustet*. Oslo, Det Norske Samlaget, 1989.

Fosse, J. (1989a), *Frå telling via showing til writing*. Oslo, Det Norske Samlaget, 1989.

Fosse, J. (1992), 'Surrealist kan fanden vere', in: *Norsk litterær årbok* 1992, p.19-24.

Fosse, J. & J. Kjærstad (1993-6), *Bøk. Tidsskrift for litteratur og teori*, 1-7/1993-1996, Oslo, Aschehoug.

Fosse, J. (2001), *Ein sommarsdag*. In: *Teaterstykke 2*. Oslo, Det Norske Samlaget, 2001.

Fosse, J. (1999), *Gnostiske essay*. Oslo, Det Norske Samlaget, 1999.

Fosse, J. (2004), *Det er Ales*. Oslo, Det Norske Samlaget, 2004.

Foster, H. (1996), *The Return of the Real*. Cambridge, MIT Press, 1996.

Foucault, M. (1977), 'What is an author'. In: *Language, Counter-Memory, Practice. Selected Essays and Interviews*. Oxford, Basil Blackwell, 1977.

Frobenius, N. (2004), *Teori og praksis*. Oslo, Gyldendal, 2004.

Gemzøe, A. & P.S. Larsen (ed.) (2003), *Modernismens historie*, Copenhagen, Akademisk forlag, 2003.

Gujord, H. (1998), 'Seinmodernisme og post-modernisme.' In: A. Dvergsdal (ed.), *Nye tilbakeblikk. Artikler om litteraturhistoriske hovedbegreper*. Oslo, Cappelen/ LNU 1998, p.221-242.

Halberg, J. (1996), *Trass*. Oslo, Kolon, 1996.

Halberg, J. (2000), *Flommen*. Oslo, Kolon, 2000.

Hamsun, K. (1976), *Sult*. In: *Samlede verker Bind 1*, Oslo, Gyldendal, 1976 (1890).

Hamsun, K. (1976a), *Mysterier*. In: *Samlede verker Bind 1*, Oslo, Gyldendal, 1976 (1892).

Ibsen, H. (1931), *Peer Gynt*. In: *Samlede Verker VI Hundreårsutgaven*, Oslo, Gyldendal, 1931.

Jansson, B.G. (1996), *Postmodernism och metafiktion i Norden*, Uppsala, Hallgren & Fallgren, 1996.

Kjærstad, J. (1984), *Homo Falsus eller Det perfekte mord*. Oslo, Aschehoug, 1984.

Kjærstad, J. (1989), *Menneskets matrise. Essays*. Oslo, Aschehoug, 1989.

Kjærstad, J. (1993), *Forføreren*. Oslo, Aschehoug, 1993.

Kjærstad, J. (1996), *Eroberen*. Oslo, Aschehoug, 1996.

Kjærstad, J. (1999), *Oppdageren*. Oslo, Aschehoug, 1999.

Kjærstad, J. (2000), 'Jeg har sett romanens lys', in: *Dagbladet* 27-11-2000.

Kjærstad, J. (2004), *Menneskets nett. Essays*. Oslo, Aschehoug, 2004.

Knausgård, K.O. (2009-10), *Min Kamp I-V*. Oslo, Oktober, 2009-2010.

Lande, F. (2006), *Frank Lande*. Oslo, Tiden, 2006.

Loe, E. (1996), *Naiv. Super.*, Oslo, Cappelen, 1996.

Loe, E. (1999), *L*. Oslo, Cappelen, 1999.

Marstein, T. (1998), *Sterk sult, plutselig kvalme*. Oslo, Oktober, 1998.

Marstein, T. (2000), *Plutselig høre noen åpne en dør*. Oslo, Oktober, 2000.

Marstein, T. (2009), *Ingenting å angre på*. Oslo, Oktober, 2009.

Moe, K. (1980), *Kjønnskrift*. Oslo, Aschehoug, 1980.

Petterson, P. (2000), *I kjølvannet*. Oslo, Oktober, 2000.

Petterson, P. (2003), *Ut og stjæle hester*. Oslo, Oktober, 2003.

Ramslie, L. (2003), *Fatso*. Oslo, Oktober, 2003.
Rottem, Ø. (1998), *Norges litteraturhistorie bind VIII. Vår egen tid: 1980-1998*. Oslo, Cappelen, 1998.
Rottem, Ø. (2002), 'Gåten Dag Solstad', In: *Dagbladet* 3-10-2002.
Rottem, Ø. (2004), 'Norsk epikk 1990-2003', In: Michelsen og Røskeland (ed.) *Nye forklaringer*. Bergen, Fagbokforlaget/LNU, 2004, p.35-51.
Rottem, Ø. (2004a), 'Intenst suggererende kortroman om sorg og savn i vesterlandsk vintermørke', In: *Dagbladet* 1-3-2004.
Solstad, D. (1987), *Roman 1987*. Oslo, Oktober, 1987.
Solstad, D. (1992), *Ellevte roman. Bok atten*. Oslo, Oktober, 1992.
Solstad, D. (2002), *16.07.41*. Oslo, Oktober, 2002.
Solstad, D. (2006), *Armand V. Fotnoter til en uutgravd roman*. Oslo, Oktober, 2006.
Stegane, I. (1994), 'Medierevolusjon og modernisme 1945-1990.' In: B. Fidjestøl (ed.), *Norsk litteratur i tusen år*. Cappelen/LNU, Oslo 1994, p.526-660.
Sunde, O.L. (1984), *Den lange teksten*. Oslo, Gyldendal, 1984.
Tjønneland, E. (1999), 'Kulturradikalismens fjerde fase.' In: *Vagant* 4/1999, p.22-27.
Ullmann, L. (1998), *Før du sovner*. Oslo, Oktober, 1998.
Ullmann, L. (2005), *Et velsignet barn*. Oslo, Oktober, 2005.
Ørstavik, H. (1997), *Kjærlighet*. Oslo, Oktober, 1997.
Ørstavik, H. (1999), *Like sant som jeg er virkelig*. Oslo, Oktober, 1999.
Ørstavik, H. (2000), *Tiden det tar*. Oslo, Oktober, 2000.

Chapter 8 – Flemish Literature

Adriaensen, B., S. de Coster & T. Sintobin (2006), 'Irony and beyond'. In: *Dietsche Warande & Belfort* 151-5/6, p.705-712.
Bassant, P. & K. Snoekx (2008), 'Gelukkig is dit maar een gedicht'. In: *Dietsche Warande & Belfort* 153-4, 2008, p.566-569.
Bastelaere, D. van (1990), 'Rifbouw'. In: *Yang* 25-144, 1989-1990, p.56-62.
Buelens, G. et.al. (2000), 'Vooraf'. In: *Yang* 36-2, 2000, p.151-153.
Bultinck, B. (2000), 'De onthoofde revolutie'. In: *Yang* 36-2, 2000, p.172-178.
Bultinck, B. (2004), 'De gulpende guirlande van de twintigste eeuw'. In: *De Morgen* 05-05-2004.
Hoste, P. (1995), *High Key*. Amsterdam, Prometheus, 1995.
Hoste, P. (2003), *Montréal*. Amsterdam, Prometheus, 2003.
Hoste, P. (2006), *Een dag in maart*. Amsterdam: Prometheus, 2006.
Hulle, D. van (2002), 'Test. 1.2.3.'. In: *Yang* 38-2, 2002, p.231-239.
Musschoot, A.M. (1994), 'Postmodernisme in de Nederlandse letterkunde'. In: Y. T'Sjoen & H. Vandevoorde (eds.), *Op voet van gelijkheid. Opstellen van Anne Marie Musschoot*. Gent, Studia Germanica Gadensia, 1994, p.203-213.

Musschoot, A.M. (2009), 'The revolution of the sixties, 1960-1970'. In: T. Hermans (ed.), *A Literary History of the Low Countries*. Rochester, Camden House, 2009, p.603-622.

Nolens, D. (2005), *Het kind*. Antwerpen, Meulenhoff/Manteau, 2005.

Nolens, D. (2008), *Stilte en melk voor iedereen*. Antwerpen, Meulenhoff/Manteau, 2008.

Peeters, K. (2007), *Grote Europese roman*. Antwerpen, Meulenhoff/Manteau, 2007.

Peeters, K. (2009), *De bloemen*. Antwerpen, Meulenhoff/Manteau, 2009.

Peeters, P. (2000), 'De handel in illusies'. In: H. Bekkering & A. Zuiderent (eds.), *Jan Campert-prijzen 2000*, Nijmegen, Vantilt, 2000, p.59-80.

Reugebrink, M. (2002), 'Wat?'. In: *Yang* 38-4, 2002, p.547-551.

Theunissen, J. (2006a), 'Een stem zegt: "We hebben zin."'. In: *Yang* 42-3, 2006, p.205-215.

Theunissen, J. (2006b), *Het einde*. Antwerpen, Meulenhoff/Manteau, 2006.

Theunissen, J. (2008), *Een vorm van vermoeidheid*. Antwerpen, Meulenhoff/Manteau, 2008.

Vaessens, T. (2001), 'Postmodernisme en leesstrategie'. In: *Neerlandistiek.nl* 01.10, 2001.

Verhaeghen, P. (1996), *Lichtenberg*. Antwerpen, Manteau, 1996.

Verhaeghen, P. (2004), *Omega minor*. Antwerpen, Meulenhoff/Manteau, 2004.

Verhaeghen, P. (2007), *Omega Minor* (translation by Paul Verhaeghen). Champaign/London: Dalkey Archive Press, 2007.

Verhelst, P. (1999), *Tongkat*. Amsterdam, Prometheus, 1999.

Verhelst, P. (2003), *Tonguecat* (translated by Sherry Marx). New York, Farrar Straus Giroux, 2003.

Verhelst, P. (2005), *Zwerm. Geschiedenis van de wereld*. Amsterdam, Prometheus, 2005.

Vervaeck, B. (1999), *Het postmodernisme in de Nederlandse en Vlaamse roman*. Nijmegen, Vantilt, 1999.

Vervaeck, B. (2006), 'Het verdriet van de wereld'. In: *Ons Erfdeel* 50-1, 2006, p.57-66.

Vervaeck, B. (2007), 'De kleine Postmodernsky: ontwikkelingen in de (verhalen over de) postmoderne roman'. In: E. Brems e.a. (ed.), *Achter de verhalen. Over de Nederlandse literatuur van de twintigste eeuw*. Leuven, Peeters, 2007.

Vervaeck, B. (2009), 'Werken aan de toekomst: De historische roman van onze tijd'. In: *Nederlandse letterkunde* 14-1, 2009, p.19-48.

Vitse, S. (2003), 'Zullen we het maar oorlog noemen?'. In: *Yang* 39-3, 2003, p.519-531.

Vitse, S. (2009), 'De hertovering van de wereld. Liefde en engagement in een gedemystificeerde wereld'. In: *Dietsche Warande & Belfort* 154-4, 2009, p.655-667.

Chapter 9 – Polish Literature

Bolecki, Wł. (1999), *Polowanie na postmodernistów (The Hunt for Postmodernists)*, Kraków, Wydawnictwo Literackie, 1999.

Czapliński, P. (2007) *Powrót centrali (The Return of the Headquarter)*, Kraków, Wydawnictwo Literackie, 2007.

Czapliński, P & P. Śliwiński (1999), *Literatura Polska 1976-1998 (Polish Literature 1976-1998)*, Kraków, Wydawnictwo Literackie, 1999.

Gorczyńska, R. (1992), *Podróżny Świata – rozmowy z Czesławem Miłoszem (Traveller of the World – Conversations with Czesław Milosz)*, Kraków, Wydawnictwo Literackie, 1992.

Heaney, S. (1988), *The Government of the Tongue*, London, Faber and Faber, 1988.

Herbert, Z. (1992), *Raport z oblężonego miasta (Report from the besieged City)*, Wrocław, Wydawnictwo Dolnośląskie, 1992.

Klejnocki, J. & J. Sosnowski, (1996), *Chwilowe zawieszenie broni (A temporary Armistice)*, Warszawa, Wydawnictwo Sic!, 1996, p. 111.

Łapiński, Z. (1993), in: *Teksty Drugie (Second Texts*, bimonthly), Warszawa, 1993, issue 1.

Miłosz, Cz. (1994), *Na brzegu rzeki (On the Border of the River)*, Kraków, Wydawnictwo Znak, 1994.

Miłosz, Cz. (1997), *Życie na wyspach (Living on Islands)*, Kraków, Wydawnictwo Znak, 1997.

Miłosz, Cz. (2003), *Wiersze tom 2 (Poems volume 2)*, Kraków, Wydawnictwo Znak, 2003.

Nycz, R. (2000) *Tekstowy świat poststrukturalizm a wiedza o literaturze (Textual World Poststructuralism and Poetics)*, Kraków, Universitas, 2000, ed. II.

Rorty, R. (1989), *Contingency, irony and solidarity*, Cambridge, Cambridge University Press, 1989.

Vendler, H. (1988), *The Music of What Happens*, Cambridge Mass. & London, Harvard University Press, 1988.

Chapter 10 – German Literature

Adorno, T. (1990), *Ästhetische Theorie*. Eds. Gretel Adorno and Rolf Tiedemann. Frankfurt am Main, Suhrkamp, 1990 [1970].

Altenburg, M. (1992), 'Kampf den Flaneuren. Über Deutschlands junge, lahme Dichter'. In: *Der Spiegel* 12-10-1992, p.308-313.

Anz, T. (ed.) (1991), *'Es geht nicht um Christa Wolf'. Der Literaturstreit im vereinten Deutschland*. München, edition spangenberg, 1991.

Assheuer, T. (1998), 'Der Schnee von gestern. Was bleibt von der Postmoderne? Die alte Realität kehrt ins neue Denken zurück'. In: *Die Zeit* 13-8-1998.

Baßler, M. (2002), *Der deutsche Pop-Roman. Die neuen Archivisten*. München, Beck, 2002.

Berendse, G.J. (2000), 'Karneval in der DDR. Ansätze postmodernen Schreibens 1960-1990'. In: H. Harbers (ed.), *Postmoderne Literatur in deutscher Sprache: Eine Ästhetik des Widerstands?* Amsterdam/Atlanta, Rodopi, 2000, p.233-256.

Biller, M. (1991), 'Soviel Sinnlichkeit wie der Stadtplan von Kiel'. In: R. Moritz & A. Köhler (eds.), *Maulhelden und Königskinder. Zur Debatte über die deutschsprachige Gegenwartsliteratur*. Leipzig, Reclam, 1998, p.62-71.

Biller, M. (2000), 'Feige das Land, schlapp die Literatur'. In: *Die Zeit* 13-4-2000.

Bohrer, K.-H. (1998), 'Erinnerung an Kritierien. Vom Warten auf den deutschen Zeitroman'. In: R. Moritz & A. Köhler (eds.), *Maulhelden und Königskinder. Zur Debatte über die deutschsprachige Gegenwartsliteratur*. Leipzig, Reclam, 1998, p.137-150.

Brussig, T. (1996), *Helden wie wir*. Berlin, Volk & Welt, 1996.

Brussig, T. (1999), *Am kürzeren Ende der Sonnenallee*. Berlin, Volk & Welt, 1999.

Brussig, T. (2004), *Wie es leuchtet*. Frankfurt/Main, S. Fischer, 2004.

Bürger, C., P. Bürger & J. Schulte-Sasse (eds.) (1982), *Zur Dichotomisierung von hoher und niederer Literatur*. Frankfurt am Main, Suhrkamp, 1982.

Dean, M.R., T. Hettche, M. Politycki & M. Schindhelm (2005), 'Was soll der Roman?' In: *Die Zeit* 23-5-2005.

Diez, G. (2005), ‚Postmodern geheilt'. In: *Die Zeit* 13-10-2005.

Engler, W. (2009), *Lüge als Prinzip. Aufrichtigkeit im Kapitalismus*. Berlin, Aufbau, 2009.

Festenburg, N. von (2005), 'Die Magie der leisen Töne'. In: *Der Spiegel* 11-6-2005.

Frank, M. (1986), *Die Unhintergehbarkeit von Individualität. Reflexionen über Subjekt, Person und Individuum aus Anlaß ihrer »postmodernen« Toterklärung*. Frankfurt am Main, Suhrkamp, 1986.

Früchtl, J. (2007), *Our Enlightened Barbarian Modernity and the Project of a Critical Theory of Culture*. Amsterdam, Vossiuspers, 2007.

Gebauer, M.(2002), 'Milieuschilderungen zweier verrückter Monologisten. Philip Roths *Portnoy's Complaint* als ein Vorbild für Thomas Brussigs *Helden wie wir*'. In: *Orbis Litterarum* 57, 2002, p.222-240.

Giesen, S. (1993), *Die Intellektuellen und die Nation. Eine deutsche Achsenzeit*. Frankfurt am Main, Suhrkamp, 1993.

Haaf, M. (2009), 'Der Postmoderne den Hintern zeigen. Ausstellung in London'. In: *Der Spiegel* 13-3-2009.

Haak, R. (2006), 'Cultural identity and Postmodern Writing in the Federal Republic of Germany, 1945-1989'. In: T. D'haen & P. Vermeulen (eds.), *Cultural identity and Postmodern Writing*. Amsterdam/New York, Rodopi, 2006, p.55-86.

Habermas, J. (1988), ‚Die Moderne – ein unvollendetes Projekt'. [reprinted] In: W. Welsch (ed.), *Wege aus der Moderne. Schlüsseltexte der Postmoderne-Diskussion*. Weinheim,VCH, 1988, p.178-192.

Hage, V. & M. Schreiber (1994), 'Gelassen wär' ich gern. Der Schriftsteller Peter Handke über sein neues Werk, über Sprache, Politik und Erotik'. In: *Der Spiegel* 49, 1994, p.170-176.

Hage, V. (1999), 'Die Enkel kommen'. In: *Der Spiegel* 41, 1999, 254-244.

Hagemann, H. (2010), *Axolotl Roadkill*. Berlin, Ullstein, 2010.

Handke, P. (1990), *Versuch über die Jukebox*. Frankfurt am Main, Suhrkamp, 1990.

Hein, J (2001), *Mein erstes T-Shirt*. München, Piper, 2001.

Herrmann, M. (2010), *Vergangenwart. Erzählen vom Nationalsozialismus in der deutschen Literatur seit den neunziger Jahren*. Würzburg, Königshausen & Neumann, 2010.

Hielscher, M. (1996), *Wenn der Kater kommt. Neues Erzählen. 38 deutschsprachige Autorinnen und Autoren*. Köln, Kiepenheuer & Witsch, 1996.

Hielscher, M. (2001), 'Geschichte und Kritik. Die neue Lesbarkeit und ihre Notwendigkeit'. In: *Zeitschrift für Literaturwissenschaft und Linguistik* 124-31, 2001, p.65-71.

Hielscher, M. (2010), 'mehr Wumms'. In: *Süddeutsche Zeitung* 13-8-2010 http://www.sueddeutsche.de/kultur/2.220/literatur-und-unterhaltung-mehr-wumms-1.987808.

Hildesheimer, W. (1991), *Gesammelte Werke*, vol. VII. Frankfurt am Main, Suhrkamp, 1991.

Hildesheimer, W. (1998), 'The End of Fiction'. In: S. Braese et al. (eds.), *Deutsche Nachkriegsliteratur und der Holocaust*. Frankfurt am Main/New York, Campus 1998, p.331-349.

Hillgruber, K. (2007), 'Lösungen für einige Welträtsel. Das Leben zänkischer Philosophen - Klaus Hoffers legendärer Roman *Bei den Bieresch*'. In: *Frankfurter Rundschau*, 29-8-2007.

Hoffer, K. (1986), *Methoden der Verwirrung. Betrachtungen zum Phantastischen bei Franz Kafka*. Graz/Wien, Droschl, 1986.

Holler, V. (2003), *Felder der Literatur. Eine literatursoziologische Studie am Beispiel von Robert Menasse*. Frankfurt am Main, Peter Lang, 2003.

Illies, F. (2000), *Generation Golf. Eine Inspektion*. Berlin, Argon, 2000.

Kaminer, W. (ed.) (2001), *Frische Goldjungs. Anthologie der neudeutschen Literatur*. München, Manhattan, 2001.

Kehlmann, D. (2007), *Diese sehr ernsten Scherze. Poetikvorlesungen*. Göttingen, Wallstein 2007.

Krause, D. (2007), *Postmoderne – Über die Untauglichkeit eines Begriffs der Philosophie, Architekturtheorie und Literaturtheorie*. Frankfurt am Main, Peter Lang, 2007.

Krauß, A. (2002), *Die Überfliegerin*. Frankfurt am Main, Suhrkamp, 2002.

Krauß, A. (2004), *Die Gesamtliebe und die Einzelliebe. Frankfurter Vorlesungen*. Frankfurt am Main, Suhrkamp, 2004.

Kunne, A. (2005), *Postmoderne contre coeur. Stationen des experimentellen in der österreichischen Literatur*. Innsbruck/Wien, Studien-Verlag, 2005.

Lamberechts, L. (2000), ‚Von der Spätmoderne zu einer resistenten Postmoderne. Über die Dynamik eines Literatur- und Kulturwandels'. In: H. Harbers (ed.), *Postmoderne Literatur in deutscher Sprache: Eine Ästhetik des Widerstands?* Amsterdam/Atlanta, Rodopi, 2000, p.59-77.

Lethen, H. (1981), *Verhaltenslehren der Kälte. Lebensversuche zwischen den Kriegen*. Frankfurt am Main, Suhrkamp, 1994.

Lewis, A. (2008), Die neue Unübersichtlichkeit. Die Lyrik des Prenzlauer Bergs: Zwischen Avantgarde, Ästhetizismus und Postmoderne'. In: H. Harbers (ed.), *Postmoderne Literatur in deutscher Sprache: Eine Ästhetik des Widerstands?* Amsterdam/Atlanta, Rodopi, 2000, p.257-286.

Luckscheiter, R. (2002), *Der postmoderne Impuls. Die Krise der Literatur um 1968 und ihre Überwindung*. Berlin, Duncker & Humblot, 2002, p.32-46.

Luedke, M. (2004), 'Die Prototypen der Wende. Thomas Brussigs Roman *Wie es leuchtet* liest sich amüsant, aber man vergisst ihn rasch'. In: *Die Zeit* 30-12-2004.

Lützeler, P.M. (1998), 'Ein deutsches Missverständnis. Die 'Postmoderne' ist keine modische Formel, sondern beschreibt präzise unsere Gegenwart – Eine Replik'. In: *Die Zeit* 1-10-1998.

Lützeler, P.M. (2005), *Postmoderne und postkoloniale deutschsprachige Literatur. Diskurs, Analyse, Kritik*. Bielefeld, Aisthesis, 2005.

Lützeler, P.M. (2010), *Bürgerkrieg global. Menschenrechtsethos und deutschsprachiger Gegenwartsroman*. München, Wilhelm Fink, 2010.

MacCormick, R.W. (1991), *Politics of the Self. Feminism and the Postmodern in West German Literature and Film*. Princeton NJ, Princeton U.P., 1991.

Maier, A. (2005), 'Meine Literatur macht, was sie will'. In: *Die Zeit* 23-5-2005.

Maier, A. (2006), *Ich. Frankfurter Vorlesungen*. Frankfurt am Main, Suhrkamp 2006.

März, U. (2010), 'Literarischer Kugelblitz. Im Koksnebel: Helene Hegemanns heftiges Romandebüt *Axolotl Roadkill*'. In: Die Zeit 21-1-2010.

Menasse, R. (1988), *Sinnliche Gewißheit*. Frankfurt am Main, Suhrkamp, 1988.

Menasse, R. (1990), 'Der Name der Rose ist Dr. Kurt Waldheim. Der erste postmoderne Bundespräsident'. In: *Die sozialpartnerschaftliche Ästhetik. Essays zum österreichischen Geist*. Wien, Sonderzahl, 1990, p.166-174.

Menasse, R. (1992), *Das Land ohne Eigenschaften. Essay zur österreichischen Identität*. Wien, Sonderzahl, 1992.

Menasse, R. (1995), *Phänomenologie der Entgeisterung. Geschichte des verschwindenden Wissens*. Frankfurt am Main, Suhrkamp, 1995.

Menasse, R. (2001), *Die Vertreibung aus der Hölle*. Frankfurt am Main, Suhrkamp, 2001.

Menasse, R. (2006), *Die Zerstörung der Welt als Wille und Vorstellung. Frankfurter Poetikvorlesungen*. Frankfurt am Main, Suhrkamp, 2006.

Menasse, R. (2007), *Don Juan de la Mancha oder Die Erziehung der Lust*. Frankfurt am Main, Suhrkamp, 2007.

Menasse, R. (2009), *Permanente Revolution der Begriffe. Vorträge zur Kritik der Abklärung*. Frankfurt am Main, Suhrkamp, 2009.

Menasse, R. (2009a), *Ich kann jeder sagen. Erzählungen vom Ende der Nachkriegsordnung*. Frankfurt am Main, Suhrkamp, 2009.

Modick, K. (2006), *Bestseller*. Frankfurt am Main, Eichborn, 2006.

Moritz, R. & A. Köhler (eds.) (1998), *Maulhelden und Königskinder. Zur Debatte über die deutschsprachige Gegenwartsliteratur*. Leipzig, Reclam, 1998, 15-17.

Müller, H.-P. (1998), 'Das stille Ende der Postmoderne. Ein Nachruf'. In: *Merkur. Deutsche Zeitschrift für europäisches Denken* 52-594/595, 1998, p.975-981.

Neuber, W. (1995), 'Die seltsame Lust an falschen Zusammenhängen. Gespräch mit dem österreichischen Schriftsteller Robert Menasse'. In: *Neue Zürcher Zeitung*. Internationale Ausgabe. 7/8-10-1995.

Ortheil, H.-J. (1987), 'Das Lesen – ein Spiel. Postmoderne Literatur? Die Literatur der Zukunft! In: *Die Zeit*, 17-4-1987.

Pilz, M. (2004), 'Geschichte wird gemacht. Thomas Brussig hat seinen nächsten Wende-Roman verfasst. Diesmal einen dickleibigen und eher ernsthaften'. In: *Die Welt* 2-10-2004.

Politycki, M. (2004), 'The American Dead End of German Literature'. In: A.C. Mueller (ed.), *German Pop Culture. How American Is It?* Michigan, University of Michigan Press, 2004, p.133-140.

Rothmann, R. (2008), 'Kleine Knochenflöte'. In: *Literaturpreis 2008 Ralf Rothmann*. Ed. Günther Rüther. Sankt-Augustin, Berlin, Konrad-Adenauer-Stiftung, 2008, p.28-36.

Ruiter, F. (1991), *De receptie van het Amerikaanse postmodernisme in Duitsland en Nederland*. Apeldoorn, Garant, 1991.

Rusch, C. (2003), *Meine freie deutsche Jugend*. Frankfurt/Main, S. Fischer, 2003.

Schirrmacher, F. (1989), 'Idyllen in der Wüste oder Das Versagen vor der Metropole. In: *Frankfurter Allgemeine Zeitung*, 10-10-1989.

Schirrmacher, F. (1990), 'Abschied von der Literatur der Bundesrepublik. Neue Pässe, neue Identitäten, neue Lebensläufe: Über die Kündigung einiger Mythen des westdeutschen Bewusstseins'. In: *Frankfurter Allgemeine Zeitung* 2-10-1990.

Schulze, I. (1998), *Simple Storys. Ein Roman aus der ostdeutschen Provinz*. Berlin, Berlin Verlag, 1998.

Serner, W. (1981), *Letzte Lockerung. Handbrevier für Hochstapler und solche die es werden wollen. Das Gesamte Werk*. Vol. 7. Munich, Klaus Renner, 1981.

Sokal A. & J. Bricmont (1998), 'Postmoderne in Wissenschaft und Politik'. [translation] In: *Merkur. Deutsche Zeitschrift für europäisches Denken* 52-594/595, 1998, p.929-943.

Späth, G. (2001), *Commedia. Roman. Durchgesehene Neuausgabe*. Göttingen, Steidl. 2001.

Stolz, D. (2002), 'A Matter of Perspective. Prose Débuts in Contemporary German Literature'. In: S. Taberner (ed.), *German Literature in the Age of Globalisation*. Birmingham, University of Birmingham Press, 2004, p.111-126.

Süselbeck, J. (2009), 'Walser light?'. Ist das 'junge Erzählen' vom Nationalsozialismus innovativ, verharmlosend oder einfach nur harmlos?' In: A. Geier & J. Süselbeck (eds.). *Konkurrenzen, Konflikte, Kontinuitäten. Generationenfragen in der Literatur seit 1990*. Göttingen, Wallstein, 2009, p.53-68.

Taberner, S. (2005), *German Literature of the 1990s and Beyond. Normalization and the Berlin Republic*. Rochester, Camden House, 2005.

Tetzlaff, M. (2004), *Ostblöckchen – Eine Kindheit in der Zone*. Frankfurt/Main, Schöffling & Co., 2004.

Timmer, N. (2010), *Do you feel it too? The Post-Postmodern Syndrome in American fiction at the Turn of the Millennium*. Amsterdam, Rodopi, 2010.

Trilling, L. (2003), *Das Ende der Aufrichtigkeit*. Transl. by Henning Ritter. München, Hanser, 1980.

Weber, C. (ed.) (1984), *Hamletmachine and Other Texts for the Stage*. New York, PAJ, 1984.

Welsch, W. (1987), *Unsere postmoderne Moderne*. Weinheim, VCH, 1987.

Welsch, W. (ed.) (1988), *Wege aus der Moderne. Schlüsseltexte der Postmoderne-Diskussion.* Weinheim, VCH, 1988.

Wittstock, U. (ed.) (1994), *Roman oder Leben. Postmoderne in der deutschen Literatur.* Leipzig, Reclam, 1994.

Chapter 11 – Spanish and Spanish American Literature

Aizenberg, E. (2002), 'Borges, Postcolonial Precursor'. In: E. Aizenberg, *Books and Bombs in Buenos Aires: Borges, Gerchunoff, and Argentine-Jewish writing.* Hanover, University Press of New England, 2002, p.102-113.

Balderston, D. (1993) *Out of Context: Historical Reference and the Representation of Reality in Borges.* Durham, Duke University Press, 1993.

Barth, J. (1967), 'The Literature of Exhaustion'. In: *The Atlantic Monthly* August 1967, p. 29-34.

Barth, J. (1980), 'The Literature of Replenishment'. In *The Atlantic Monthly* January 1980, p. 65-71.

Berg, K. (2008) *Javier Marías's Postmodern Praxis. Humor and Interplay between Reality and Fiction in his Novels and Essays.* Saarbrücken, VDM Verlag Dr. Müller, 2008.

Bertens, H. (1997), 'Introduction'. In: H. Bertens & D. Fokkema (eds.), *International Postmodernism.* Amsterdam/Philadelphia, John Benjamins, 1997, 3-13.

Bolaño, R. (2004a), *Distant Star.* Tr. Chris Andrews. New York, New Directions, 2004.

Bolaño, R. (2004b), 'Literatura y exilio'. In: *Entre paréntesis.* Madrid, Anagrama, 2004, p. 40-46.

Bolaño, R. (2008a), *Nazi literature in the Americas.* Tr. Chris Andrews. New York, New Directions, 2008.

Bolaño, R. (2008b), *2666.* Tr. Natasha Wimmer. London, Picador, 2008.

Borges, J.L. (1962), *Ficciones.* Edited by Anthony Kerrigan. Tr. Anthony Kerrigan, Alastair Reid and others. New York, Grove Press, 1962.

Borges, J.L. (2005), *Obra poética, 2 (1960-1972).* Madrid, Alianza, 2005.

Borges, J.L. (1975), *A Universal History of Infamy.* Tr. Norman Thomas di Giovanni. New York, Penguin Books, 1975.

Borges, J.L. (1981), 'The Argentine Writer and Tradition'. In: *Labyrinths. Selected Stories and Other Writings.* Edited by Donald A. Yates and James E. Irby. Tr. Donald Yates, James E. Irby, John Fein, Dudley Fitts, Julian Palley and others. Harmondsworth, Penguin Books, 1981, p. 211-220.

Casanova, P. (2004), *The World Republic of Letters.* Cambridge, Harvard University Press, 2004.

Corral, W. (2006), 'Roberto Bolaño: Portrait of the Writer as a Noble Savage'. In: *World Literature Today,* nov.-dec. 2006, p. 47-50.

Elmore, P. (2008), '2666: la autoría en el tiempo del límite'. In: E. Paz Soldán et alii (eds.), *Bolaño salvaje.* Canet de Mar, Candaya, 2008, p. 259-292.

Fokkema, D.W. (1984), *Literary History, Modernism, and Postmodernism*. Amsterdam/Philadelphia, John Benjamins, 1984.

Grohmann, A. (2005), 'Javier Marías'. In: M. E. Altisent & C. Martínez-Carazo (eds.), *Dictionary of Literary Biography. Vol 322: Twentieth Century Spanish Fiction Writers*. Detroit, Thomson Gale, 2005, p. 148-159.

Kunz, M. (2008), 'Femicidio y ficción: los asesinatos de mujeres de Ciudad Juárez y su productividad cultural'. In: *ConNotas. Revista de crítica y teoría literarias*, 6: 11, 2008, p. 117-153.

Larsen, N. (1990), 'Postmodernism and Imperialism: Theory and Politics in Latin America'. *Postmodern Culture* 1-1, 1990, http://muse.jhu.edu/journals/postmodern_culture/v001/1.1larsen.html.

Lasdun, J. (2010), 'Glittering with Intent'. In: *The Guardian* 21-11-2010, p. 12-13

Lozano Mijares, M. (2010), 'Postmodernism and Spanish Literature'. In: L. Martín-Estudillo and N. Spadaccini (eds.), *New Spain, New Literatures*. Nashville, Tennessee, Vanderbilt University Press, 2010, p. 183-202.

Manzoni, C. (ed.) (2002), *Roberto Bolaño: la escritura como tauromaquia*. Buenos Aires, Corregidor, 2002.

Marías, J. (1997), 'Jorge Luis Borges desvalido'. In: *Miramientos*. Madrid: Alfaguara, 1997, p. 23-28.

Marías, J. (2001), *Dark Back of Time*. Tr. Esther Allen. New York, New Directions, 2001.

Marías, J. (2005), *Your Face Tomorrow. Fever and Spear*. Tr. Margaret Jull Costa. New York, New Directions, 2005.

Marías, J. (2006), *Your Face Tomorrow. 2: Dance and Dream*. Tr. Margaret Jull Costa. New York, New Directions, 2006.

Marías, J. (2008), *Sobre la dificultad de contar*. Madrid, Real Academia, 2008.

McHale, B. (1987), *Postmodernist Fiction*. New York/London, Methuen, 1987.

Mendoza, E. (1998), 'El extraño caso de Javier Marías'. In: *El País*, 18-11-1998.

Molloy, S. (1972), *La diffusion de la littérature hispano-américaine en France au XXe siècle*. Paris, Presses Universitaires de France, 1972.

Navajas, G. (1987), *Teoría y práctica de la novela postmoderna*. Barcelona, Edicis del Mall, 1987.

Ortega, J. (1997), 'Postmodernism in Spanish-American Writing'. In : H. & D. Fokkema (eds.), *International Postmodernism*. Amsterdam/Philadelphia, John Benjamins, 1997, p. 315-326.

Puente, M. I. de la. (2008),'Formas de representar la violencia en algunas escenas de la literatura latinoamericana'. In: *Revista Question*, Autumn 2008, http://perio.unlp.edu.ar/question/numeros_anteriores/numero_anterior18/nivel2/articulos/ensayos/delapuente_1_ensayos_18otono2008.htm

Sarlo, B. (2007), *Borges. Un escritor en las orillas*. Barcelona, Siglo XXI, 2007.

Sorensen, D. (2007), *A Turbulent Decade Remembered. Scenes from the Latin American Sixties*. Stanford, Stanford University Press, 2007.

Steenmeijer, M. (1996), 'Sporen van Borges'. In: *Mythenbouwers van de Nieuwe Wereld*. Amsterdam, Wereldbibliotheek, 1996, p. 76-85.

Steenmeijer, M. (2009a), 'Tiempo rimado, tiempo cojo: una lectura bilingüe de Marías'. In: A. Grohmann and M. Steenmeijer (eds.) (2009), *Allí donde uno diría que ya no puede haber nada. Tu rostro mañana de Javier Marías*. Amsterdam/New York, Rodopi, 2009, p. 133-147.

Steenmeijer, M. (2009b), *Moderne Spaanse en Spaans-Amerikaanse literatuur. Een geschiedenis*. Amsterdam, Wereldbibliotheek, 2009.

Steenmeijer, M. (2011), 'Captar lo que otros no han reflejado: la recepción nacional e internacional de la narrativa de Javier Marías' (forthcoming 2011).

Thiher, A. (1984), *Words in Reflection. Modern language theory and postmodern fiction*. Chicago, Chicago University Press, 1984.

Van Alphen, E. & M. Bal (eds.) (2009), *The Rhetorics of Sincerity*. Stanford, Stanford University Press, 2009.

Villoro, J. (2010), 'Roberto Bolaño: The Future Battle'. In: *Review: Literature and Arts of the Americas*, 80: 43/1, 2010, p. 9-18.

Chapter 12 – American Literature

Annesley, J. (1998), *Blank Fictions. Consumerism, Culture and the Contemporary American Novel*. London, Pluto Press, 1998.

Annesley, J. (2009), 'Review Essay: David Foster Wallace'. In: *Journal of American Studies* 43-1, 2009, p.131-134.

Barth, J. (1988), *Lost in the Funhouse: Fiction for Print, Tape, Live Voice*. New York, Anchor Books/Doubleday, 1988.

Barth, J. (1984), 'The Literature of Exhaustion'. In: idem, *The Friday Book. Essays and Other Nonfiction*. Baltimore, Johns Hopkins University Press, 1984, p.62-76.

Blazer, A.E. (2002), 'Chasms of Reality, Aberrations of Identity: Defining the Postmodern through Bret Easton Ellis's *American Psycho*'. In: *Americana: The Journal of American Popular Culture* 1-2, 2002. [Online] Available at: http://www.americanpopularculture.com/journal/articles/fall_2002/blazer.htm [accessed at 4 October 2010].

Boswell, M. (2003), *Understanding David Foster Wallace*. Columbia, University of South Carolina Press, 2003.

Burn, S. (2003), *Infinite Jest: A Reader's Guide*. New York, Continuum Books, 2003.

Burn, S. (2008), '*Infinite Jest* 10th anniversary'. In: *The Times* 17-9-2008). [Online] Available at: http://entertainment.timesonline.co.uk/tol/arts_and_entertainment/the_tls/article4772351.ece [accessed at 4 October 2010].

Cioffi, F.L. (2000), "An Anguish Become Thing': Narrative as Performance in David Foster Wallace's *Infinite Jest*'. In: *Narrative* 8-2, 2000, p.161-181.

Confessore, N. (2000), 'Finite Jest'. In: *The American Prospect* 19-6-2000, p.86-88.

Dulk, A. den (2008), 'Voorbij de doelloze ironie. De werken van Dave Eggers en David Foster Wallace vergeleken met het denken van Søren Kierkegaard'. In: L. Derksen, E. Koster & J. van der Stoep (eds.), *Het postmodernisme voorbij?*. Amsterdam, VU Uitgeverij, 2008, p.83-98.

Dulk, A. den (2011), 'Wallace and Wittgenstein: Literature as Dialogue Concerning the Real World'. In: Sébastian Hüsch (ed.), *Philosophy and Literature and the Crisis of Metaphysics*. Würzburg, Verlag Königshausen & Neumann, 2011.

Eggers, D. (2001a), *A Heartbreaking Work of Staggering Genius*. London, Picador, 2001.

Eggers, D. (2001b), *Mistakes We Knew We Were Making* [appendix to: Eggers, *A Heartbreaking Work of Staggering Genius*]. London, Picador, 2001.

Eggers, D. (2002), *You Shall Know Our Velocity*. San Francisco, McSweeney's, 2002.

Ellis, B.E. (1991), *American Psycho*. London, Picador, 1991.

Federman, R. (1988), 'Self-reflexive Fiction'. In: Emory Elliott (ed.), *Columbia Literary History of the United States*. New York, Columbia University Press, 1988, p.1142-1157.

Foer, J.S. (2002), *Everything Is Illuminated*. London, Hamish Hamilton, 2002.

Foer, J.S. (2005), *Extremely Loud & Incredibly Close*. Boston, Houghton Mifflin, 2005.

Fogel, S. & G. Slethaug (1990), *Understanding John Barth*. Columbia, University of South Carolina Press, 1990.

Franzen, J. (2002), 'Why Bother?'. In: idem, *How To Be Alone. Essays*. London, Fourth Estate, 2002, p.55-97.

Goerlandt, I. (2006), "'Put the Book Down and Slowly Walk Away': Irony and David Foster Wallace's *Infinite Jest*'. In: *Critique: Studies in Contemporary Fiction* 47-3, 2006, p.309-328.

Harris, C.B. (1983), *Passionate Virtuosity: The Fiction of John Barth*. Urbana, University of Illinois Press, 1983.

Holland, M.K. (2006), "'The Art's Heart's Purpose': Braving the Narcissistic Loop of David Foster Wallace's *Infinite Jest*'. In: *Critique: Studies in Contemporary Fiction* 47-3, 2006, p.218-242.

Hultkrans, A. (1997), 'Books – *A Supposedly Fun Thing I'll Never Do Again* by David Foster Wallace'. In: *Artforum* 35-10, 1997, p.15-22.

Hutcheon, L. (1995), *Irony's Edge: the Theory and Politics of Irony*. London, Routledge, 1995.

Kakutani, M. (2000a), 'Clever Young Man Raises Sweet Little Brother'. In: *The New York Times* 1-2-2000. [Online] Available at: http://www.nytimes.com/2000/02/01/books/books-of-the-times-clever-young-man-raises-sweet-little-brother.html [accessed at 4 October 2010].

Kakutani, M. (2000b), 'Critic's Notebook: New Wave of Writers Reinvents Literature'. In: *The New York Times* 22-4-2000. [Online] Available at: http://www.nytimes.com/2000/04/22/books/critic-s-notebook-new-wave-of-writers-reinvents-literature.html [accessed at 4 October 2010].

Kamphuis, M. (2005), 'Interview Jonathan Safran Foer: "Schrijven is voor mij iets als samen zingen, rond een kampvuur"'. In: *Filosofie Magazine* 7, 2005, p.28-31 [Publication in Dutch].

Kierkegaard, S. (1989), *The Concept of Irony: with Continual Reference to Socrates; Together with Notes of Schelling's Berlin lectures*. Princeton, Princeton University Press, 1989.

Kierkegaard, S. (1992), *Concluding Unscientific Postscript to Philosophical Fragments Volume 1*. Princeton, Princeton University Press, 1992.

Korthals Altes, L. (2008), 'Sincerity, Reliability and Other Ironies – Notes on Dave Eggers' *A Heartbreaking Work of Staggering Genius*'. In: Elke D'hoker & Gunther Martens (eds.), *Narrative Unreliability in the Twentieth-Century First-Person Novel*. Berlin, Walter de Gruyter, 2008, p.107-128.

Leclair, T. (1996), 'The Prodigious Fiction of Richard Powers, William Vollmann and David Foster Wallace'. In: *Critique: Studies in Contemporary Fiction* 38-1, 1996, p.12-37.

Mattson, K. (2002), 'Is Dave Eggers a Genius? Rebelling and Writing in an Age of Postmodern Mass Culture'. In: *Radical Society* 29-3, 2002, p.75-83.

Max, D.T. (2009), 'The Unfinished'. In: *The New Yorker* 9-3-2009, p.48-61.

McCaffery, L. (1993), 'An Interview with David Foster Wallace'. In: *Review of Contemporary Fiction* 13-2, 1993, p.127-150.

McConnell, F.D. (1977), *Four Postwar American Novelists. Bellow, Mailer, Barth, and Pynchon*. Chicago, University of Chicago Press, 1977.

McHale, B. (1987), *Postmodernist* Fiction. New York, Methuen, 1987.

McLaughlin, R.L. (2004), 'Post-Postmodern Discontent: Contemporary Fiction and the Social World'. In: *Symploke* 12-1/2, 2004, p.53-68.

Miller, L. (1996), 'Interview – David Foster Wallace'. In: *Salon* 9-3-1996. [Online] Available at: http://www.salon.com/09/features/wallace1.html [accessed at 4 October 2010].

Murphet, J. (2002), *American Psycho. A Reader's Guide*. New York, Continuum Books, 2002.

Myers, B.R. (2005), 'A Bag of Tired Tricks'. In: *The Atlantic Monthly* 5-2005, p.115-120.

Nichol, B. (2009), *The Cambridge Introduction to Postmodern Fiction*. Cambridge, Cambridge University Press, 2009.

Nichols, C. (2001), 'Dialogizing Postmodern Carnival: David Foster Wallace's *Infinite Jest*'. In: *Critique: Studies in Contemporary Fiction* 43-1, 2001, p.3-16.

Scholtens, W.R. (1995), 'Inleiding'. In: Søren Kierkegaard, *Over het begrip ironie*. Amsterdam, Boom, 1995, p.7-31.

Scott, A.O. (2000), 'The Panic of Influence – Review of *Brief Interviews with Hideous Men*'. In: *The New York Review of Books* 47-2, 2000, p.39-43.

Solomon, D. (2005), 'The Rescue Artist'. In: *The New York Times* 27-2-2005). [Online] Available at: http://www.nytimes.com/2005/02/27/magazine/27FOER.html [accessed at 4 October 2010].

Stack, G.J. (1977), *Kierkegaard's Existential Ethics*. Tuscaloosa, University of Alabama Press, 1977.

Suglia, J. (2004), 'Bret Easton Ellis: Escape from Utopia'. In: *Youth Quake Magazine* 27-5-2004. [Online] Available at: http://www.youthquakemagazine.com/author_articles/breteastonellis.htm [accessed at 4 October 2010].

Timmer, N. (2010), *Do You Feel It Too? The Post-Postmodern Syndrome in American Fiction at the Turn of the Millennium*. Amsterdam, Rodopi, 2010.

Wallace, D.F. (1990), 'The Empty Plenum: David Markson's *Wittgenstein's Mistress*'. In: *The Review of Contemporary Fiction* 10, 1990, p.217-239.

Wallace, D.F. (1996), *Infinite* Jest. Boston, Little, Brown & Company, 1996.

Wallace, D.F. (1999), *Brief Interviews With Hideous* Men. Boston, Little, Brown & Company, 1999.

Wallace, D.F. (1988), 'Fictional Futures and the Conspicuously Young'. In: *The Review of Contemporary Fiction* 8, 1988.

Wallace, D.F. (2002), 'E Unibus Pluram: television and US fiction'. In: idem, *A Supposedly Fun Thing I'll Never Do Again. Essays and Arguments*. London, Abacus, 2002, p.21-82.

Wallace, D.F. (2009), *This Is Water. Some Thoughts, Delivered on a Significant Occasion, about Living a Compassionate Life*. New York, Little, Brown & Company, 2009.

Waugh, P. (1984), *Metafiction: the theory and practice of self-conscious fiction*. London, Methuen, 1984.

Weber, B. (2008), 'David Foster Wallace, Influential Writer, Dies at 46'. In: *The New York Times* 14-9-2008. [Online] Available at: http://www.nytimes.com/2008/09/15/books/15wallace.html [accessed at 4 October 2010].

Wiley, D. (1997), 'Interview – David Foster Wallace'. In: *The Minnesota Daily* 27-2-1997. [Online] Available at: http://www.badgerinternet.com/ ~bobkat/jestwiley2.html [accessed at 4 October 2010].

Worthington, M. (2001), 'Done with Mirrors: Restoring the Authority Lost in John Barth's Funhouse'. In: *Twentieth-Century Literature* 47-1, 2001, p.114-136.

Young, E. & G. Caveney (1993), 'Introduction'. In: idem (eds.), *Shopping in Space. Essays on America's Blank Generation Fiction*. New York, The Atlantic Monthly Press, 1993, p.i-iv.

Young, E. (1993a), 'Children of the Revolution'. In: E. Young & G. Caveney (eds.), *Shopping in Space. Essays on America's Blank Generation Fiction*. New York, The Atlantic Monthly Press, 1993, p.1-20.

Young, E. (1993b), 'Vacant Possession'. In: Elizabeth Young & Graham Caveney (eds.), *Shopping in Space. Essays on America's Blank Generation Fiction*. New York, The Atlantic Monthly Press, 1993, p.21-42.

Young, E. (1993c), 'The Beast in the Jungle, the Figure in the Carpet'. In: E. Young & G. Caveney (eds.), *Shopping in Space. Essays on America's Blank Generation Fiction*. New York, The Atlantic Monthly Press, 1993, p.85-122.

About the Authors

Brigitte Adriaensen (1975) obtained her PhD from the University of Leuven in 2005, and is now Assistant Professor in Hispanic literature at the Radboud University Nijmegen. Her international publications are situated in the fields of Spanish and Spanish American literature. She published *La poética de la ironía en la obra tardía de Juan Goytisolo* (Verbum, 2007) and *Pesquisas en la obra tardía de Juan Goytisolo* (Rodopi, 2009). Currently, she is collaborating with Maarten Steenmeijer on a NWO research project concerning the reception of Jorge Luis Borges in World literature.

Yra van Dijk (1970) is Assistant Professor at the University of Amsterdam, and literary critic at the national newspaper *NRC Handelsblad*. Her PhD-thesis, *Leegte die ademt* (Vantilt, 2006), was concerned with the meaning of typographic blanks in the modern poem. Her recent focus in research and teaching has been on digital literature, and on ethics and the holocaust in contemporary literature.

Allard den Dulk (1978) is Lecturer in Modern Philosophy and Aesthetics at the Faculty of Philosophy of the VU University Amsterdam. His research focuses on the analysis of philosophical themes in contemporary American literature and film. For more information and publications, go to: http://www.allarddendulk.nl.

Sebastian Groes (1973) is Lecturer in English Literature at Roehampton University UK. In 2010 he published two monographs: *The Making of London* (Palgrave) and *British Fiction in the Sixties* (Continuum). Groes is a Series Editor of *Contemporary Critical Perspectives* (Continuum), which includes volumes on J.G. Ballard, Ian McEwan, Kazuo Ishiguro, and Julian Barnes.

Monica Jansen (1966) is Lecturer in Italian Literature at Utrecht University (NL) and at the University of Antwerp (BE). In 2002 she published a monograph on *Il dibattito sul postmoderno in Italia: in bilico tra dialettica e ambiguità* (Cesati) and in 2006 she co-edited *The Value of Literature in and after the Seventies: the Case of Italy and Portugal* (Igitur). Jansen is a Series Editor of *Texts/Testi mobili* (Peter Lang), which includes volumes on Italian crime fiction after the 1990s.

Ewout van der Knaap (1965) is Associate Professor of German Literature at Utrecht University. Recent publications include *Die (k)alte Sachlichkeit. Herkunft und Wirkungen eines Konzepts* (Königshausen & Neumann, 2004, ed.), *Uncovering the Holocaust. The International Reception of Night and Fog* (Wallflower, 2006, ed.), and *Nacht und Nebel. Gedächtnis des Holocaust und internationale Wirkungsgeschichte* (Wallstein, 2008). A critical edition of poetry by Ernst Meister is forthcoming (Wallstein, 2011).

Arent van Nieukerken (1957) is Lecturer of Slavic Literature at the University of Amsterdam. He is the author of two books (written in Polish): *Ironiczny Konceptyzm* (Ironic Conceptualism), devoted to Polish Modernism (Kraków, 1998), and *Perspektywiczno´s´c Sacrum* (The Holy in Perspective) about the romantic poet Cyprian Norwid (Warszawa, 2008). Foreign member of the Polish Academy of Science (PAN).

Suze van der Poll (1975) is Lecturer in Scandinavian Literature at the University of Amsterdam. She wrote several articles on contemporary Norwegian literature, which was also topic of her dissertation in 2009. In 2011 Van der Poll published, together with Rob van der Zalm, a book on the Norwegian playwright Henrik Ibsen (Amsterdam, Arbeiderspers).

Ellen Rutten (1975) is affiliated as a Postdoctoral Fellow to the Bergen-based project *The Future of Russian*, which studies the impact of new media on Russian language. At the at the University of Bergen she also leads the research project *Web Wars*, on memory wars in digital media. She is editor of the new-media journal *Digital Icons*, and author of the monograph *Unattainable Bride Russia* (NWUP, 2010).

Guido Snel (1972) is Lecturer in Modern European Literature at the University of Amsterdam. He contributed to John Neubauer's and Marcel Cornis Pope's *History of the Literary Cultures of East-Central Europe* (John Benjamins, 4 volumes). He published among others *Alter Ego. Twenty Confronting Views on the European Experience* (Amsterdam UP, 2004) as well as three novels (in Dutch) and a large number of literary translations (from Bosnian/Croatian/Serbian).

Maarten Steenmeijer (1954) is Professor of Modern Spanish and Spanish American Literature and Culture at the Radboud University Nijmegen. His latest publications include *Allí donde uno diría que ya no puede haber nada. Tu rostro mañana de Javier Marías* (2009, volume edited with Alexis Grohmann) and *Moderne Spaanse en Spaans-Amerikaanse literatuur. Een geschiedenis* (2009).

Thomas Vaessens (1967) is Professor in Dutch literature and Chair of the Dutch Department at the University of Amsterdam, and Academic director of the National graduate School for Literary Studies (OSL). His publications in Dutch literature include monographs about Modernism, Postmodernism, poetry and intermediality, and Late Postmodernism. He is a (founding) member of the Editorial Board of the *Journal of Dutch Literature*.

Sven Vitse (1981) is Lecturer in Modern Dutch literature at Utrecht University. His PhD-thesis (*Een woestijn die de stad verpulvert*, Brussels 2008) is about poststructuralist theory and Dutch avant-garde and postmodernist fiction of the 1970s. A collection of his essays on literature appeared in 2010: *Tekstbestanden* (Het Balanseer).

Sabine van Wesemael (1963) is Lecturer in French Literature at the University of Amstredam. She published several books on contemporary French literature, including *Michel Houellebecq, le plaisir du texte* (L'harmattan, 2005), *Les relations familiales dans le roman contemporain* (with Murielle Lucie Clement, L'Harmattan, 2008), *Le roman transgressif contemporain: de Bret Ellis a Michel Houellebecq* (L'Harmattan, 2011).

Index

Index of Subjects

1960s 17, 43, 80, 85, 94, 95, 110, 119, 134, 135, 138, 151, 152, 155, 162, 187, 210, 212-213, 226, 227-229, 250, 258-259, 264, 286, 294

1980s 8, 12, 13, 15, 35, 42, 43-45, 60-65, 70, 76, 78, 79-80, 81, 83, 84, 85, 95, 96, 97, 116, 119, 121, 134-136, 150, 151, 162, 164, 175, 178, 186, 188-189, 196, 210, 213, 227, 229-230, 246, 248

Addiction 44, 233, 236, 239
Aesthetic life 232-234
Aestheticism 153, 154, 189, 194, 261
Agency 80, 236
Alienation 46, 94, 98, 100-101, 106-108, 113, 161, 218
Allegory 85, 91-92, 181, 264
Altermodernity 18, 194-195, 267
Ambivalence 15, 18, 53, 57, 58, 75-76, 79, 84, 85, 119, 122, 131, 253
Anti-postmodernism 13, 37, 51, 89, 174, 248
Anti-realism 93, 94, 106
Anything goes 171, 181, 194, 200, 230, 251
Apocalyptic 84, 90-92, 163
Artificiality 176, 179, 228, 234, 237, 264
Authentic inauthenticity 19, 172
Authenticity 10, 12, 18, 34, 56, 60, 71, 76, 98, 149, 154, 156, 161, 163, 165, 171, 173, 176-177, 189, 199, 207, 211, 264, 269
Authority (literature and...) 13, 44, 63-65, 88-89
Autobiography 20, 22, 47, 68, 83, 95-96, 121-123, 130, 138, 145, 148, 171, 172, 181, 217, 258, 271
Autonomy (of literature) 22, 84, 127, 138, 155-156, 187-188, 191, 244, 264
Avant-garde 13, 43, 55, 80, 81-85, 118, 128, 132, 151, 155, 169, 186, 195, 209, 221, 259, 264, 273

Balkan war 20, 39, 118, 123-127, 129, 132, 189, 199, 259
Barbarism 79, 89-91, 115, 188, 256
Barcelona 212-213, 219
Bildung 64
Blogosphere 37
Boom 212-213
Breach between language and reality 100

Cannibali (giovani) 79, 81-82, 90
Caricature 67, 71, 215
Chaos theory 153
Commitment 15, 19, 20-21, 79, 86-87, 90, 91, 94, 122, 132, 149-165, 173, 177, 187, 189, 232, 233, 261
Communication 158, 173-175, 226, 239, 255
Communism (end of) 20, 31, 38, 116-117, 122, 168, 170, 173-176, 180, 199, 258, 264
Community 65, 82, 85, 146, 156, 158, 163, 169, 176-177, 179, 182, 225-241
Constructivism 169, 171
Conversation 150, 151, 157-158, 230, 240-241
Crime 82, 85, 87, 109, 111, 121, 129, 223-224, 254, 270
Criollismo 209
Critical postmodernism 13, 81, 82, 84-86
Cultural activism 21, 86, 90
Cultural Studies 10, 13, 38-39
Culture industry 17, 173-174, 187-188
Cynicism 8, 14-15, 28, 31, 32, 60, 70, 72, 75, 105, 120, 164, 233-236, 248, 253, 270

Deconstruction 9, 12, 13, 14, 29, 32, 55, 63, 64, 66, 69, 82, 86, 106, 153, 160, 162, 163, 227, 253, 271
Deconstructive philosophy 63, 162, 163, 227, 253, 271

Depression 102
Devaluation of literature 64-65, 70-72, 76
Dialectics 78, 79, 81, 84, 88, 168, 185-202
Dialogue 90, 139, 146, 219-224, 235, 239
Dictatorship (Chilean) 210, 211, 219, 221-223
Dictatorship (Spanish) 212, 215, 216
Digression 224
Disintegration of ideological and moral frames of reference 99
Dispositif 90
Diversity 154, 158, 178
Documentary fiction 20, 74, 119-132, 191
Documentary imperative 20, 123, 124
Double coding 80, 172, 174, 181, 254, 264
Double-bind 84-85

Early postmodernism 11, 15, 151, 187
East and West 116-117, 126-127, 132, 168, 187, 192, 196-198
Eclectic 62, 64, 100-101, 113, 136, 200
Ego-documents 95, 199
El Hogar 209
Ellipsis 224
Engagement 22, 57, 58, 60, 65, 69, 70-72, 73, 78-80, 96, 103, 126, 131, 132, 189, 195, 199, 202, 208, 210-211, 230, 234, 238, 241, 253
Enlightenment 39, 42, 49, 188
Epic 77, 78, 80, 82-84, 86-87, 137, 198
Essentialism 8-14, 60
Ethical life 232-234
Ethics 18-22, 64, 78, 85, 86, 87, 88, 90, 125, 188, 250
Ethics (literature and...) 18-22, 64, 65-66, 87, 250
Europe – East, Central and West 116-118, 128, 175-177, 259
Evil 11, 110-111, 177-178, 207, 211, 218-224
Exhaustion; 'literature of exhaustion' 209, 228-229

Exile 119, 123-124, 126, 132, 168, 219
Existentialism 85, 210, 263
Experience (crisis of) 78, 90

Farce 120, 215
Fascism 88, 116, 121-122, 158, 173, 187, 202, 216, 220-224, 268
Federal Republic Germany 186, 189, 190, 192
Fiction/non-fiction 19-20, 22, 66, 87, 128
Fictionality 20, 78, 91, 137, 168, 172, 228-229
Fin de Siècle 71, 168, 169
Formentor meetings 212
Frankfurt School 188, 202
Freedom; negative (freedom-from), positive (freedom-to) 232
French Theory 10, 43
Futurism 169

Gallimard 208
Game, literature as a 209-210, 223
Gatekeepers 72, 170, 188
German Democratic Republic 186, 192, 193, 196-198, 202
Giovani cannibali (young cannibals) 79, 81-82, 90
Goodness 169-170, 179, 180
Grand narratives 20, 38, 44, 45, 63, 78, 136, 145, 147-148, 162, 197
Gruppo 63 85
Gruppo 93 84-86, 255

Hard memory 39
Highbrow 31, 68, 81, 87, 173
History 8, 16, 20, 28, 29, 32-39, 42, 50, 52, 54, 55, 56, 61, 62, 69, 72, 76, 78, 82, 84, 96, 115, 117, 119, 120, 121, 122, 123, 125, 127, 130, 131, 132, 134, 138, 141, 142, 150, 151, 152, 153, 154, 155,

157, 158, 159, 162, 168, 169, 173, 176, 182, 187, 196, 198, 200, 202, 209, 213, 214, 218, 219, 221, 223, 246, 249, 250, 251, 259, 260
History (end of)   78, 117
History (return, end of)   115, 123
Holocaust   20, 121, 123, 153, 154, 191-192, 201, 222, 259
Hybrid postrealism   97

Ideology   33-35, 83, 84, 117, 119, 120, 122, 152, 153, 162, 197, 199, 255
Impegno   78, 79, 86-87, 254
Indifference   15, 16-17, 32, 73, 156, 233
Infamy   121, 124, 127, 129, 214, 220, 222
Intellectualized postmodernism   62, 63, 64, 73
Intertextuality   29, 80, 88, 135, 137, 147, 173, 182, 220, 260-261
Ironic relativism   104-106
Irony   8, 11, 14, 15-16, 18, 19, 31, 34, 35, 52, 60, 70, 73, 82, 104, 105, 127, 128, 150, 152, 156-157, 160, 164, 165, 172, 173, 175, 177-179, 180, 181, 198, 211, 218, 220, 224, 226, 229, 230, 231-234, 235, 236, 241, 248, 253, 261, 270, 272

Janus head   84-86
Jargon (of postmodernism)   10, 15, 17, 46, 100
Journalism (literature and...)   11, 16, 49, 54, 61-62, 65, 72, 74, 79, 87

La Croix du Sud   208
La nueva novela española   213
La nueva novela hispanoamericana   212-213
Late postmodernism   8, 10, 14, 16, 18-22, 23, 28, 38, 39, 48-57, 60, 61, 63-76, 78-79, 84, 86-92, 97-113, 130, 134, 137, 139-147, 170, 172-174, 176, 179, 183, 208, 218, 245, 249
Laying bare the device   171
Leavisite tradition   45, 48-51
Liberal humanism   8, 9, 12, 18, 43, 60, 61, 64, 66, 67, 69, 71, 76, 250, 251
Literature of exhaustion   209, 228-229
Literature of replenishment   209
Loss of identity   98-100
Love   19, 34, 73, 80, 98, 102, 106, 145-146, 158, 161, 176, 181, 201, 214, 240, 274
Lowbrow   81, 90

Mainstream   13, 15, 61, 81, 137, 174, 250
Mass literature   170, 173
Mass-media culture   32, 48, 49, 50, 173, 174, 182, 192
Master narratives   29
Melancholy   88, 130-131, 256
Memoir   123, 154, 259
Memorandum   80, 82-83, 86
Memory   16, 28, 31, 35, 38, 39-40, 48, 51, 55-57, 88, 90, 98, 109, 111, 112, 130, 137, 140, 141, 159, 197, 207-224, 211, 216-218, 219, 221, 259, 278
Metafiction   43, 55, 78, 84, 89, 91, 94, 151, 213
Metatheoretical debate   38, 39
Minimalism; 'minimalist realism'   10, 16, 105, 137, 139-141, 226, 227, 229-231
Modern society   97, 143
Modernism   13, 18, 42, 45, 48-57, 58, 62, 134-135, 168, 169-170, 172, 177-178, 188, 197, 209, 213, 216, 250, 263, 264, 270
Modernist fiction   215
Modernity   12, 39, 48, 56-57, 58, 84, 89-90, 176, 179, 188, 195, 199, 201-202, 212, 255, 264
Morbid humor   105

Moscow Conceptualism 29-30, 33, 246, 248
Mutation (anthropologic) 81
Mythpoesis 82

Nationalism 20, 117, 119-123, 129, 132, 212, 222
Nazi Germany 123, 131-132, 154, 187, 201, 259
Neo-avant-garde 80, 84-85
Neo-leftism 36
Neo-Marxist 80-81, 84-86, 254
Neorealism 19, 80, 113
Neue Lesbarkeit 190-191
Neues Erzählen 190
Neurotic symptoms 100
New emotionalism 37
New Italian Epic 78, 80, 82-84
New realism 168, 173-174, 179, 180
New sincerity 15, 23, 28, 30-33, 35-40, 73, 76, 172, 174, 226, 247, 248, 249, 253, 270
Nihilism 46, 86, 97-106, 150-151, 156, 177, 189, 230
Nomadic subject 160-162
Non-fiction 19-20, 22, 38, 54, 66, 74, 79, 87, 128, 192, 234, 260
Nostalgia 20, 38, 163, 176, 197
Nouveau roman 16, 56, 94, 96, 104, 119, 121, 151
Novaia iskrennost' (New sincerity) 15, 28, 30-33, 35-40

Objectionable formalism 97
Ontological and epistemological doubts 78, 87, 94, 95, 106, 112, 113
Originality 60, 63, 71, 76, 80, 261
Ostalgie 197

Pact (autobiographical, fictional) 87, 121-122, 128, 130

Parody 90, 197, 215, 273
Performative knowledge 85, 86, 92, 269
Performativity 34, 78, 85, 86, 92, 138, 143, 144.147, 269
Perversion 13, 90, 107-108, 223-224
Photography 128-132, 148, 238
Plagiarism 120,
Playful postmodernism 62-64, 82, 187, 214, 227, 251
Political activism 36-37, 163-164
Political engagement 189, 208-210
Politicized postmodernism 29
Politics (literature and...) 13, 18, 23, 37, 66, 69, 84, 87, 116-118, 134-136, 182
Pop art 10, 17, 63, 151, 170
Popular culture 31, 62, 70, 79, 82, 173
Pornography 102-103, 201
Post-Fordism 83
Post-political, the 20, 117-118, 125
Post-postmodernity 8, 14, 21, 28-33, 37, 39-40, 54, 80, 87, 226, 229, 246, 247, 249, 270
Postcolonialism 190, 210
Poststructuralism 63, 85, 150, 152, 155, 186
Public space (literature and...) 48
Pulp 68, 79, 82

Readymades 29
Real presences 177
Realism 21, 29, 45, 52-55, 57, 78-79, 86-87, 93-113, 134, 137-138, 139, 142, 155, 168-182, 191-202, 220, 223, 230, 257
Reality 10, 14, 16, 19-22, 31, 42, 43, 47-48, 50, 53, 55, 56, 62, 63, 64, 65, 71, 72-75, 76, 77-92, 93-113, 116, 118, 123-126, 129, 130, 131, 132, 136, 137, 138, 141, 142, 147, 148, 153, 154-156, 160, 177, 180, 182, 191, 193, 194, 200, 202, 208, 209, 210, 214, 215, 216,

218, 220, 222, 223, 225-241, 249, 251, 259, 260, 264
Reflexivity   21-22
Relativism   8-18, 32, 34, 43, 47, 51, 60-67, 73, 74, 76, 78, 85, 86, 90, 91, 104, 105, 106, 136, 156, 177, 262
Representation   13, 47, 48-49, 50, 51, 52, 53, 86, 95, 142, 142, 155, 177, 186, 210, 215, 220, 222-224, 273
Return of fictionality   168, 172
Rhetorics of sincerity   14, 40, 211, 224, 249, 269
Rietveld Academy of Fine Arts   28, 245
Risk society   90
Rolling Stones   197

Samizdat   116
Scepticism   43, 72, 216, 218, 229, 235, 239
Self-reflection   29, 50, 137, 147, 186, 226
Self-reflexivity   13, 21-22, 47, 52, 151, 160, 210, 228
Semantic pluralism   29
Siege of   20, 118-119, 123-132, 176
Sincerity   10, 12, 14, 15, 18, 19, 23, 27-40, 60, 73, 76, 91, 160, 163, 169-183, 195, 199, 211, 224, 225-241, 247-249, 253, 265, 269, 270, 272
Social critical novel (Spanish...)   212
Socialist realism   29, 170, 195
Society of spectacle   79, 90
Soft memory   40
Solipsism   193, 229, 231, 235, 239
Soviet trauma   33-40
Spanish Civil War   212, 216-217
Stalinist repressions   35
Starbucks   36
Subversiveness   16, 57-58, 119, 150, 187, 198, 237
Sur   208

Tate Gallery   18, 55, 194, 167
Television   22, 37, 47, 48, 50, 72, 81, 83, 136, 173, 190, 238, 256
Terrorism   11, 20, 66, 95, 108, 129, 153, 189, 244
Testimony   88, 223, 255
Theatricality   33-34, 269
Transatlantic writer   219
Transgression   29, 100, 102, 107-108, 113, 123, 136
Transición   216
Transmediality   21, 82, 86, 90, 144, 148
Trauma (historical...)   37, 39, 157, 216, 221, 246
Trust   34, 50, 235-236
Truth   10, 12, 14, 18, 20, 32, 55, 60, 64, 73, 78, 81, 87-89, 110, 138, 142, 148, 151, 156, 160, 180, 193, 196, 200, 227, 235, 238, 250

Uncertainty   21, 42, 44, 51, 52, 55-57, 58, 83, 84, 227, 229
Universal values   8-14, 17, 64, 72, 76, 222
Unreality   228-231, 237, 238
Unreliability   43-44, 130, 216, 223-224
Urgency   47, 235-236, 238, 240, 244, 255
Utopian thinking   162-164, 196

Violence   91, 101, 104, 108-113, 129, 150, 152, 158, 164, 217, 220, 222-224, 228

Wall, Berlin   122, 196, 197
World republic of letters   208, 213

Xenophobia   70, 128, 129, 132, 198

Index of Names

The notes are not included.

Acker, Kathy   153
Ackroyd, P.   43, 49
Adams, Lorraine   19
Adorno, Theodor W.   81, 155, 188
Agamben, Giorgio   85
Albahari, David   118, 126
Alcalay, Ammiel   125
Ali, Monica   47
Alphen, Ernst van   40, 211, 224
Altenburg, Matthias   190
Altman, Robert   198
Amis, Martin   11, 21, 43, 44, 47-49, 57, 62, 67
Ammaniti, Niccolò   78, 79, 90, 91
Antonello, Pierpaolo   81, 86, 88
Arnold, Matthew   11, 12
Arntzen, Knut Ove   134, 145
Austen, J.   43, 50
Auster, Paul   62, 125

Badiou, Alain   164
Bal, Mieke   40, 211, 224
Balcells, Carmen   212
Balderston, Daniel   210
Ballard, J.G.   49
Balzac, Honoré de   98, 109, 110
Banville, J.   43
Barbusse, Henri   96
Baricco, Alessandro   78, 79, 84, 89-91
Barilli, Renato   89
Barker, Nicola   46
Barnes, Julian   42, 43, 46, 48, 49, 57, 63, 151
Barral, Carlos   212, 214
Bart, Andrzej   181
Barth, John   209, 228, 229
Barthes, Roland   9, 152

Bassler, Moritz   197
Baudrillard, Jean   13, 43
Bauman, Zygmunt   68
Beck-Nielsen, Claus   138
Becker, Torsten   190
Beckett, Samuel   190
Beigbeder, Frédéric   96
Benet, Juan   218
Berg, Karen   215
Bernhard, Thomas   192
Bertens, Hans   8, 210, 211, 221
Bewes, Timothy   15
Bialoszewski, Miron   171
Biller, Maxim   190
Binding, Paul   142
Blagg, Alex   35
Blanckeman, Bruno   95-97
Blinchoe, N.   47
Blisset, Luther   82
Bloch, Ernest   200
Błoński, Jan   173
Bolaño, Roberto   208, 211, 218-224
Bolecki, Włodzimierz   171
Bon, François   19, 74, 96
Boon, Louis Paul   151
Booth, Wayne   22
Borges, Jorge Luis   16, 119, 121, 208-211, 218-221
Boym, Svetlana   31
Božović, Velibor   129
Bradford, Richard   45
Brakman, Willem   151
Brener, Aleksandr   30
Breton, André   94, 95
Bricmont, Jean   13, 189
Brinkmann, Rolf Dieter   192
Brooks, Peter   143
Brussig, Thomas   19, 74, 187, 196-198
Bukowski, Charles   35
Bulhak, Andrew C.   10, 17

Burke, Kenneth 22
Butor, Michel 94, 105
Byatt, A.S. 19, 43

Cabrera Infante, Guillermo 213
Caillois, Roger 208, 209
Calabese, Stefano 91
Calvino, Italo 63, 78, 81
Campbell, Aifric 19, 21, 74
Carey-Thomas, Lizzie 195
Carter, A. 43, 51
Cartland, Barbara 80
Carver, Raymond 189
Casadei, Alberto 82
Cela, Camilo José 214
Céline, Louis-Ferdinand 190
Cercas, Javier 216
Ceserani, Remo 81, 83
Chotjewitz, David 192
Christensen, Lars Saabye 21, 137, 141-145, 147, 148
Chwin, Stefan 172
Claudel, Philippe 96, 97, 108, 112, 113
Claus, Hugo 151
Coe, Jonathan 21
Compagnon, Antoine 64
Conover, Ted 19
Conrad, Joseph 43, 127, 128, 189
Cormack, Alistair 50, 51
Cortázar, Julio 213, 219
Coupland, Douglas 62, 73
Covacich, Mauro 92
Cozarinsky, Edgardo 119
Crews, Frederick 10, 12
Critchley, Simon 88
Cuder-Domínguez, Pilar 53
Čudina, Marija 118
Currie, Mark 50, 150

Darrieussecq, Marie 96
De Man, Paul 152
De Michele, Girolamo 85
De Wispelaere, Paul 151
Dean, Martin R. 193
Deleuze, Gilles 13
De Lillo, Don 83
Delibes, Miguel 214
Delville, Michel 99, 105
Derrida, Jacques 9, 13, 30, 43, 63, 162, 168, 227
Despentes, Virginie 96
Dickens, Charles 19, 48
Dijk, Yra van 227
Doctorow, E.L. 151
Donnarumma, Raffaele 86
Dorgelès, Roland 96
Doyle, Arthur Conan 46
Drabble, Margaret 52
Drndić, Daša 116, 119, 124, 130, 131, 132
Dulk, Allard den 15, 31
Duras, Marguerite 94, 95, 105
Dyer, Geoff 47

Eagleton, Terry 162
Ebert, Teresa 17, 62
Echenoz, Jean 94, 101, 105
Eco, Umberto 80, 81, 84, 181
Eggers, Dave 19, 47, 73, 74, 226, 227, 231-241
Eliot, G. 43
Eliot, T.S. 174, 178
Ellis, Bret Easton 17, 62, 230
Elmore, Peter 224
Epstein, Mikhail 30-33
Ernaux, Annie 96
Esposito, Roberto 85
Esterházy, Péter 119
Etkind, Alexander 39, 40

Februari, Marjolijn 21, 60, 63-67, 69, 72, 76, 105
Federman, Raymond 228
Ferron, Louis 151
Fiedler, Lesley 80, 187
Finkielkraut, Alain 22
Flaubert, Gustave 46, 200
Foer, Jonathan Safran 19, 73, 74, 186, 226, 227, 234, 237-241
Fokkema, Douwe 8, 209
Forster, E.M. 51
Fosse, Jon 21, 135, 137, 139-142, 144, 148
Foster, Hal 16, 21, 88
Foucault, Michel 13, 63, 210
Fowles, John 43
Franco, Francisco 212, 215, 216
Friedrich, Caspar David 88
Frobenius, Nikolaj 138, 144, 147
Fuentes, Carlos 171, 213
Fukuyama, Francis 62, 162
Furedi, Frank 13

Gailly 99
García Márquez, Gabriel 213
Garland, Alex 47
Genette, Gérard 94
Gibson, Andrew 18
Ginsberg, Allen 179
Glavurti, Miro 118
Goethe, Johann Wolfgang 198
Gombrowicz, Witold 19, 168, 171-173, 175, 176
Gordimer, Nadine 189
Gorky, Maxim 11
Goytisolo, Juan 213
Gramsci, Antonio 87
Grass, Günther 144, 191, 196
Green, Jeremy 10
Gruenter, Undine 190

Grunberg, Arnon 15, 17, 60, 63-65, 67, 72-76, 105, 143
Gujord, Heming 134

Habermas, Jürgen 68, 84, 188
Hagemann, Helene 191
Halberg, Jonny 143
Handke, Peter 187, 198, 199
Hardt, Michael 83
Head, D. 45, 53
Heaney, Seamus 176
Hegel, Georg Wilhelm Friedrich 200
Heidegger, Martin 85
Heißenbüttel, Helmut 192
Hemon, Aleksandar 20, 116, 124, 127, 129
Herbert, Zbigniew 170, 173, 175, 176, 182
Hettche, Thomas 190, 193
Hildesheimer, Wolfgang 189
Hitler, Adolf 221
Hoffer, Klaus 189
Hoffmann, E.T.H. 199
Homer 135
Horkheimer, Max 188
Hoste, Pol 150, 151, 152, 154
Houellebecq, Michel 18, 21, 83, 96-108, 113, 141, 143
Huelle, Paweł 172, 173, 181
Humm, Maggie 10
Hutcheon, Linda 15, 16, 84, 150, 213, 241

Ibsen, Henrik 145
Ignatieff, Michael 17
Ivanjicki, Olja 118

James, Henry 43
Jameson, Fredric 15, 81, 86, 150, 162, 165
Jansen, Johannes 190
Jansen, Monica 21
Jaruzelski, Wojciech 175

Jongstra, Atte 151
Joyce, James 55, 135, 190

Kaczyński, Jaroslaw 182
Kaczyński, Lech 182
Kafka, Franz 48, 189, 219
Kaminer, Wladimir 192
Kang, Minsoo 10
Kehlmann, Daniel 191
Kellendonk, Frans 76
Keller, Gottfried 200
Kermode, F. 43
Kiberd, Declan 22
Kibirov, Timur 33
Kierkegaard, Søren 231, 232, 234
King, Bruce 53, 54
Kiš, Danilo 16, 20, 116, 118-131
Kjaerstad, Jan 135-137
Konwicki, Tadeusz 171
Kracht, Christian 190
Krauß, Angela 193
Kunz, Marco 223

La Porta, Filippo 82
Lancaster, John 46
Lande, Frank 138
Larbaud, Valéry 94
Larkin, P. 43
Lawrence, D.H. 43
Leavis, F.R. 18, 43, 57
Levi, Primo 132
Lihn, Enrique 219
Lipovetsky, Mark 31, 37, 38
Lipovetsky, Gilles 99, 106, 107
Litt, T. 46, 47
Loe, Erlend 138
Lukács, Georg 200
Lukashenko, Alexander 37
Luperini, Romano 84
Lyotard, Jean-François 9, 13, 20, 63, 84, 162

Madonna 62
Magris, Claudio 89, 90
Maier, Andreas 193
Manzoni, Celina 221, 222
Marías, Javier 208, 211-218
Marías, Julián 217
Marstein, Trude 144, 145
Martín-Santos, Luis 213
Marx, William 64
May, Karl 200
McCarthy, T. 42, 48, 55, 56, 57
McEwan, Ian 11, 12, 16, 42, 43, 48-51
McHale, Brian 45, 213, 215, 228
McKenzie Wark, Kenneth 91
McWilliam, Candia 46
Medvedev, Kirill 35-37
Mehmedinović, Semezdin 116, 118, 123-129
Menasse, Robert 187, 200-202
Mendiluce, Luz 221
Mennes, Paul 150
Mihajlovich, Vasa 120
Milić od Maćve 118
Milošević, Slobodan 122
Miłosz, Czesław 119, 123, 168-170, 173, 174, 177-182
Mitchell, D. 46
Modiano, Patrick 96
Modick, Klaus 20, 190-192
Moe, Karin 135
Mouffe, Chantal 117
Murdoch, Iris 52, 54
Musil, Robert 190
Musschoot, Anne Marie 151
Mussgnug, Florian 86, 88
Mutsaers, Charlotte 76, 151

Nabokov, Vladimir 127, 128
Nalkowska, Zofia 123
Nieukerken, Arent van 19
Nolens, David 150, 156, 157, 160, 161, 165

Norris, Christopher 15, 150, 165
Norwid, Cyprian 168

Ørstavik, Hanne 141, 144-148
Ortheil, Hanns-Josef 188, 189, 192
Osmolovskii, Anatolii 30
Oster, Christian 99

Palandri, Enrico 81
Pamuk, Orhan 20, 138
Parra, Nicanor 219
Pasolini, Pier Paolo 81
Peeters, Koen 150, 151, 156-159, 165
Perec, George 20, 94
Petrella, Angelo 85
Petterson, Per 137, 141, 144, 145, 148
Pinochet, Augusto 219, 221
Pleşu, Andrei 116, 117
Politycki, Matthias 193
Poll, Suze van der 20
Portoghesi, Paolo 84
Powers, Richard 270, 272
Prigov, Dmitrii 15, 27-29, 33-36, 38
Proust, Marcel 94, 95
Putin, Vladimir 37
Pynchon, Thomas 63, 151, 153, 154, 186

Rajewski, Irina 91
Ramette, Philippe 88
Ramslie, Lars 143, 145
Ransmayr, Christoph 151, 202
Ray, R. 47
Reiter, Hans 223
Reitz, Edgar 198
Reugebrink, Mark 155
Rilke, Rainer Maria 174
Risi, Marco 91
Robbe-Grillet, Alain 48, 55, 56, 94-102, 105-110, 112
Robberechts, Daniël 151, 152

Rorty, Richard 15, 18, 181
Roth, Patrick 190
Roth, Philip 17, 196
Rothmann, Ralf 195
Rottem, Øystein 134, 135, 145
Rouaud, Jean 96
Różewicz, Tadeusz 171
Rubinstein, Lev 38
Ruiz Taggle, Alberto 221
Rushdie, Salman 43, 44, 47-49, 51, 57, 151
Russel, Peter 217
Rymkiewicz, Jaroslaw Marek 182

Sage, Lorna 52
Šalamun, Tomaž 125
Salavaire, Lydie 96
Sánchez Mazas, Rafael 216
Sarlo, Beatriz 210
Sarraute, Nathalie 94, 95, 105
Sartre, Jean-Paul 103
Saviano, Roberto 87
Scalfari, Eugenio 89, 90
Schädlich, Joachim 196
Schindhelm, Michael 193
Schirrmacher, Frank 190
Schulz, Bruno 128, 171
Schulze, Ingo 198
Schwarzenegger, Arnold 10, 13
Schwob, Marcel 220
Sebald, W.G. 20, 119, 130, 131, 141
Šejka, Leonid 118
Self, Will 46
Shields, David 47
Shishkoff, Serge 120
Simon, Claude 94, 96, 105
Siti, Walter 87
Smith, Ali 46
Smith, Zadie 22, 42, 47, 48, 51-55, 67
Snel, Guido 20, 29, 39
Sokal, Alan 13, 189

Solstad, Dag 138, 144, 147, 148
Sontag, Susan 118
Sorokin, Vladimir 34
Späth, Gerold 189
Štajner, Karlo 123
Stalin, Jozef 40, 121, 222
Stasiuk, Andrzej 172, 181
Stefanovski, Goran 117
Stegane, Idar 135
Stellardi, Giuseppe 85
Sterne, Laurence 200
Sunde, Ole Robert 135
Świetlicki, Marcin 177
Szymborska, Wislawa 170, 173, 174, 182

Tabucchi, Antonio 78, 79, 87-89
Tarantino, Quentin 79
Tellkamp, Uwe 194
Theunissen, Jeroen 150, 156, 157, 162, 164, 165
Thiher, Allen 213
Thomas, S. 47
Thorne, M. 47
Timmer, Nicoline 87
Tjønneland, Eivind 145
Tode, Emil 115
Tokarczuk, Olga 172, 181
Tondelli, Pier Vittorio 81
Tournier, Michel 94
Toussaint, Jean-Phillipe 56, 94, 99, 105
Treichel, Hans-Ulrich 194
Trilling, Lionel 199
Tryzna, Tomek 169, 173, 179-181

Ugrešić, Dubravka 118, 122, 126
Ullmann, Linn 141, 144

Vaessens, Thomas 39, 105, 227
Van Bastelaere, Dirk 152
Van Hulle, Dirk 155

Vargas Llosa, Mario 213
Vasta, Giorgio 83
Vattimo, Gianni 80, 81, 85, 89
Vercier, Bruno 113
Verhaeghen, Paul 150, 151, 154, 157, 165
Verhelst, Peter 150, 151, 153, 154, 157, 165
Vernooy, Robert 76
Vervaeck, Bart 151, 155, 157
Viart, Dominique 95, 96, 97, 113
Vila-Matas, Enrique 219
Villoro, Juan 219, 224
Virno, Paolo 83
Vollman, William T. 119
Vonnegut, Kurt 186, 189

Wallace, David Foster 15, 73, 226, 227, 230, 232-241
Warhol, Andy 62
Wassmo, Herbjørg 147
Waugh, Patricia 227, 228
Wawerzinek, Peter 190
Welsch, Wolfgang 188
Wenders, Wim 198
Wesemael, Sabine van 21
Winter, Leon de 76
Witkacy [Witkiewicz, Stanislaw Ignacy] 171
Wolf, Christa 196
Woolf, Virginia 55

Yourcenar, Marguerite 94
Yurchak, Alexei 31, 37, 38

Zagajewski, Adam 174
Zaimoğlu, Feridun 190
Zeeman, Michaël 76
Zeh, Juli 194
Zwagerman, Joost 21, 60, 62-66, 70-72, 76, 105